ONE OF THE GUYS

ONE OF THE GUYS

Girls, Gangs, and Gender

Jody Miller

University of Missouri–St. Louis

New York   Oxford
OXFORD UNIVERSITY PRESS
2001

Oxford University Press

Oxford   New York
Athens   Auckland   Bangkok   Bogotá   Buenos Aires   Calcutta
Cape Town   Chennai   Dar es Salaam   Delhi   Florence   Hong Kong   Istanbul
Karachi   Kuala Lumpur   Madrid   Melbourne   Mexico City   Mumbai
Nairobi   Paris   São Paulo   Shanghai   Singapore   Taipei   Tokyo   Toronto   Warsaw

and associated companies in
Berlin   Ibadan

Published by Oxford University Press, Inc.,
198 Madison Avenue, New York, New York, 10016
http://www.oup-usa.org
Oxford is a registered trademark of Oxford University Press

Library of Congress Cataloging-in-Publication Data
Miller, Jody, 1966–
    One of the guys : girls, gangs, and gender / Jody Miller.
        p.   cm.
    Includes bibliographical references and index.
    ISBN-13 978-0-19-513078-2 (pb : alk.) — ISBN-13 978-0-19-513077-5 (hc : alk.)

    1. Female juvenile delinquents—United States.   2. Juvenile delinquents—United States.
3. Gangs—United States.   4. Gang members—United States.   I. Title.

HV9104 M55 2000
364.36'082'0973—dc21   00-035693

Printing (last digit): 10 9 8 7 6
Printed in the United States of America
on acid-free paper

For Marty Schwartz—
with admiration and appreciation

CONTENTS

FOREWORD

I am grateful for the publication of Dr. Miller's *One of the Guys* for many reasons. I am grateful because it significantly advances our understanding of female street gang members, because the research was so deliberately designed to yield comparative findings about these young women, because the author's gendered perspective is both palatable and informative, because the volume covers a host of issues I've long felt were important in gang research generally, and because the author uses her respondents' own words to illustrate her discoveries. There is more here, in my view, than in any single work yet produced on the nature and place of gang girls in America.

I come to this view as one who initiated a girl gang study several decades ago in almost total absence of a guiding literature. Where was Jody Miller when I needed her in those days? I had taken over the direction of a large study of street gangs in Los Angeles that, I soon found, was concerned only with male gang members. As I developed a pattern of broad field observations, I was quickly alerted to the presence of numerous young females who were attached in semi-autonomous ways to the males, yet no research attention was being devoted to them. And so we developed a research proposal, later funded by a federal agency, to explore these girls' lives and perspectives. Over a three-year period, we identified 200 female members linked to four large male gangs containing 576 male members.

How could it be that the originators of the research ignored 26 percent of the members of these gangs? Feminist scholars in criminology have been asking a similar question ever since and have, over time, launched a series of inquiries and studies that are well documented in Dr. Miller's review of the literature. One can study male gangs without reference to their female constituents, but only at a cost to a world that does, after all, contain *two* sexes. And one can study female gangs or gang members—as many have done—without reference to the males in their worlds. But the fault is the same, as is the loss. Dr. Miller's research, clearly emphasizing the perspective of her female respondents, makes it clear nonetheless that many of those perspectives are affected by necessary accommodations to male gang members. There is a serious attempt here, in the author's words, "to expand feminist accounts of female offenders by providing a nuanced portrayal of the complex gender experiences of girls in gangs."

Beyond this, my satisfaction in reading *One of the Guys* comes from two general sources: the design of the research and its coverage of specific concerns I consider important—issues often overlooked or underplayed in much gang research. Regarding the design, Dr. Miller has deliberately planned a *comparative* study, far more so than is normally the case. First, she was careful to interview both gang members and nongang girls from the same sources and neighborhoods. The contrast locates gang members in their own social context, showing us the special nature of gang girls as gang members, beyond their situation in clearly disadvantaged communities. Gang girls are different, but we can only appreciate the differences through comparisons with nongang girls.

Second, Dr. Miller carries out her study in two contrasting cities, Columbus and St. Louis. Columbus, a newcomer to gang problems, is more representative of thousands of communities that have only confronted the gang problem in the last decade. St. Louis had gang problems in its distant past and has again had to deal with them more recently. The problems of poverty, deindustrialization, and ghettoization are more severe in St. Louis, as Dr. Miller effectively demonstrates. Its gang problem, therefore, is more severe, although not as uniformly as we might anticipate. We find that Columbus suffers from the impact of the "supergangs" of Chicago, while gang activity in St. Louis more fairly resembles early gang patterns found in Los Angeles and other cities. The differences are instructive and remind us properly that while we can generalize about street gangs, we had best do so while recognizing that they reflect their different community contexts.

The third contrast, drawn explicitly by Dr. Miller and implicitly in many of the statements of her female respondents, is that between male and female gang members. She makes it clear that while there are differences—in crime levels and severity, in victimization experiences, and in perspectives on sexual relations—the very fact of gang membership nonetheless yields similarities between male and female members. Such similarities include the impulsiveness of much gang crime, the importance of gang rivalries to group cohesiveness, the preponderance of individual profit rather than group gain as a motive for drug sales, and the intermember variation in behaviors and characteristics. Paradoxically, it is the comparative analyses that give clarity to the similarities in these areas.

These comparisons—gang/nongang, intercity, and intergender—comprise one source of my satisfaction with this work. The second is a series of issues that particularly caught my attention, listed here so the reader may be alerted to them in the process of reading this work:

1. The attention paid to definitional issues, so often ignored in writings on gangs.
2. The use of the girls' quotes to *illustrate* rather than to *prove* the points being made.
3. The use throughout, in a more or less ethnographic study, of tabular data that demonstrate the behavior patterns being described.
4. The demonstration that gang (group) processes overwhelm differences attributable to ethnicity.

5. The reference to gang structures—especially in Chapter 5—to clarify gang similarities and differences.

6. New material on factors leading to gang joining, most notably in Chapter 3; the impact of neighborhood peer networks; gang members within the family; and the push outward emanating from family dysfunction, including abuse.

7. The emphasis on variations between girls and between gangs and an almost anti-journalistic insistence on the avoidance of stereotyping.

8. The clarification of victimization, both as a pattern prior to gang joining and as a dramatically increased risk as a function of joining.

9. The description of several patterns of sexual relations (and their absence), that refute the simplistic "toys for boys" stereotype.

10. The exposition of gang girls' perspectives and strategies for dealing with gender issues. For example, in Chapter 8 Dr. Miller describes how her respondents differentiate themselves from other girls and know that they are denigrated by them. She finds (in a new perspective I have not seen among prior writers) that her girls steadfastly maintain a myth of genuine equality with the boys, despite their multitudinous descriptions to the contrary. She then describes the various strategies that gang girls use to deal with their gender in a male-dominated setting, by which they find a set of balances to meet their needs. She labels it a "patriarchal bargain"—one that occurs to me has no place for a feminist gang member but is a fine setting for a good feminist scholar such as Dr. Miller.

Where do we go from here, given the kind of foundation Miller and others have provided? Several directions seem obvious. First, we will benefit from more deliberately designed comparative studies: gang versus nongang, communities of different characteristics, male versus female, traditional versus newer gang structures, and so on. Second, we will reap special benefits from more efforts at longitudinal designs of the sort not possible in Miller's work. Third, and almost nonexistent in gang literature to date, will be careful study of the after-gang life of both males and females. What is the cost—in lifestyle, education, occupation, marriage, health, and other areas—of immersion in gang life as a youth? The victims of gang crime cry out, and properly so, for retribution and restitution. Few cry out for the gang members, yet they too are victims. We need to assess both sets of costs. For better or worse, as Dr. Miller aptly demonstrates, gang members are a part of our communities.

Malcolm W. Klein
University of Southern California

ACKNOWLEDGMENTS

In September 1987, I was a senior in Ohio University's visual communication program, preparing to graduate and become a photojournalist. As a first generation college student—the second in my family to attend university—the importance of going to college had been instilled in me by my parents from an early age. But I never considered, much less understood, the idea of graduate school. I was earning a women's studies certificate, and so enrolled in the second sociology course of my college career—a seminar on violence against women taught by Professor Martin D. Schwartz. Although I couldn't have known it at the time, this was to be the start of my academic career.

Marty has a gift for recognizing potential in undergraduates and for committing himself to mentoring them. He literally changed the course of my life. Since my time with him at Ohio University, others have followed after me. Although we see each other infrequently, Victoria Pitts, Carol Gregory, and I have an inexplicable bond with one another because of our mutual connection with Marty. I dedicate this book to Marty Schwartz because he helped me discover my voice, taught me to think critically, and, over the years, has remained both a generous colleague and an understanding and supportive friend.

There are a number of additional people to thank. First, members of my dissertation committee and other professors who supported and encouraged my work as a student: Barry Glassner, Malcolm Klein, Philippa Levine, Cheryl Maxson, and Barrie Thorne (formerly) at the University of Southern California; Mary Margaret Fonow, Judith Mayne, and Ruth Peterson at The Ohio State University. I experienced intellectual growth through my interactions with each of them, and each guided me, in various ways, toward more rigorous scholarship. With regard to the current project, Barrie Thorne's work on gender has strongly influenced my perspective. Mac Klein and Cheryl Maxson piqued my interest in gangs and have continued to provide me with a number of opportunities to work together. Cheryl has been especially generous with her time and insights throughout the project. And without question, it was the urging and insistence of Mac that made this book a tale of two cities.

The research on which the book is based was funded by the National Institute of Justice's Dissertation Fellowship Program (grant # 95-1642394) and the University of Southern California's Haynes Dissertation Fellowship Award, as well as by grants from the University of Missouri Research Board and University of Missouri–St. Louis Research Award programs. Of course, the opinions expressed in the book are my own and do not necessarily reflect those of the funding agencies. Thanks to Winnie Reed and Rosemary Murphy at the NIJ for their efforts; Letty Baz, Frances Fitzgerald, Eli Heitz, Dora Lara, and Judith Webb at USC; and Cathy McNeal, Brenda Stutte, and Pattie Tierney at UM–St. Louis for their administrative expertise and support. My editors at Oxford University Press, Jeffrey Broesche and Lisa Grzan, have been a tremendous help as I completed the final manuscript; thanks also to Layla Voll, with whom I originally worked at Oxford.

A number of individuals in Columbus and St. Louis facilitated the research. Ronald Huff made the project possible in Columbus by opening his networks and putting in good words for me. He is, as Cheryl Maxson dubbed him, "the nicest man in the gang field." Jodi Rice in Columbus and Olivia Quarles in St. Louis served as youth advocates for the project, and both were generous with their time and insights. In Columbus, I also appreciate the assistance of Carol Johnson and Anne Japinko at Rosemont Center; Jane Carter, Joanne Carter, John Cerbi, and Walt Wheeler at the Detention Center; and Duane Casares at Directions for Youth, as well as Lieutenant Bowditch , Detective Alexander, and Detective Metco with the Columbus Police Department.

In St. Louis, thanks to Jamala Rogers and Olivia Quarles with SafeFutures, Maureen Filter Nolan formerly with SafeFutures, Peggy Calvin and Lisa LaGrone at Health Street, Josephine Gillespie at the Detention Center, Beverly Humphrey at Madison Tri-A, Kristi Rackley at Juvenile Probation, and Tracy Vinson and Linda Sharpe Taylor at Provident Counseling. Thanks also to Lori Reed and Laurie Mitchell for transcribing audiotapes, Tommie Vales for assistance with data entry and analysis, Toya Like for indexing, and Niquita Vinyard for completion of some of the St. Louis interviews. Rod Brunson was a world-class research assistant and friend upon my move to St. Louis. He completed many of the interviews in St. Louis, and his great rapport with and deep empathy for young people come through in the quality of his transcripts. I look forward to watching his, Toya's, and Niquita's careers blossom in years to come.

There are a number of additional people to thank, all of whom have helped me in various ways over the course of the project. Bob Bursik, David Curry, Kathy Daly, Walter DeKeseredy, Suzanne Hatty, Ron Huff, Claire Renzetti, Jackie Rogers, Marty Schwartz, Norm White, and Richard Wright have read and commented on drafts of chapters, and Scott Decker, Finn Esbensen, Mac Klein, and Cheryl Maxson generously read the work cover to cover, pushing me to move forward when I needed that extra boost. Thanks to my supportive group of friends and colleagues at the Department of Criminology and Criminal Justice at UM–St. Louis, including—in addition to the afore-mentioned—Eric Baumer, Jennifer Bursik, Bruce Jacobs, David Klinger, Janet Lauritsen, Kimberly Kempf-Leonard, Rick Rosenfeld, and Al Wagner. Wednesday nights at Hugos certainly contributed to the completion of this project. And Zoe Curry is always a breath of fresh air when I need it most.

Throughout the project, a number of additional friends have supported me through personal crises and encouraged my work when I struggled: Julie Pinyan; Greg Stiers; Michael, Linda, and Jim Fairchild; Kim Huisman; Ameena Hussein; Marilyn Morton; Janet Curry; Carlos Royal; Claude Louishomme; Fahim Uvais; Vik Dhawan; Linda Schmidt; and Elicka Peterson. Dyan McGuire dragged me away from the computer and out of the house at key moments when I needed it. Spending time with Sarah Morton, Tari Vales, and Veronica Fluker provided me with insight into what it's like to be young women negotiating in the world today. They've taught me about resiliency and courage; they're also a lot of fun. My parents, Linda and Jerry Miller, have consistently encouraged my work. Thanks most of all to my mother for her unwavering love and support.

Finally, I want to thank the young women who participated in this project. Although a few remained suspicious, most were generous with their time and thoughts, some amazingly so. Each touched my life and expanded my understanding of the world. I still laugh out loud every time I read the transcript of my interview with Traci—may she never lose her silly, playful side. More than anything, I see these young women as incredibly resourceful, though not always in the most productive ways, in building lives and identities in a hostile and often dangerous world. To borrow from my friend Tari, "You gotta give 'em their props."

ONE OF THE GUYS

Perspectives on Gangs and Gender

> Gang girls . . . are not, by and large, attractive by conventional standards either with respect to their physical appearance or behavior. . . . [They are] "a loud, crude group of girls who not only curse and are sexually active, but who take no pride in the way they dress." . . . Programs which seek to teach the girls how to dress, use cosmetics, and comport themselves find eager recruits, but sometimes with grotesque results which are comical despite their underlying pathos.
>
> —Short and Strodbeck, 1965[1]

> In defiance and in defense, they have broken away from male gangs, creating a language, a style, and a culture outsiders cannot penetrate. They roam the streets staking out territory, dealing drugs, and asserting their strength and independence. . . . Cops on the streets say women are often more violent, more brutal than men. And they say much of their crime is now related to gang activity.
>
> —ABC News correspondent, 1990[2]

These passages represent two poles on a continuum of representations of young women in gangs. In the first instance, girls are hapless and pathetic, sexually mistreated on the streets as a result of their individual maladjustment. In the second, they are dangerous "street feminists," blazing a trail of equality through their adoption of violence and aggression. Both, of course, are caricatures. But each contains a deeply entrenched belief about women that must be reckoned with to gain a better understanding of young women's involvement in gangs. Although feminist scholars have challenged the long-standing view of women's crime as resulting from maladjustment to appropriate femininity, the competing themes of women's victimization and volition continue to permeate much of the research on women and crime, including the study of young women in gangs.[3] As a result, even much contemporary feminist scholarship on girls' gang involvement remains bound, though often in subtle ways, to these dichotomous characterizations of young women's experiences.

Moreover, much contemporary scholarship on women and crime is bound by another set of tensions equally in need of address. As Daly and Chesney-Lind discuss in their seminal article on feminism and criminology, research on women and crime tends to take one of two approaches: one (the gender-ratio problem) emphasizing gender differences, the other (the question of generalizability) tending to focus on uncovering gender similarities.[4] As I will show, each of these approaches also speaks to the issues of victimization and volition and likewise continues to contribute to the dichotomous treatment of women's offending. This book represents an attempt to bridge these divides while presenting an analysis of female gang involvement that critically examines how girls in gangs construct and negotiate their day-to-day lives.

Attention to young women in gangs has expanded in the last decade, representing the convergence of two phenomena: the reemergence of scholarly interest in gangs among criminologists beginning in the late 1980s and increased attention to women's involvement in crime more generally—a topic that grew in popularity beginning in the 1970s and gained momentum through the 1990s. The 1980s and 1990s witnessed monumental national growth, both in gangs and in the renewed academic study of gangs. Part of this attention comes from extensive evidence of the proliferation of gangs across the United States into a "growing number of large and small cities, suburban areas, and even some small towns and rural areas."[5] According to Malcolm Klein, an estimated 1,000 communities across the United States now report having gangs, with the largest growth since 1985.[6] This is an issue I will return to in Chapter 2. For now, let me simply note that research suggests that gang structure and organization, activities, and criminal involvement, as well as ethnic and gender composition, vary within and across these sites.[7]

One consequence of this renewed interest in gangs has been much improved information with regard to young women's gang participation. Recent evidence shows that young women are much more involved in gangs than was previously believed. While data from official sources tend to underestimate the extent of girls' gang membership,[8] a number of recent studies with juvenile populations estimate that young women approximate 20 to 46 percent of gang members and that in some urban areas, upwards of one-fifth of girls report gang affiliations.[9] In fact, despite the minimal attention young women in gangs received prior to the contemporary era, there is evidence that the level of girls' involvement in gangs is not a new phenomenon. For instance, Klein's and Moore's work on gangs in the middle decades of the 1900s suggest that during that time girls constituted between one-fourth and one-third of active gang members.[10]

A major concern regarding contemporary gangs is their disproportionate involvement in serious and violent crime. Although gang structures and patterns of criminal involvement vary across gang contexts, there is nonetheless consistent evidence that serious criminal involvement is a feature that distinguishes gangs from other groups of youths.[11] In addition, research suggests that this patterns holds for female as well as male gang members, such that young women in gangs have higher offending rates than their non-gang counterparts, female and male.[12] Consequently, both feminists and criminologists have turned attention to girls in gangs, and work on the topic has flourished.

As I indicated at the outset, interest in girls in gangs also should be situated within the broader context of the recent attention female offenders have garnered in general. Buttressed by the fact that most serious criminal offenders are male, the field of criminology, historically, has been a masculinist enterprise, interested primarily in understanding men's offending. Much gang research has paralleled this larger trend in the field. The emphasis on gangs as a principally male phenomenon has been a long-standing tradition in the study of gangs.[13] As a result, early work that took note of female gang members focused on individual maladjustment and the presumably "sexual" nature of these girls' delinquency. And gang research was not alone in this regard—these mischaracterizations of women's crime, often sexualized, were the norm in the field throughout most of its history.[14]

The growth of the modern women's movement brought about new attention to women offenders, challenging the dominant paradigms regarding gender and crime. This was a result of two phenomena. First, feminist perspectives were introduced into the field in conjunction with increases in the number of women criminologists. These changes brought about the recognition, long absent in the field, that female offenders are worthy of scholarly attention in their own right.[15] Second, new attention to female offenders resulted from concern and speculation of a convergence in women's and men's patterns of crime as the women's movement brought about greater gender equality in contemporary society.[16] Both of these trends remain significant, as each continues to shape contemporary criminological research about women's participation in crime and about girls in gangs. In addition, each revisits the themes of victimization and agency evident in the opening passages of this chapter—themes, as I've noted, that continue to haunt feminist scholars as we strive to gain better understandings of the gendered nature of women's lives.

THE SEARCH FOR GENDER SIMILARITIES: GENERALIZABILITY AND CONSTRUCTS OF WOMEN'S AGENCY

Much of the debate regarding the study of women and crime centers on the tension between the gender-ratio approach noted earlier and the question of generalizability. For over a century, theories developed to explain why people commit crime have actually been theories of why *men* commit crime. Some contemporary scholars have thus been keen on the question of whether, or the extent that, these theories can explain *women's* participation in crime. Moreover, feminist scholars have posed the question: "Can the logic of such theories be modified to include women?"[17]

Nonetheless, a routine strategy in criminology when dealing with samples that include males and females has been to test whether the given theoretical constructs can account for the offending of both groups, paying little attention to how gender itself might intersect with various factors to create different meanings in the lives of women and men. Scholars who have attempted to test whether traditional theories can be generalized to women have focused on such things as the family, social learning, social bonding, delinquent peer relationships, and, to a lesser extent, strain and deterrence. This has become a common approach within the gang literature as well.[18] For the most part, these studies have found mixed results. As Kruttschnitt summarizes, "It appears that the factors that influence delinquent development differ for males and females in some contexts but not others."[19]

Parallel with this approach toward theory generalization, which searches for gender similarities—and despite the overall lack of success in finding uniformity across gender—there has been a plethora of scholarship couched in terms of various "liberation" hypotheses. As I noted earlier, recent attention to female offenders has resulted not only from the introduction of feminist perspectives to criminology but also *in response to* feminism—based on speculation that inroads against gender inequality would also increase women's involvement in crime, particularly crime traditionally committed by men. At their extreme, these approaches tend to do one of two things. The first is essentially to erase gender, depicting women offenders as equals to men and paying little attention to the importance of gender as an entrenched feature of the social organization of society. Second, as suggested by the ABC News passage opening this chapter, some discussions actually continue to emphasize gender differences, but in this case suggest that women are in fact more violent or more dangerous than men are. This is a particularly popular approach in media depictions of women offenders.[20]

The original treatise on the relationship of the modern women's movement to women's participation in crime is outlined in Freda Adler's *Sisters in Crime.* The basic premise is that as women move from traditional "female" roles into more masculine ones and the protective factors associated with femininity diminish, women will take on more masculine characteristics, and this will result in an expansion in women's participation in traditionally "male" crimes, particularly crimes of violence. Simon's *Women and Crime* gives a similar account of the rise of female offenders, but focuses on changes in criminal opportunities available to women as a contributing factor to their presumed increases in crime, which Simon suggests would primarily be property offenses. For the most part, the prediction of substantial increases in women's crime has been refuted.[21] However, despite evidence to the contrary, the idea that women's rates of crime are converging with men's remains a popular one.[22]

Recent scholarship in this vein has focused important attention on the economic and social dislocations experienced by men *and* women in urban inner-city communities. There is considerable evidence that the growth in urban crime through the 1980s and early 1990s, including the proliferation of gangs, resulted in part from the rapid deterioration of living conditions for many Americans caused by structural changes brought about by deindustrialization.[23] These problems were further fueled by the influx of crack cocaine into many urban neighborhoods.[24] Focusing on similarities in the experiences of women and men in these communities, some scholars suggest that women's crime is increasing more rapidly than men's crime and that women make up an increasing share of serious offenders.[25]

Specifically, these scholars locate the reasons for these presumed changes in women's patterns of offending in economic transformations that, they argue, have lessened the relevance of gender on the streets and have increased women's opportunities for participation in a variety of crimes. Much of this work has focused on either gangs or the drug trade. For instance, Baskin, Sommers, and Fagan suggest that the convergence of economic marginality and the growth in drug markets have resulted in a lessening of social control over young women, who have developed role models on the street that guide them toward increased participation in these contexts. They suggest: "Women in inner city neighborhoods are being pulled toward violent crime by the same forces that have been found to affect their male counterparts. As with males, neighborhood, peer and addiction factors have been found to contribute to female initiation into violence."[26] These authors conclude that "women's roles and prominence have changed in transformed neighborhoods," such that there exist "new dynamics of crime where gender is a far less salient factor."[27] Similarly, Bourgois describes what he calls the "redrawing [of] the gender line on the street," noting that women in inner-city communities "are in the midst of carving greater autonomy and rights for themselves," including increased participation in drug dealing and other street crime.[28]

Some of the literature on young women and gangs has also been influenced by these notions that changing gender relations are resulting in greater autonomy among women on the streets, resulting in a convergence of their behavior with that of young men in gangs. For instance, several scholars have suggested that new autonomous female gangs have emerged in recent years—a reflection, it is argued, of women's challenges of and emancipation from male oppression. Taylor, for instance, suggests that the socioeconomic consequences of deindustrialization are such that "cultural definitions of women [are] changing," as are "areas [such as street crime] that have been male-dominated." As a result, Taylor suggests, "Today, without much fanfare, women are participating in gangs and crime as never before in urban America." He describes African American women in Detroit gangs as having "moved into more serious modes of independence and operation" and concludes: "The influence of the drug commerce has played a key role in black female emancipation."[29]

In sum, one approach toward explaining women's offending has been to test whether theories developed to explain male crime can be generalized to explain female crime. In a similar vein, a number of recent scholars have suggested that gender is no longer relevant on the streets—that changing patterns in society, including economic transformations, have resulted in changing patterns within drug and criminal subcultures, leading to greater female autonomy. With this autonomy, they argue, come female offenders who participate in crime like their male counterparts. As I document in the next section, feminist scholars raise important critiques of both such approaches.

THE SEARCH FOR GENDER DIFFERENCES: GENDER RATIOS, VICTIMIZATION, AND GENDERED RESISTANCE

Feminist scholars recognize gender as a key element in the social organization of society and, consequently, as a key factor in understanding women's and men's experiences. Researchers that attempt to be gender neutral, in the search for generalized patterns, are unable to address this pivotal issue and instead take 'or granted that variables or constructs have the same meanings for females and males. While feminist scholars recognize the importance of structural conditions such as racial and class inequalities in shaping women's offending and participation in gangs, they are nonetheless quite critical of the kinds of work described in the previous section. Notably, while the generalizability approach looks to find out whether the same processes are at work in explaining women's and men's crime, scholars in this tradition can't account for the gender ratio of offending—that is, men's disproportionate involvement in most crime. This is also a place where scholarship on women's presumed "emancipation" on the streets falls short. Men continue to commit the vast majority of street crime, including violent crime; moreover, as I will detail later, there is extensive evidence that the streets continue to be dominated by men.

The question of whether women's proportion of serious offending has increased over the last decades remains debatable. Most evidence for this increase comes from arrest data, making it difficult to disentangle changes in police behavior from changes in women's behavior. Moreover, even if women's proportion of offending has increased in recent years, it is still the case that the vast majority of serious crime is committed by men. For instance, according to the FBI's Uniform Crime Report for 1995, women accounted for 9.5 percent of homicide arrestees, 9.3 percent of robbery arrestees, 17.7 percent of arrestees for aggravated assault, and 11.1 percent of those arrested for burglary.[30] Feminist scholars who address the gender-ratio problem thus raise the following pivotal questions: "Why are women less likely than men to be involved in crime? Conversely, why are men more crime-prone than women?"[31]

Even scholars who argue that the proportion of violent crime committed by women has increased do not fully contend with contradictory data in their own studies.[32] Nonetheless, their emphasis on the importance of structural dislocations for explaining women's and men's crime remain important. Feminist scholars also have been attentive to the structural conditions of race and class inequality that shape women's offending and participation in gangs.[33] For instance, a number of feminist scholars have described gangs as a means for inner-city youths to adapt to oppressive living conditions, including poverty, neighborhood crime, lack of opportunities, racism, and, for girls, gender-specific limitations such as subordination to men and childcare responsibilities.[34]

The difference is that feminist scholars continue to insist on the importance of gender in shaping women's crime and girls' participation in gangs. Consequently, they are quite critical of work such as that of Baskin and her colleagues, Bourgois, and Taylor, rejecting the notion that gender has become less salient or that women have become more autonomous on the streets. While bringing important attention to racial and class inequalities, much of this work does so in ways that unnecessarily ignores the continuing importance of gender inequality. As Maher aptly notes, scholars who suggest that gender has lost its relevance on the streets confuse women's *activity* with equality.[35]

There is overwhelming evidence that gender inequality remains a cornerstone of the urban street scene; this belies the assertion of women's movements toward equality on the streets.[36] In fact, Wilson's work suggests that structural changes may have *increased* cultural support for violence against women.[37] For instance, while much of the focus regarding women's increased autonomy has emphasized the significance of crack markets in expanding women's opportunities, most research on crack markets challenges the assertion that women have become less constrained by gender inequality, instead documenting the opposite—that crack markets have narrowed women's opportunities, exacerbating and intensifying their degradation and devaluation.[38] Likewise, even when women do participate in traditionally "masculine" crimes, they must accommodate features of gender inequality in order to do so successfully.[39]

These questions have led researchers to pay attention to gender differences and to develop theories that can account for variations in the patterns and extent of women's and men's offending.[40] Moreover, much of the feminist work that began with the gender-ratio problem as a starting point has now moved beyond this question to a broader understanding of gendered lives.[41] One such approach is to theorize about gender as situated accomplishment. Gender is conceptualized as "more than a role or individual characteristic: it is a mechanism whereby situated social action contributes to the reproduction of the social structure."[42] Women and men "do gender," or behave in gendered ways, in response to normative beliefs about femininity and masculinity. This performance of gender is "the interactional scaffolding of social structure"[43]—both an indication and a reproduction of gendered social hierarchies.

This approach has been incorporated into feminist accounts of crime as a means of explaining differences in women's and men's offending, especially participation in violent crimes. Violence is described as "a 'resource' for accomplishing gender—for demonstrating masculinity within a given context or situation."[44] Examining violence as masculine accomplishment helps account for women's relative lack of involvement in these types of crimes, just as this approach offers an explanation for women's involvement in crime in ways that are scripted by femininity (e.g., prostitution). In addition, this approach has the potential to account for differences resulting from racial and class inequalities, with the recognition that constructions of femininity and masculinity vary across these important contexts.[45] However, the approach has tended to leave unexplained women's participation in violent street crime, and arguably at least some young women's involvement in gangs, except as an anomaly. In fact, Braithwaite and Daly suggest that although some women may engage in violent behavior, because their actions transgress normative conceptions of femininity, they will "derive little support for expressions of masculine violence from even the most marginal of subcultures."[46]

Instead, attention to gender inequality has led many feminist scholars to examine the impact of women's victimization as an explanatory factor for their crime. In the context of gangs and elsewhere, feminist scholars have played a significant role in bringing attention to the overlapping nature of women's criminal offending and victimization. This research focuses attention on "the gendered and sexed contexts that bring adolescents to the street [and] the gendered and sexed conditions of survival on the street."[47] There is evidence, for example, that a number of female offenders, including young women in gangs, have histories of childhood victimization or find themselves in abusive relationships as adults.[48] Chesney-Lind suggests that often women's efforts to escape and resist abuse are then criminalized, resulting in a process that punishes women and girls for their victimization.[49]

This conceptualization of women's actions as resistance to oppression often carries through to feminist scholars' explanations of women's participation in aggressive behaviors such as violent crime. In highlighting the "blurred boundaries" of women's victimization and offending, a number of scholars suggest that women's use of violence is qualitatively different from that of men. These authors suggest that women use violence as a protective measure, in response to their vulnerability to or actual victimization. This approach has been adopted by feminist scholars to explain both girls' gang behavior and women's involvement in other forms of street crime.

For instance, in her ethnography of a Brooklyn drug market, Lisa Maher notes that women adopt violent presentations of self on the street as a strategy of protection. She explains: "'Acting bad' and 'being bad' are not the same. Although many of the women presented themselves as 'bad' or 'crazy,' this projection was a street persona and a necessary survival strategy."[50] Maher notes that the women in her study were infrequently involved in violent crime and most often resorted to violence in response to threats or harms against them. She concludes, "Unlike their male counterparts, for women, reputation was about 'preventing victimization.'"[51]

Likewise, Campbell suggests that while men routinely adopt instrumental aggression, women's aggression tends to be expressive, unless they find themselves in contexts in which instrumental aggression is necessary for self-protection. When she turns her attention to gangs, Campbell thus differentiates between gang girls' use of violence and the violence of their male counterparts. Among young men, Campbell suggests, "Violence is power, and it is directed at other gangs and local youth because gang members want recognition and respect on their own turf. Violence is a measure of being someone in a world where all hope of success in conventional terms is lost."[52] In contrast, she describes young women's aggression in a very different manner:

> Fear and loneliness—in their families, their communities, and their schools—are the forces that drive young women toward an instrumental view of their aggression. They know what it is to be victims, and they know that, to survive, force must be met with more than unspoken anger or frustrated tears. Less physically strong and more sexually vulnerable than boys, they find that the best line of defense is not attack but the threat of attack. . . . There is nothing so effective as being in a street gang to keep the message blaring out: "Don't mess with me—I'm a crazy woman."[53]

Joe and Chesney-Lind draw much the same conclusion in their comparison of male and female gang members' use of violence:

> [F]or boys, fighting—even looking for fights—is a major activity within the gang. . . . For girls, fighting and violence are part of life in the gang—but not something they necessarily seek out. Instead, protection from neighborhood and family violence is a major theme in girls' interviews. . . . For girls, violence (gang and otherwise) is not celebrated and normative; it is instead more directly a consequence of and a response to the abuse, both physical and sexual, that characterizes their lives at home.[54]

In these accounts, even when women's physical aggression is offensive in nature, it can still be understood as a defensive act because it emerges as resistance to victimization. I suggested at the outset of this chapter that feminist accounts of women's offending, including girls' gang involvement, often continue to be constrained by the narrow conceptions of women suggested by the opening passages. These descriptions of gender and aggression are illustrative. Here, young women's actions are circumscribed by gender so completely that their participation in violence is conceptualized exclusively as response to threat.

While this explanation of girls' behavior moves beyond the early image of individual pathology, it nonetheless keeps girls thoroughly and almost exclusively bound by gender. Here young women are not victims of biology and maladjustment, but are victims of male oppression—victims whose actions always reflect resistance or response to that oppression. Women's agency is thus narrowly defined. The important factors that scholars such as Baskin and her colleagues uncover—especially the importance of peers and the status that some young women *do* get for their participation in violence—are overlooked. Thus if some scholars can be accused of overlooking the significance of gender, many feminist criminologists are equally guilty of overemphasizing gender differences.[55]

BRIDGING THE SIMILARITIES/DIFFERENCES DIVIDE

The impulse for such an approach is clear, particularly in light of the intensity of ongoing debates that attempt to erase gender or define women's violence as more dangerous and socially troubling than men's violence. Many feminist scholars have resisted examining women's agency beyond its capacity as "resistance to victimization" precisely because of the tendency to overlook the significance of gender oppression when it isn't explicitly at the foreground and because our work occurs in the shadow of various "liberation" hypotheses. Research that examines women's participation in violence without paying sufficient attention to how "gendered status structures this participation"[56] cannot adequately describe or explain this behavior. The problem is that neither can research that *overemphasizes* gender.

Because gender differences are overemphasized in many feminist accounts of aggression, similarities in experiences across gender are ignored, including similarities in the contexts that shape decisions to behave in these ways. For instance, it is likely that not all of women's street violence can be viewed as resistance to male oppression, that, in fact, some elements of women's motivation to commit violent crimes are similar to those of men. For instance, in certain contexts, norms favorable to women's use of violence exist, and these norms are not simply the consequence of avoiding victimization, but also result in status, recognition, and support for expressions of presumably "masculine" forms of violence.[57] Part of the problem may be that narrow conceptions of masculinity and femininity are hidden within these analyses, specifically "within the parameters of the white middle class (i.e., domesticity, dependence, selflessness, and motherhood)."[58] Simpson and Elis suggest that such a passive feminine ideal is likely "much more relevant (and restrictive) for white females," and presumably middle-class females, than it is for other women.[59]

Obviously, this is not to suggest that victimization and gender inequality are unimportant for understanding women's use of violence, but to call attention to the need to recognize variations in women's experiences.[60] For instance, we need to recognize that some of women's participation in violent crime likely results from the same factors that motivate men—for instance, "the frustration, alienation and anger that are associated with racial and class oppression"[61] and that, in some instances, gender is not the salient motivating factor.[62] Thorne points out that gender "may be more or less relevant, and relevant in different ways, from one social context to the next."[63] This does not mean that gender is unimportant or that gender doesn't shape criminal behavior, but that its significance is variable. Moreover, the importance of gender can't be assumed at the outset but needs to be empirically discovered.[64]

I make this point in particular with regard to situational motives for crime, which should be recognized as distinct from the question of larger etiological factors.[65] And this is especially important to consider in the context of gangs, given extensive evidence of the importance of group dynamics and processes in shaping youths' offending.[66] As I will document, gender plays a role in gang girls' participation in violent delinquency—defining, for instance, appropriate targets, methods, and frequency. However, these decisions are also patterned in important ways by larger dynamics within gangs, such as group processes shaping notions of threat and respect and the normative responses to such phenomena.

Many young women in my study gave accounts of their gang involvement that resonated with research on male gang members. At the same time, they offered evidence of the distinctively gendered nature of their gang activities. These contradictions highlight the tension I noted earlier with regard to taking a gender-similarities versus a gender-differences approach. It is not so much that I am arguing for a "middle ground," if there is such a thing. Instead, I point to important feminist research in fields outside of criminology that makes the case that while gender is and should remain central to our analyses, research that overemphasizes gender differences essentializes behavior rather than understanding its complexities.[67] Instead, we need to recognize and explore both between-gender similarities and within-gender differences, as well as differences across gender.[68] Feminist explanations of gender and crime are strengthened when these insights are taken into account.

GIRLS IN GANGS: VICTIMIZATION, RESISTANCE, AND AGENCY

Throughout the preceding sections, I have discussed issues related to women in crime broadly, while also linking these issues to research on gangs. Now let me make the connection of these issues to gang research more explicit. As Short and Strodbeck's opening remark illustrates, traditional gang research emphasized the auxiliary and peripheral nature of girls' gang involvement and often resulted in an almost exclusive emphasis on their "failed" femininity and their sexual activities with male gang members. Often these young women were depicted as particularly physically unattractive, and their roles were described in narrow terms—as weapons carriers, decoys or spies for infiltrating rival gangs, sexual outlets for male gang members, instigators or provokers of conflict between male gangs, and as cat fighters, fighting one another for the attention of male gang members.[69]

These early biases are well documented by contemporary gang scholars, who have worked to develop more inclusive and gender-attentive studies of gangs. Moreover, while feminist research clearly documents the operation of gender inequality within gangs, much contemporary feminist scholarship also has been devoted to examining the significance of gang life for the young women involved.[70] In particular, feminist scholars have been attentive to the ways in which gender inequalities intersect with class and racial oppression to shape young women's gang involvement. As Campbell summarizes, "The gang represents for its [female] members an idealized collective solution"[71] for dealing with a myriad of problems in their lives, including, as I noted earlier, limited educational and occupational opportunities and gender inequality, in addition to the powerlessness of underclass membership they share with males in their communities.

In a recent review of the literature on female gang involvement, Curry notes that scholars typically interpret girls' experiences in gangs through one of two frameworks: the "liberation hypothesis" or the "social injury hypothesis."[72] Viewed as a continuum, several studies fall at the poles of these competing frameworks,[73] while most fall somewhere in between. Regardless, most of this research documents the ways in which gender oppression is reproduced within gangs. Notably, while many studies describe young women's internalization of sexist attitudes and beliefs, they typically frame gender inequality as a situation that young women react to and against, rather than participate in.[74]

Scholars who emphasize the social injuries caused by gang involvement focus on the gender inequality within these groups, as well as the negative long-term consequences of gang involvement for young women. Gang girls face a number of risks and disadvantages associated with gender inequality. For instance, in his ethnography of a Kansas City gang, Fleisher documents the extensive exploitation and abuse that gang girls experience at the hands of their male gang peers.[75] In addition, Moore notes that some of the male gang members she spoke with admitted that female members were often viewed as possessions or "treated like a piece of ass," despite young women's attempts to be treated as equals.[76] This devaluation of young women can lead to girls' mistreatment and victimization because they aren't seen as deserving of the same status and respect as their male counterparts.[77] In addition, young women in gangs are at risk for a number of problems into and within their adult lives. Whereas many opportunities for legitimate success are already gravely limited for young women living in impoverished communities, the negative consequences associated with gang membership, as well as public response to gangs and to women in urban communities, can exacerbate the situation further.[78]

Studies that can be classified as supporting a "liberation hypothesis" focus on the gang as a site for young women to overcome gender oppression. Evidence for this perspective comes mainly from several studies that document the development of independent female gangs. For instance, as I discussed earlier, Taylor has suggested that new, autonomous female gangs have emerged in recent years as a result of young women's challenges of and emancipation from male oppression. He describes African American women in Detroit gangs as having "moved into more serious modes of independence and operation," suggesting that "black female emancipation" has resulted.[79]

An interesting feminist modification of Taylor's "emancipation" thesis can be found in Lauderback, Hanson, and Waldorf's description of an autonomous female gang in San Francisco—the Potrero Hill Posse (PHP)—whom they characterize as "doin' it for themselves."[80] PHP was a drug-selling gang that came about after several of the young women became dissatisfied with a "less than equitable . . . distribution of the labor and wealth"[81] that had been part and parcel of their previous involvement selling drugs with male gang members. While their views on men are described as "decidedly negative,"[82] the young women in PHP described their all-female gang as providing mutual support and a sense of family.

It's important to note that despite Taylor's claim, there is no evidence that independent female gangs account for more than a very small percentage of young women's gang involvement. For instance, based on interviews with 110 female gang members in three sites, Curry found that only 6.4 percent of girls described being in independent female gangs, while 57.3 percent described their gangs as mixed-gender and another 36.4 percent said they were in female auxiliaries of male gangs. Likewise, Nurge found that the majority of girls she interviewed in Boston were in groups that were in some way mixed-gender rather than female-only, and my own research supports this as well.[83] Nonetheless, Lauderback and his colleagues' theme regarding the supportive, almost familial, relationship the young women in PHP described having with one another is echoed in other scholarship on young women and gangs.

While rejecting the notion that gangs can be emancipatory, many studies concentrate on the "sisterhood," support, and companionship that young women find among their female gang peers. These studies bridge the liberation/social injury divide by focusing explicitly on the gang as a site for young women to combat victimization and resist the devaluation and exploitation of women in their communities. Researchers argue that young women turn to gangs, in part, as a means of protecting themselves from violence and other family problems and from mistreatment at the hands of other men in their lives. Within the gang, girls' friendships provide an outlet for members to cope with abuse and other life problems.[84] In addition, Campbell suggests that being in a gang provides young women with a means of resisting the narrow confines of traditional femininity. She notes that "gang girls see themselves as different from their [female] peers. Their association with the gang is a public proclamation of their rejection of the lifestyle which the community expects from them."[85]

While Campbell emphasizes the importance of female friendships within gangs, she also notes that young women frequently accept rather than challenge gender inequalities within gangs and reinforce norms governing young women's behavior in their interactions with one another. She notes, for instance, that the sexual double standard young women apply to male/female relationships tends not only to disadvantage them in their relationships with young men but also interferes with the strength of their own friendship groups.[86] However, few studies have paid sufficient attention to *why* many young women choose to uphold gender inequality within their gangs. Returning to Lauderback and his colleagues' study, they note—but others' discussions of their research often fail to mention—that the young women in PHP actively exploited *other* women, procuring drug-addicted women to provide sex for the men who frequented their crack houses. Sex-for-crack exchanges in drug houses are widely recognized as among the most abusive of illicit sexual exchanges,[87] and the members of PHP are described as reviling the women who work for them in this capacity.

This raises an issue—often avoided by many feminist scholars—about women's accountability for their participation in crime, especially crimes of violence that clearly victimize others.[88] While the images of female solidarity, sisterhood, and resistance to oppression within gangs are seductive ones—and are in some ways true—there is another side to girls' gang involvement (and women's crime) that has to be addressed. For instance, failing to grapple with women's use of violence beyond its function as "resistance to victimization" means that "we will continue to fail women and children who have suffered at the hands of women."[89] Part of the hesitancy to deal with women's violence is that doing so may draw attention away from the fact that violence is a predominantly male phenomenon and may be perceived as substantiating or supporting sensationalized accounts of female offenders. But it need not do either. In fact, neglecting the topic is to our detriment. Kelly notes:

> [In the past,] our caution and irritation at "women do it too" statements were justified, since the speaker was seldom concerned about the issues, and usually motivated by a desire to dismiss feminist analysis. But today, avoiding the issue of women's use of violence represents as much of a threat as we previously felt talking about it did. If we fail to develop feminist perspectives we are handing over the issues to the professionals and the media.[90]

Moreover, ignoring this aspect of women's lives means that these women are not given the space to be fully human. The dilemma is that by resisting the negative connotations of "street feminism" that the opening passage and some recent accounts suggest, a rather romantic notion—one of sisterhood and solidarity—tends to replace it. But neither image is really accurate. Refusing to grant the complex realities of women's lives—good and bad—means we too end up circumscribing their agency, and the result is a narrowing of our ability to fully appreciate and understand their experiences.

Likewise, if we hope to understand how gender inequality is reproduced, we must grapple not just with men's treatment of women and with male-dominated institutions but with "how women remain vested in the gender system,"[91] including how and why women sometimes actively participate in oppressing other women. We need to ask: What do *women* get out of maintaining gender inequality? This question extends well beyond the context of gangs or crime,[92] but it is particularly relevant for girls in gangs because many of their beliefs and harmful actions are targeted at other young women. While I would not argue that changing women's attitudes and behaviors is the solution to gender inequality, I do suggest that this is an issue that feminist criminologists have neglected in theorizing women's lives.

The passages that open this chapter illustrate deep-seated beliefs about women that continue to pervade our explanations of girls' participation in gangs. As I have illustrated here, recent feminist scholarship often continues to revisit the themes we struggle to overcome. Broadening our focus provides a strategy for disrupting these frameworks. Without question, we must continue to examine the roles that gendered victimization and resistance play in shaping young women's decisions about whether and how to participate in gangs. But explanations that reduce everything to gender are insufficient, as "gender alone does not account for variations in criminal violence"[93] or other facets of gang activities. Our reluctance to view women's crime in terms other than as resistance to gendered victimization constrains our abilities to fully document women's lives. In the context of girls in gangs, overemphasized gender differences fail to account for the variable and fluid nature of gender, and they downplay shared circumstances in the lives of young women and young men. In addition, we need to broaden our meanings of "resistance" to also include those gender strategies adopted by girls and women that ultimately and even purposively uphold women's oppression. Only in doing both can we adequately address those aspects of young women's lives that involve harmful actions—against themselves and others.

THE PRESENT STUDY

My interest in young women's gang involvement emerged from a long-standing concern with the experiences of "at-risk" girls.[94] As a graduate student in Los Angeles in the early 1990s, the setting would have seemed a perfect one for a study of girls in gangs, as southern California has long been dubbed the "gang capital" of the world.[95] But several things drew me to the Midwest and to the cities—Columbus, Ohio, and St. Louis, Missouri—that provide the settings for my study of girls in gangs. As I noted early in this chapter, a unique feature of gangs in the contemporary era is their proliferation across the United States into a number of cities without previously identified gang "problems." Although research on girls in gangs was limited until recently, the majority of work that had been done on the topic occurred in Los Angeles or places like it—cities with long histories of gangs.[96] In addition, most prior research has focused on Chicana or Latina gang members, with very little attention, for instance, to primarily African American gangs.[97]

Thus the Midwest, and particularly Columbus and St. Louis, provided the opportunity to explore girls' gang involvement in new settings. Both are examples of "emergent" gang cities, where young people's creation of and involvement in gangs has occurred since the mid-1980s.[98] In addition, as compared to a number of traditional gang cities such as Los Angeles, New York, or Chicago, the racial composition of Columbus and St. Louis is predominantly white and African American, and gangs in both cities are primarily African American. However, the socioeconomic contexts of Columbus and St. Louis are vastly different—while St. Louis is characteristic of a number of cities adversely affected by deindustrialization, Columbus is one of the few Midwestern cities to experience both economic and population growth in recent years. These differences are worth consideration with regard to their influences on the nature of gangs and of girls' gang involvement. In addition, much of the in-depth work on young women in gangs has focused on older populations, though research indicates that young women tend to get into gangs at younger ages than young men do and to exit earlier.[99] My work focuses explicitly on young women who are primarily in their early to mid-teens.

A number of scholars have lamented that gang research has often been bound to single cities, or even individual gangs, making contrast across locations difficult. My focus on girls' gang involvement in two cities—similar in their size, ethnic composition, and recent gang "problems," different in their socioeconomic experiences—while still limited, does provide some basis for comparison and is structured to do so. Moreover, as Chapter 2 will describe in more detail, in addition to interviews with girls in gangs in each city, I also interviewed young women in the same neighborhoods and communities who were not in gangs. This allows at least an exploratory investigation of the differences that might exist among girls that help account for why some girls join gangs while others in the same communities do not.

My goal for the book is to provide an overview and analysis of young women's gang involvement that takes seriously girls' perspectives on their lives. My approach incorporates a number of the insights of feminist criminologists regarding the gendered nature of young women's experiences. In addition, I remain attentive to the possibility of overlapping similarities in young women's accounts with those that previous researchers have uncovered regarding young men. I pay critical attention to variations in girls' experiences, the existence of inequalities between girls, and the ways in which and reasons that some young women participate in and support the exploitation of other girls. In doing so, I hope to expand feminist accounts of female offenders by providing a nuanced portrayal of the complex gender experiences of girls in gangs.

Chapter 2 provides a more detailed discussion of the study settings, as well as an account of the methodology and related issues and a description of the young women who participated in the study. My goal is to present detailed portraits, both of girls' pathways into gangs and their experiences of gang life. I begin by framing girls' gang involvement within the broader contexts of their lives. Chapter 3 considers the circumstances that lead young women to join gangs. Here I compare gang and nongang girls in Columbus and St. Louis with regard to characteristics that might shape decisions to choose or avoid gang involvement. I also provide evidence from in-depth interviews with gang girls to illustrate the predominant themes in girls' discussions of getting into gangs.

Moving to the foreground of gang life, Chapters 4 and 5 discuss the nature of young women's gangs in Columbus (Chapter 4) and St. Louis (Chapter 5), including young women's discussions of the structures, characteristics, and activities of their gangs. Chapter 6 examines the issues of crime and violence in gangs, with particular attention to how gender shapes girls' participation in gang crime. Chapter 7 examines victimization risk within gangs, focusing on both the overlapping nature of offending and victimization and how gender structures girls' victimization risk within gangs. Chapter 8 addresses girls' gender ideologies within gangs, including their perceptions of self and of women more broadly. In particular, I focus on girls' resolutions of the contradictions of being both "female" and "gangsters." I conclude (Chapter 9) by discussing the implications of the study for feminist theories of women's involvement in the urban street world.

2

Studying in "New" Gang Cities

S ince the mid-1980s, gangs have sprung up in a number of cities where they had not previously been observed. Scholars have made much of the contrast between these emergent gang cities and cities with chronic gang problems.[1] However, there may also be important variations *across* emergent cities. This is a question I examine in my research with regard to girls' gang involvement, but to do so, let me provide more information about what are believed to be the causes of this recent growth in gangs. Most evidence suggests that the proliferation of gangs is a result of the independent development of gangs within cities, rather than organized gang migration.[2] There also is compelling evidence that much—but not all—of the new growth in gangs has been spurred by the deterioration in living conditions for many Americans resulting from rapid deindustrialization.[3]

These changes have ushered in the growth of an urban "underclass"— disproportionately poor African American and Latino/a individuals living in conditions of entrenched poverty in inner-city communities characterized by intense racial and economic segregation and a precipitous decline in social services for those left behind.[4] The lack of alternatives resulting from such conditions is believed to have contributed to the growth of gangs in many cities, and recently it has meant that youthful gang members—given less opportunity for maturing out of gangs into the formal economy—are more likely to extend their gang and criminal involvement into adulthood.[5] As Jackson observes, "Higher crime rates and more youth gangs are among the unintended consequences of the nation's pattern of postindustrial development."[6]

However, in cities with less severe economic problems these explanations may carry less weight.[7] A second contributing factor may be the diffusion of gang culture through popular media attention to gangs and the commercialization of gang style.[8] Music, films, the news media's attention to gangs, and the resulting popularity of "various aspects of gang culture"[9] such as clothing, hand signs, and tattoos—all add to youthful identification with gang culture. Cultural diffusion may help explain the simultaneous growth of gangs in so many communities across the United States, contributing to the formation of what Spergel and Curry describe as "copycat gangs."[10] Groups of youths who otherwise simply might be involved in minor delinquent activities adopt gang names for themselves; when this occurs, they may be recognized and responded to as such by others in their community and by institutions with social control capacities. Klein and

Crawford have noted that group processes operate in gangs such that negative sanctions from external sources may strengthen the groups' cohesiveness; thus response to youths who begin to adopt gang names may exacerbate the problem.[11]

As I considered possible settings for my study of girls in gangs, these issues helped guide my choices. I wanted to examine female gang involvement in new or emergent gang cities; I also hoped to find cities that would provide an interesting comparison by virtue of their socioeconomic differences—one that fit with the literature's dominant view of gang proliferation, one that seemed to challenge it. Maxson and Klein's national gang migration survey[12] provided an initial pool of midwestern cities with emergent gang problems; then I used social and economic indicators from the 1990 U.S. Census to compare possible sites. St. Louis fits very well with the underclass explanation of gangs, while Columbus emerged as perhaps the least typical gang city, experiencing both economic and population growth in the last decade. In addition, both have comparably sized metropolitan areas, and each is composed primarily of whites and African Americans. Their combined similarities and differences made them optimal choices for my undertaking.

STUDY SETTINGS

Urban analyst David Rusk examines the effects of deindustrialization in the context of what he calls cities' elasticity. Noting that most people across the United States now live in suburbs and that most jobs are located there, Rusk describes elastic cities as those capable of capturing suburban growth and inelastic cities as those that cannot. He explains:

> An inelastic area has a central city frozen within its city limits and surrounded by growing suburbs. It may have a strong downtown business district as a regional employment center, but its city neighborhoods are increasingly catch basins for poor Blacks and Hispanics. . . .
> In an elastic area suburban subdivisions expand around the central city, but the central city is able to expand as well and capture much of the suburban growth within its municipal boundaries. Although no community is free of racial inequities, minorities are more evenly spread throughout the area.[13]

Inelastic cities typically have greater racial and economic segregation, population decline within the city limits, wide city–suburban incomes gaps, and a city government in distress—"squeezed between rising service needs and eroding incomes."[14] Elastic cities, in contrast, have reduced segregation, lower city–suburban income gaps, and a city government with a broader tax base with which to meet the community's needs. St. Louis is one of eight large midwestern cities that Rusk characterizes as having *zero* elasticity. In contrast, Columbus is described as *highly* elastic.[15]

Table 2-1 County/City Comparisons, Columbus and St. Louis*

	Franklin County	Columbus	St. Louis County	St. Louis City
Population	961,437	632,958	993,529	396,685
Percent Black	15.9%	22.6%	13.9%	47.5%
Percent White	81.5%	73.2%	84.2%	50.9%
Median Household Income	$30,375	$26,651	$38,127	$19,458

*Columbus is located within Franklin County, while St. Louis County and the county of St. Louis City are separate jurisdictions.

Source: U.S. Census, 1990.

Table 2-1 provides a comparison of Columbus and St. Louis and their surrounding counties. As Rusk suggests, Columbus and St. Louis are characterized by very different relationships with their surrounding communities. Columbus is housed in Franklin County; the county has just under one million residents, roughly two-thirds of whom reside within the city limits of Columbus. St. Louis and St. Louis County are in a rather unique situation—the city officially separated from the county in the late 1800s,[16] locking its political boundaries in a way that has ultimately been quite detrimental. Using Rusk's characterization, St. Louis city literally has zero elasticity—the Mississippi River and East St. Louis, Illinois, are to its west and St. Louis County surrounds it in Missouri, giving the city no room to expand.

Columbus and Franklin County also have much less racial diversity than St. Louis and St. Louis County. While under one-fourth of Columbus's population is African American, nearly half of St. Louisans are African American.[17] Looking at the counties, it appears that Franklin County has more African Americans—15.9 percent of the population, compared to 13.9 percent of the population in St. Louis County. However, taking account of the number of African Americans in Franklin County who reside within Columbus city limits, in fact only 3 percent of Franklin County residents who live outside the city are African American.

With regard to income, residents of Columbus have a median income over $7,000 higher than St. Louis city residents and a city/county income gap that is smaller than that of St. Louis and St. Louis County. It appears, then, that Columbus is characterized by a more even distribution of individuals by income level (though not by race), while St. Louis typifies urban underclass cities with regard to racial and economic segregation.

Looking at changes in each city over time helps to illuminate these issues. The greater Columbus metropolitan area grew in population by 89 percent from 1950 to 1990. Significantly, the city population grew by 69 percent during this period, capturing a total of 40 percent of the overall growth within its boundaries.[18] This was accomplished by aggressively expanding the city limits—annexing unincorporated areas surrounding the city. While Columbus was 39 square miles in 1950, by 1990 it was 191 square miles—a change of 385 percent.[19]

In contrast, the population in the city of St. Louis declined sharply during this period, lacking the possibility of Columbus's strategy of physical expansion because of its locked political boundaries. In 1952, St. Louis was the eighth largest U.S. city, with a population over 850,000.[20] By 1990, the population had dropped by approximately 54 percent to less than 400,000 people. Decker and Van Winkle note, "So precipitous was the population decline, that the city of St. Louis is now the second smallest central city in the nation relative to the size of its metropolitan statistical area."[21] Along with this population decline, racial segregation in the city has increased, making St. Louis one of the ten most racially segregated cities in the United States.[22]

St. Louis has been distressed not just by population loss but also by considerable deindustrialization. While the economy in St. Louis traditionally has been dependent on manufacturing jobs, the reduction in a number of industries since the 1970s—notably the automotive and aerospace industries—resulted in a sharp reduction in available jobs, diminishing the economic circumstances of many city residents, particularly those without an advanced education.[23] In contrast, Columbus sustained economic growth during this period. While the city experienced a 14 percent decline in manufacturing jobs, simultaneous job growth was 40 percent.[24] The vast majority of this growth was in the service sector.[25]

Despite the dramatic differences between Columbus and St. Louis, there remains continuity between them. Given the apparent racial segregation in Franklin County, illustrated by the paucity of African Americans living outside the Columbus city limits, it may be that Columbus's elasticity masks disparities within the city itself. Although it has not experienced the devastating effects of deindustralization confronted in St. Louis, Columbus nonetheless remains a city with significant racial inequalities. Much of Columbus's economic growth, while within the city limits, has occurred in suburban areas. There remain substantial pockets of impoverished neighborhoods within the city, and, given the relatively small population of African Americans, these economically isolated neighborhoods also tend to have high concentrations of poor African Americans.

Table 2-2 provides comparative data on a number of socioeconomic indicators for African Americans and whites in Columbus and St. Louis. While the median household income of African Americans in Columbus is nearly $6,000 higher that of African Americans in St. Louis, the black/white disparity in each city is similar. In St. Louis, African Americans' median income is about 60 percent of the median income of whites, while in Columbus, this figure is approximately 69 percent. Likewise, one-third of African American families in St. Louis are living in poverty, compared to over one-fourth of their counterparts in Columbus. In St. Louis, the percentage of African Americans in poverty is nearly four times that of impoverished white families in St. Louis, while in Columbus, African Americans are over three times as likely as whites to be poor.

In comparative terms, African Americans in Columbus are better off than their counterparts in St. Louis—with a higher median income, lower unem-

Table 2-2 Select Socioeconomic Characteristics by Race, Columbus and St. Louis

	COLUMBUS		ST. LOUIS	
	African American	White	African American	White
Median Household Income	$19,750	$28,583	$13,803	$23,121
Percent of Families Below the Poverty Line	26.8%	8.6%	33.5%	8.9%
Percent Female-Headed Families	46.9%	16.8%	56.3%	20.0%
Median Income, Female-Headed Households with Children under Age 18	$8,791	$14,948	$7,698	$11,834
Percent Poverty, Female-Headed Households with Children under Age 18	52.6%	37.8%	57.5%	42.9%

Source: U.S. Census, 1990.

ployment rates, and lower rates of poverty. In relative terms, however,—comparing gaps between blacks and whites—racial disparities in Columbus are not considerably lower than those in St. Louis. In fact, *both* the Columbus and St. Louis metropolitan areas are among the ten most racially segregated with regard to their public school systems.[26] In addition, despite the economic growth experienced in Columbus in recent decades, disparities between African Americans and whites in the county have been increasing. For instance, while the poverty rate for whites remained stable (at 9.6 percent) from 1980 to 1990, it grew for African Americans—from 26.4 percent in 1980 to 29.3 percent in 1990.[27] Thus, while St. Louis provides a much better fit with scholars' focus on the socioeconomic contexts in which much of the recent growth of gangs has occurred, Columbus also fits this model in some ways, despite its overall economic vibrancy.

THE RESEARCH PROCESS*

As I noted in Chapter 1, my goal for this study is to provide a detailed portrait of young women's gang involvement, situated in the larger contexts of their lives. In doing so, I hope to expand the ways we think, not just about girls and gangs, but also about the nature of gender and crime. To achieve my goal, I needed to locate young women willing to share some of their life experiences with me, and I had to design my research in a way that would capture the complexities of their lives. I accomplished this by incorporating

---

*The interested reader can find the bulk of the more technical methods in the End-notes.

a number of research strategies, including the use of multiple methodologies and a comparative study design.[28]

The work is based primarily on in-depth interviews with girls in gangs, but it also includes surveys with gang and nongang girls and supplemental information on the characteristics of the neighborhoods that the young women call home. Interviewing girls in Columbus and St. Louis allowed me to explore variations that emerge in different contexts; in addition, survey interviews with at-risk young women who are not in gangs provided useful comparative information concerning differences in life experiences that help explain why some girls join gangs while others in the same communities do not. My hope for the project was to come away with a deeper understanding of girls' gang involvement, including why girls join gangs, the nature of gangs and gang life for girls, and the meanings of gang involvement, with particular attention to how gender shapes each of these issues.

Young women were recruited to participate in the study with the cooperation of a number of organizations working with at-risk youths, including a range of social service and juvenile justice agencies. Table 2-3 shows the sources of respondents.[29] A total of 94 girls were interviewed, including 48 gang members (21 in Columbus, 27 in St. Louis) and 46 nongang girls (25 in Columbus, 21 in St. Louis), all of whom described themselves as living in areas with at least some gang activity.[30] There are several limitations to my study resulting from the sampling. First is the problem of relying on interviews with young women who have come to the attention of authorities. Having done so means that it is likely that my sample overrepresents young women who have been in trouble. I did not have adequate access to young women who may be in gangs but have not come to the attention of the juvenile justice system or social service agencies, and it may be that they have different backgrounds or experiences that I have been unable to discover. For instance, one concern with using a sample of girls who've been in some trouble is that it might exaggerate the extent to which gang girls are involved in delinquency. Importantly, however, as I'll discuss in Chapter 6, even with this overrepresentation of girls who've been in some trouble,[31] it is still the case that only about one-third of the gang girls I interviewed were involved in ongoing serious offending.

Table 2-3 Source of Respondents (N = 94)

	Gang Members (N = 48)	Nongang Girls (N = 46)
Detention Facilities	19 (40%)	13 (28%)
Residential Shelter	8 (17%)	14 (30%)
Community Agencies	11 (23%)	12 (26%)
Schools	9 (19%)	7 (15%)
Snowball Referral	1 (2%)	0 (0%)

In addition, a portion of my sample were girls in facilities. Gangs may have different meanings to youths who are locked up or living in residential facilities than they do to youths who are living in the community. For instance, experiencing sanctions for activities related to gang involvement might alter girls' perceptions about the positive features of their gangs. On the other hand, gangs may take on special significance for youths in new or nontraditional settings as a means of fitting in. In fact, as I will discuss, the residential shelter in Columbus could almost be considered a breeding ground for gang involvement. Girls who entered the facility got to know other girls who were gang members and sometimes decided to join gangs as a result. For instance, Brandi joined Veronica's gang because she became friends with Veronica in placement and looked up to her. Three other young women I interviewed at the facility who were not gang members were contemplating joining at the time that we spoke.

However, it's important to point out that these girls were not gang members only during their time in placement. Instead, because the shelter where they lived was not a locked facility, young women routinely went AWOL to spend time on the streets and with their gangs. In fact, their frequent runaways sometimes interfered with my research, as I would show up to interview a young woman only to learn that she had taken off and would have to wait to reschedule until she turned back up. In addition, although a substantial minority of the gang members were interviewed in the local detention center in each city, this was not a long-term placement in either community. Instead, most youths were there subsequent to arrest but prior to adjudication. Thus I was interviewing young women not about experiences in the distant past but about activities they were currently or quite recently involved in within their communities.

Finally, the sample is relatively small. My experience was that it was both difficult and time-consuming to gain access to gang members, particularly young women. This was especially the case in Columbus, where more than a year's worth of effort yielded only twenty-one interviews with young women in gangs. Given the size of my sample and its nonrepresentativeness, my goal here is not to generalize about girls in gangs but to provide a rich analysis of both the nature of girls' gang involvement and the meanings they attribute to their gangs. What I lack in breadth I hope I've made up for in depth.

Girls were identified as gang members for the study through self-nomination—that is, they were classified as gang members when they said they were. This has become a standard method for identifying gang members in survey research, and it is widely believed to be the most reasonable approach for doing so among the limited options available.[32] Nonetheless, as with any method, self-nomination is not foolproof. One potential problem is having "wannabes" claim to be gang members when they aren't actually involved. And although there's no way to be sure this didn't happen in my study, one way to deal with the problem is to check the veracity of girls' reports, especially as they compare to other girls' descriptions of gangs and other available information.

For instance, I believe I identified one such young woman in Columbus. She was at the shelter care facility and hung out with Veronica and Brandi, whom I mentioned before. Initially she talked about wanting to join Veronica's gang, and she later told me that she had joined. However, she was unable to answer even the most rudimentary questions about the gang in ways that were consistent with what I had heard from other girls. Without challenging her, I simply ended the interview early, paid her for participating, and discarded it. I found no other instances where girls didn't provide adequate information; consequently, I take them at their word.

I began interviewing in Columbus in early 1995 and finished there in early 1996. Interviews in St. Louis began in the spring of 1997 and were completed that fall. Each interview began with the completion of an extensive survey; young women who identified themselves as gang members were then asked to participate in a follow-up in-depth interview about their gang involvement.[33] The interviews were voluntary, and respondents were promised strict confidentiality.[34] Interviews were conducted primarily in private offices, interview rooms, or secluded spots in visiting rooms, with a handful taking place in respondents' homes.

Once young women were approached about the study and agreed to speak with me, I began by providing them with a written description of the research, which I read aloud.[35] All of the girls who were approached agreed to be interviewed. The interviews were face-to-face and conducted one-on-one. I started by asking the young women to provide the names of two intersecting streets near their homes. While not as precise as an actual address, the information provided a means of gathering information about the neighborhoods where girls lived. Then we moved to an extensive survey interview, which included a wide range of questions to explore factors that may be related to gang membership for young women—for instance, family, school, neighborhood, and peers.[36] Girls who self-identified as gang members also were asked a series of questions about their gang, including things like what the gang is like and how and why they became involved. The survey interviews took anywhere from one-half hour to two hours to complete. Gang-involved girls then were asked to participate in a follow-up interview, which we either completed just after the survey or within a few days.

The in-depth interviews were semistructured with open-ended questions; all but one were audiotaped. The goal of these interviews was to gain a greater understanding of the nature and meaning of gang life for young women. The in-depth interviews were organized around several sets of questions. We began by discussing girls' entry into their gangs—how and why they became involved, the process of joining the gang, and what other things were going on in their lives at the time. Then we discussed the structure of the gang—its history, size, leadership, and organization and their place in the group.

The next series of questions concerned gender within the gang; for example, how females get involved, what activities they engage in and whether these are the same as the males' activities, and what kind of males and females have the most influence in the gang and why. The next series of questions explored gang involvement more generally—what being in the gang means, what kinds of things they do together, and so on. Then I asked how safe or dangerous they feel gang membership is and how they deal with risk. I concluded by asking them to speculate about why people their age join gangs; what things they like, dislike, and have learned by being in the gang; and what they like best about themselves. This basic guideline was followed for each interview, although when additional topics arose in the context of a conversation, we often deviated from the interview schedule to pursue them.[37] In Columbus, girls were paid ten dollars for each interview; in St. Louis, they were paid ten dollars for each survey and ten or twenty dollars for each in-depth interview, depending on the site.

When conducting research of this type, the procedure is often not nearly as straightforward as this description suggests. For instance, at one particularly slow point during my Columbus interviews, I became anxious to locate more gang members and turned to a not-uncommon method other researchers have employed—paying respondents to refer their friends and associates. I approached two of the most "hardcore" gang girls I had interviewed, both of whom were staying in a residential facility but who frequently went AWOL back to the streets. One of the girls came through for me beautifully, providing several referrals (all within the agency) that gave my research the jumpstart it needed. The other created what proved to be quite a sticky situation for me, which ultimately resulted in a mutual and fortunately amicable decision that I would terminate my interviews at this agency.

A particularly ingenious young woman, this girl decided she could cash in on my project by initiating new members into her gang. I arrived at the center one weekday morning, eager to complete several interviews scheduled for the day. As I headed up the walkway, the supervisor rushed out the door and informed me that the campus had experienced gang activity overnight and the place was in a bit of an uproar. One girl had been taken down to the pool the previous evening and beaten into a gang; another initiation, the staff had learned, was slated for that evening. My concern grew to anxiety when I realized that at least one of the girls was someone I had planned to interview. Not only would she have received an additional ten dollars for being a gang member (because she would be completing *both* the survey and in-depth interview), but her cottagemate who arranged the interview also would have received ten dollars for the referral. As a direct result of my research and the economic incentives attached to it, a young woman had joined a gang—a potentially life-altering decision.

Although the staff was gracious in accepting my profuse apologies for my unwitting role in the scheme, I nonetheless decided—and was met with no protest—that I would pull out of the site. It was a difficult decision to make because I had struggled for so long to locate gang girls in Columbus. Ultimately I believe it was the right thing to do. My presence had stirred up trouble for the agency, and I had an ethical obligation to back away, regardless of the cost to me. Before leaving, I spotted the young woman who arranged the interview for me. She was hanging around outside with a group of friends, and I pulled her aside and explained why I was leaving. She feigned obliviousness, but was nonetheless cordial about my precipitous exit and inability to conduct the interview or to pay her for the referral.

The situation was complicated even more because the director of the agency wanted to file formal assault charges against this young woman. The girl who was beaten in was uncooperative, though it didn't stop rumors from surfacing among the other girls that she was a potential snitch. The director, whom I had known for a number of years since working as a volunteer there as an undergraduate, began questioning me about my perceptions of the extent of the young woman's gang involvement. My promise of confidentiality prohibited me from answering the questions, but my long-standing relationship with the director—who had taken me under her wing when I was younger—as well as my feelings of culpability for the incident made me feel even worse about my silence. Moreover, if charges were filed and authorities questioned me, I was concerned about the ramifications. Fortunately the incident died down, and my exit from the agency also ended my further involvement in the problem. From my experience such complications, while stressful and troubling, are not unusual. Rather, the story should serve as a reminder of the problems with this type of research, where seemingly harmless decisions have the potential for quite detrimental consequences.

Table 2-4 provides demographic information about the young women in the study. In Columbus, approximately three-fourths of the sample were African American or multiracial and one-fourth was white. All of the re-

Table 2-4 Demographic Characteristics ($N = 94$)

	Gang Members ($N = 48$)	Nongang Girls ($N = 46$)
Race		
African American	39 (81%)	33 (72%)
White	5 (10%)	7 (15%)
Biracial or Multiracial	4 (8%)	6 (13%)
Age		
12–13	7 (15%)	7 (15%)
14–15	19 (40%)	23 (50%)
16–17	19 (40%)	12 (26%)
18–20	3 (6%)	4 (9%)
Mean Age	15.3	15.2

spondents in St. Louis were African American, with the exception of four multiracial girls. Columbus respondents were also slightly younger than the respondents from St. Louis. The mean age of girls in Columbus was 14.8 (14.9 for gang girls and 14.7 for nongang girls), while in St. Louis, girls' mean age was 15.6 (15.6 for gang members and 15.7 for nongang).

The range in girls' ages is also worth consideration. Interviewing adolescents, especially the younger ones, means staying attuned to developmental issues and how these may shape the research process. For instance, research suggests that, when compared to both older and younger youth, youths ages twelve to fourteen—especially girls—are more self-conscious, have slightly lower self-esteem and more unstable self-images, and are particularly sensitive to others' perceptions of them.[38] Moreover, these changes are heightened by being in new environments, especially places like junior high schools (or placement facilities), which are often characterized by conflict, gossip, and rumors.[39] It's not surprising then, that I found that the older girls typically opened up more during the conversational parts of the interviewing. This isn't to discount the handful of younger girls who were very talkative, but they were not always as focused or self-reflective as the older girls. Formal operational thought—or the ability to think theoretically—is believed to have developed by later adolescence;[40] thus the older girls also tended to have more insight into their behaviors than the younger ones did.

Perhaps this point is best illustrated with an example. Erica was seventeen years old when I interviewed her, and she had been in her gang for about two years.[41] She was quite insightful about her gang involvement and its costs and benefits to her as a person. At times, she was downright ambivalent about it. She explained:

> In some ways [being in the gang] makes me feel like a person, like actually somebody. But, in other ways, it's like, I don't know. It's, it just doesn't feel right. I mean, 'cause sometimes I sit back and I think that there are other things that I could be doing to get that respect or that attention without bein' in a gang.

For Erica, it was specifically her self-concept that the gang seemed to interfere with most. She noted, "It's just not the right picture of my life would be to be part of a gang." In particular, she grappled with the persona that being a gang member required her to project: "I gotta be more aggressive than I have to be with my friends. 'Cause I mean, if I really wanted to I could be a nice person. But around them, I, sometimes I just don't act like that. I act like I'm some real mean bully-type person." Even among the older girls who did not express ambivalence about their gangs, they still tended to bring the sort of sophisticated insight about their lives that Erica's discussion illustrates. On the other hand, younger girls were less able to think about their experiences in such terms. These are important considerations to bear in mind in later chapters, when I examine the meanings of gang involvement for young women.

FIELD RELATIONS

Successfully capturing the nature and meaning of girls' gang membership is not an easy task. For a variety of reasons, respondents may choose to be circumspect about the nature of their activities and may choose to conceal elements of their lives they consider incriminating, embarrassing, shameful, or simply private. The secretive nature of gangs can exacerbate this problem, as can social distances resulting from factors such as gender, race, class, and age.[42] Social distances that include differences in relative power can result in suspicion and lack of trust. For instance, Taylor and colleagues point out that "[a]dolescents may choose a form of political resistance—that is, choose not to speak about what they know and feel—to people they see as representing or aligning with unresponsive institutions and authorities."[43] Overcoming these obstacles can only be achieved by building rapport, ensuring and reassuring confidentiality, and establishing trust. I used a number of approaches to facilitate this process.

First, my research approach proved useful for establishing rapport. The survey interview began with relatively innocuous questions (demographics, living arrangements, attitudes toward school) and slowly made the transition from these to more sensitive questions about gang involvement, delinquency, and victimization. In addition, completing the survey interview first allowed me to establish a relationship with each young woman, so that when we completed the in-depth interview, there was a preexisting level of familiarity between us. In particular, in the course of the survey when a young woman described participating in serious delinquency—including, in some instances, brutal acts of violence—I had the opportunity to respond in a nonjudgmental manner. This provided a layer of understanding that facilitated frank discussions when we revisited these issues during the in-depth interviews.

In fact, a nonjudgmental *manner* is just the beginning—to explore the meanings individuals attribute to their experiences, it is necessary to make the additional effort to actually try to understand and share in their subjective views.[44] A goal of qualitative research is to capture and describe the world from the points of view of the research participants. Quite simply, this means making the effort to put oneself in their shoes. One measure of my success at this endeavor came from a conversation I had with a friend of mine—a fellow grad student at the time—who was transcribing some of my interviews. She was amazed and somewhat disturbed at my reaction during one of the interviews. A young woman described to me that she had recently started carrying a gun to school to protect herself, after having been repeatedly threatened by a group of girls who had lately gone so far as to brandish knives. My spontaneous reaction was, "You have to protect yourself," while my friend Lori said hers would have been, "What! You took a gun to school?" To the extent that my intuitive reactions to girls' stories reflected an understanding of their points of view, my efforts to develop rapport and trust were boosted.

In addition, I worked to ensure trust in the young women I interviewed through my efforts to protect their confidentiality. This went beyond simply stating my intentions and instead involved actually showing young women I was serious about protecting them. For instance, when girls accidentally disclosed their own or a friend's name on tape, I immediately stopped, erased the name, and played the tape back before continuing the interview. Likewise, I stayed aware of our surroundings to ensure against eavesdropping. There were times when I paused during interviews because agency staff or other youths appeared to be within hearing range, and I even moved to more private settings to complete a few interviews when, upon asking them, girls indicated they would be more comfortable doing so. I was proactive in reacting to the immediate environment and did not wait for a sign of discomfort from respondents. In fact, often I remained much more concerned than they were. Ultimately, I believe these actions engendered greater trust among the young women who spoke to me, as evidenced by some of what they disclosed.

Finally, providing respondents with the opportunity to act as teachers can afford them with a sense of meaning and importance. This is particularly the case for young women in gangs, for whom adolescence, coupled with marginalization and membership in a socially stigmatized group, has routinely meant that they are denied the opportunity to be heard and have their perspectives taken seriously.[45] One way in which I indicated that I viewed them as teachers was to incorporate aspects of their language into our discussions—in some cases substituting their language for my own (e.g., "set" instead of "gang"), but more often by asking them what terms they would use when talking with one another in order to indicate my interest in learning their language and meaning systems.[46] Mind you, there is a delicate balance to maintain. Had I tried to talk like them, it probably would have undermined my credibility. They clearly recognized our differences, and an overincorporation of their language would have made me look like a "poser."

In addition, I paid close attention to and took seriously respondents' reactions to themes raised in the interviews, particularly instances in which they "talked back"[47] by labeling a topic irrelevant, pointing out what they saw as misinterpretations on my part, or offering corrections. In my research, young women talked back the most in response to my efforts to get them to articulate how gender inequality shaped their experiences in the gang. Despite stories they told to the contrary, many maintained a strong belief in their equality within their gang. Consequently, I developed an entire theoretical discussion around the contradictory operation of gender within the gang (the subject of Chapters 7 and 8). As the research progressed, I also took emerging themes back to respondents in subsequent interviews to see if they felt I had gotten it right. In addition to conveying that I was interested in their perspectives and experiences, this process also proved useful for further refining my analyses.

Each of these efforts helped me build rapport and trust among the young women I interviewed. In settings where multiple interviews took place, word of mouth about the project tended to be positive, which encouraged more girls to participate and to feel comfortable opening up during interviews. In fact, on one occasion when I was interviewing a gang member referred by a friend at the shelter care facility, she hesitated when I began asking questions about her gang's criminal activities. I paused, asked whether she was uncomfortable with the line of questions, and she said yes and asked that I wait while she took a break. I suspect that she left the room to speak to the gang member who had referred her; when she came back she appeared reassured and comfortable and expressed no further ambivalence in talking to me.

This is not to suggest that all of the interviews ran smoothly. While I have noted the ways that positive word of mouth benefited the project, it was also sometimes the case that being too well known to potential respondents posed problems. Because I was interviewing both gang and nongang girls, I tried to keep the project from being labeled a "gang" study. However, there were occasions when it became clear to me that there was too much "buzz" following me around and that the focus of a lot of the talk was about gangs. On several occasions, I decided to temporarily pull out of a given site to allow talk of the project to die down, after girls who were concerned about being labeled gang members expressed reservation about opening up to me. In fact, agency personnel sometimes exacerbated the problem. Despite my requests to the contrary, staff members frequently described the project as about "gangs" in front of potential respondents. In the most disturbing incident, I was just beginning to interview a girl at the shelter care facility when a staff member burst into the room and loudly announced, "Hey, do you wanna interview me? I know a lot about gangs!" Fortunately the young woman ended up being an out-of-town placement who didn't meet my sample criteria. It remained a problem, however, that occasionally slowed the research process.

An additional potential problem worth more detailed consideration is the issue of social distances and their influence on the interview process. In this regard, it is revealing to compare my experiences interviewing young women with those of Rod Brunson and Niquita Vinyard, my research assistants in St. Louis. Rod is an African American male who grew up in North St. Louis, where many of the respondents were from, while I am a white female. We are both in our early thirties, though most girls assumed I was younger.[48] Niquita is an African American female in her early twenties, from the suburbs north of the city, middle-class, and educated. Originally, we planned for Rod to interview young men for a related project while Niquita and I interviewed young women. When—due to project delays—Rod began interviewing young women, he felt initial discomfort that gender would be an obstacle, but found instead that many girls were much more comfortable opening up to him than the young men had been.[49] We also discovered that the way young women responded to us sometimes varied and appeared to be shaped both by race and by gender.

Perhaps because many of the girls we interviewed had had less than positive experiences with other adult men in their lives, they responded to Rod—an older African American male who was empathetic and interested in their lives—as a paternal figure and felt quite safe disclosing and talking at length with him (and without prompting) about their experiences of victimization. One girl even asked him to adopt her; another tried to fix him up with her aunt. Conversely, while young women disclosed victimization to Niquita and me, there was rarely an instance in which they appeared comfortable, let alone desirous, to speak about these experiences in detail. While feminist researchers have sometimes assumed that women are more comfortable discussing victimization with other women, Currie and MacLean recently suggested that this is not the case; in fact, in some instances women are more comfortable speaking with sympathetic males. These authors point out that gender dynamics operate, not just in mixed-gender settings but also in single-gender settings, so that "regardless of how 'sisterly' a feminist researcher may feel toward other women, there is no guarantee that respondents perceive other women as necessarily supportive."[50] In fact, given the strength of girls' victim-blaming attitudes towards other young women who were mistreated (see Chapters 7 and 8), it is remarkable they shared with us as much as they did.

In my case, it may be that our perceived similarity in age, perhaps coupled with social distances created by race and class differences, was a source of uneasiness for some young women, hindering their willingness to open up to me about these issues.[51] In Niquita's case even more, their similarities of race and age, in conjunction with their class differences, meant that she had the most difficulty getting girls to open up to her about aspects of their lives they felt could be scrutinized. Niquita was also a new mother at the time of the interviews, and she sometimes found herself following up with questions about the responsibilities of motherhood that seemed to make a handful of girls defensive.

On the other hand, we also found that my differences from respondents—particularly in relation to race—often were beneficial once trust had been established. Taylor and her colleagues suggest that one advantage of social distance is that it "may elicit explanations that are assumed to be known by someone with insider status."[52] Reading Rod's transcripts against ours, we found instances in which girls assumed shared understandings with Rod, while they took more time to explain things, especially to me. In addition, as I previously suggested, social distances facilitate respondents' recognition of themselves as experts on their social worlds. Many of the girls were cognizant of the "controlling images"[53] used to describe aspects of their lives. Consequently, in some instances, young women responded to me in ways that purposely challenged common stereotypes about adolescents, inner-city youths, and gangs. For instance, Tamika told me:

Some people stereotype, they just stereotype gang members to be hardcore and to always be shootin' at somebody. They don't stereotype people that that could be a gang member but still they could go to school and get straight As. That's stereotyping because I know, I know a few gang-bangers who go to school, get straight As, hit the books but still when they on the street, you know, they take good care of theirs. They takin' care of theirs in school and they takin' care of theirs on the street and I don't think that's right to stereotype people.

Richardson has noted that "people organize their personal biographies and understand them through the stories they create to explain and justify their life experiences."[54] For some of the young women I spoke to, I believe participating in the interviews was both empowering and illuminating because they were able to reflect on their lives in ways typically not available to them. An additional consideration, however, is the ways in which the interviews provided girls with the opportunity to refine the stories of their lives, blurring the ways their actual experiences fit with their *stories* of their experiences. These stories are shaped by "already established cultural standards,"[55] including those of the larger culture and, for gang members, of the gang itself.

When I interviewed girls in institutional environments, for example, it often was clear that the setting shaped how they perceived their lives and, consequently, what they told me. Agar has suggested that out-of-context reports often are not completely accurate and may present a more exaggerated, glamorous, or smooth picture than is warranted.[56] For some girls, being locked up, even for a short time, led to introspection and ambivalence about their gang involvement that likely would not have occurred in other settings. Being in an environment where they were unable to hang out with their friends, and instead were experiencing negative consequences for their activities, led some girls to vacillate between their attachment to the gang and their desire to "do good" on the outside. One young woman even vacillated throughout our interview. In one breath Traci was utterly enthralled with gang life—throwing signs for me and talking about the gang in a very animated manner—and in the next breath exclaimed that she was getting out of the gang when she was released to straighten up her life.

However, as Richardson's comments suggest, this does not make the interviews inherently less "trustworthy" than interviews gathered in other contexts. To make such an argument, one would have to assume that contexts exist that do not shape individuals' immediate perceptions of their lives—a position I find untenable. The context in which my interviews were completed, as with any context, simply provided a *particular* slice of life, and this is what's important to keep in mind.

In addition, gangs themselves have particular stories that get refined through telling and retelling. These stories become part of the normative structures of gangs, even when they are not consistently enacted in behaviors. For instance, Klein has noted that violence is a "predominant 'myth system' "[57] within gangs, even though there is often much more talk about violence than actual violent behavior. When analyzing girls' discussions of their gang involvement, I have been careful in attempting to tease out their experiences from the frames they adopt to explain their experiences. While girls' stories of the gang are significant for what they reveal about constructed norms and values within the gang, read carefully, their descriptions of activities sometimes provide evidence that challenges the stories they tell.[58] Thus, the interviews actually provide two sets of findings—evidence of the nature of gang girls' social world, and the cultural frames they use to make sense of their experiences.[59] In the chapters that follow, I weave these findings together to provide a window into the lives of girls in gangs in Columbus and St. Louis.

3

Getting Into Gangs

Gang membership doesn't happen overnight. Research shows that youths typically hang out with gang members for some time—often as much as a year—before making a commitment to join.[1] Moreover, there are pushes and pulls even earlier in life that increase the likelihood that young people will associate with gangs in the first place. The goal of this chapter is to explore girls' pathways into gangs by painting a picture of the broader contexts and precipitating events that lead young women to spend time with gang members and to join gangs.

On the whole, cities like Columbus and St. Louis have not had gang problems long enough to have intergenerational gang involvement within families. Consequently, gangs remain concentrated among adolescents and young adults. The young women in this study typically began hanging out with gang members when they were quite young—around age twelve on average—and they joined at an average age of thirteen. In fact, 69 percent of the girls in the sample described joining their gangs before they turned fourteen.[2] In considering girls' motives for joining gangs, it is important to keep their youthfulness in mind.

Three themes emerged in my research with regard to the life contexts that contribute to girls' gang involvement, at least among the kinds of gang girls in my sample. What's notable is that they emerged independently, both in the surveys—as factors distinguishing gang from nongang girls—and in the in-depth interviews, as contexts that young women attributed to their becoming gang-involved. First were girls' neighborhood contexts and their exposure to gangs via both neighborhood peer and other friendship networks. A second theme that emerged for some young women was the existence of serious family problems, such as violence and drug abuse, which led them to avoid home, contributed to their weak supervision, and pushed them to attempt to meet social and emotional needs elsewhere. Finally, many young women described the strong influence that gang-involved family members—particularly older siblings in Columbus and siblings and cousins in St. Louis—had on their decisions to join.

While each young woman revealed her own trajectory into gang life, there were many common circumstances across girls' stories. In fact, the three themes noted here rarely stood alone in young women's stories of how they came to join their gangs. Instead they were overlapping in girls' accounts. As each told of individual life experiences, most recounted complex pathways into gangs that involved, in varying ways, the themes I've just de-

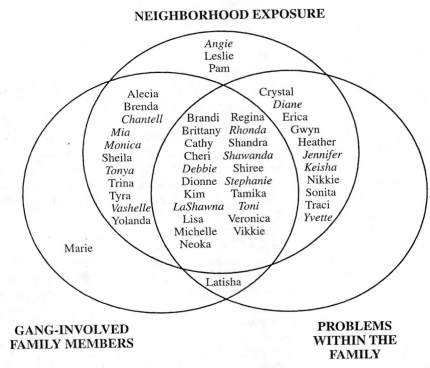

NEIGHBORHOOD EXPOSURE

Angie
Leslie
Pam

Alecia   Crystal
Brenda   *Diane*
Chantell   Brandi   Regina   Erica
Mia   Brittany *Rhonda* Gwyn
Monica   Cathy   Shandra Heather
Sheila   Cheri   *Shawanda* *Jennifer*
Tonya   *Debbie* Shiree   *Keisha*
Trina   Dionne   *Stephanie* Nikkie
Tyra   Kim   Tamika   Sonita
Vashelle   LaShawna *Toni*   Traci
Yolanda   Lisa   Veronica *Yvette*
             Michelle Vikkie
Marie   Neoka

Latisha

GANG-INVOLVED   **PROBLEMS**
FAMILY MEMBERS   **WITHIN THE**
                                FAMILY

Figure 3-1 Pathways into Gangs
Note: Girls whose names are italicized report regular involvement in serious delinquency.

scribed. Before I delve into each of these themes in greater detail, it is important to have a clear picture of the extent of their interrelationships and how they differed for gang and nongang girls.

Blending our discussions during the in-depth interviews with data from the survey, Figure 3-1 illustrates how young women accounted for their gang involvement. Girls were classified as having neighborhood exposure to gangs when they said there was a lot of gang activity in their neighborhood or they reported gang members living on their street. Gang-involved family members included girls with a sibling in a gang or with multiple family members in gangs or girls who described another family member (e.g., a cousin or aunt) as having a decided influence on their decision to join. Girls with family problems included those with three or more of the following: violence between adults in the home, having been abused, drug or alcohol abuse in the family, or family members in jail. Four additional girls who did not report three of these were also categorized as such because of their discussions of the impact of family problems. These included Heather, who was sexually abused by multiple members of her family; Rhonda and Latisha, who reported frequent abuse and witnessed physical violence among adults in the family; and Jennifer, whose parents were killed in a car crash, the loss of whom she felt was a turning point in her life.

What's striking about Figure 3-1 is the extent to which young women reported multiple dimensions of these risk factors. Taken individually, a majority of girls fit within each category. Ninety-six percent described living in neighborhoods with gangs (of these, 69 percent explicitly described their neighborhood and peer networks as factors in their decisions to join). Likewise, 71 percent recognized family problems as contributing factors, and 71 percent had siblings or multiple family members in gangs or described the influence of gang-involved family members on their decisions to join. In all, 90 percent of the gang members in the study report two or more dimensions of these risk factors, and fully 44 percent fit within the overlap of all three categories.[3] In Figure 3-1, the names of young women involved in ongoing serious delinquency are italicized. It is notable that only one-third of the gang members were involved in serious offending. The majority of girls, despite their gang involvement, were not.[4]

Figure 3-2 provides a similar picture of nongang girls' exposure to the risk factors highlighted by gang girls. Nongang girls were classified using the same survey criteria as gang girls. In addition, Cherise was classified as having family problems despite not mentioning three of the five listed here because her mother was in jail and she had been shuffled between foster homes and residential facilities from the time she was six. Young women listed outside the diagram met none of these criteria, though they nonetheless had some exposure to gangs. Several things are notable in comparing Figures 3-1 and 3-2. First, while the vast majority of gang girls (90 percent) fit in overlapping categories, only one-third of the nongang girls experienced multiple risk factors for gangs, and only four nongang girls (9 percent, versus 44 percent of gang girls) reported all three dimensions. These data will be broken down individually in Tables 3-2 through 3-4. Those contexts most likely to be shared between gang and nongang girls were neighborhoods that exposed them to gangs, which 59 percent of nongang girls reported. However, only 26 percent of the nongang girls reported serious family problems, compared to 71 percent of gang girls. Likewise, 71 percent of gang members reported significant gang-involved family members, while only one-third of the nongang girls had gang members in their immediate family or multiple gang members in their extended family. Thus, while the majority of nongang girls had gangs around them, most didn't have other experiences that could tip the scales in favor of gang involvement.

Nonetheless, many of the nongang girls did have friends in gangs, and a sizeable minority had considered joining. In all, 35 percent of the nongang girls said that half or more of their friends were gang members (as indicated by italicized names in Figure 3-2). Likewise, 28 percent (boldface names) said they had considered joining a gang themselves. However, only three young women—Denise, DeeDee, and Cherise—were seriously contemplating joining or had specific plans to join in the future. As I noted in Chapter 2, each of these girls was in the shelter facility in Columbus where a number of young

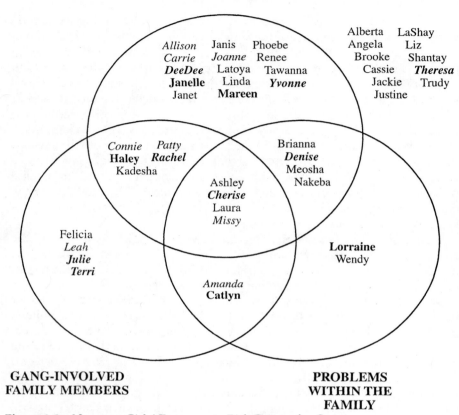

Figure 3-2 Nongang Girls' Exposure to Risk Factors for Gangs.
Note: Girls whose names are italicized report half or more of their friends are gang members; girls whose names appear in boldface have considered joining gangs.

women were gang-involved. Later in the chapter, I will discuss in more detail nongang girls' accounts of why they considered joining gangs and why they avoided them. First, let me turn my attention back to gang girls' descriptions of how they got into gangs. Although I will discuss each of these themes—neighborhood and peer networks, gang-involved family, and family problems—separately, I will keep their overlapping nature at the forefront, building a layered picture of how young women get into gangs.

NEIGHBORHOOD CONTEXTS AND NETWORKS

Scholars long have recognized that factors such as neighborhood characteristics, poverty, and limited opportunities are associated with the extent and nature of gangs in communities.[5] Recent studies of female gang involvement likewise have made the connection between these factors and young women's participation in gangs.[6] In fact, many scholars have pointed to the gang as a means for inner-city youths—male and female—to adapt to the oppressive living conditions imposed by their environments. According to Joe and Chesney-Lind, "The gang assists young women and men in coping with their lives in chaotic, violent, and economically marginalized communities."[7]

In Chapter 2 I described the overall character of Columbus and St. Louis. In both cities there is substantial racial inequality, but on the whole Columbus is more socioeconomically stable than St. Louis. But what about the neighborhoods of the girls in my sample? Table 3-1 compares citywide characteristics with the average characteristics of the neighborhoods that the young women called home.[8] In both cities, the vast majority of girls in the study lived in neighborhoods that were economically worse off and more racially segregated than the city as a whole. Their neighborhoods had substantially lower median incomes and higher rates of poverty and unemployment than the citywide averages. In fact, in Columbus, the averages in Table 3-1 are skewed slightly because of Leslie's inclusion. From one of the wealthiest, most exclusive, and "whitest" suburbs in Columbus, she joined her gang after running away from home and meeting members in the neighborhood where she stayed.

While the gap between the city and girls' neighborhoods was not greater in St. Louis than Columbus, young women in St. Louis nonetheless were drawn from more segregated and economically devastated neighborhoods, on average, than were young women in Columbus. In fact, two-thirds of the gang members in St. Louis lived in neighborhoods that were 80 percent or more African American.[9] Although Table 3-1 does not provide information on the nongang respondents, it is worth noting how they compare to the gang girls in the sample. The nongang girls interviewed also tended to come from racially segregated and economically troubled neighborhoods. However, on average, they were in neighborhoods that were slightly better off

Table 3-1 City and Neighborhood Characteristics

	City	Gang Members' Neighborhoods
Columbus		
Median Income	$26,651	$19,625
Percent Poverty	17.3%	29.3%
Percent Unemployment	5.9%	13.2%
Percent African American	22.6%	55.8%
St. Louis		
Median Income	$19,458	$14,933
Percent Poverty	24.0%	41.2%
Percent Unemployment	10.6%	18.2%
Percent African American	47.5%	72.0%

Source: U.S. Census, 1990.

than gang girls' neighborhoods. For instance, the median income and percent poverty for nongang girls in Columbus were $21,298 and 30.4 percent, respectively; in St. Louis they were $18,246 and 35.6 percent, respectively.

Gang and nongang girls also did not differ considerably with regard to characteristics often associated with poverty, such as family structure, adult unemployment, or educational attainment. Half of the gang members and 43 percent of the nongang girls lived with a single parent, most often their mother. Eleven gang members (23 percent) lived in two-parent families, compared to one- hird (fifteen) of the non-gang girls. Ten gang members (21 percent) and eight (17 percent) nongang girls lived with extended family, most often grandmothers or aunts, while three gang members (6 percent) and three non-gang girls (7 percent) lived in other settings (foster homes, with friends).

However, among Columbus gang girls in particular, these figures mask a tremendous amount of mobility. For example, Veronica said she would stay with her father for a while, then move to her uncle's, then in with her boyfriend's family and back again. Sonita described living with her mother, but spending most of the previous year and a half as a runaway. In all, eight gang members in Columbus (38 percent of the sample there) described moving back and forth between various locations, staying no more than a few months at a time in any given household. Four of the nongang girls in Columbus (16 percent) also described such movement, while these discussions were largely absent in St. Louis. Most likely, these differences are the result of my greater reliance on girls in facilities in Columbus (see Chapter 2).

The vast majority of girls in both cities reported that at least one of the adults in their household worked: 83 percent of the gang members and 87 percent of the nongang girls. Fourteen of the gang members (29 percent) and ten of the nongang girls (22 percent) reported that no one in their household had graduated from high school, while the majority reported that at least one household member had graduated from high school (29 percent of gang members and 35 percent of nongang girls) or had some training or college education beyond high school (40 percent and 39 percent, respectively). Nonetheless, most young women lived in impoverished, racially segregated neighborhoods.

Living in these neighborhoods means living in places with substantial amounts of crime.[10] In recent times, it often also means living in neighborhoods with street gangs. It goes without saying that to join a gang a young woman must have some exposure to gangs—at least the one she's joining. It's useful, then, to examine girls' descriptions of the extent of gang activity in their neighborhoods and the meanings they attribute to it. An important component of this is the extent to which they view gangs in the neighborhood as having facilitated or contributed to their decisions to join.

Table 3-2 illustrates girls' characterizations of the extent of gang activity in their neighborhoods. In both Columbus and St. Louis, the vast majority of young women described some exposure to gangs in their neighborhoods. As I noted in Chapter 2, some level of exposure to gangs was a criterion for in-

Table 3-2 Exposure to Gangs

	Gang Members (N = 48)	Nongang Members (N = 46)
There is a lot of talk about gangs around the neighborhood	38 (80%)	31 (67%)
There is a lot of gang activity around the neighborhood	40 (83%)	25 (54%)*
There are other gang members living on the same street	39 (81%)	21 (46%)*
There are rival gangs close by	35 (73%)	26 (57%)

*$p < .05$.

clusion in the sample, both for gang and nongang girls. My interest here, however, is the extent and proximity of gang activity in girls' neighborhoods. As Table 3-2 shows, gang members were significantly more likely than nongang girls to report "a lot" of gang activity in their neighborhoods and to note that there were other gang members who lived on their street.[11] While the vast majority of the gang members (96 percent, as shown in Figure 3-1) described gang activity in their neighborhoods in these terms, just over half of the nongang girls did so. While all of the girls in the study could be characterized as at risk for problem behaviors and detrimental life consequences, only half of them had joined gangs. It appears then, that coupled with other factors, living in neighborhoods with gangs in close proximity increases the likelihood that young women will choose to become gang-involved themselves.

Documenting the existence of gang activity in girls' neighborhoods provides one piece of the puzzle. But what meanings do gang-involved girls attribute to gangs in their neighborhoods, and to what extent do they perceive neighborhood gangs as having had an impact on their decision to join? Because one goal of my study was to try to come away with an understanding of gang life from girls' points of view, this is an important line of inquiry. Other scholars have suggested that gangs can function to alleviate the boredom experienced by inner-city youths, who have few options for recreation or entertainment. John Quicker summarizes, "To be in a gang is to be part of something. It means having a place to go, friends to talk with, and parties to attend. It means recognition and respected status."[12] In addition, many scholars talk about the protective functions of gangs.[13] A number of the young women in my study had been victims of crime prior to as well as after joining gangs. Many articulated a specifically gendered sense of protection that they saw resulting from being in gangs that were predominantly male. While this was not a theme young women explicitly talked about in their discussions of why they decided to join, nonetheless it's an important topic that will receive more attention in Chapter 7.

Not surprisingly, the majority of the gang girls suggested that their decision to become gang-involved stemmed in part from exposure to gangs through their neighborhood peer networks. Most often, they described a process in which they began to hang out with older gang-involved kids around the neighborhood as they reached adolescence, and these associations eventually led them to want to join. For instance, Angie, fifteen when we spoke, had joined her gang at age eleven. She described how changes in her neighborhood shaped her desire to become a gang member:

> It's like, our neighborhood started changing a little bit, people started movin' in and out, and I was associating with the people who moved in and out, you know, and I was just, then, they was, a lot of 'em was in gangs, or things like that, and I wanted to be in a gang.

Because she was so young when she joined, it was a couple of years before she became actively involved. Instead, it appears that the older members thought it was cute that a young girl from the neighborhood wanted to be a member, but had few expectations for her participation. She explained:

> They was just like, "Hey, you wanna be a member?" I was like, one day, and I was like, "Yeah, yeah! I wanna be one, I wanna be one, I wanna be one!" Then they put me in and I was in, but then I, and as the years went by that's when I started really gettin' involved wid 'em, but then [at that time] I didn't, I didn't see them that much.

Chantell also described her neighborhood context as the overriding factor leading to her gang membership. Fourteen when we spoke, she became gang-involved at age twelve. Chantell lived with her mother, grandmother, and siblings in a neighborhood where gangs were "just like everywhere." She described her childhood as one in which she grew up with gangs. She explained, "When I was little, I mean when I was young, I grew up around 'em. Just grew up around 'em, basically. Then when you grow up around 'em and you see 'em so much, until you want to get initiated."

At the time she decided to join, many of Chantell's neighborhood friends also were joining, as well as her older sister. "It was like a lot of gang-banging, I mean, it was just like, people were just like gettin' in it and having fun." Although she was somewhat torn about joining—"like wondering should I or shouldn't I, stuff like that, or what would happen if I did, or if I didn't"—eventually she decided to go ahead. "I was around 'em so much, the things they did I did," she explained, "so I said, since I grew up with 'em, I'm already hanging out with 'em, couldn't be no difference, so."

Chantell's comments about seeing other young people "gettin' in it and having fun" were echoed by a number of young women who described joining gangs in part because of their desire to belong to a neighborhood group, fit in, and have fun. This was especially the case for girls who joined quite young. Crystal joined at age twelve, noting, "You see other people doing it and you just think it's cool." And Nikkie, who also joined at twelve, explained, "If you ain't in it you just be . . . you just be feelin' left out. You be like, 'oh they all in a gang and I'm just sittin' here.'" As a result, she said, "I was like, 'I wanna get in it.' And I got in it." Latisha joined at twelve and explained, "It's fun. That's why I joined, 'cause it was fun and I seen what they was doing and I thought it was fun and it was cool or whatever." Likewise Pam joined at thirteen and noted:

> They just [were] having fun, going to parties, kickin' it, staying out all night, new clothes, new shoes, selling drugs and all that. I wanted to be like that too. I wanted to wear name brand shoes, name brand clothes, I wanted my hair done and everything just like that so that's what I done.

In addition, residential instability appeared to be a factor shaping the influence of neighborhood gangs on girls' decision making. Over half of the gang members in the sample (52 percent in both cities) described having moved within the year prior to our interview, and two-thirds had moved within the previous two years. In comparison, 28 percent of the nongang girls had moved in the last year, and 48 percent within the previous two years. Moreover, these figures do not include such things as running away from home or spending time in detention or placement facilities—experiences that a large number of girls (especially in Columbus) reported and that are indicative of further residential instability. While this instability is likely related to other family and economic problems that may be linked to risks for gang involvement, it is also the case that, upon arrival in a new environment, becoming involved with a local gang provides young women with a means of fitting in with a new crowd and becoming known. As Shawanda described, "I just needed some friends; [joining the gang] was a quick way to make me a friend." In fact, several girls explicitly described joining gangs upon moving to new places, and, as I've noted, others decided to join when they met gang members in residential facilities.

For instance, Traci had only recently moved to Columbus when we spoke, and likewise had recently joined her gang. She explained that moving to a new city, she "wanted to be like other people." At the same time she began noticing "all these blue scarves and red scarves and stuff," she got to know the neighbor in the apartment above hers—a young man who was a member of a neighborhood Crips set. Shortly thereafter she joined the gang and began going out with the young man. Traci felt that joining the gang was a way both to make friends and to fit into her new environment. LaShawna was sent to Columbus to live with relatives when she was thirteen, and had been gang-involved since age twelve in the large city where she previously lived. In Columbus she became gang-involved when she "hooked up with" another gang member in a residential facility, where her knowledge of "big-city" gangs provided her with status and reputation.

A handful of young women, mostly in Columbus, described becoming gang-involved as a result of friends' involvement rather than through neighborhood peer networks. Jennifer, Leslie, and Heather joined their gangs after a close friend introduced them to other gang members. For instance, Heather said of her decision to join: "I [was] at my friend Chad's house and they [gang members] had just came over 'cause they was friends with Chad's, and we just started talkin' and hangin' out and then they started talkin' about a gang and it's like that, I just got in there." Likewise, Jennifer joined her gang after her best friend introduced her to the OG ("Original Gangster," i.e., a leader). She explained, "My friend was already in it and she would come over and she'd talk about all the, how it's real, it's just real cool to be in and everything like that." Once Jennifer met the OG, she began spending time with the other gang members and eventually was allowed to join.[14]

Leslie had run away from home and became friends with a gang girl she met at a local shelter for teen runaways. She returned home, but later "ran away with my friend. And she took me down there and introduced me to [the gang]." Leslie talked to the OG, who "told me that I would, it was an easy way to be protected and, um, I wouldn't have any problems. I wouldn't have to worry about money, food, clothing, a place to stay, 'cause I'da have all that because I was in the gang." At the point we interviewed, Leslie was pregnant and planning to sever her ties to the gang. Her outlook on it was decidedly negative. Of her initial conversation with the OG and decision to join, she surmised, "It was a bunch of lies . . . and I fell into the trap and believed him."

JM: And why do you say it was a lie now?
LESLIE: Because I was almost in the gang for about a year and a half. And, just bein' in there, you didn't go anywhere. You, um, you really didn't, I mean, succeed in anything 'cause the stuff that you were doin' was wrong. And, half, that's why half of 'em, half the guys are in here [the detention center] now, it has to do with some kind of gang-related somethin'.

Although gang girls in St. Louis reported similar rates of residential instability as gang girls in Columbus, a number of them described having recently moved to relatives' neighborhoods. Young women in St. Louis were more likely to describe their neighborhood gangs as wary of outsiders, and thus new people—unless they were the relatives or friends of youths in the neighborhood—were less able to quickly assimilate into the local gang as girls in Columbus described.[15] Pam, for instance, joined her neighborhood gang when she was thirteen. She said, "I grew up with some of them, went to school with some of them, and by me knowing them I just knew the other ones 'cause they used to be around." Much like Chantell, Pam joined because she'd "been knowing them anyway all my life for real." But she described a gang with somewhat tighter boundaries than what Chantell had described. Pam explained that for someone to join her gang:

> They just got to be known or something. You can't just be no anybody. They got to know you or they been knowing you or they grew up with you or something like that or you family. Other than that, they just don't put you in there like that. . . . 'Cause anybody that is in the gang, everybody grew up together

for real. It's just not like no anybody, like they gonna get anybody. You want to be in this gang? It ain't like that. You got to know a person, you got to grow up around it or be around it.

Tyra articulated much the same beliefs as Pam, noting, "If you ain't in our streets or nothin', live on our streets, you ain't joining nothin'." She said she joined her gang because "I grew up in that neighborhood with them." Moreover, Tyra suggested that part of the nature of gangs in St. Louis is attributable to how dangerous many neighborhoods are. She explained: "Growing up on the North Side [of St. Louis], you got to be like that 'cause everywhere you look, you turn around and somebody is getting killed. I don't care what nobody say, I think the North Side worse than any side."

Very few of the young women described getting involved with their gangs because their boyfriend was a member. In fact, only three girls—Rhonda, Marie, and Stephanie—described this as a specific motivating factor. This is not to suggest that young women didn't have boyfriends, including within their gangs. For instance, Traci became gang-involved at around the same time her gang-involved neighbor became her boyfriend. But she didn't attribute her desire or decision to join the gang as having to do with him. Instead she said, "I just wanted to join, I don't know why, when I moved out here [to Columbus] I just *had* to join a gang." It is significant that only a handful of girls described a relationship with a boyfriend as a factor influencing their decision to join a gang, with most describing broader neighborhood peer networks as having greater importance. This finding challenges some long-held beliefs about young women in gangs, but also is in keeping with other research that suggests that, despite being overlooked by many scholars, girls' friendships are an important factor for explaining both their gang involvement and their delinquency.[16]

While neighborhood and friendship networks help answer the questions of how and why girls come to join gangs, these remain only a partial explanation. In fact, as Figure 3-1 illustrates, often there are other precipitating factors to consider. Many young women described problems in their family lives that led them to spend time away from home, out on the streets, and with gang members. In addition, like their relationships with friends in the neighborhood, having gang-involved family members was significantly related to girls' gang involvement in both Columbus and St. Louis. In the next section, I discuss further the impact of family problems on girls' gang involvement; then I return to the issue of gang-involved family members.

FAMILY PROBLEMS AS PRECIPITATING CIRCUMSTANCES

The family has long been considered crucial for understanding delinquency and gang behavior among girls.[17] Problems such as weak supervision, lack of attachment to parents, family violence, and drug and alcohol abuse by family members all have been suggested as contributing to the likelihood that girls will join gangs.[18] My study provides additional support for these conclusions, based on comparative findings from survey interviews and from young women's accounts of why they joined gangs.

As Table 3-3 illustrates, gang members were significantly more likely to come from homes with numerous problems than were the young women who were not in gangs. Gang girls were significantly more likely to have witnessed physical violence between adults in their homes and to describe having been abused by adult family members. In addition, gang members were much more likely to report that there was regular drug use in their homes. Most importantly, gang members were significantly more likely to describe experiencing *multiple* family problems—with 60 percent describing three or more of the five problems listed in Table 3-3 and 44 percent reporting that four or more of these problems existed in their families. In fact, only *three* gang members—Angie, Brenda, and Chantell—said there were none of these problems in their families, compared to nine (20 percent) of the nongang girls.

In addition, a number of gang girls had been sexually abused or raped in the context of their families.[19] In all, twenty-five (52 percent) of the gang members in my study reported having been sexually assaulted, and they described a total of thirty-five instances of sexual assault. Of these thirty-five incidents, twenty-three of them (66 percent) were committed by family members or by men whom the young women were exposed to through their families. Eight of these assaults were committed by immediate family members (e.g., girls' fathers, brothers, and in one case her mother). Eight were committed by extended family (e.g., girls' cousins, grandfathers, uncles), and seven were committed by individuals that young women came into contact with through their families. For instance, Tamika was raped by her stepfather's brother, Vikkie by her mother's boyfriend's friend, Yolanda by her uncle's friend, and Brittany by her aunt's boyfriend. While fewer nongang girls had been sexually assaulted (ten of forty-six or 22 percent), like the

Table 3-3   Problems within the Family

	Gang Members (N = 48)	Nongang Members (N = 46)
Witness to Physical Violence between Adults	27 (56%)	12 (26%)*
Abused by Family Member	22 (46%)	12 (26%)*
Regular Alcohol Use in Home	27 (56%)	17 (37%)
Regular Drug Use in Home	28 (58%)	8 (17%)*
Family Member in Prison/Jail	35 (73%)	31 (67%)
Three or More Family Problems	29 (60%)	11 (24%)*
Four or More Family Problems	21 (44%)	6 (13%)*

*$p < .05$.

gang girls, two-thirds of these assaults (eight of twelve) occurred in the context of the family.

For many young women, home was not a particularly safe place. Turning to young women's descriptions of their decision to join a gang, it is not surprising that the majority (though by no means all) noted family problems as contributing factors. The ways in which family problems facilitated girls' gang involvement were varied, but they shared a common thread—young women began spending time away from home as a result of difficulties or dangers there, and consequently sought to get away and to meet their social and emotional needs elsewhere. Often young women specifically said that their relationships with primary caregivers were problematic in some way. A number of researchers have suggested that "the gang can serve as a surrogate extended family for adolescents who do not see their own families as meeting their needs for belonging, nurturance, and acceptance."[20] Regardless of whether gangs actually fulfill these roles in young women's lives, it is clear that many young women believe that the gang will do so when they become involved.[21]

The most common family-related themes described by young women as contributing to their gang involvement were drug addiction and abuse.[22] While 58 percent of the gang members described regular drug use in their homes, ten girls (21 percent) explicitly discussed the impact of their mother's crack or heroin addiction. Drug-addicted parents, while not necessarily described as abusive, often were quite neglectful, leaving girls feeling abandoned and unloved, but also not providing necessary supervision over their time and activities. Moreover, given the intense degradation of many drug-addicted women on the streets, these particular young women likely dealt with the trauma of having knowledge of or even witnessing their mother's involvement in such situations.[23]

Keisha was fourteen when we spoke and had joined her gang the previous year. She described her neighborhood as "nothin' but Folks and Crips" and attributed her decision to become a gang member to her sense of abandonment resulting from her mother's drug addiction. She explained: "My family wasn't there for me. My mom smokin' crack and she act like she didn't wanna be part of my life, so I just chose the negative family, you know what I'm saying?" Likewise, Crystal described joining her gang at a time when she was "fighting with my mama 'cause she was on drugs."

Shandra got to know members of her gang "walking to school, back and forth to school and I would see them in the mornings and after school and after awhile I just [started] hanging around smoking weed and just kicking it with them." She elaborated:

Right around the time that I started hanging with them I had just got put out of school and had tried to kill myself not too long before that 'cause I was just, you know, I had run away from home and I was just dealing with a lot of stuff. 'Cause my mother is on drugs real bad, and her and her boyfriend used to be fighting all the time and I just, I don't know, I guess I just didn't want to be around that. So I chose to be around the gang.

Shandra said after she "just used to kick it with them [gang members] so much, one day I just woke up and I just say I wanna be one of them, and then I told them and then they jumped me in the 'hood." She was twelve when she joined her gang. Shandra's mother knew she had become gang-involved "because I started coming in late and I be high when I came in, I started dressing like a gang member, wearing all stars and khakis and stuff like that." But she explained, her mother "didn't really say nothing about it." At the time, Shandra said she "felt close to" the other gang members and "bond[ed] with them like they [my] family." When she first joined, she continued, the gang was so "important for me that I did anything I could to get respect from the OGs and just, you know, be down for [the gang]. It was important because I wanted to feel, I guess, accepted to the gang, accepted in the gang."

In addition to their belief that joining a gang would fill emotional voids, a number of these young women said that a lack of supervision attributable to their mother's addiction also was a contributing factor. Veronica, for example, joined her gang when she was "gettin' ready to be twelve," after her older brothers had joined. She said the gang was "right there in my neighborhood . . . then I seen that my brothers, 'cause I seen my brothers get put in. So then I said I wanna be put in." At the time, she explained, "I was just doin' what I wanted to 'cause when I found out my mom was doin' drugs and stuff. So she wasn't never in the house, so she didn't know."

Likewise, Yvette explained, "My mama, she on drugs, [we] used to fight and stuff. Me and her don't get along . . . [and] my father, he just ain't been around." Yvette said because of her mother's drug habit, when she was growing up her mother often "made me stay out late and stuff like that." Eventually Yvette "just started hanging out with" gang members in her neighborhood, whom she described as also being unsupervised. "I just hung around with some people that can do what they want to do, stay out late, whatever, go home when they want to go home, I'm hanging out with them." She said, "It was like, I wasn't going to school a lot so I got with them. We was having so much fun. Most of them didn't go to school so I felt like I didn't need to go to school. . . . I had fun with the gang so I became one of them." Although her mother was unhappy and threatened Yvette when she found out about her gang involvement, Yvette said, "It was like too late for her to try and change me."

Another theme that emerged in some girls' discussions of how they became gang-involved was the impact of being physically or sexually abused by family members. In most of these cases, violence and victimization in the family precipitated girls' decisions to avoid home, and several girls described running away from home and living for extended periods with friends—often exposing them to gangs. In a few cases, being placed outside the home as a consequence of abuse also had the unintended consequence of exposing girls to gangs and gang members. Erica's story is a case in point.

Erica was seventeen when we spoke and had joined her gang when she was fifteen. She lived with her father and stepmother for most of her childhood, until her father and uncle raped her at the age of eleven, whereupon she was removed from the home. Since that time she had been shuffled back and forth between foster homes, group homes, and residential facilities and had little contact with her family because they turned their backs on her. Erica explained, "I didn't have *no* family. Because of the incidents with my dad and my uncle. After that, they just deserted me and I didn't, I had nothin' else." Although she said her stepmother was the primary person who raised her, their relationship was severely damaged by the rape. "She doesn't, she doesn't believe it. I mean, even after he [dad] pleaded guilty she still doesn't believe it."

Erica's childhood up to that point had been filled with violence. Her father was physically abusive toward her stepmother, herself, and her siblings, and as a young child, Erica had witnessed her mother being raped. Both her father and stepmother had spent time in jail, and there was heavy alcohol and drug use in the home as she was growing up. As a result, she described herself as a physically aggressive child. She explained, "In elementary school before I even knew anything about gangs, I'd just get in a lot of fights." In fact, her nickname in elementary school was "Iron Mike," in recognition of her Tyson-like characteristics. Her initial contact with gangs came when she was fourteen and living in a foster home. During her stay there, she met a group of kids and began spending time with them:

> I didn't know 'em, but I just started talkin' to 'em. And, they always wore them blue rags and black rags and all that. And, I asked them, I said, "Well you part of a gang?" And they tell me what they're a part of. So, it was like, everywhere I went, I was with them. I was never by myself. If they went out to [a] club I went with them. If they did anything, I was with them. And, um, we went down to some club one night and it was like a whole bunch of 'em got together and um, I asked to join.

Erica said she joined the gang "just to be in somethin'" and so that it could be "like a family to me since I don't really have one of my own." She felt that being in the gang allowed her to develop meaningful relationships. She explained, "People trust me and I trust them. It's like that bond that we have that some of us don't have outside of that. Or didn't have at all. That we have inside of that gang, or that set." Nonetheless, as I described in Chapter 2, Erica expressed some ambivalence about being in a gang because it involved antisocial attitudes and behaviors that she didn't see as being part of who she really was, particularly as she neared adulthood. Her decision to join, however, was in part a search for belonging and attachment.

Likewise, Brittany described a terribly violent family life. She lived in a household with extended family—twelve people in all—including her mother, grandmother, stepfather, and an adolescent uncle who was physically abusive. Her aunt's boyfriend had sexually assaulted her at the age of five, but family members didn't believe her. Although she didn't know her father, who was in jail, she had early memories of him physically abusing her mother. Moreover, she felt very disconnected and unloved by her family and also described being isolated at school: "I didn't have no friends, used to always get teased. . . . My grades started going down, I started getting real depressed, started skipping school, smoking weed after school and stuff." Brittany saw the gang as a means of finding love. She explained: "I felt that my family didn't care for me . . . that when I was on the streets I felt that I got more love than when I was in the house so I felt that that's where my love was, on the streets, so that's where I stayed." And although she did not admit to doing so herself, Brittany noted, "My best friend got initiated [into the gang] by having sex with twelve boys."

Other young women also focused on myriad family factors in explaining their gang involvement. Diane's experiences are exemplary of how family problems could compound in a way that ultimately leads to gang involvement. When we spoke Diane was fifteen and was among the most deeply entrenched gang members in the sample. She had joined her gang at eleven, but she was only ten when she began hanging out with members, including the seventeen-year-old young man who lived next door:

> I think I was about ten and a half years old and we started hanging out over there, over at his house and all his friends would come over and I just got into, just hangin' out, just becomin' friends with everybody that was there. And then I started smokin' weed and doin' all that stuff and then when I turned eleven it was like, well, 'cause they seen me get in fights and they seen how my attitude was and they said, "Well I think that you would be, you would be a true, a very true Lady Crip."

The time she spent with the gang and her decision to join were predictable results of her life history up to that point. As a young child, the family moved around a lot because her father was on the run from the law. Her father dealt drugs out of their home and had a steady stream of friends and clients moving in and out of the place. Exposed to crime and drugs at an early age, Diane tried marijuana for the first time at age nine. She noted, "I was just growin' up watchin' that stuff." Her life changed dramatically when she was ten and her father was sent to prison, leaving her care to her drug-addicted mother. Diane explained:

> We didn't have very much money at all. Like, my mom was on welfare. My dad had just gone to jail. My dad had just gone to prison for four years. . . . My mom was on drugs. My, see my dad, always sellin' acid, quaaludes, cocaine and my mom was on, just smokin' marijuana and doin' crack. Back then she was just real drugged out, had a lot of problems and it was just me and my little brother and my little sister and that's all that was goin' on, besides

me goin' to school and comin' home to seein' my mom do whatever, hit the pipe, and goin' next door and hangin' out.

Diane remained very dedicated to her gang and fellow members, noting passionately, "I *love* my cousins [fellow Crips]. I *love* 'em." This was in large part because of what they provided her when she felt she had little else. She elaborated, "That neighborhood's not a good neighborhood anyway, so. I had nothin' to look forward to, but these people they helped me out, you know? I mean, I was a young kid on my own. . . . I was just a little girl, my dad's gone and my mom's on drugs." Diane's father had been released from prison when we spoke, but was locked up again—as was Diane—for an armed robbery they had committed together. Ironically, her close bond with her father, and the knowledge she'd gained from him about how to commit crime, had resulted in a great deal of status for her among her gang peers. She noted, "My dad is just so cool. Everybody, everybody in my little clique, even people that aren't in my set, just my regular friends, they all love my dad."

As these young women's stories illustrate, a multitude of problems within families can increase young women's risk for gang involvement. This occurs through girls' attempts to avoid home and to meet social and emotional needs, as a result of ineffective supervision over their activities and, in cases like Diane's, by showing young women through example that criminal lifestyles are appropriate. These problems are exacerbated when young women live in neighborhoods with gangs, which provide a readily available alternative to life at home. Moreover, older gang members appear "cool," and their seemingly carefree lifestyle and reputed familial-like bonds to one another are an appealing draw for young girls with so many troubles at home.

GANG INVOLVEMENT AMONG FAMILY MEMBERS

Some girls who lack close relationships with their primary caregivers can turn to siblings or extended family members to maintain a sense of belonging and attachment. However, if these family members are gang-involved, it is likely that girls will choose to join gangs themselves. Moreover, even when relationships with parents or other adults are strong, having adolescent gang members in the family often heightens the appeal of gangs.[24] As Table 3-4 illustrates, gang members were significantly more likely than non-gang girls to report family members in gangs. Most importantly, gang members were much more likely to have siblings in gangs and were more likely to have two or more gang-involved family members.

These relationships were actually somewhat different in the two sites—with the relationship between girls' gang membership and that of her family being most marked in St. Louis. In Columbus, gang girls were not sig-

Table 3-4   Gang Membership among Family Members

	Gang Members (N = 48)	Nongang Members (N = 46)
Gang Member(s) in Family	38 (79%)	25 (54%)*
Sibling(s) in Gang	24 (50%)	8 (17%)*
Multiple Gang Members in Family	29 (60%)	13 (28%)*

*$p < .05$.

nificantly more likely than nongang girls to have a family member in a gang—57 percent of gang members had family in gangs versus 48 percent of nongang girls. By comparison, all but one of the gang members in St. Louis (96 percent) reported having at least one gang-involved family member. In fact, a greater percentage of nongang girls in St. Louis (62 percent) described having a family member in a gang than did gang members in Columbus (57 percent). Moreover, St. Louis gang members were the only group for whom a majority reported having more than one gang-involved family member. In all, twenty-one St. Louis gang members (78 percent) described having multiple gang members in the family, compared to 38 percent of Columbus gang members, 29 percent of nongang girls in St. Louis, and 28 percent of nongang girls in Columbus.

However, gang members in both cities were significantly more likely to report a gang-involved sibling than nongang girls. In all, 52 percent of St. Louis gang members and 48 percent of Columbus gang members had siblings in gangs, compared to 19 and 16 percent of the nongang girls in these cities, respectively. In St. Louis, nine gang girls reported brothers in gangs and ten reported sisters; in Columbus, eight gang girls had brothers in gangs and three had gang-involved sisters. Overall, 35 percent of the gang members had brothers who were gang members, and 27 percent had sisters in gangs. In addition, four gang members—two in each city—described having parents who had been in gangs.

Turning to young women's accounts of how they became gang-involved and the role family members played, there also are notable differences between the two sites. In Columbus, all of the young women who described the influence of a family member mentioned a sibling or siblings. In St. Louis, on the other hand, eight girls pointed to siblings, while twelve identified cousins or aunts who prompted their decision to join. Gang girls in St. Louis also were more likely to talk about the influence of *female* family members, be they sisters, aunts, or cousins. Perhaps as a consequence (as I discuss in Chapter 8), gang girls in St. Louis were more likely to talk about the importance of their friendships with other girls in the gang, while most gang girls in Columbus identified more with young men.

In general, the greater influence of extended family members on girls' gang involvement in St. Louis was striking. The likely explanation lies in the socioeconomic differences between the two cities and their effects on the strength of extended family networks. As I noted earlier, the young women in Columbus tended to live in neighborhoods with higher than average rates of poverty and racial segregation than the city as a whole. However, the neighborhoods of girls in Columbus were somewhat better on social and economic indicators than the neighborhoods of girls in St. Louis. Moreover, while there are pockets of concentrated poverty in Columbus, St. Louis exhibits much larger geographic areas blighted by intense poverty, racial isolation, and population loss, resulting in large numbers of vacant lots and abandoned buildings in many of the poorest neighborhoods.

So how might these differences relate to the tendency for St. Louis gang members to say that extended family networks, rather than immediate family, drew them into gangs, while this simply was not the case in Columbus? I would suggest that the answer may lie in families' responses to entrenched poverty conditions. Research has shown that African American families living in poverty often rely to a great degree on extended family for economic, social, and emotional support.[25] Given the more detrimental economic conditions in St. Louis, it may be that extended family networks are stronger there than in Columbus. This would help explain why St. Louis gang members seemed to spend more time with their relatives outside the immediate family and, consequently, why those relatives had a stronger influence on girls' decision making with regard to gangs. Regardless of which family members have an impact, it is clear that having family members who are in gangs increases the likelihood that girls will perceive gangs as an appropriate option for themselves as well.

More often than not, young women who joined gangs to be with or like their older siblings did so in the context of the types of family problems noted earlier. Veronica was a case in point. Her mother's drug addiction left her and her siblings unsupervised; when her older brothers began hanging out with the neighborhood gang, she followed suit. In fact, she went on to tell me, "Then my *little* brother wanted to get put in it. And he was like only about six. [Laughs] They told him no."

Similarly, Lisa was thirteen when we spoke and had only recently joined her gang. Her brother Mike had been a member of a Folks gang for several years, and when the family relocated to another area of Columbus, he decided to start his own set of the gang in their new neighborhood. Lisa was among its members. Prior to Mike starting his own set, Lisa hadn't considered joining, but nonetheless said she "claimed [Folks] because that's what my brother was so I wanted to be like that too." Their mother had died when Lisa was eleven, and she described their father as physically abusive and distant. She felt very close to her brother and said her desire to be with him was her primary reason for joining his gang.

Several weeks before Lisa joined, her brother's girlfriend Trish—who was also Lisa's best friend—was initiated. Lisa explained, "One day Trish was like, 'Well you wanna be true?' And I was like, 'Yeah.' And they was like,

'All right.' And they took me behind the railroad tracks and kicked the shit outta me and I was in it [Laughs]." Lisa was initiated into the gang on the same day as her boyfriend and another male friend of theirs. A primary concern for her was to make a good impression on her brother. She explained:

> The boys was scared. They was like, "Man, I don't know, I don't know." And then I was like, I just looked at my brother. Then I looked at my friend and I looked at them boys and I was like, "I'll go first." So I just did it, I think . . . why I did it then is just to be, I don't know. Just to show them, my brother, that I was stronger than them boys.

Although she enjoyed what she described as the "fun and games" that she had with her brother and the other gang members, Lisa was actually ambivalent about being in a gang. She told me, "Right now I wish, I kinda wish I never got into it but I'm already in it so, like, um, I just, I don't know. I don't think I'm gonna be that heavy as my brother is, like all the time, you know, yeah, yeah." Lisa was especially concerned for her brother, who took his gang involvement quite seriously, which she perceived as putting his physical safety at risk. She explained, "My brother, when he was little, he was a little geeky little kid that wore glasses. But now he's like, you know, and I don't understand it but uh, I wish he was still a little kid that wore glasses." Nonetheless, she felt being in the gang allowed her to spend time with him. She surmised, "We all just hang out all the time. We just are always together. If you see me you see my brother. If you see my brother you see his girlfriend. If you see me you see my boyfriend. I mean, it's just like that."

In fact, a number of young women described joining their gangs in order to be around and meet the approval of their older brothers regardless of whether—like Lisa and Veronica—they had family problems at home. When Tonya was younger, she said she noticed "my brother just started wearing red all the time, all the time." She continued, "then after school . . . he just kept going outside. All these dudes and girls used to have fun, selling drugs and having money and stuff. And then I just wanted to do it. I thought it would be fun so I joined. I tried to join and then my brother let me join." Tonya said her initiation into the gang involved "just a couple of my brother's friends, he didn't let nobody really [cause me] pain for real, like really beat me up. They was just beating me up so I would have to fight back. I had some bruises, busted lip, in another minute it was gone, it was cool." What wasn't gone was Tonya's belief that "I had gained my brother's respect and stuff." Only thirteen at the time, she said "in the beginning I was like a little shortie. I didn't sell drugs, I didn't run around shooting or none of that." Her involvement increased, however, when she began "going out with one of my brother's friends," who provided her with drugs, which, she said, was "how I started selling dope."

Monica was also thirteen when she joined her brothers' gang. She had four older brothers, between the ages of twenty and twenty-eight at the time she joined, all of whom were members of the same Crips set. Sixteen at the time we spoke, she remained the youngest member of her gang and said she joined because she "wanted to be like" her older brothers. Monica described that she "always followed them around" and explained, "All four of my brothers were in so I was like, 'all right, I wanna be in a gang.' So I used to ride around with them all the time. And then my brother asked me, he said, 'Do you wanna be down or what?' . . . And I was like, 'Fine, I'll do it.' So I did." Perhaps because of the adult role models in her family and because she "grew up around it," Monica, like Diane, was one of the most committed—and consequently delinquent—gang members that I spoke with. She told me, "I'm down for real, I'm down for life." Diane's strong gang commitment resulted from gang members filling a caregiving niche unavailable to her from her family while her father was in jail. In contrast, Monica's commitment was the result of her close bonds to her family.

A number of the young women in St. Louis, as I noted earlier, described the influence of extended family members—most often cousins, but sometimes also aunts. All of these young women talked about spending quite a bit of their time at their relatives' homes, sometimes but not always when they lived in the same neighborhoods. Trina joined her gang when she was eleven; both her cousins and aunts were members, and she described "just being around over there, being around all of them" growing up. Trina said her aunts and cousins had dressed her in gang colors from the time she was young, and she surmised, "I just grew up into it."

Likewise, Shiree described her gang as "a family thing," and Alecia also said her gang involvement was "like a family thing." Alecia explained, "My auntie first moved on [the street] where I live now . . . [and] I started visiting my cousin." The gang evolved from "everyone that was growing up in that 'hood. . . . I seen all my relatives, not my father and mother, but you know, all my relatives in it and then I came over just like that." She said, "It ain't like they talked me into it or nothing." But eventually she and her mother and siblings moved to the same block, further solidifying her gang affiliation.

Vashelle said she joined her gang "because my family, all of my cousins, my relatives, they was Bloods already and then I moved over there because my cousin was staying over there so I just started claiming [the gang]." While in general Vashelle believed that girls joined gangs for "little stuff, they want a family or something," she argued that these were not her own motives. She explained, "It's just something I wanted to do because my cousin was in it so I wanted to be hanging around. . . . I ain't no follower. It's something I wanted to do and by them doing it was just more influence on me."

In some cases conflict in girls' immediate families increased the time they spent with relatives. Vickie began spending time with a gang-involved cousin when she became frustrated at home and "just wanted to get out of the house." She explained, "My mama always wanted me to babysit. I got tired of doing that. She always yell and stuff, she come home from work and start yelling. Like that kind of stuff and I got tired of hearing that. I need somebody to hang out with where I wouldn't be home half of the time." She turned to her cousin and "just started hanging out with him." The members of his gang, she said, "was like, 'you gonna do something [to join]?' I was like, I just gotta do what I gotta do," and so she joined.

As the preceding stories have illustrated, in some cases girls' trajectories into gangs are more heavily influenced by neighborhood dynamics, in others by severe family problems, and in still others by close ties to gang-involved family members. Dionne is perhaps the best illustration of how all of the factors I've described thus far—neighborhood context, family problems, and gang-involved family members—can come together to fuel girls' gang involvement. Dionne grew up in a housing project with gangs, where she had four male cousins who were members. She had been physically and sexually abused repeatedly by her mother's boyfriend, who was also her father's brother.[26] She explained:

> When [I] was little my uncle tried to have sex with me and stuff. I was like eight or seven, you know, and I told my mama in her sleep. I told my mama what happened, I woke her up out of sleep. You know she told me, she say, I'll get him when I wake up. For real, when she woke up, he ain't do nuttin' but tell her, "Aw, she lyin'. She just wants some attention." You know, and she hit me 'cause, you know, she thinkin' I'm just sayin' somethin'. I was mad though, and he thought he could take advantage by keep on doin' it.

There was also drug and alcohol abuse in the home, her mother had spent time in jail, and her mother and mother's boyfriend were violent toward one another. Dionne noted, "My mama, you know, me and my mama didn't get along. . . . My uncle [her mother's boyfriend], you know, we didn't get along. It was like, you know, he couldn't stand me, I don't know why. . . . He told me to my face, 'I hate you,' he say, 'I hope you die.'" Consequently, Dionne said "I used to like goin' to school, 'cause to get away from home." Eventually she began running away and spending time on the streets around her housing project with her cousins and other gang members. "I just started hangin' with 'em and doin' what they did then, and they, it was like, they, you know, was used to me hangin' around." When she was eleven, one of her cousins tattooed the gang's name and her nickname on her forearm. Dionne was drunk when her cousin tattooed her, but she said that afterwards the tattoo "made me feel big and stuff, you know?" While she was abused and felt neglected and disparaged at home, Dionne said being with the gang "be kinda fun, you know, bein' around all your little friends, just chillin' or somethin'."

NONGANG GIRLS' PERCEPTIONS OF GANGS

As Figure 3-2 showed, most of the nongang girls in the sample did not experience the same risk factors for gangs as the young women in gangs. Most notably, only a small percentage had gang-involved siblings and only

Table 3-5   Nongang Girls' Reasons for Not Joining Gangs

	All nongang Girls (N = 46)	Multiple Risk Factors (N = 15)	Some Gang Involvement (N = 21)
Gangs are violent, risky, dangerous	12 (26%)	3 (20%)	5 (24%)
Personal safety concerns	10 (22%)	6 (40%)	5 (24%)
Don't want to get in trouble	4 (9%)	2 (13%)	2 (10%)
Gangs are stupid, do stupid things	9 (20%)	3 (20%)	3 (14%)
Wouldn't do the things you have to do	4 (9%)	2 (13%)	1 (5%)
Want to be down but not in it	3 (7%)	2 (13%)	3 (14%)
Moral opposition, gangs are bad	6 (13%)	2 (13%)	2 (10%)
Not that kind of person	11 (24%)	2 (13%)	3 (14%)

around a quarter had multiple family problems such as those described by girls in gangs. Despite these differences, 35 percent of the nongang girls described half or more of their friends as gang members, and 28 percent had considered joining a gang. It's important, therefore, to explore nongang girls' perceptions of gangs, including why girls who have the opportunity choose to avoid gangs, as well as what the appeal of gangs is for some nongang girls. In the survey interview, young women were asked if they had ever considered joining a gang, and then, in an open-ended question, were asked why or why not. Table 3-5 provides a summary of nongang girls' responses to the question of why they didn't join gangs. In addition, while as a rule I did not conduct in-depth interviews with nongang girls, there were three young women—Denise, Rachel, and Julie—with whom I did. This was because each described being quite involved with gangs but insisted they were not gang members and, in Rachel and Julie's cases, were adamant that they would not join in the future. All three were from Columbus. Although they are only three cases, they nonetheless offer insights into both the appeal of gangs and those factors that may help some young women resist joining gangs even when they are gang-identified.

Young women described a number of reasons for not joining gangs, and many young women listed more than one reason for not joining. Although the numbers are small, Table 3-5 lists responses for all nongang girls, then for the fifteen girls with multiple risk factors for gangs, and finally for girls with some gang involvement—either they have friends in gangs, have considered joining, or both. Although no one response dominated, responses did tend to cluster around several themes: concerns about the violence and trouble associated with gangs, an unwillingness to do "stupid" things or follow explicit gang rules, and a sense of moral opposition or an image of oneself as different from gang members.

More than anything else, many young women described the violence associated with gangs as a deterrent against involvement. Sometimes this was stated generally. As Carrie noted, "It's an easy way to die." Likewise, Janelle said, "People die 'cause of that stuff," and Latoya concurred, "Everybody around there is dying." Angela said being in a gang "won't do anything but get you killed." Julie said she considered joining, but changed her mind after a "good friend got killed." Having someone close to them injured or killed solidified a belief in the dangers of gangs; as Laura noted, "You can get hurt over them, my cousin did." Some young women were explicitly concerned with their own safety. Janet said she was "afraid of getting hurt," and Denise said "I don't feel like getting beat up." Terri said she considered joining "to see what it felt like" but after she saw the film *Banging in Little Rock*, she changed her mind, deciding she "didn't want to get beat up." In addition to violence, young women noted other problems associated with gangs, most notably getting in trouble or going to jail. Allison said, "A lot of my friends are in jail because of being in a gang." Brianna summed up, "You either gonna get killed or go to jail."

Another theme young women discussed had to do with their perceptions of gang members' behaviors or the rules and expectations associated with gang involvement, which a number of nongang girls classified as "stupid." Yvonne summarized, "Everybody say you can't get out, it's stupid, why should I fight for someone else, for colors?" Linda concurred, "It's stupid, they're fighting over a color." Catlyn provided a litany of problems she had with gangs: it's hard to get out, harassment, pressure to go to meetings, pressure to hurt others, being approached by other gangs. Like other young women, she concluded that gangs are "stupid." Meosha said she wouldn't join because of "the way you have to get in, beat up by a bunch of girls or do it to [have sex with] the king." Likewise, Renee said "It's not nothing to be happy about. I know from my friends what you gotta do to get in and I wouldn't put up with it." Cassie noted, "I think it's dumb and fake. There is no real gangs in Columbus, people are just wannabes I think."

Finally, a number of young women expressed their moral opposition to gangs or their belief that they are "not that kind of person." Jackie surmised, "I think it's devilish stuff," and Janis explained, "I don't like gangs." Ashley was adamant about her distaste for gangs, which was partly a result of seeing all the trouble her gang-involved older sister had gotten in: "I hate gangs, [there's] too much violence. I just don't like 'em. If you ask me I don't think there should be any gangs." LaShay said simply, "It's not me," and Trudy said, "I don't see anything in it." Tawanna explained, "I don't have time for that gang stuff." Connie noted, "The way I was raised was to be against gangs," and Janelle said, "It's the wrong choice." She explained, "I'm better off without joining anything, better off how I am." Alberta said, "I'm the type of person, I'd rather be by myself," and Angela noted, "It's not for me, what are you getting out of it? [Being in a gang is] not getting you anywhere." Finally, Felicia said, "I got too much going for myself to let a gang drag me down."

Some nongang girls, however, did hang out with gangs and considered joining. DeeDee was in the shelter facility and planned to join a Crips set. She said, "It's fun. Knowin' that a whole bunch of people got your back." Cherise was at the same facility and also wanted to join, she said, " 'cause my friend [Veronica]'s in it, for protection, stuff like that." Catlyn said she considered joining because it "seemed like they were so cool with each other, had each other's back, like fun," but eventually decided the negative aspects of gang life outweighed the positives. And Lorraine said she considered joining at one point " 'cause so much was going on with me, moving out and stuff like that, with my mom giving me up, it would be my new family." But she changed her mind after moving in with her sister because she said she "got used to staying at my sister's."

As I noted earlier, Julie, Rachel, and Denise had many close friends in gangs, and we talked at length about their gang involvement and why they hadn't joined. I conducted exploratory interviews with them to learn more about their associations with gang friends and resistance (or reservation, in Denise's case) to joining gangs. Julie was thirteen when we spoke, and both her brother and boyfriend were gang members, but in rival gangs. Most of her friends were gang members, though she didn't associate with one particular gang or set. Rachel was fifteen and hung out primarily with members of Folks sets, though not exclusively. Denise was seventeen and was affiliated with a local Crips set, but vacillated about whether she wanted to join. Each represents a different point on a continuum of gang connections. Their stories are important for what they reveal about the meanings of gangs in their own lives and in contrast with the discussions of gang girls.

Julie was attracted to gang members as friends because, she said, "They're more fun [and] they're more bold" than people who aren't in gangs. She continued, "I don't like hangin' around dull people. I'm one of those people who needs excitement. And just, they're crazy. And I like hangin' around people that are crazy." When I ask her to elaborate, she explained: "Just, like, they'll do anything, like anything. Like, my boyfriend, if I say I want a pair, I want a pair of new shoes, he goes up to the store and he'll rob the store for a pair of shoes. He's just, they're crazy. Don't think about what could happen to them." Although she hung out with gang friends and committed crimes with them, she didn't take part in specifically gang-related crimes or conflicts between rival gangs. She explained, "I'm not gonna have to spend a few years of my life in jail because of . . . a gang. I mean, if I'm gonna do somethin', I'm gonna do it for myself not for a clique."

Julie's gang friends came from different gangs, and she knew them from a variety of places. They included friends she'd grown up with; people she met at the mall, movie theaters, skating rinks, and the detention center; and people she met through relatives and other friends. She was clearly drawn to certain elements of the excitement of gang life, particularly her friends' delinquent involvement and overall "craziness." However, she was strongly opposed to joining a gang because of the limitations it would place on her. When I ask her what the benefits of *not* being a member were, she told me:

> Just, like, I can hang out, I mean, if I was a Crip I couldn't hang out with some of my friends that are Bloods 'cause they don't get along. And just, I guess, being able to hang out with who I want. And, wearing what color I want. I mean, that's stupid that, in a certain gang you're not allowed wearin' a certain color.

Like Julie, Rachel expressed a strong resistance to joining gangs because she didn't want a group identity to subsume her individual identity and because she wanted the freedom to act in ways she chose. She was drawn to gang members for the same reasons as Julie and was also heavily involved in delinquent activities with her gang friends. She was a close friend of LaShawna, a gang member at the shelter facility in Columbus who attended the same school as Rachel. Rachel explained:

> How I see it is you can do anything you can if you're not in a gang than if you are. You know what I'm saying? . . . I can do all the same stuff they do and if I don't wanna do it no more then I don't gotta lose my life. Like if you get in a gang and do this and that, you can get, like, like, if you're in the gang and you do something that you're not supposed to then you get Vs [violations]. Vs is where your OG, the leader of the gang, can come and give you how many ever blows to the head. So, you know what I'm saying, I can mess up on my own and don't worry about getting no Vs, so. I ain't tryin' to get in no gang.

Both Julie and Rachel had a strong sense of self as individuals. As Rachel said, "I don't claim nothin' but Rachel." It is notable that neither young woman reported family conflict in the survey interview. Julie answered no to each of the five questions in Table 3-3, while Rachel answered yes only to having had a family member spend time in jail (which 67 percent of non-gang girls reported). Perhaps because each had strong relationships with adults in their families, they didn't have the same desire for belonging that many gang members described. Rachel even said as much:

> Now, if I lived in [the shelter facility] like half these girls, I think I would be in a gang 'cause I would like, like, if I didn't have no one who cared for me, looked out for me, did this and that for me, then I would get in a gang 'cause that's what most girls get in the gang for. But, see, I got my mom. I got my family that loves me. My mom takes good care of me, you know what I'm saying.

Unlike Julie and Rachel, Denise was affiliated with a specific gang and clearly aligned herself with them. She said, "A Blood is a Slob to me. . . . I see somebody dressed in all dred [red], I look at 'em and go, 'Psssh, whatever.' And I ain't even in a gang but I still call 'em Slobs." The set she associated with didn't have any female members, but she and a female friend had been hanging out with them for the last year. Members had invited her to join, and she was considering it, but at the time we interviewed she said, "I don't think I'm ready to join." The following conversation illustrates the nature of her vacillation:

JM: You said that sometimes you think you want to be a member and sometimes you don't?

DENISE: Yeah, 'cause sometimes we be sittin' there chillin' and they all come out with guns and stuff, you know what I'm sayin'. They load they shit. They look better than the police. They just look hard, you know what I'm sayin'. They all got money. Everybody, all of 'em got money. And it ain't just like one dollar bills. They all got hundreds. And flashin' 'em. Everybody come over there. Nobody disrespect 'em. 'Cause they too scared. They just hard.

JM: So those are the things that are appealing about it?

DENISE: Yeah.

JM: And then what are some of the reasons that you haven't made that leap yet?

DENISE: 'Cause goin' in jail and some of the crimes they be doin'. They like, like you walk down the street and they just mess with somebody just to mess with somebody. They ask this dude if he got a quarter. He was like "no, I don't got no quarter." So they just beat him up. For a stupid quarter. And they didn't need it but, you know what I'm sayin'? Just somethin' to do.

JM: And you, and so why does that make you not want to join?

DENISE: 'Cause what you gonna beat somebody up over a quarter for? And then they got confrontations with the Slobs. They just be all, they always with them, messin' with them. I ain't tryin' to get shot.

Denise was drawn to the excitement of gang life and the respect gang members got from others around them, but she also had both moral and safety concerns that kept her from joining. At the time we spoke, she had been able to enjoy many of the benefits of the gang without putting herself at tremendous risk. She explained: "It's fun, man. [They] give you money. It's fun. You get high. You usually gotta buy, but, they sell it, they buy it for you. They smoke wit' you. They got cars, rides, you don't have no car, you like, call 'em up, 'you wanna take me to the mall?' They like, 'yeah, I'll drop you off, hold on.'"

An important element of the interviews with Julie, Rachel, and Denise is that they highlight the fluid nature of gang boundaries. On the one hand, each girl articulated that she was clearly not a gang member, yet each participated on some level in the activities of gang members, if not gangs. Julie said that her friends in rival gangs always tried to get her to "set each other up," yet they trusted her not to set them up. She hung out with them and committed crimes with them despite her connections with rival gangs. Rachel had actually assisted her friends in initiating new members when they were short-handed. She explained, "I'm not supposed to jump people into a gang unless you're in a gang," but LaShawna asked her to and "I'd practically do anything for her, 'cause that's my heart." And Denise was privy to many gang members' crimes. These young women derived some of the same meanings from their gang involvement as gang members, especially delinquent recreational activities and excitement. But they hadn't felt the need for belonging that many gang members described as motivating their decisions to join gangs.

CONCLUSION

This chapter has illustrated the range of circumstances that help pave girls' pathways into gangs. Notably, some of their discussions clearly parallel the discussions young men provide with regard to their decisions to join, particularly the strength of neighborhood peer networks. Young women join gangs because they perceive these groups as capable of meeting a variety of needs in their lives, both social and emotional, and sometimes economic. Previous research has suggested that a number of factors—among them socioeconomic context, family problems, and peer influences—contribute to girls' gang involvement. My research offers further support for these findings by comparing the experiences of gang and nongang girls and also details in concrete ways the various trajectories through which some young women join gangs while others are able to avoid gang involvement.

My work suggests the strong influence of three overlapping factors— exposure to neighborhood gangs, problems within the family, and having gang-involved family members. The vast majority of gang girls described their decision to get into a gang as involving interactions between two or more of these factors. So, for instance, girls who grew up in close proximity to gangs, particularly those with serious family problems, became aware of gangs and often chose these groups as a means of meeting social needs and avoiding home. In addition, my study found that (mostly adolescent) kinship networks had a strong relationship to girls' gang involvement. Girls with older siblings or relatives in gangs often looked up to those family members and, particularly but not always when there were other problems at home, sought to spend time with them on the streets and around their gangs. Notably, gang members in Columbus who said family members had an impact on their decision to join named siblings; in St. Louis they were more likely to mention cousins or other extended family members.

Finally, my research offers further support for the importance of family problems in facilitating many girls' gang involvement. Moore's work found strong evidence, comparing male and female gang members, that young women recounted more cases of childhood abuse and neglect and more frequently came from homes where wife abuse and other family problems were present.[27] My study fills in an additional piece of the puzzle by comparing female gang members with their nongang counterparts. Not only do female gang members come from more troubled families than do their male counterparts, as Moore's work shows, but they also come from more troubled families than do at-risk girls who don't join gangs. Even among the handful of girls I interviewed who associated with gangs but didn't join, this appeared to be the case when contrasted with gang girls.

Moreover, my discussions with young women shed some light on how these family problems led to gang involvement. Often when relationships with primary caregivers were weak or ineffective, girls began spending time with the older adolescents who were hanging out on the street or around the neighborhood. For instance, drug-addicted parents led young women to feel neglected and abandoned and did not provide needed supervision over their time and activities. For other young women, physical or sexual abuse or other conflicts in the household precipitated their spending time away from home. Given their likelihood of living in neighborhoods where gangs were present and having older siblings or relatives in gangs, these groups were readily available for girls to hang out with and eventually, over time, step into.

This chapter has primarily focused on what could be classified as background processes shaping gang involvement. However, once young women join gangs, gang involvement itself produces new situations and expectations. Hagan and McCarthy have suggested that one limitation of much criminological research is the "tendency to discount foreground causal factors theoretically and instead focus on background and developmental variables."[28] This is an especially important insight for studying gangs, given the group norms, expectations, and processes that govern gang life. In the coming chapters, I thus move my discussion to the foreground of gang life—exploring the nature, structure, and activities of gangs; gang-related delinquency and victimization; and the importance of gender in shaping gang girls' lives.

Gangs and Gang Life in Columbus

"I didn't cry at all," Diane recalled. "I'm surprised I didn't cry. But after sixty seconds, I was down on the ground, just like, 'ooh, ooh.'" Diane's gang initiation involved getting jumped for one minute by three of the young women in her gang. The group met in a field behind someone's backyard. She was eleven at the time, and though four years had passed, she remembered the incident in detail. "It was like, 'you ready, you ready?' I was like, 'Yeah, I'm ready.' I was like, 'do I get to fight back?' They was like, 'Do what you gotta do.' . . . [Then] they just started throwin' their punches." She tried to fight back, but the three-to-one ratio was too much for her. Once the sixty seconds were called, she picked herself up off the ground and was encircled by her new partners.

> They was like, "Oh give me some love, give me some love." And then they all gave me a hug and then I got down on my right knee and they, they put my flag over my right shoulder and they blessed me with the flag, they blessed me into their set.[1]

In Chapter 3 I described some of the precipitating factors leading to girls' gang involvement. Here I focus on what these groups are like. In this chapter, my focus is on girls' gangs in Columbus; Chapter 5 will turn to gangs in St. Louis. As I have noted, young women typically hung out with their gang for upwards of a year before deciding to join. The actual initiation into the group was often an important rite of passage, as young women moved from affiliation with their gang to full membership.[2] A girl's willingness to subject herself to an assault at the hands of the gang's members signaled her induction into the group, which in exchange promised her love, respect, and belonging. Diane, now reflecting on the other side of the initiation process, surmised, "If you can take a beat down from us, we're gonna take care of you and we're gonna love you forever."

So what makes these groups *gangs*, and what distinguishes them from other adolescent friendship groups? Researchers are embroiled in considerable debate about this question. Because gangs have proliferated rapidly over the last decade or so, some suggest that it is problematic to establish specific criteria to determine what constitutes a gang, as doing so results in an absence of the flexibility necessary to account for variations across time and place.[3] On the other hand, it is difficult to compare gangs across sites without some level of standardized definitions—otherwise, the meaning of comparisons becomes questionable. The goal, then, is to adopt a definition flexible enough to capture differences, but with some level of stability for comparison. Malcolm Klein's definition is probably the most influential and longstanding. He suggests three features that characterize gangs. Gangs are groups of youths that

> (a) are generally perceived as a distinct aggregation by others in their neighborhood, (b) recognize themselves as a denotable group (almost invariably with a group name) and (c) have been involved in a sufficient number of [illegal] incidents to call forth a consistent negative response from neighborhood residents and/or enforcement agencies.[4]

Probably the major debate in the field is whether this last element—criminal involvement—should be part of the definition. Its inclusion, some argue, is necessary to highlight that crime is a focal point of the group and to distinguish gangs from more prosocial youth groups. Others suggest this is precisely the problem: Making crime a defining feature of the gang privileges one negative characteristic of the group while downplaying other positive elements and overlooking gangs' similarities to other youth groups. James Short, for instance, notes that "many gangs who commit delinquent acts are not so much criminally inclined as concerned about such matters as participation in youth culture, and getting by." Moreover, he suggests that crime need not be a defining feature of gangs to distinguish them from other youth groups, as their self-determination and lack of adult sponsorship are sufficient to do so.[5] These are vexing debates, which I circumvent in my study by again relying on self-nomination. That is, I define a girl's peer group as a "gang" when she herself classifies it as such. In doing so I have a standardized measure that also allows me to explore a potential range of youth groups considered by their members to be gangs.[6] Although I didn't adopt crime in my definition, the vast majority of girls themselves—including all of them in Columbus— nonetheless highlighted criminal activities as defining features of their gangs.[7]

I will come back to how Columbus girls define their gangs momentarily. First, let me briefly describe their gangs in terms of size, age range, gender composition, and other general characteristics. Except for Jennifer, who was a member of an all-female gang I call the Gangster Girlz, all of the young women in Columbus were members of Folks, Crips, or Bloods sets.[8] Although they adopt nationally recognized gang names, gangs in Columbus are what Ronald Huff calls "homegrown"—that is, they are not the result of the organized migration of gangs from other places, but are primarily Columbus youths who have formed gangs on their own, emulating what they see and learn about from other places.[9] Police estimates at the time of my research suggested that Columbus had approximately thirty active gangs with four hundred to one thousand members.[10]

Young women in Columbus described their gangs as small groups with relatively narrow age ranges. In fact, 85 percent of these groups had memberships of thirty or less: Six girls reported twenty or fewer members in their sets, and eleven described twenty to thirty members. Only three said their gangs had forty-five to fifty members—but each of these girls said they hung out primarily with a smaller clique of gang friends.[11] Columbus gangs also were primarily adolescent groups. On the one hand, only around half of the girls (ten of twenty-one) reported that all of their members were twenty or younger, while the rest said their gangs included members who were twenty-one or older. However, almost without exception, these groups were primarily teenagers with either one adult who was considered the OG ("Original Gangster," i.e., the leader) or just a handful of young adults. Only Monica was in a gang whose members were not mostly adolescents—at sixteen, she was the youngest member of her set, and her thirty-one-year-old brother was the oldest. In addition, six girls described having members in their gangs under thirteen years old, while the majority did not.

With regard to race, girls' gangs in Columbus were principally African American, though some gangs were racially mixed, with a small number of white members as well.[12] Recall from Chapter 2 that nearly one-fourth of the gang girls I spoke with in Columbus were white; with the exception of Lisa, whose brother had started his own set and was her OG, these girls— Cathy, Diane, Heather, and Jennifer—were members of mainly African American gangs and were either the only or one of several white members. Most of the African American girls described being in all-black gangs, though a few mentioned having a handful of white members.

Except for Jennifer's Gangster Girlz, all of the Columbus gangs were described as integrated, mixed-gender groups.[13] The vast majority of these gangs were predominantly male: Sixteen girls (80 percent) described their gangs as having more males than females, and of these, fourteen (70 percent) were in groups in which girls were one-third or fewer of the members.[14] In fact, more than half of the girls (55 percent) reported that there were five or fewer females in their gangs. By and large, girls were a numeric minority in these mixed-gender gangs and, on the whole, were not treated as equals. Nonetheless, they held fast to the notion of gender parity within their gangs. In fact, although the girls described some gender differences in activities among gang members, most did not describe a specific gender organization of the group, and instead argued that males and females were equal partners.[15] As Chantell, among others, asserted repeatedly, "It's all the same, it's all the same."

GANG DEFINITIONS: WHAT MAKES THEM GANGS?

The girls I spoke with in Columbus had been in their gangs on average for just under two years. Most had joined between six months and two years prior to our interviews, but the range included Lisa and Tamika, who had joined within weeks of our conversations, and LaShawna, who had been involved in gangs for five years. Although I counted their peer groups as "gangs" when they classified them as such, I nonetheless remained interested in how and why the young women defined these groups as gangs. At minimum, most scholars classify youth groups as gangs when they are recognized by others and see themselves as discernible groups. More restrictive definitions include such things as participation in delinquency, symbolic systems such as colors and signs, gang names, initiation procedures, and minimum size requirements.[16] In fact, what is striking is the extent to which young women used these same characteristics when describing their gangs.

Girls' explanations for why their groups were gangs included three primary foci: the recognition their gang received from others, the elaborate symbolism they adopted to signify that the group was a gang, and their participation in a variety of delinquent endeavors, most notably conflicts with other groups that called themselves gangs. Angie, for instance, surmised:

> It's a lot of us, and that forms a gang. And then, we don't always do, we don't do a lot of violence, you know, [but] that's what makes them a gang, and plus the violence that they do makes them a gang. Everybody wanna join it, so that's why they call it the gang. 'Cause we have a lot of people and everybody be wantin' to get in.[17]

Likewise, Erica explained, "To me, it's just 'cause it's, it's a group of us, we all walk around sportin' certain colors. We can only wear certain colors. And it's like people look at us and that's exactly what they think—there's a gang. And they respect us for that. They won't bother us." Most girls highlighted symbolism and gang rivalries—in fact, except for the Gangster Girlz, all of girls' gangs in Columbus adopted colors, hand signs, and symbols for their gangs, and all of the girls described having rival gangs with whom there was some level of conflict. "[What makes it a gang is] the name, the way we write it, the stackin', the prayer, the throwin' it up,[18] Folk and all that. The colors, blue and black," noted Keisha. And Traci added, "Because . . . we fight against, you know, we fight Bloods and stuff. And we wear our scarves and everything."

Lisa specifically noted territoriality in her description of the gang. In fact, the vast majority of girls in Columbus (90 percent) described their gangs as having some designated area—often as small as a block—that they claimed as their own.[19] What made her group a gang, Lisa illustrated, was that its members

> claim their territory. They wear their colors. They uh, they just claim that turf. And if, like someone else comes up wearin' the wrong colors, I don't care if you don't have a rag on or not. If you got this color on, a shirt, a hat or anything, you're gettin' beat up.

Territoriality among many of these gangs appeared to be somewhat loosely defined—more so than in traditional gang cities. Only six girls (29 percent) described their gangs as being comprised solely of youths from the same neighborhood, and they were most likely to report that their gang claimed this as its territory or 'hood. Cathy said her gang's 'hood was "just mainly one street," while Brandi noted that territories change according to "parts of the street." She explained, "If you walkin' down like one street wearing red, then, then you end up fightin', it's like one neighborhood's Folks neighborhood, then there's Slobs,[20] then there's Crips, stuff like that."

Nine girls (43 percent) reported that members of their set were from different parts of the city but all hung out together in a particular area. Despite this, most girls described having a territory but nonetheless tending to "just get around everywhere." This was facilitated by various sets' affiliations with one another—members of Crips and Folks sets were "cool" with each other and sometimes hung out together, as did members of different Bloods sets. Consequently, many girls described a broad division of the city by sides of town—North Side, East Side, West Side, South Side—and designated these as particular gangs' territories. Their linkages were informally based, however, and were not part of organized gang groupings like those "supergangs" or gang nations found in bigger gang cities like Chicago and Los Angeles. In fact, young women were cognizant of the difference between Columbus gangs and "big city" gangs. Diane surmised:

> Some places it's where you live, that's your gang. Where you live at. What block you live on or whatever. But in Columbus, it ain't really about that. It's just whatever clique you with. You could live on the West Side but your set could be on the East Side. Or you could live on the East Side and your set could be or the West Side. It's, in Columbus, it's all based up in North Side, East Side, West Side, or South Side. You know? It's like, like how in New York it's, oh I live, I stand on this block or I stand on this block or I stand on this block. Here it's, I stay out east, I stay out west, I stay out south.

Young women's perceptions of the differences between Columbus and other cities expanded beyond territoriality to a broader recognition that gangs in Columbus, though potentially dangerous, were less violent than gangs in other places. Diane and Monica, whom I described in Chapter 3 as among the most committed gang members I spoke with, were particularly vocal in their articulation of this position. As Monica surmised, "Columbus is small time compared to like Cleveland . . . and all that. We, we is small time." Comparing her mostly adult gang with the primarily adolescent gangs around her, Monica observed that "all the little kids wanna be down":

> What I see with most thirteen and fourteen year olds is that they just will not, well, some of 'em, it just seems like they say they're down with a gang just to say they down. And I mean, if they say they down then it's going to be mostly just their friends. . . . It's probably just their friends. But I know I'm down for real, down for life.

Likewise, Diane complained, "To me, Columbus is very weak. 'Cause there's just so many fakes out there. . . . People, they say, 'Ok, I'm a Crip. And this is my, these are my six friends right here so we're all gonna fight and beat each other in and now we're Crips.' " In fact, she wasn't far off the mark in her lament. Recall from Chapter 3 Lisa's description of her gang: Her brother Mike had been a Folks member before they moved to a new neighborhood, and he then decided to start his own set. Just as Diane asserted, Mike had thus far initiated six people, including his girlfriend Trish, his younger sister Lisa, her boyfriend, and three other friends.

Descriptions like this one do tend to characterize these gangs as "small time"—at least compared to popular imagery of gangs, if not actual gangs in other cities. Diane felt a more authentic claim to gang membership than many of the other gang-involved youths she saw around her, in part because her OG, C-Loc, had been a member of a notorious Crips gang in Los Angeles before he came to Columbus. Consequently, Diane felt a link with those "real" gangs we hear about so much. Before further detailing the activities of Columbus gangs, the next section examines these types of links to "big city" gangs, as well as other forms of gang proliferation and diffusion described by Columbus gang members.

GANG DIFFUSION AND CROSS-CITY TIES

As I noted, Diane described her OG as having been gang-involved in Los Angeles before migrating to Columbus. In all, five young women identified their OGs as having come from some place other than Columbus, including Diane, as well as LaShawna, Sonita, Leslie, and Cathy. Describing her gang, Diane explained:

> See I'm in the Gangster Crips and they broke off of Rolling 20s because the OG, C-Loc, he came from Los Angeles, he was a Rolling 20. . . . Gangster Cs is just a set broke off the Rolling 20s set and that's been around, Gangster Crips has been around since C-Loc came down here [to Columbus].

In fact, Diane's gang was among the most organized and criminally sophisticated that I encountered in Columbus. However, it is important to note that C-Loc did not move to Columbus to start the gang, but rather was on the run as a teenager and ended up there. As I indicated earlier, Ronald Huff's work in Columbus provides compelling evidence that gangs there have not emerged as a result of any sort of organized gang migration. Huff *did* find evidence of individual youths moving to Columbus with their families. Often their knowledge of gangs resulted in their being emulated or looked up to by Columbus youths, providing ample opportunities for them to become involved in preexisting gangs or to start their own sets.[21] Nonetheless, most did not become involved in gangs as well-developed as Diane and C-Loc's.

LaShawna was a case in point. Originally from New York, she moved to Columbus at age thirteen and subsequently spent the bulk of her adolescence moving back and forth in various residential facilities. It was at one of these facilities—in fact, during an earlier stay at the one where I interviewed her—that she first joined a Columbus gang. Upon meeting gang members there, LaShawna painted a dramatic picture of how she ended up in the city. I asked how she became involved, and she explained:

LASHAWNA: There was this girl Georgina, and uh, she . . .
JM: You mean here at [the facility]?
LASHAWNA: Yeah. She asked me what I was claimin'—'cause I always used to wear black and white—and, um, I told her Folks. And she said, "For real?" She told me that she was a leader and everything. I said, "Oh, I'm down here for uh, protection, uh, my friends, my G sent me down here for protection."
JM: 'Cause you have family down here?[22]
LASHAWNA: Yeah, that too. And plus, you know, I did somethin'. So they sent me down here and so I hooked up with her and then she got me in my rank and everything, showed me the ropes, kicked some lit to me and some knowledge. And then, after that, she made me a queen.[23]

LaShawna's story, to me and to everyone in Columbus, was that she had committed a serious crime while in her New York gang and was sent away for protection. Unverifiable, it provided her with a "rep" in Columbus, which she used to gain status among her peers. Eventually she started her own set—designating herself as the OG—which she created mostly by recruiting youths she met within facilities and at school, as well as on the streets when she was AWOL from her placements. At the facility where I interviewed her, she and her gang friends would routinely go AWOL and spend time hanging out with other gang members on the streets for a few days before being picked up or returning to the facility voluntarily.

Cathy described a somewhat similar occurrence. Her OG, Anthony, moved to Columbus from Chicago and joined her gang when he arrived. Rather than starting his own gang, Anthony gained status among his Columbus gang peers by playing up his connection to a hardcore gang city like Chicago, and gradually he became the OG. Cathy explained:

[Anthony] just came down here, and like the Bloods down here, he started hangin' out with people and it was like, he knew so much about it and talked to them so much, it was like everybody started looking up to him. And then when people wanted to get initiated they just went to him.

Thus one source of gangs' diffusion—though a relatively small one—appears to result from youths like C-Loc, LaShawna, and Anthony bringing knowledge about gangs from other places and using this knowledge to become established in their new settings. In addition, Tamika said several members of her gang had moved to Columbus from Detroit. They did not come to Columbus to start a new set, but came to visit friends and eventually relocated, joining a local gang. According to Tamika, these young men maintained their ties to gang members in Detroit, and their connections expanded her gang's cross-city ties, as members of her gang would travel to Detroit for visits.

In addition, recall from my discussion in Chapter 2 that scholars have recently attributed an additional source of gang proliferation to the mass media's diffusion of gang culture. In talking with young women about their gangs, I found it striking that a number of them gleaned their information about gangs from popular culture. During my conversation with Keisha, for instance, I followed up on a comment she had made about her gang not "looking for trouble." As she responded, her shift focused and she began to describe a scene from a popular movie about gangs, blurring the boundaries between her own gang and the gang in the film:

JM: So you said that usually your set doesn't just go out looking for trouble?

KEISHA: Right. We go out and have fun, but there's, uh, like in the movie *Menace II Society*, you know how like when, alright, you know when they, Kane got shot, he had that white T-shirt and they was like, bitch I need that thing, and they went to the emergency room? Like if something like that happened at a party, whoever did it, they gone. They gone. You know what I'm sayin'?

Keisha actually continued to make parallels between scenes in the film and what would happen if those events occurred in real life with members of her gang. In doing so, she seemed to be illustrating a process by which she had learned how the gang should act based on what she viewed in a film, and she associated her own gang with the popular image of gangs. Notably, Keisha was unable to describe specific events in her gang that were parallel to those in the film, instead focusing on "what ifs."

Likewise, young women had little sense of the history and origin of their gangs. Instead, many seemed more interested in their mythic connections to gangs in general or to the media construction of gangs, rather than expressing knowledge of their own sets' histories. Even Monica, one of the most knowledgeable and hardcore of the members I spoke with, knew little about the history of her gang. When I asked her, she commented, "I don't even know. And that's, that's really embarrassing to sit here and tell you that I don't know about [it]." When I asked Stephanie if she knew the origins or history of her gang, she said she knew a little about it because she and other members of her gang had rented a movie from the video store and had watched it over and over. In fact, as my conversation with Erica illustrates, many young women had little actual knowledge of the history of gangs in general:

JM: Do you know how long [your gang]'s been around? Or like the history of it, how it got started?
ERICA: No, but I can find out. I heard there's a movie out on it, how the gang originated, got formed.
JM: You mean like the Folk gang?
ERICA: No, just gangs here, how they got formed.
JM: Do you know the name of it, the movie?
ERICA: Um, I think it's *Panther*, that's coming out now, *Panther*. They say that's s'posed to be the one that's . . . talking about how gangs first got formed and how and why and stuff. It's just come out. I want to see it. It looks good, you know, really good.
JM: Yeah. So do you know about your own set? How they got started?
ERICA: Nnhnn [no].
JM: Or, how long they'd been around before you joined 'em?
ERICA: Nnhnn [no].

One thing notable about young women in Folks sets was that part of the diffusion of gang culture they picked up on was politicized, as when Erica made the connection between *Panther*—a film about the emergence and history of the Black Panther Party—and the origins of gangs. I mentioned earlier that Sonita's and Leslie's OGs were from outside Columbus; specifically, they were from Chicago. Both were members of Folks sets, as was Erica. Like them, most of the girls in Folks sets—all of whom traced the origins of Folks to Chicago—would tell me (though they self-identified as gang members), "It's not a gang, it's an organization." However, the distinction for them was not particularly clear-cut. The following conversation with Lisa is illustrative:

JM: How long has [your brother's] set been around, do you know? Do you know the history of how it got started?[24]
LISA: I know the history of how the Folks got started but not of how his set got started.
JM: So how did the Folks get started?
LISA: In Chicago, I guess, it's one of the kings. I ain't really real familiar with it all but we didn't always used to be a violent gang, so they say. But, um, one of the kings got, went to jail or somethin' and someone killed him or somethin' and they all just, a Blood killed him or somethin' and that's when, 'cause we're not, we don't consider ourself a gang. We consider ourself an organization. But, I mean, people like the judges and stuff consider us a street gang but, we don't consider ourself a gang. We're an organization.
JM: And how do you distinguish between a gang and an organization? Do you know?

LISA: No.
JM: Just that that's the name that you call yourselves?
LISA: Yeah.

In fact, leaders of the Gangster Disciples in Chicago, who are under the Folks nation, adopted the term *organization* with the explicit intent of reframing public perceptions, if not the actual behavior of the group, to highlight its role in community activism and revitalization while shifting attention away from its criminal endeavors. Predecessors of the Gangster Disciples were among those Chicago gangs that became politically active during the 1960s, and these groups were involved in what ended up being controversial federally funded gang programs during that time.[25] One of the Gangster Disciples leaders, Larry "King" Hoover, remains a contentious political figure, even after spending more than two decades in prison for murder. In 1995, Hoover was indicted by federal law enforcement for drug conspiracy. While he claims to be a political prisoner, kept locked up to squelch his political activities in urban black communities, law enforcement alleges that Hoover has run the Gangster Disciples' narcotics organization from prison since the early 1970s.[26]

Several girls in Columbus made reference to Larry Hoover, though only Lisa mentioned him by name, calling him "King Hoover." She explained to me that Hoover had choked on a chicken bone and was deceased, and consequently that Folks were not permitted to eat chicken on Fridays (the day he supposedly died). With more accuracy, Sonita, describing her gang's connections to Chicago, surmised, "That's where half of 'em are and that's where our OG came from, that's where we started to learn about the leader [Hoover], why he was in jail for I think murder or something like that, robbery or something." Leslie drew the most vivid connections between her gang and Folks gangs in Chicago, as the following conversation illustrates:

LESLIE: Our gang was started up in Chicago. . . . The guy, our leader had came back down from Chicago and started his set up north. And, then, it's just grown from there.
JM: Like, what, the north end of Columbus?
LESLIE: Yeah. The north, like, right off of [a main street].
JM: OK. And so, the leader that you're referring to, would he be the leader of just your set, or other sets?
LESLIE: Yeah. He's just a leader of our set. . . . Then, you have, like, the highest one, the highest one that we have, he doesn't live in Ohio. He lives in Chicago. And he's the leader, like, of all sets.
JM: And does anybody have any contact with him?
LESLIE: The leader . . . of our set has contact with him. But, we really don't know who it is. We just know there is one. But we don't know who it is.

For the most part, young women's descriptions of their gangs' ties to gangs elsewhere were less direct connections than filtered-down gang lore.[27] With the exception of Diane, who was a Crip, only young women from Folks gangs described explicit connections to gangs elsewhere; among them, even when they knew of members in Columbus who had direct ties to gang members in Chicago, this didn't appear to shape the day-to-day activities of their gangs in Columbus. Likewise, Diane did not describe ongoing relations with C-Loc's gang in Los Angeles, and none of the other Crips or Bloods gang members reported direct ties to gangs outside of Columbus. Instead, Columbus gangs appear to be in keeping with John Hagedorn's description of the emergence of gangs in Milwaukee: These groups "tend to follow big-city gang traditions, borrow ideas about big-city gang structure, and respond favorably to the image of big-city gangs [while] the use of big-city names and symbols by local gangs indicates a process of cultural diffusion rather than structural ties."[28]

MEMBERSHIP, INITIATIONS, AND STATUS ISSUES

Regardless of how "small time" these Columbus gangs were compared to gangs in other places, they had real meaning for the young women involved. One way gangs are meaningful is through their perceived exclusivity. Being chosen to join a group with delineated boundaries—one that presumably doesn't let just "anyone" join—brings feelings of pride, accomplishment, and belonging. The pull of feeling like you're part of something is a powerful one for many young people. Recall from Chapter 2 that although Erica expressed some reservations about her gang involvement, she nonetheless said that "in some ways" being in the gang "makes me feel like a person, like actually somebody." Diane concurred, "Being a Crip means . . . that I'm to be respected."

Most young women described their gang involvement as providing a sense of empowerment. Lisa described girls in gangs as feeling like, "Aw, I'm hard, you know, you can't beat me up." And she confirmed, "When you're in a gang, that's how you feel. You just feel like, oh my God, you know, they got my back. I don't need to worry about it." Erica agreed: "People don't bother you, especially if they don't know you and they know that, that you're in a gang. They don't bother you. It's like you put that intimidation in somebody." Describing how joining the gang made her feel, Leslie surmised, "I felt like, yeah now I'm gonna be cool, I'm gonna be Miss Thang in the gang and walk around Miss Bad Butt. Nobody can mess with me now because I'm in a gang."

Given the gangs' provision of empowerment and members' beliefs that it afforded protection, gang members valued particular traits in seeking out new members and assessing current ones. Young women's descriptions of the qualities that make a good gang member were parallel for females and males: first, they should be tough, willing and able to fight; second, they should be loyal, true, and "down for the gang." Loyalty and toughness were seen as going hand-in-hand. As Diane noted, "They're gonna be down for theirs, they're gonna be ready to fight for theirs." In the following conversation, Cathy elaborated:

JM: What do you look for in someone when they want to join the gang, like what do you expect out of them?
CATHY: Um, to be true to our gang and to have our backs. I mean, we don't want nobody that's been out here wantin' to be a Crip or been, you know, false flaggin'[29] with Crips or somethin'. We don't want that.
JM: What does it mean to be "true" to the gang?
CATHY: Like, if you say you're a Blood, you be a Blood. You wear your rag even when you're by yourself. You know, don't let anybody intimidate you and be like "take that rag off," you know, "you better get with our set," or something like that.
JM: OK. Anything else that being true to the set means?
CATHY: Yeah, I mean, just you know, I mean it's, you got a whole bunch of people comin' up in your face and if you're by yourself they ask you what you're claimin', you tell 'em. Don't say "nothin'."
JM: Even if it means getting beat up or something?
CATHY: Mmhmm [yes].

Some girls suggested that the gang would test potential members before allowing them to join. Lisa said her brother would have the individual steal something or would purposely get into a fight to see whether his companion would jump in and assist. Erica described a less explicit testing process that simply emerged as the potential member associated with the gang over time. I had posed the same question that began my dialogue with Cathy:

ERICA: [We expect] that they're not a punk. And that when something goes down that they're there.
JM: What do you mean by "punk"?
ERICA: Well, they're not a scaredy cat. 'Cause when you join something like that, you might as well expect that there's gonna be fights. I mean, just a lot of stuff. And if you're a punk, or if you're scared of stuff like that, then don't join.
JM: OK, so how do you know ahead of time?
ERICA: Actually you can tell. Just like, the people, the Folks I hung around with before I got put in, I fought all the time when I was with them. I mean, even when I wasn't in it I fought all the time. I never backed down from anybody. I didn't care either. So they knew I wasn't gonna [be a punk]. You can mostly just tell. If you hang around with them before you're put in it, and they test you before you're put in with things to see if you'll do it. And that was mostly what was with mine. I fought all the time when I was with them.

In fact, most young women told me that the initiation itself was an important event for determining whether someone was "gang material." Heather explained:

> When you get beat in if you don't fight back and if you just like stop and start cryin' or somethin' or beggin' 'em to stop and stuff like that, then they ain't gonna, they'll just stop and they'll say that you're not gang material because you gotta be hard, gotta be able to fight, take punches, stuff like that.

Girls' descriptions of their own initiations paralleled these same themes. The specifics of initiations varied across gangs. Several girls described a timed fight or beating, as Diane illustrated in the opening of this chapter. Most took a set number of punches or "blows" to the head or chest, and a few recounted walking through a line-up of gang members, each of whom threw punches as the initiate passed by. Several girls also described committing a crime as part of their initiation. Kim and Jennifer each committed a robbery, Keisha shot up a school building and started a fire in a wooded lot, and Cathy confronted and fought a rival gang member.

While Diane was jumped by females, Heather and Tamika described being jumped in by male members of their gangs. Heather recounted:

> There's like a bunch of people around and then one comes in and you start fighting with that one then you fight with that one for about two minutes and then another one comes in and you fight 'em both for a while and then they just gradually pull a bunch of 'em in and then all of a sudden you're gettin' your butt beat. [Laughs]. . . . I cried a little bit, but I didn't show it 'cause I was cussin' at 'em. I was mad at 'em. I was like, "I can't believe you guys beat me up. I hate you guys." [Laughs] They's like, "Well you wanted to be in the gang." I was like, "You're not supposed to be hittin' me that hard." [Laughs] 'Cause I was beat up real bad. I had a black eye and some bruises all over me, and these red marks around, kick red marks all over my head and stuff. I was so mad. I was crying. I was like, "I hate all you guys." They was like, "You wanna fight again?" I was like, "Yeah, what's up." I was mad.

On the other hand, Tamika suggested that the three members who jumped her in took it easy on her: "They was just like, they was taggin' me. It hurted, but you know it *really* didn't hurt. . . . They wasn't tryin' to hurt me. They was just tryin' to do what they had to do so I could just get in real quick." As was the case with most initiations, Tamika had been partying—drinking and smoking marijuana—when the initiation took place, in her case at a hotel party. Consequently, she said, "I ain't feel nothin' 'cause I was so high."

By far the most common form of initiation described was to take a set number of punches to the head or chest. Most girls who "took blows" for their initiation described being prostrate at the time. Veronica explained, "You take six blows to your head and your chest. You get down with your left knee on the ground and you throw up your Folks sign."[30] Leslie's description was more detailed:

I had to be punched in the chest by this girl, by my friend that was there. She punched me in my chest six times. And I had to put the Folks sign up and then I had to say "Folks live forever" four times. The whole time she was punching me in my chest. . . . You have to be down on one knee and one knee in the air, and if . . . like if you fall or somethin' or start cryin' or somethin' they would say, "Well you can't be in it 'cause you're not strong enough."

Unlike the girls who described being prostrate when they received their blows, Cathy and Lisa walked through a line of gang members to receive them. Cathy explained: "It was like, five was on this side and five was on this side. I walked through the middle and got hit five times in the head and then got another rag at the end." She had already received one rag during the first part of her initiation, which involved confronting and fighting a rival gang girl. Cathy described the entire process—including her decision to join—as spur of the moment. She had been hanging with the gang for some time; her sister had been a member for about a year.

It was just like, all of us was [out] one day and there was like this girl. She was a Crip. And it's the same girl my sister had to beat up to get in it. And she started sayin' somethin' to me and den my sister, they was just all like, you know, "Beat her up, beat her up! And you'll be a Blood." And I was like, "OK." So I beat her up. And then after I was done, it was like the top leader of the gang handed me a rag.

As I noted earlier, Cathy was not the only young woman whose initiation involved committing a crime in addition to being assaulted by her gang's members. In fact, Jennifer's Gangster Girlz was the only gang that did not require submitting to a physical assault as part of their initiation, and this was one reason Jennifer was drawn to her gang over the other gangs she saw around her. She explained that she didn't like "Crips, Folks, and Bloods 'n stuff like that" because she considered their initiations brutal and degrading: "Like you have to get jumped by five girls and you're not allowed to fight 'em back. Or you have to go down a line and they have bats 'n stuff that they can hit you in the head with and you can't hit 'em back. . . . I just look at them like, I'm sorry, but I couldn't even go through it." It wasn't the violence per se that Jennifer disliked about other gangs' initiations; instead, it was the element of submission—allowing yourself to be attacked without fighting back—that she found troubling. In fact, her own initiation involved quite a bit of violence: She committed a series of crimes with other members, including jumping a group of girls, and then "jacking a geeker [robbing an addict]." To Jennifer's mind, she was an active participant in these events, not the object of the Gangster Girlz' attack, making her initiation a collaborative process rather than one of submission.

While the specifics of girls' initiations differed, they were all variations on a theme—the testing of an individual's ability to withstand physical confrontation and do so in the name of the gang. Although their talk was tough and most girls described enduring physical assaults that many of us would define as fierce, there were also plenty of allusions in girls' conversations similar to Tamika's description of gang members taking it easy on initiates. In fact, while young women argued that the qualities of toughness and loyalty were of utmost importance in choosing members, there was also evidence that in some of their gangs, the most important qualification was simply the desire to be a member. Recall from Chapter 3 Angie's description of being initiated when she was eleven—she hadn't been involved in any gang activities, but simply lived on the block and looked up to the older youths she saw around her. It wasn't until she was a few years older that she began spending significant amounts of time on the streets and with her gang.

There were other examples as well. Returning to Tamika's initiation at the hotel party, she explained that once she was initiated, her friends Vernessa and Janet, who were also at the party, decided to join as well. Their initiations occurred shortly after hers and involved being jumped by Tamika herself. She explained, "Two of my other girls, after I got jumped in, then they wanted me to jump them in so I did that. . . . I was like, 'You want me to do it real quick?' They was like, 'Yeah.' I was like, 'Well you know, come on then.' And I just tagged 'em a couple times for three minutes and it was over." Curious as to the contrast between gang members' descriptions of the seriousness with which decisions were made to let individuals join and Tamika's description of her friends' impromptu initiations, I pressed the issue.

JM: [This was the] same night?
TAMIKA: Yep.
JM: And did [your girls] hang out with [the gang] beforehand?
TAMIKA: It was like, it's me, my two, my other two girls that was in [the detention center with me]. . . . It's just always us three just kickin' it with my boyfriend, my brother [both members of the gang]. 'Cause Vernessa, she like[s] my boyfriend's brother. So you know, and we both know how to stack. We know how to do all that. And she was like, "Oh, I wanna be down. I done seen you get in and I wanna get in now." I was like, "Alright." And so we just started boxin', so I just did it.
JM: So you just [boxed with her to let her in]?
TAMIKA: Yep.
JM: And so how come she didn't have to fight three people [like you did]?
TAMIKA: Because I, there ain't no other females in it but us three. And so if another female, I had to box with [male members] because there was no other females to do it so they had to do it. And then, since I was a female, that's why I had to box with [the girls] to put them in.

This dialogue illustrates the extent to which many of these youth gangs are ephemeral groups, less organized and sophisticated than they portray themselves or are portrayed as by others. "Partyin' all day, all night, goin' into the next day partyin'," Tamika's friends impetuously decided to join the gang, and just as spontaneously, gang members allowed them to do so and allowed their newest member to perform the initiation. The period of testing that girls describe as occurring in theory often simply did not occur in practice. LaShawna, for instance, had recently initiated a young woman into her gang who had never fought before. In fact, her friend Rachel, who was not a gang member (see Chapter 3), even helped with the initiation, which took place in the hallway at school. Of the new initiate, Rachel told me, "She's never been in a fight before but how she got jumped in. That was her first fight ever."

Likewise, Lisa said her brother's girlfriend Trish, who he initiated into his gang, had never been in a fight before. Trish was "sexed" into the gang: Unlike Lisa and the others, who walked through a lineup and were punched, Trish's initiation involved having sex with Mike, who wore his rag and "said some little prayer or something" during intercourse.[31] Lisa said that as a consequence Trish's status was different than hers—Trish was a "queen"[32] while Lisa was a gang-banger, and she noted that Trish, because of her status, could not move up "the ranks" (see later) in the gang. Describing the difference, Lisa said:

> A gang-banger goes out and fights. Trish don't have to fight if she don't want to. She can just claim, that's it. But she, she fights. Well, she ain't never fought yet. But she would if it came down to it. Like, if another rival gang came up she would fight 'em. Or they would end up fightin' her. One or the other.

In fact it's likely, despite many girls' claims to the contrary, that gang members' lack of serious concern with initiates' qualifications may be a gendered phenomenon—that is, that young women are held to less stringent standards than young men. This issue will be explored in greater detail in Chapters 6–8, but it is worth at least mentioning here. Leslie articulated the position, suggesting to me that "guys are more important to the gang than girls are." It's harder for male gang members to join and to leave the gang, she explained, " 'Cause I mean, you can always find a girl that'll be willing and easier to join a gang."

Most young women remained resistant to Leslie's argument because it called into question the empowerment they drew from the gang. Nonetheless, their stories revealed that girls' devaluation was something they struggled with even as they sought to ignore its existence, both within the gang and in others' perceptions of female gang involvement. In particular, young women were disturbed by the sexual connotations sometimes attached to girls' gang membership, as evidenced by the existence of sexual initiations such as Trish's. All of the young women were familiar with being "sexed into" gangs, and in fact most said this was an option even within their own sets. However, none admitted to having been sexed in, and they held strong derogatory feelings about those girls who were.

The reasons for this are apparent in the connection Monica made between sexing-in and her fight to be recognized as an equal to male gang members.

This was less of a problem for her within her gang, she noted, because she got her respect "right off the bat" by choosing to be initiated by male rather than female members. She explained: "Instead of taking six [punches] from the girls I took six from four guys. . . . So the girls, they had nothin' to say about me bein' a punk, neither did the guys." Her frustration, she said, stemmed from others' perceptions of her as a female gang member:

> They be showing these little movies on TV, like well, the females have to get sexed in and the males have to get jumped in and like that. You know, you seen 'em on TV. And [people], they just figure, well if you a girl gang member then you got sexed in. And I really didn't. I wasn't even down for nothin' like that.

As we shall see, young women also dealt with the devaluation of females within their own gangs. The consequences of this devaluation, as well as how and why girls dealt with it, are the subjects of Chapters 7 and 8. Next I continue my focus on status issues by examining gang leadership and member ranking systems within Columbus gangs.

LEADERSHIP AND MEMBER RANKINGS

Although much research has suggested that gang leadership tends to be shifting and unstable,[33] all of the young women I spoke with in Columbus described their gangs as having one leader, whom they called their OG.[34] Recall that these gangs were primarily adolescent groups, and those with adults typically described just one or several young adult members with whom leadership rested. Eleven girls described their OG as twenty-one or older, while ten had leaders who were twenty or younger.[35] In addition, leadership in these gangs was almost exclusively male. With the exception of LaShawna, who reported being the OG of her gang, all of the girls in mixed-gender gangs described their OG as male. In fact, a number of young women told me that only males could be leaders.

As I noted earlier, with the exception of Monica, all of the girls were in gangs in which the majority of members were adolescents. In fact, several girls described adult leadership that appeared to be supervisory in nature. For instance, Erica was in a large Folks set with a twenty-four-year-old OG. She hung out with a small group of adolescent gang friends who would check in with their OG rather than hang out with him on a regular basis. She explained:

> He's the leader, just like when we have meetings he's the one that does the meetings. We have to . . . like when we take off and run from here [go AWOL from the residential facility], we go and see him. It's like he's, I don't know, he's like our probation officer. We check in with him all the time, so he knows

how we're doin' and all that he's doin'. And, like, if we're doin' somethin' wrong, out of the gang, that we know we're not supposed to, he'll check [correct] us for it.

It appears that young women accepted the OG's leadership uncritically, particularly when he was an adult. Of the juvenile OGs, young women reported that these young men had earned that rank because "he's been in the gang for a long time," or, in cases like Lisa's brother Mike, because he "got enough rank from doin' whatever he did to get that rank [e.g., "dirt," serious crime]" that he could start his own set. Young women viewed their OGs with both reverence and fear. Veronica described her OG as follows: "He's just crazy, but we gotta listen to 'im. He's just the type that if you don't listen to 'im he gonna blow your head off. He's just crazy." Likewise, I asked Keisha what it was about her OG that made the members want to listen to him. She replied:

I mean, that's the top. That's the top G. If you don't do [what he says], he can shoot you. He can kill you. So to defy him, you have some fear in your heart in a way. Like if you was the leader and you told me to shoot this Slob and I didn't do it, I's like backin' down, I'm gettin' my ass kicked for the simple fact I'm disobeyin' you.[36] And that's a no-no. I came close to doin' that. Talked back to 'im. Got slapped. [Laughs] Got slapped pretty hard too. I never do that again. Our leader, I'd say he about 6'9", close to seven feet, I'm not gonna fuck with him. Don't nobody wanna fuck with him. That's the big dog. Can't hang with the big dog, you better stay your ass on the porch with the poodles. I know for the fact that I'm stayin' on the porch. I ain't comin' off the porch. When it comes to him, no, no, no, no. His hands is like twice [the size] of Shaq's [Shaquille O'Neil's].

Six girls (29 percent) did report that there was a "high-ranking" female in their gang, in a few cases considered the female OG, who was under the male OG. Describing this situation in her gang, Keisha surmised:

There's this girl. She up high, she's like second best. You know what I'm sayin'? You can like, if the leader's like gone somewhere you can go to her. I mean, she's like a vice president. You know, the president and vice president. She like that. But she his peon and I'm her peon.

Often girls were high-ranking or gained status in the gang because of their connections either to the leader or to other high-status males. Veronica described the girl with the most power in her set, who was "kind of like the leader for the girls," as the OG's "sister or his cousin, one of 'em." His girlfriend also had status, though Veronica noted that "most of us just look up to our OG." Several of the young women I interviewed whose brothers were in their gangs also described feeling that they gained recognition in part because of this relationship. Tamika said, "Everybody know me, everybody know me as Stan's little sister." And Monica noted that she got respect partly "because my brothers is up there," but also because the other members "know what I'm all about." In fact, young women appeared to have two routes to status—via their connections to influential males in the gang and, like male gang members, by being tough and true to the set.

While the OG was at the top of gangs' ranking systems, usually girls described additional hierarchies within the group. Some of the previous discussion has alluded to gang members "moving up the ranks." In fact, three-fourths of the Columbus gang members I spoke with noted some role specialization within their groups, though few (15 percent) described age-graded roles, and just under one-third (30 percent) described specific roles for males and females. The role specialization they described did not involve the types of subgroupings found in traditional gangs; instead, they were based on a loose hierarchy of ranks that members could move up in based on the amount of dirt (crime, fights) they did for the gang.[37]

Nearly all of the girls described a relatively uncomplicated set of ranks that members could move up in over time or by "putting in work" for the gang. Usually these included a series of three to five ranks. For instance, Lisa described that "there's like Foot Soldier One, Foot Soldier Two, Foot Soldier Three, and then there's like Chief Enforcer after that." Monica said, "Like we have a Governor and then on down. We got OG, Governor, and then just regular gangsters—Gs—and all that shit." Leslie described a set of ranks that were gender differentiated, the language adopted from Chicago's Gangster Disciples, with whom her gang was loosely connected (see earlier):

> When you first enter the gang the guy is a Disciple; the girl is like the Disciple or Disciple Princess, somethin' like that. But the second level is the guy will move up he's still a Disciple, but he's a Disciple Prince. Then the girl is a Disciple Princess. Then, when you move up to the third level it's just Prince and Princess. Then, the highest one you can get for a girl is, it changes around to Princess Disciple. Then that's the highest for a girl. A Prince Disciple is like the one before the highest for a guy.

Almost uniformly, girls said that there were not particular roles or jobs assigned to individuals according to their rank. As Sonita noted, "Just everybody do everything." Only Diane described a more complicated series of ranks that involved criminal specialization. The ranks in her gang included nine for females and ten for males. She explained:

> Everybody's rank is different. Everybody's rank has a, has somethin' to do. Like my rank, I'm Governor. My position is to go out and find licks [robbery targets]. I go and set up the licks. I keep the money. I, like, money, like when we sell drugs we keep our own money. But I keep track of like, like who's doin' what. You know what I'm sayin.' So I keep track of who's doin' what. I go and set up licks. . . . Like who we're gonna rob. So that's all money.

This pattern of organization was likely influenced by the particular knowledge Diane's OG C-Loc brought from his Los Angeles gang.

As I noted, members could move up in rank by "putting in work" for the gang, including both economic crimes and fights with rival gang members. In addition, young women reported that rank came from the length of time that members were involved in the gang, which was believed to coincide with knowledge about the gang. Monica said in her set ranks were determined "just [by] the length of time you been in there." And Keisha said, "The longer you're in it, the higher you go." Most girls, however, described criminal acts ("doing dirt") as a way to raise one's rank. Lisa said members could raise their rank by "beatin' up somebody or somethin', or like fightin' a rival gang, somethin' like that," while Chantell also mentioned carjacking. Sonita summarized the process in her gang:

SONITA: It's like, steps you gotta do. First become a foot soldier, and that's just gettin' in, learnin' about it, then you become a G and that's when you know almost everything about it. And you done did something to get your G or whatever, earn it. . . .

JM: What kind of things would you do to earn a G?

SONITA: Whatever they told you to do. Shoot at somebody, go beat somebody up, go steal a car, go do a whole bunch of stuff they tell you to do, anything they tell you to do you gotta do it. Without gettin' caught.

Like other girls' discussions of leadership, Sonita's reiteration that "anything they tell you to do you gotta do it" reveals girls' experience of gang leadership as authoritarian. However, these examples also illustrate that girls were describing pretty typical forms of delinquent activities as a means of raising rank and gaining status in the gang—for instance, getting into fights and stealing cars. Although shooting at someone and car-jacking were mentioned, on the whole young women were not describing the types of sensationalized crimes—homicides, drive-by shootings—typically associated with gangs. I will discuss gangs' and gang members' criminal endeavors in greater detail in Chapter 6, but the relatively mild nature of the gang crime girls described is noteworthy. In part, this was because girls tended to be excluded from the most serious forms of gang crime. This is also, however, indicative of the nature of gangs in Columbus at the time of my interviews. A relatively new phenomenon in the city, comprised primarily of adolescents with little or no intergenerational dynamics, these groups did not involve complex organization, tended not to be involved in economic crimes in any sophisticated way, and were not particularly violent. In fact, although the number of gang members had increased in Columbus and the number of juveniles arrested for carrying concealed weapon had nearly tripled in the few years prior to my study, arrests for violent offenses among this group had thus far remained stable.[38]

LIFE IN THE GANG[39]

Malcolm Klein has often reported that gang members spend much more time talking about their criminal endeavors than engaging in them. Instead, he suggests, youths' time with their gangs tends to be relatively mundane, punctuated with occasional acts of serious crime that become the fodder for much ongoing conversation and discussion.[40] In Columbus, most gang girls' time was spent simply hanging out with other gang members, and the primary everyday activities gang members described were either noncriminal or nonserious forms of delinquency. For instance, when I asked girls to describe a typical day with their gang friends, their responses were nearly uniform. Brandi said:

> A typical day would be sittin' back at the park or somethin' like that or one of our friend's houses, or a gang member's house, gettin' drunk, gettin' high and, you know, watchin' TV, listenin' to the radio. Actually, we listen to tapes and stuff, stackin' and all this stuff.

And Veronica remarked:

> Most of the time is on a weekend, like a Friday or a Saturday. We just be, like, when we was over at my cousin's house, we just be sittin' there watching TV, everybody puttin' in money, orderin' pizzas and stuff. Just listen to music, dancin'. They be sittin' around playin' with guns, drinkin' and stuff, smokin' weed. That's really, that's all. Crackin' on people. [Laughs]

Nikkie described a similar scenario:

> We just, it's just like we got a, our OG, he got a house and his girlfriend live with him, and we all be over there playin' video games and stuff. We just be havin' fun. And sometimes we go to the movies, sometimes we steal cars, um, we don't do nothin' else really.

As did Monica:

> Play cards, smoke bud [marijuana], play dominos, play video games. That's basically all we do is play. You would be surprised. This is a bunch of big kids. It's a bunch of big old kids in my set. They will fight over a Nintendo game in a minute. They, I mean, they will seriously go out into the front yard and go to blows over a Nintendo game. They just big ol' kids. We just have fun playin' around and stuff like that but when it come time to get down to business, you gotta get down to business.

For Monica and Diane, "getting down to business" meant involvement in planned criminal activities such as drug sales in Monica's case and drug sales, robberies, and property crimes in Diane's case. Most of the young women, however, reported much less organized involvement in crime. For the majority, delinquent endeavors tended to be sporadic, unplanned, and happened upon rather than specifically intended. Fights occurred routinely, particularly when gang members spent time, as they often did, walking around the neighborhood or hanging out in public places like parks or malls. However, these fights weren't necessarily with rival gang members. For instance, Erica said that she and her friends would walk around the neighborhood "pick[ing] on people" and "beating people up." Explaining their behavior, she said, "If somebody's bored and they have nothin' to do, then they'll start a fight." Likewise, Traci said she and other members of her set would routinely "go out and look for trouble, like go out and look for fights and stuff, start trouble and stuff." Veronica said sometimes they fought "with people that's not even in gangs" who "mess with" them while they're hanging around on the streets. I will focus in greater detail on gangs' and gang members' involvement in delinquency and conflicts with other groups in Chapter 6. My main point here, however, is to highlight that the bulk of gang members' activities in Columbus do not revolve around organized, serious crime.

In addition to hanging out together, nearly all of the young women in Columbus described their gang as having regular meetings (90 percent), along with specific rules or codes that members were expected to follow (95 percent). This seemed to be in keeping with the loose but supervisory leadership that many girls characterized their gangs as having. Although most girls described seeing one another on a daily or near-daily basis, they reported having more formal meetings, typically once a week or once or twice a month. The meetings were usually planned ahead of time and were held in the same location each time—for instance, at a park, parking lot, or someone's house. Sonita's set met once a month, either "at a school in they field or at somebody's house in they yard." She said, "The OG'd go around tellin' everybody so they won't miss it." Erica said her set had meetings "mostly every Friday night," at a place she described as a "closed off area," like a fenced lot. Her gang was large, and she hung with a smaller group of about fifteen. Of the rest, she said, "We just don't all hang out, like all fifty of us really, except for at the meetings."

Young women said the meetings were usually to "take care of business," which typically involved discussing what was going on with rival gangs. Heather explained:

They say, like, you know, they'll say like, "Some Slobs have been doin' this," you know, "We need to get a couple people to take care of that problem," or you know what I'm saying, it's more like a business meeting really. It really is. And then, they just, everyone just talks about what's been going on and, you know, things that need to be taken care of, and that's about it.

Diane said her set had meetings twice a week, usually at a member's house, where they discussed not only what was occurring with rival gangs but also their plans for making money:

> Everybody brings bud [marijuana] and forties [40-ounce bottles of beer]. Sit there and get fucked up, talk about what we're gonna do, what we plan on doin' for the next week, how we're gonna make money, who's tryin' to trip, who is after us, who we're after and it's just set up.

Monica said the members of her set, which only had fifteen members, saw one another often enough that they only had meetings on special occasions, such as when "you all gotta sit down and discuss something for real, like discuss puttin' somebody else down [initiating them] or something like that." At such times, they usually met at "somebody's house, [the] closest house to where you at or whatever."

Young women also described a number of different rules or codes of conduct they were expected to follow. For example: They were supposed to attend scheduled meetings, they were not allowed to date members of rival gangs, they couldn't back down when confronted by rival gang members, and gang business was supposed to be kept within the gang. Chantell explained, "Like, your flag, if you drop it, you can't drop it, that's disrespectin' [the gang], 'cause it touched the ground. And, can't wear dred [red], stuff like that. You can't be throwin' up Slobs, you can't be throwin' up that stuff, you always have to throw 'em down."

Another code of conduct within the gang that many young women discussed was that members should get along with one another—"have love" for each other regardless of personal differences or conflicts. The majority of girls mentioned this as a rule in their gang. Chantell noted, "That's like your brothers and sisters, so you should get along." LaShawna said, "You're not supposed to fight one another," but admitted that it happened on occasion:

> Sometimes they beef and everything and then they just squash it. Like forget about it, or they make up. Whatever, show each other love. Regardless, if they get into a scrap [fight], though, and one of us is there that's over them, we make 'em show 'em love anyway. Just tell 'em to squash it and if they don't they get a violation.

In addition, there were rules against using crack cocaine, even though many members reportedly sold it. Young women had strong feelings against smoking crack because they saw the effects of the drug around them. Keisha said, "That's just not allowed. I mean, that's like disrespectin' yourself and your members. You gonna smoke crack you might as well just go ahead and join the Slobs." Their attitudes about the drug, in fact, seem to be in keeping with recent anti-crack conduct norms that have arisen throughout the United States in response to the personal and social devastation wrought by the drug.[41]

The rules described here were common across gangs; they were mentioned by numerous girls from different sets. The typical consequence for breaking a rule was a violation, though in the case of cross-gang dating, the individual might be beaten out of the gang. Both Brandi and Diane described incidents in their sets when this occurred. Like their discussions of initiations, however, while young women insisted on the importance of the rules they described, in the course of conversation they also provided evidence of the transgression of these same rules. Decker and Van Winkle note the existence of informal rules such as these in St. Louis, which they describe as "evolv[ing] out of practice, lore, or common sense."[42] Likewise, these Columbus gangs appeared to have adopted rules or codes of behavior from a variety of sources, though their application remained inconsistent.

MOTHERHOOD, PREGNANCY, AND DATING IN THE GANG

Inevitably, one element of girls' involvement in mixed-gender gangs is romantic relationships with young men. Ten young women (48 percent) in Columbus said that they had a boyfriend in the gang.[43] And although other researchers have focused attention on how motherhood shapes girls' gang involvement,[44] in Columbus only LaShawna and Keisha had a child, and neither were their child's primary caregivers. Both described their babies as being in the custody of relatives. LaShawna was pregnant again when we spoke, and Keisha had two miscarriages in addition to the child she had. Two other girls reported a total of four pregnancies, each of which ended in miscarriage or abortion,[45] and Leslie was pregnant when we spoke, with plans to leave her gang. In fact, Keisha had her child before she joined the gang, and saw pregnancy and motherhood as things to avoid during her gang involvement. As the following conversation illustrates, this appeared to be an opinion shared by her female gang peers:[46]

JM: What about when a girl gets pregnant? Have you known anybody that got pregnant?
KEISHA: [Shakes her head]
JM: You've never known anybody in your set who's gotten pregnant?
KEISHA: Not for the simple fact, we don't wanna bring our babies into no gangs so we use condoms. If you don't use condoms we ain't giving it up. That's just the way it is. That's on us females, we already had that discussion amongst us six.

Other young women concurred. In fact, about half of the girls said that gangs were no place for young women to have babies and that they either made sure it didn't happen or their impending motherhood led them to leave the gang. The other half described young women staying involved in the gang, but curtailing their involvement until the child was born. Sticking with the first group, Erica told me that none of the girls in her gang had children, explaining, "They're not stupid. I think they use protection. I mean, if they were to get pregnant they probably would end up having an abortion." She continued, "They're just into that gang, I mean just like . . . to hang out with their friends and like to party. They don't want to have no kids when they're havin' fun like that and partyin'. They're just not thinkin' about that then." Traci said members of her gang were about to initiate a young woman when they found out she was pregnant. Although other members considered letting her in, Traci was adamant that she should not join: "She got a life to live, she gotta take care of her baby 'n stuff now. And I told 'em that she shouldn't. . . . I was like, 'Well, we can't have you in here.' " And Veronica said the only girl in her gang she knew to have been pregnant dropped out: "She had got pregnant and she had the baby, she ain't never come back around to no sets or nothin'."

One reason young women resisted bringing children into the gang was that they believed once the child was born in the gang, they were affiliated for life. Referring to the same young woman, Veronica continued:

> They wanted, they wanted to bless her baby in . . . but she said "no." They tried to bless my cousin's little boy in. Said the little prayer and stuff. It was silly. [Laughs] I was like, my kids ain't bein' in no gang. 'Cause my boyfriend be talkin' about, "Yeah, you have my baby, my son gonna be bad and he gonna be in a gang, and he gonna do this." And I'm like, no. I don't think so. Like, my child ain't gon be bad.

Like other stories about gangs that young people sometimes believed, the idea that a child born in the gang was forever marked as a gang member was a powerful one.[47] Chantell told me, "If the father and the mother's in a gang, the baby's already in it." In fact, Keisha's resistance to having children while in the gang was about this very point. When I asked what initiated her conversation with the other girls about not getting pregnant, she responded:

> I brought it up for the simple fact, when I joined in, most of the girls didn't know that. I was like look y'all know when you get pregnant, that's, your baby [is a] future Folk, and he gotta grow up in the gang. And it's like, naw fuck that. I don't want that to happen. Just for the simple fact that's my son. I wanna teach him to be somethin' different. I want him to go to college. I want him to play football and basketball.

Leslie, as I mentioned, was pregnant when we spoke. Her boyfriend was also a member of her gang. Although she was in the detention center awaiting adjudication, she insisted that once she got out she was leaving her gang so that her child wouldn't be part of the gang life. She explained:

> The leader, he tried to tell you, he tried to tell the guys to get their girls pregnant, so then that would be—'cause they try to say if a child is born into a

gang then they're always going to be [in the] gang from birth to death. . . . And I mean, I've already told my boyfriend, I said my baby is not gonna have nothin' to do with no gang. You may be in a gang but don't bring it around my kid.

As I will discuss in greater detail in Chapters 7 and 8, these young women's insistence that they would not expose their own children to the gang, despite their own involvement, seemed an indication of how girls saw gangs fitting into their lives—specifically, for many girls, gang affiliation was viewed as an adolescent phenomenon that they would move away from as they entered into adulthood. However, as I noted earlier, just as many young women described knowing girls in the gang who remained active members after the birth of their children. One of the young women in Diane's set had a child when she was fifteen and was still an active member five years later when Diane and I spoke:

Collette has a little girl named Porsha and she's five. . . . Everybody just took care of her [when she was pregnant], everybody just took care of her like she was our, like she would get taken care of. Because her mom and dad aren't around either. And she was, she was fifteen when she had her baby. She's twenty now. And everybody just took care of her. Just like a regular person would take care of a pregnant lady. And when she had her baby, she slowed down a little bit but she was still, you know, in the household, comin' over, she'd be taken care of, sellin' bud or whatever and all that. One time she went to jail and they took Porsha away from her. [When there was a drug bust at the house] she was there, was caught there. They didn't catch no dope on her 'cause she keep, she would keep dope in her baby's diaper. So they didn't catch any on her. But still she went to jail just for, like drug sales. But she got bonded out and nothin' ever happened with that.

Leslie had a family in the suburbs whom she had run away from when she joined her gang. They were willing not only to take her back but also to accept and support her arriving baby. Perhaps Collette maintained her gang ties after the birth of her child because she had fewer options, as her parents were not in her life. Other young women said that when girls were pregnant, they typically weren't involved in the gang's "dirty work." Leslie said other girls she knew "sat on the porch" during their pregnancy, but would resume active involvement once the child was born. Likewise, Monica described what happened when one of the young women in her gang was pregnant: "They don't expect her to go out there and sell nothin' like that, or smoke bud or nothin'. But if, if she wasn't sick or havin' morning sickness or whatever, she would come out and play cards and play dominos and then get back home when she got tired." It appears, then, that young women had flexibility in the decisions they made once they became pregnant. Some girls found pregnancy a compelling reason to leave the gang, while others continued their affiliation and other members were happy for them to do so.

Returning to the issue of dating, it is notable that despite the fact that nearly half of the girls I spoke with in Columbus had gang boyfriends, they consistently downplayed this as a significant element of their gang interactions and resisted talking with me about dating. As I alluded to earlier, this was likely a means of disputing the possibility of my categorizing them or girls in general as sex objects within their gangs. In fact, five girls, Cathy, Chantell, Erica, Heather, and Nikkie, said that members of their sets did not go out with one another. Heather said that they were "all buddies," and Erica said that they "just have that friendship relationship and nothing crosses that." Cathy conceded, "I mean, sometimes it would happen but very rarely. I mean, just because they're more cool with each other and you know, more like brothers and sisters than boyfriend and girlfriend."

The girls who reported that there was some dating within their gangs described it simply as an inevitable result of spending time together. Lisa said, "Most of the time it works out that way . . . because you're all the time around them and it just, it just happens." Diane concurred:

> It just works like, say you's a guy, saw a girl. Like say he was in my set, you like me and I like you, why not? We're both Crips. Why not go for it. Now, if you like me and, now just say you is a guy. If you like me and I didn't like you, then hopefully I would be woman to say, well, look, you're my cousin[48] and I just wanna keep it like this. Just as you bein' my cousin.

Most girls were vague about the inevitable tensions that arose as a result of dating relationships and break-ups, but a few alluded to the problem. Stephanie said that while girls in her set went out with guys from the same set, "All [the boys] do is just play them. I know their boyfriends play them hard. They be goin' out having sex with every girl." Nikkie said members of her set could get a violation—a punishment for breaking the gangs' rules that involved being beaten up or getting a set number of "blows"—for "playing" another member. "If you go with 'em and you play 'em or somethin', they'll like, you will get in trouble for it. You can't go with somebody and play 'em. They'll like, they'll hit you on your head like five times."

However, this punishment seemed to apply more to females who "played" or cheated on their boyfriends than the reverse. In fact, Nikkie herself said the boys "tell us like, 'we'll play girls in a minute,' and they don't care. And they'll tell you to your face if they went with you or whatever." Keisha had a boyfriend in the gang who cheated on her with another girl in the gang. Of the *girl*, she said, "That's disrespect, that's real disrespect." Describing their relationship afterwards, Keisha said, "We ain't cool no more. For the simple fact she did it to my boyfriend, and, know what I'm sayin'? We still, we in the gang, I got love for her but, as far as verbally talkin' to her, no. We have nothin' to say to each other." Just as Anne Campbell documented in her groundbreaking study of young women's gang involvement in the early 1980s,[49] Keisha's hostility was focused not on the boyfriend who cheated on her but on the girl with whom he cheated. Moreover, she described no punishment or violation meted out to her boyfriend for his behavior, but she was expected to get along with the offending parties for fear that she would get "bitched at" or worse by the leader.

CONCLUSION

This chapter has provided an overview of the nature of young women's gangs and gang life in Columbus. Their groups were relatively small in size—with 85 percent having thirty or fewer members; they were composed primarily of African American adolescents, the majority of whom were young men. Although they drew on nationally recognized gang names and gang symbolism, for the most part young women's gangs in Columbus were local groups with ephemeral ties to other gangs and gang cities. And while criminal involvement was clearly a feature of their gangs, nonetheless, these groups' primary activities centered on much more typical adolescent activities—primarily, socializing with one another and looking to have fun. Organizationally, it is notable that girls described their gangs as having structured leadership and initiation processes, as well as meetings, rules, and internal rankings of members.

I also have highlighted several aspects of the gender organization of these groups, which I will examine in closer detail in later chapters. To summarize at this point, it is noteworthy that most young women described their gangs as mixed-gender but said that girls were a numeric minority. Leadership in these groups was almost exclusively male; even when girls described female members who were "high-ranking," they typically did not view these young women as leaders. They also described "sexing-in" as a form of initiation for female members, and some alluded to different expectations for male and female members with regard to their fighting abilities. As I will describe in Chapters 6 and 7, these gendered expectations played themselves out in complex ways with regard to members' "getting down to business" for the gang and affected the status and treatment of female members as a result. Before I return to these issues, Chapter 5 provides an overview of girls' gangs in St. Louis and highlights the similarities and differences across these two cities.

Gangs and Gang Life in St. Louis

With Rod K. Brunson and Niquita Vinyard

U nlike Columbus, St. Louis has a long, though disjointed, history of gangs. I noted previously that both cities were chosen for my study because they are representative of emergent gang cities. In St. Louis, this is a qualified truth. Maxson and Klein's national gang migration survey[1] places the onset of St. Louis gangs at 1985. However, as Decker and Van Winkle note in their detailed study of St. Louis gangs, these groups have waxed and waned there for the last century. Importantly, these scholars found no evidence that contemporary gangs in St. Louis have any ties to the St. Louis gangs that last appeared in the 1960s.[2]

It's difficult to get accurate statistics on gangs and gang members. The only systematic data gathered about gangs come from law enforcement agencies—and much of this can hardly be considered truly systematic, as there is substantial evidence that politics have a strong influence on how police agencies define and respond to their gang problems.[3] Recall from Chapter 4 that police estimates in Columbus at the time of my research suggested there were thirty active gangs, with four hundred to one thousand members. This was up from the estimates they provided Maxson and Klein in 1992, when Columbus was said to have ten to twenty-five gangs and over two hundred members. By 1998, the Columbus Police Department had reversed its official policy on gangs, claiming that the city had no recognized street gangs.[4] In comparison, the St. Louis Police Department described an estimated nine hundred-plus gang members in 1992. By 1998, responding to a survey by the National Youth Gang Center, police reported that the city had approximately seventy-five active street gangs with thirteen hundred members. But there's a catch: St. Louis gangs were characterized by the police department as 100 percent male.[5]

Certainly our research contradicts this, as we had no trouble locating female gang members to participate in the project there. In fact, the young women in the St. Louis portion of the study described their gangs as having more female members than I found among the gangs I researched in Columbus. This was both the result of interviewing girls from more varied gang structures (e.g., mixed-gender, female gangs affiliated with male gangs, autonomous female gangs) and because girls described being a larger proportion of the members in mixed-gender gangs in St. Louis. Whereas twenty of the twenty-one gang members I interviewed in Columbus described their gangs as mixed-gender, in St. Louis twenty-two girls (81 percent) described being in mixed-gender gangs, three girls were in an all-female gang that affiliated with a male gang in the same neighborhood, and two more described being in an autonomous female gang.[6]

Table 5-1 provides a comparison of the gender composition of mixed-gender gangs in Columbus and St. Louis. In both cities, the preponderance of girls in mixed-gender gangs were in groups that were majority male, though on the whole, St. Louis girls' gangs tended to have more female members. In Columbus, seventeen girls (85 percent of those in mixed-gender gangs) described their gangs as having more males than females; in St. Louis, fourteen of twenty-two girls (64 percent) did so. In fact, about one-third of the girls in both cities were in gangs with one-fifth or fewer female members. However, the young women in Columbus were a more clear and consistent minority in their gangs than were the young women in St. Louis. Half of the girls in St. Louis were in gangs with more than one-third female members, and over one-third (37 percent) were in gangs in which females were half or more of the members. In contrast, only 25 percent of Columbus girls were in gangs with more than one-third female members, and only three described girls as half or more of the members. Moreover, over half of the Columbus girls (55 percent) reported five or fewer females in their gangs, compared to only six (27 percent) of the girls in St. Louis. Differences in the gendered structure and gender ratios of girls' gangs appear to have consequences with regard to girls' relationships with other members, male and female, as well as how they experience gang life. I will spell out many of these issues in detail in Chapters 6, 7, and 8.

While nearly one-fourth of the gang members I interviewed in Columbus were white, all of the girls in St. Louis were African American (89 percent) or multiracial (11 percent). Their gangs were almost exclusively African American as well. Only four young women (15 percent) described having non-African Americans in their gangs. This included Rhonda, who said her gang had nearly equal numbers of African Americans and Latinos, along with a handful of whites and one Asian American; Dionne, who said that two of the thirty-eight members of her gang were white; and Sheila and

Table 5-1 Gender Composition of Mixed-Gender Gangs

	Columbus (N = 20)	St. Louis (N = 22)
Majority male	17 (85%)	14 (64%)*
Half male/half female	2 (10%)	5 (23%)
Majority female	1 (5%)	3 (14%)
Females one-fifth or fewer members	6 (30%)	7 (32%)
Females one-third or fewer members	15 (75%)	11 (50%)
Five or fewer female members in gangs	11 (55%)	6 (27%)

*Total equals 101 percent; percentages have been rounded off to the nearest whole number.

Cheri, both of whom were in predominantly African American gangs with one or several Latino and American Indian members. Recall from Chapter 2 my characterization of St. Louis as one of the ten most racially segregated cities in the United States. This, combined with the strength of neighborhood ties in defining the boundaries of St. Louis gangs (see later), probably helps explain why St. Louis gangs appear to be somewhat less multiracial in character than those in Columbus.

GANG STRUCTURES: A COMPARISON

The expanding number of gangs and cities with gangs has resulted in increased attention to the issue of gang structure. Klein and Maxson have been at the forefront of this research and have documented five gang types in cities around the country: traditional, neotraditional, compressed, collective, and specialty.[7] The importance of learning more about gang structures, these scholars point out, is to correct the widely held view of gangs as monolithic groups. They note, "If gangs can be differentiated with respect to a few predominant structural types, then differential intervention and control practices may be developed (and presumably will thereby be more effective)."[8] Klein and Maxson suggest that a series of dimensions are important for determining gang types: size, age range, duration, whether or not subgroupings and territoriality exist, and versatile versus specialized crime patterns. These are useful for comparing girls' gangs in St. Louis to those in Columbus.

As I noted in Chapter 4, Columbus gangs tended to be small groups: All of the girls described their gangs as having fifty or fewer members, and 85 percent were in gangs with a membership of thirty or less. St. Louis gangs were characterized by more variation and somewhat larger gangs: fourteen girls (52 percent) described their gangs as having thirty or fewer members, nine girls (33 percent) were in gangs with thirty-five to fifty members, and four girls (15 percent) reported that their gangs had more than fifty members.[9] In fact, these numbers don't fully reflect the size of many of the St. Louis gangs, as a number of young women described the existence of some subgrouping, particularly with regard to age. They typically provided information on the number of members in their individual subgroup, thus underestimating, for the purpose of Klein and Maxson's classification, the gang's actual size. Debbie, who was twenty years old and had been in her gang for ten years, explained why she felt it was difficult to provide an accurate count of the number of members: "I mean it's just like [people who were involved] when they was younger, you still down? Young ones you meet, now all of them is in it, too many to count."

Moreover, as I noted earlier, three young women described being in a female gang that was affiliated with a male gang in the same neighborhood. While they provided numbers on the size of their female group, in subsequent parts of their interviews the distinction between theirs and the male gang became somewhat blurred. Yvette, for instance, was a member of the 2-1s, a female Crips set so-named because its territory was the 2100 block of a local street. Her group affiliated with the 2-2s, a mixed-gender gang who claimed the 2200 block of the same street. In fact, their territories were loosely shared and also expanded several blocks deep. In the following dialogue, Yvette explained the relationship between the 2-1s and the 2-2s:

NV: Why is it all girls? It's all girls because the guys have a set?
YVETTE: They have they own. We wanted our own gang for real, you know.
NV: Why did you all want to break away and kind of be separate from the males?
YVETTE: We ain't separate, for real. That's just what they call us.
NV: So you all do hang out with them?
YVETTE: Yeah.
NV: But [do] you do activities with them?
YVETTE: Yeah.

Despite her vision of the two gangs' connections, the information Yvette provided with regard to the size of her gang—fifteen members—was limited not just to the female members, but to the older female subgroup within the 2-1 gang. Crystal, who was also a 2-1 but in the younger subset, characterized the gang as larger (twenty-six members), but noted that she was counting both the older and younger members of her set. Before I discuss this issue of subgroups in more detail, let me first provide an overview of the age range young women in St. Louis gangs reported.

Recall that girls' gangs in Columbus were principally comprised of adolescents. Just over half reported having young adults in their gangs, but typically they were only one or a handful of the members; only Monica described a gang that included a sizeable number of adults. She also was one of only two girls who said there was a member over thirty. In contrast, girls in St. Louis were more likely to report having adult members in their gangs. In all, nineteen St. Louis girls (70 percent) reported having adults in their gangs, and six girls (22 percent) said there were members over age thirty in their gangs. Importantly, they characterized these groups as comprised of adolescents and young adults, rather than as primarily adolescent groups.

What might account for these differences? One explanation could simply be my sampling, rather than actual differences between the two cities. However, the works of Huff in Columbus and Decker and Van Winkle in St. Louis suggest that there are real differences between the two cities that my data are capturing. Young women in both cities could provide little information with regard to their gangs' formation. Consequently I cannot assess the question of duration—that is, how long their gangs had been in existence. However, given that the onset of gangs in both cities was around the mid-1980s, I can confidently speculate that all of the young women were members of gangs with relatively short histories. This makes it unlikely that the wider age range of members in St. Louis was attributable to longer gang traditions. Instead, the difference probably lies in the divergent socioeconomic circumstances of the two cities.

Recall from Chapter 2 that while Columbus has continued to thrive economically since the 1950s, St. Louis has been typical of midwestern cities devastated by the changes brought about by deindustrialization. A number of gang scholars have noted that in communities such as St. Louis, gang members have a more difficult time "maturing out" or leaving the gang because they find themselves with very limited options in the formal economy.[10] Thus, a likely explanation for the greater number of older members in St. Louis girls' gangs is that a larger portion of youths who joined in their early to mid-teens have hung on to their gang affiliations into young adulthood for economic reasons. In addition, the much stronger neighborhood character of St. Louis gangs, as I will discuss later, was probably a contributing factor as well: Unless young people left their neighborhood they likely didn't leave the gang, even if their ties to the group lessened with age.[11]

Perhaps because of the greater age range within their gangs, many young women in St. Louis described these groups as having age-based subgroupings. In all, nineteen young women (70 percent) reported having some form of age-grading within their gangs. Several young women provided age-based gang names: Vashelle and Brittany spoke of the OGs and the BGs (Baby Gangsters), and Shandra described having OGs, Gs, YGs (Young Gangsters), and BGs. On the whole, what they described were not rigid distinctions, but rather cliques of youths who hung out with similarly aged others in the gang. Regina, who was thirteen, explained: "The people that be like [under] fifteen, we all be together, and like fifteen to seventeen, they be together." In Mia's gang, she described that members around fifteen to nineteen years old hung together, as did nineteen- to twenty-five-year-olds. Likewise, Pam reported that her gang friends were "seventeen and up" but that there was another "little group that claim [the gang], they are the same age like thirteen to fifteen." She explained that "they be in they own little group and we be in our own little group 'cause we don't hang with them, they young." Pam speculated, however, that the "little girls look up [to us], want to be like us." Shawanda, who was sixteen, said her gang had no organized age-grading, but said younger members, "twelve-, fourteen-[year-olds] are little locs." And Tonya noted that while her gang didn't have different sets by age, they did differentiate between themselves and younger kids who hung around the gang: "Little kids like about eleven are like, 'What's up Blood, what's up Blood?' We call them shorties, 'cause they want in the gang, we call them shorties."

Importantly, young women did not describe specific role specialization that distinguished between older and younger members. Their gangs were not so organized as to require such specialization. Latisha explained, "Basically [everyone] do the same things." And Shandra said, "We all do the same things for real." Neoka explained, "It ain't no certain duties for nobody for real, unless you take it upon yourself to do it." Moreover, despite the fact that members cliqued by age, young women described that they would come together when necessary. Pam illustrated, "They do they own thing, we do our own thing. We don't get in they mix unless they fight somebody bigger, then we'll help them. But other than that, we just our own crowd."

Nonetheless, older and younger members did recognize informal differences in their activities, suggesting that who chose to do what seemed to be influenced by age. Shawanda explained: "It ain't no difference, they all be the same group, it's just the little locs, they young and they got the energy to burn. . . . We do stuff too but not as much as the little locs." In particular, young women suggested that criminal involvement was shaped by age. Ironically, many members of the younger cliques viewed the older members as involved in more serious forms of crime; older members viewed younger ones in this way. For the most part, this contradiction lies in the types of crimes younger versus older girls defined as "more serious," as there was general agreement about the crime patterns of younger and older members. On the whole, girls emphasized the more symbolic crime of younger members—fighting with rivals over gang colors and signs, for instance, while older members were described as involved in more economic crimes. Vashelle, who was only fourteen but hung with older members, observed:

[We] just be out there trying to get that money for real. Don't nobody over there be pumping up they gang but the young people. All the older people just get money. But they gonna still fall when it's time to fall with they 'hood. As far as running around and throwing up gang signs and stuff, it ain't even about that no more unless the younger people over there doing it.

Comparing her younger clique to the older one, Regina noted, "We don't do some of that [criminal activities], we just hang around, not like they [older members] do. But they steal cars and sell drugs and stuff." Likewise, Shawanda said that for the older members, the gang was "about money." Yvette, who was seventeen, agreed: "I'm about my money. . . . Fuck all that fighting and banging and shit, you know what I'm saying." Pam, who was eighteen, concurred:

PAM: The younger crowd, they ain't on our level. They go around and do stupid stuff.
JM: Like what do you mean?
PAM: Like taking people bikes, stealing stuff out of the store, getting caught, getting caught with guns and stuff like that. They just get theyself in trouble for nothing.

In fact, older members described changes in their own behavior as they aged. Shandra said her participation in gang rivalries was more intense when she was a new member, but became less important to her over time "because I been from [the gang] for so long." She explained: "When I first joined, it was [so] important for me that I did anything I could to get respect from the OGs and just, you know, be down for [the gang]. It was important because I wanted to feel, I guess accepted to the gang, accepted in the gang." Pam observed, "That's why they label them as little locs, the little group, 'cause they young. They ain't know for real, they just be on that level where they want to be in a gang, they just want to fight." I questioned her about whether she thought she had behaved differently when she was younger, and she said, "Yeah, going around C[rip]-World and all that, yeah, I don't even do that no more." When I asked her why not, Pam asserted, " 'Cause that was childish. That's just kicking up stuff, making some enemies doing that." Yvette agreed: "We used to like jump people. Now it's just like [we only fight] if somebody want to start something with us. . . . We don't do all that stuff like we used to."

For the most part, the older girls attributed these changes to growing up.[12] As they got older, making money became more important, fighting lost its appeal, and, in many instances, other responsibilities took hold. Yvette and Pam both noted that as they and their gang friends got older, more and more of them had kids. Challenging rival gang members and fighting over colors, Yvette said, was "just getting so old, you know what I'm saying." She suggested that because "most of my partners got kids," they "don't do all that stuff like we used to do." In contrast, she said of one young women in her gang, "She don't got no kids. . . . She like, she don't care what she do 'cause she don't got no kids or nothing that would get hurt." On the whole then, many young women in St. Louis gangs, particularly the older ones, described their ties to the gang as economic ones—as Vashelle asserted, "just trying to make they money." Their descriptions lend credence to my suggestion that some St. Louis gang members choose to stay involved in their gangs longer as a result of the more limited economic opportunities in the city, and their perceptions that gang ties provide them with a network of monetary opportunities, albeit criminal ones.

In addition, the duration of individuals' gang ties is likely influenced by the strength of neighborhoods in shaping gangs' territoriality. Recall that while Columbus gangs were territorial, gang girls there characterized their turf as rather fluid. Not so in St. Louis. As Decker and Van Winkle point out, St. Louis has a long history of steadfast neighborhood boundaries. These have influenced the nature of gang territoriality there for the last century and, with the reemergence of gangs in the 1980s, provided ready-made perimeters for emergent gangs' territories.[13] In all, 93 percent of St. Louis gang members (twenty-five of twenty-seven) described their gangs as territorial; the two who did not (both members of an all-female gang) nonetheless described their gang as neighborhood- and family-based. Depending on the size and location of girls' gangs, their territories encompassed anywhere from a city block, an area spanning several blocks, a local park, and/or the space surrounding their housing project.

Because of the loosely defined nature of territoriality in Columbus, gang girls there did not suggest that potential members had to come from the same neighborhood in order to join. But as I mentioned in Chapter 3, young women in St. Louis gangs were much more wary of outsiders and less willing to let youths from outside the neighborhood join their gangs. Alecia explained that members of her gang don't "really let nobody join, you know, like the only people that join is people that grew up there or something like that. Like everybody close to you." Likewise Tonya said that her gang "didn't really have no outsiders. It was like everybody was in the neighborhood." Yvette concurred: "You can't be too involved if you don't live over there." And Latisha said her gang's territory was their neighborhood, where "everybody just grew up together." Vashelle perhaps best articulated the neighborhood basis of St. Louis gang territoriality and its contrast with that of Columbus:

We don't let nobody join from outside. Everybody over there who in a gang over there, who pump up [our gang] been pumping this up for a while. Now you try to come over there and talk about you want to join a gang and stuff, they gonna look at you like you crazy, talking about joining a gang, you know what I'm saying. . . . It ain't like it's no club or something. It's a little club when you say, "I want to join this" and "I want to join that." It ain't no club or nothing. [If] you already done been a Blood [and] you come over there . . . and now you want to start pumping up [our set] 'cause you done been over there for a while, I understand that, but as far as coming over there and saying you want to be in a gang, it ain't even all about that. Somebody gonna look at them like they really dumb.

Recall from Chapter 4, the actions Vashelle calls "dumb" and "crazy" were precisely those that many young women in Columbus described about how they became involved in gangs there.

As I noted earlier, only two young women in St. Louis said their gang did not claim a territory. Both Shiree and Yolanda were in a small all-female gang called N.W.O. (No Way Out). In part, their gang was not territorial because they shared their block with members of a larger mixed-gender gang that was territorial. Yolanda said that while "there's other gang members on the block, we don't get into it, we cool with everybody. Everybody on the block cool with everybody." As I will detail in Chapter 8, these young women in the all-female gang provided a description of their group that was somewhat different than that provided by girls in mixed-gender gangs. While Yolanda said N.W.O. did "have fights and everything," and they "pump up our set or whatever," she suggested that their gang was more about "friendship." Shiree concurred, noting that the gang provided "a safe haven, you know. I know if I have a problem they gonna be by my side no matter what. If I have one, just the same if they have a problem, I'm gonna be by they side, you know, it's comfort." It was because of the different focus of their gang that N.W.O. appeared to get along with the other gang members on the block: They were not particularly criminally active and specifically were not involved in drug sales. As such, they didn't pose a territorial threat to members of the other gang.

The final characteristic for Klein and Maxson's typology of gang structures is whether the gang is involved in versatile or specialized patterns of criminal behavior. While I will discuss gang-related crime in detail in Chapter 6, at this point it is worth noting that in both cities, gang and gang members' crime can best be characterized as versatile. The gang members in St. Louis appeared to be more deeply involved in drug sales than those in Columbus, but most girls in both places reported that members of their gangs sold drugs. In addition, they committed a wide variety of additional gang-related and other crimes: vandalism, fighting, stealing, robbing, shooting, and so on. In Columbus, all of the girls characterized their gangs as criminally involved; in St. Louis, only Marie—a member of the Gangster Disciples whom I will talk about more later—did not provide evidence that her gang was involved in some illegal activities.

Based on the dimensions I have outlined here—size, age range, duration, subgrouping, territoriality, and crime patterns—it appears that the girls' gangs in St. Louis have more diverse gang structures than the girls' gangs in Columbus. All of the girls I interviewed in Columbus were in gangs that can be characterized as compressed: They were small, without subgroups, with a narrow age range, a duration of ten years or less, some territoriality, and criminal versatility. Some of the young women I interviewed in St. Louis described gangs that fit this category as well. Of the eight young women who did not describe subgroups within their gangs, six were in gangs with fewer than twenty members and one said her gang had thirty-six members. All seven of these girls (26 percent) described gangs that fit the criteria of a compressed gang. In addition, one young woman, Sheila, described a gang that fit Klein and Maxson's designation for a collective gang: She described approximately one hundred members in her gang, but it had not developed subgroups, making her group appear to be "a kind of shapeless mass of adolescent and young adult members that has not developed the distinguishing characteristics of other gangs."[14]

However, the majority of girls in St. Louis (70 percent) described groups that can best be characterized as neotraditional gangs. These groups, according to Klein and Maxson, resemble potential traditional gangs in the making: Their duration is "probably no more than ten years,"[15] but they are of medium size with around fifty to a hundred members,[16] age-based cliques have evolved, and they are quite territorial. But as I indicated in note 9, there is evidence that gang involvement has declined in St. Louis over the last few years, and police suggest a splintering of gangs there as well. Consequently, the likelihood that these groups will emerge into traditional gangs does not appear to be great. On the whole, my findings, in keeping with other evidence about the two cities, suggest that St. Louis has a more diverse array of gang structures as compared to Columbus.[17]

CULTURAL DIFFUSION AND ITS EFFECTS ON GANGS

There are other features that differentiate between the gangs I studied in Columbus and St. Louis. Much of this variance appears to result from the cultural influences shaping gangs in both cities. In Chapter 4, I described the strong influence of Chicago gang style on the nature of girls' gangs in Columbus. This is even more apparent when these gangs are compared to girls' gangs in St. Louis. Despite the closer proximity of St. Louis to Chicago, almost without exception the gang members in St. Louis did not describe ties—loose or otherwise—to gangs in Chicago. One reflection of this is girls' gang affiliations. In Columbus, over half of the young women I spoke with (57 percent) were members of Folks sets, which trace their origins to the Chicago-based Gangster Disciples. In contrast, of the young women interviewed in St. Louis, fifteen (56 percent) were members of Crips sets, nine (33 percent) were Bloods, two were members of N.W.O., and only one young woman, Marie, described her gang—a Gangster Disciples set—as having ties to Chicago.

Whereas five young women from Columbus said their OGs were from Chicago or elsewhere, in St. Louis not even Marie described direct ties of this sort to Chicago. Nonetheless, much of her description of her gang paralleled girls' descriptions in Columbus. For instance, Marie called her set an organization rather than a gang and was unique among St. Louis gang girls in describing a series of "different ranks" in her gang, including "foot soldier, leader, security guard, body guard, all that stuff." She also downplayed the gang's involvement in criminal activities; instead, she commented: "I saw the positive stuff they was doing and I wanted to be a part of it." The conversation continued:

RB: Like what kind of positive stuff were they doing?
MARIE: They try to set examples for young people, young kids that want to grow up and be in a gang. They try to tell them that's not the way to be, that's not the way to lead your life. They try to help out the community, do community things, helping elders clean up and stuff like that.

As I noted in Chapter 4, these prosocial activities are part of at least the rhetoric of the Gangster Disciples in Chicago. There is wide debate about whether they are indicative of this group in action. In fact, one recent study suggests that compared to other street gangs, Chicago's Gangster Disciples have developed "many characteristics of emerging organized crime groups."[18] Whether this was the case in St. Louis is unclear. Marie was the only young woman in St. Louis who said her gang was not involved in criminal activities, though she did say that members drank and smoked marijuana. And she was the only Gangster Disciple interviewed.

Her gang also shared a number of features in common with the Columbus gangs that were distinct from many other St. Louis gangs. These in-

Table 5-2 Gang Characteristics

	Columbus (N = 20)*	St. Louis (N = 27)
The gang has established leaders	20 (100%)	14 (52%)†
There are initiation rites or rituals	20 (100%)	17 (63%)†
The gang has a territory that it claims	18 (90%)	25 (93%)
The gang has regular meetings	18 (90%)	14 (52%)†
The gang has specific rules or codes	19 (95%)	19 (70%)
It has special colors, symbols, signs, or clothes	19 (95%)	27 (100%)

*One missing case.
†$p < .05$.

cluded having established leaders, regular meetings, and standardized initiation rituals. Table 5-2 provides a comparison of girls' gangs in Columbus and St. Louis gangs with regard to these and several other characteristics. Girls' gangs in St. Louis were significantly less likely to have established leadership, initiations, or meetings and were somewhat less likely to have rules or codes that were expected to be followed. Most of the gangs in both places, as I noted earlier, were territorial; all of the gangs, save Jennifer's Gangster Girz in Columbus, described adopting forms of gang symbolism such as colors and signs.

Despite their differences, which I will say more about later, young women in St. Louis defined their gangs in ways that were very much in keeping with Columbus girls' explanations of what made their groups gangs—with an emphasis on recognition, symbolism, rivalries, and crime. Tonya explained:

> I guess what made us a gang was, shoot, I don't really know, but I guess because we used to go [dress in] red all the time. We out there throwing signs, write out gang signs all along the walls and vacant buildings and stuff. We would go into different neighborhoods and get into fights with other gang members, like Crips you know, stuff like that.

Alecia said what made 2-1 a gang was members "claiming they set, like fighting as a group and throwing up they gang signs, saying 2-1 and all that." Brittany commented: "What makes them a gang? Well you down for each other. You down to kill for one another. You there for each other, showing the love like sisters and brothers." Likewise, Shawanda said that "nobody else can get the respect and love that we got for each other. We just a crew that call ourselves SLC. . . . It stands for Street Love and Cash." Neoka explained, "What makes it a gang is because everybody gonna be down for it, everybody behind each other you know what I'm saying." And Shandra: "I guess what makes them a gang is they hang out in a certain neighborhood that they chill in and they wear blue. . . . They Crips so that's what makes it a gang and they do things that gangs do like kill people and sell drugs and stuff."

What's interesting about St. Louis gangs is that a number of members, in my study and in Decker and Van Winkle's, attributed the development of gangs there to the 1988 movie *Colors*, about the Los Angeles Crips and Bloods. Because of the strong neighborhood ties in St. Louis, there were already groups of youths who hung around together. *Colors* provided the labels:

JM: How long has your gang been around, do you know? Do you know how it got started?

PAM: All the gangs came up when this movie came up, Crips and Bloods [*Colors*], that's when all the gangs started coming. There wasn't no gang, there wasn't no such thing as a gang, it was just a group. They had they own little group. Like it would be a group like HTGs, we were GIBs, Gangsters in Black, Hill Top Gangsters and all that. It wasn't no gang, no Bloods, no Crips, it was just groups.

JM: So after the movie came out?

PAM: After the movie came out they seen the colors and everybody who was wearing blue got to claiming Crips and everybody who was wearing red got to claiming Blood. But before that everybody used to hang together. But when that came out, people went they own ways and be what they wanted to be and that's what made it enemies. 'Cause I was with you when we was little so why would you grow up to be on this side and I'm on this side? So that's how it be kicking off.

Pam had been a member of her gang since she was thirteen and had hung out with them since she was eight—right around the time the group's members began considering it a gang. Younger girls, who had been involved in their gangs for a shorter period of time, had less sense of the history of the groups. For instance, Trina, who was twelve and appeared to be a relatively peripheral member of her gang, said that the Bloods "started over in Puerto Rico." Most young women didn't know the histories of their gangs, and, much like Monica in Columbus described, it was partly because they simply hadn't thought about it. Tyra speculated, "The boys really made it up, the boys in my 'hood." And Shawanda said while she didn't know the history of her gang, "I could find out, our OGs are like twenty-six, twenty-five [years old], so it would have to be like when they was young." Neoka had been passed down a story about the history of her gang, although the dates she provided didn't quite match up:

RB: Do you know how it got started or how long it's been around?
NEOKA: For six years.
RB: Do you know any of its history, how it got started?
NEOKA: This old man, OK, this was back in 1986. This old man was stay-

ing over there at Potomac, and him and a couple of his friends used to go sit on the corner and drink all the time. So one day the man moved on Potomac and his friends came over there and he told them, when they call him, it was 2-5, his pager number. So from there on out they started calling him 2-5 and then we became 2-5 Gangster Crips. I don't know where it came from, how, but that's the story.

The adoption of Crips and Bloods affiliations among preexisting neighborhood adolescent groups and the virtual absence of Chicago-based influences meant that much of the cultural diffusion picked up by Columbus gangs were not characteristic of these St. Louis gangs. Like gangs in Columbus, St. Louis gangs were "homegrown" in that they emerged primarily from within rather than without.[19] Nonetheless, because of their knowledge of the cultural lore surrounding the Bloods and Crips, St. Louis gangs took on the rivalry between groups, along with the symbolic systems of these gangs—colors, hand signs, tattoos, the designation of left and right sides of the body (e.g., wearing caps tilted to one side, hanging rags from one side, etc.), graffiti, and so on. But the organizational nature of Chicago's Gangster Disciples/Folks Nation does not appear to have found its way into St. Louis. Many of the girls' gangs in Columbus, regardless of whether they were Folks, or Crips and Bloods, were influenced by the diffusion of Chicago-style gang organization. As I described in Chapter 4, these Columbus gangs weren't actually well-organized criminal entities. But young women did describe having standardized initiation rituals and established leaders who often were adults to the larger membership's adolescence, and most girls said their gangs had regular meetings at designated locations. These features were not prominent in St. Louis girls' accounts of their gangs.

Take the example of initiations. As Table 5-2 showed, the majority of St. Louis gang girls (63 percent) did report that their gangs had some form of initiation ritual. However, these initiations often did not have the same character as those described in Columbus—which almost uniformly involved some form of physical confrontation. In St. Louis, those gangs that had initiations were more flexible about what they entailed. Partly this may have been because they were girls. Decker and Van Winkle found that young women's initiations into gangs in St. Louis were less likely to involve physical confrontations than were young men's.[20] Vikkie said that "the things the boys do [to get initiated] is tougher than, we didn't have it easy, but it was easier. They had it harder."

In all, ten girls (37 percent) described a physical confrontation with members of their gang. As Shandra characterized it, "I had to fight my way in. . . . They jumped me in the 'hood." Regina said she had to "fight some people older than me [in the gang] . . . until they told [us] to stop." Only Yolanda described the ritualized punching characteristic of many Columbus gang initiations. She said every member punched her in the arm four times and said "N.W.O.!" Shiree, who was a member of the same gang, said she "got jumped in," but she was older when she joined, while Yolanda was just thirteen.

Six more girls (22 percent) described a variety of activities they say gained them entrée into their gangs: Vikkie committed a car-jacking, got a tattoo, and said she also "had to go around and see a girl and hit her. Any girl that stare at me funny I had to hit her." Marie said she was blessed into her gang, and "they said a prayer over me."[21] Debbie "beat up" a rival gang member, and Sheila had her nickname and the gang's name tattooed on her right arm. Likewise, Dionne "got my tattoo" and, along with one of her companions, "snatch[ed] this lady's purse." She explained:

It was a alley on the side of her house, and she was standin' on the front and I walked up both her steps and grabbed her purse and I was like, you know, snatchin' it from her, "Go on and give me the purse, gimme the purse, you better gimme the purse!" And the lady was like, "Lemme go! What are you doin'? Are you crazy?" You know. And I'm pullin' the purse from her like, "Give it here!" You know, hollerin' at her, yellin' at her real loud. Then all of a sudden, you know, she fell, she fell to her knees and I just snatched the purse and ran through the alley.

Dionne took the purse and showed it to "this dude named Martin, he da oldest out of all of 'em [in the gang]. . . . He was you know, like 'aw, she did it for real too,' you know." The final of these six girls—Brenda—would not specify how she was initiated, but did say that girls have to "do something with a nigga to get in a gang." She alluded to having been sexed into her gang, as did Yolanda, in speaking about her previous gang experience. Recall that Yolanda was a member of N.W.O. when she was interviewed. However, before that she had briefly been a member of a mixed-gender gang, and she indicated she had quit that gang because sexual behavior became a continued expectation after her initiation, and it "was too much for me." She explained, "I was already initiated but they wanted me to do too much, you know, like I ain't gonna do it for nobody so I left it alone."

The rest of the girls in St. Louis said they did not go through an initiation. Shawanda said that while she wasn't initiated, her gang did sometimes have initiations, and they typically involved getting a tattoo. Finally, ten girls (37 percent) reported that their gangs did not have initiations; instead, being a member came from growing up in the neighborhood and spending time on the streets. The following conversation with Tyra is illustrative:

RB: How did you start hanging out with [the gang]?
TYRA: I grew up in the neighborhood with them. That was my street.
RB: When did you decide to become a member?
TYRA: I didn't decide, I was just already initiated.
RB: Just by growing up over there you [were] automatically a member?
TYRA: Yeah.

RB: So you didn't have to do anything special to join or anything to prove you would be a good member?
TYRA: No.

Likewise, when asked about initiations Vashelle replied, "It ain't like that, you know what I'm saying, it ain't like a cult or something. It ain't nothing like that." And Neoka explained, "Once I started hanging out with them, I was automatically a member." Discussing initiations, Pam surmised:

> That's some gangs, but not our gang. Some gangs you do that [go through an initiation] but you don't got to do that to get in no gang, you know what I'm saying. Why would you have to do it to every dude just to get in the gang? I would rather be by myself if I got to do that. All you have to do is be real. You be real, then you real to that gang. You ain't got to be whupping nobody in the gang, get jumped by fifteen people to be in the gang like they have it on TV, it ain't like that. They do that 'cause they want to do that. They might do that up in they gang: "In order to join our gang, you gotta do this, you gotta do that." We ain't have that. It's all about being real.

Many young women's descriptions of gang leadership paralleled their discussions of initiations. The same resistance they had to being told what to do in order to get in the gang was mirrored in their perceptions of having a leader. Recall that all of the young women in Columbus said their gang had a leader—one individual who was considered *the* leader. Only around half of the girls in St. Louis (52 percent) said they had leaders, and of these, just five girls (nineteen percent) described having a specific leader from whom the other members took instructions. These included Marie (the Gangster Disciple); Yolanda and Shiree, who were members of N.W.O.; and Dionne and Mia.[22] Marie and Mia actually said their gangs had both a male and a female leader. Dionne reported that the leader of her gang was in jail, but that the members still talked about him as if he were their leader: "Everybody, you know, always talkin' 'bout well, he [the] OG, you know, he's the biggest one out of all of 'em, he tells them all what to do." She said the next oldest male in her gang, Martin, took over the OG's duties since he was locked up: "The one that's in jail now, he put Martin in charge after that."

In contrast, the majority of girls who said that their gang had leadership (33 percent of the sample) described it as much more diffuse, suggesting for instance that the older (adult) members were looked up to by the younger ones, and consequently were influential. Although Shawanda said her gang had leaders, when asked if there was one leader she responded, "Not for real. The OGs, people look up to them." In fact, she was resistant to the idea, described routinely in Columbus, of having one leader who told other members what to do. Shawanda insisted that "ain't nobody no leader over me." Likewise, Latisha said there wasn't a leader, but that the leaders were "the OGs, the oldest people, the people that's the oldest." And Neoka explained that while there were leaders in the form of influential members, "We don't have nobody that straight tell us what to do."

In addition, around half of the young women in St. Louis (48 percent) said their gangs did not have leaders. Vikkie asserted, "We didn't want no leader." And Yvette explained, "We don't consider anybody no leader. We all lead our own self. It's not like we got to have somebody tell us what to do, nothing like that." Alecia concurred: "Ain't nobody no leader." As did Pam: "Ain't no leader. Everybody their own person." However, many of these young women did concede that some members influenced others' behavior. Trina explained: "It's like if one person do one thing and everybody gonna follow behind that person. But if like another person do another thing, somebody else follow right behind him. So I guess it's like a leader each day or something. Whatever they'll do, we'll do."

In fact, the young women who said their gangs did not have leaders characterized the influence of older members in much the same way as girls who defined these older members as "leaders." For instance, Vashelle said, "There ain't no leader. . . . The OGs is like a leader, they the ones that order the little things. Ain't no leaders or nothing like that." The following conversation with Shandra is also illustrative:

RB: Was there somebody that you considered the leader?
SHANDRA: No, we just had the OGs. I guess they was considered the leaders.
RB: What does OG stand for?
SHANDRA: Original Gangsters, they the older ones. They was the first gang members, they were the first, you know what I'm trying to say. . . . They made the gang.

Given these similarities between girls who answered "yes" or "no" to the question of whether their gangs had established leadership, Table 5-2 probably inflates the number of girls in St. Louis with gang leaders, for the purpose of comparing their groups to those in Columbus. Aside from the five girls who specifically described having the kind of leadership that all of the girls in Columbus described, responses to the question seemed to be simply a matter of interpretation in St. Louis. Ultimately, it seems fair to conclude that the vast majority of girls' gangs in St. Louis did not have leadership like that of girls' gangs in Columbus but instead had much more fluid leadership of the sort described in other cities not influenced by the Chicago model.[23]

Two further considerations illustrate some differences between girls' gangs in Columbus and St. Louis: meetings and gang rules. As Table 5-2 indicates, 90 percent of gang girls in Columbus said their gangs had meetings; only 52 percent of girls in St. Louis indicated that this was the case. Of those gangs that had meetings in St. Louis, most were characterized by less regularity than those in Columbus. Marie and Dionne, both of whom had a gang leader, described the most consistent and organized meetings. Marie explained that members got together "every month or every other month, for meetings to let you know what they gonna go about doing that month." Dionne even reported that members were "not supposed to smoke or drink at the meetings or nothin' like that."

Others described less routine meetings that typically were called when something was about to go down with rivals or when the group planned criminal activities. Shandra explained, "The OGs usually call the meetings, and we get together in like a park or in the 'hood, something like that." Tyra remarked that her gang "had meetings about somebody been doing something, like if they hanging out with the same group that shot at them, something like that. . . . They have meetings about what they gonna steal and all that. Everybody vote and stuff like that." Likewise, Vikkie said her gang had meetings "when we want to get on somebody, rob somebody, steal somebody car, we'll have a meeting and we'll just plan it."

Although 70 percent of the girls in St. Louis responded "yes" to the question of whether their gang had rules or codes, few spoke about them in any detail during their interviews. One theme that did emerge with some consistency was the rule that members were not supposed to fight with one another. However, without established leadership and given members' resistance to being controlled, rule enforcement was another question. Many young women in Columbus spoke of violations—physical punishments meted out to members who broke the rules. However, only two girls— Shandra and Dionne—described any formalized rule enforcement in their gangs. Shandra described what she called regulating: "When they regulate you the OGs jump you. It's like a whupping like they your parents and when you do bad you get a whupping for it, that's what it's like and they regulate you and they jump you." And Dionne said members "get mouth shots and chest shots for fightin' each other." Asked what she meant by "shots," Dionne explained, "You get punched in the mouth, and they can knock your teeth out if they wants to, and they can punch you on your chest." The conversation continued:

RB: Does that ever happen?
DIONNE: Yeah, this one girl got her teeth, her teeth missing 'cause she gots so many mouth shots.

In fact, Dionne remembered one gang meeting where she said a fight broke out between two members, Robert and Patti, "the girl [whose] teeth gone." Dionne recalled that the fight "had somethin' to do with her sellin' drugs for him." Her gang's acting OG stopped the meeting to break up the fight, but not before Robert had "beat her up real bad, you know. . . . He just beat her down, you know, crushed her." Dionne explained:

They was fightin' and, you know, Martin, he's like, "Hold on," you know, "Hold on, we gotta break this up. If y'all don't stop right now, y'all ain't gonna," you know, "Y'all's gonna get it." . . . He stopped the fight to give them a mouth shot and a chest shot. She got two mouth shots and he got fourteen chest shots and a mouth shot.

The event, which Dionne characterized as a "fight" despite the fact that Robert "crushed" Patti, ended with both of them being punished by the acting OG. In addition, that Patti had lost some teeth as a result of the "mouth shots" she took in the gang is indicative of Martin's established and apparently unquestioned (at least by Patti) leadership. These facets of her gang's organization are, as I have indicated, much more characteristic of girls' gangs in Columbus than most of the girls' gangs in St. Louis.

In contrast, most St. Louis gang girls described informal rule enforcement. Brittany explained that members will "argue and hit each other. If two girls get into it, they can argue but if they get to [physically] fighting the whole group gonna jump on them." Likewise, Gwyn said if two members get into a fight, "Everybody will break it up." Brittany's and Gwyn's accounts are typical of most St. Louis girls' descriptions of the inevitable fights within their gangs, and the enforcement of the rules against fighting. As such, they illustrate the more diffuse and consensual, rather than authoritarian, nature of most St. Louis girls' gangs and gang leadership. These differences between girls' gangs in Columbus and St. Louis appear to be related to the evolution of their gangs in the two sites. In Columbus, despite gangs there being a homegrown phenomenon, girls described gang formation that typically was not based on pre-existing friendship groups, and many of their perceptions of what a gang should be had been imported from the outside and specifically based on the Chicago model. On the other hand, in St. Louis it was often the case that preexisting neighborhood-based friendship groups learned about gangs and adapted their groups accordingly, resisting (or perhaps not even exposed to) the more dogmatic features characteristic of some gangs.

STATUS AND EVERYDAY LIFE IN ST. LOUIS GANGS

Despite the fact that many St. Louis gang members did not describe having initiations and stressed the importance of neighborhood ties in facilitating gang affiliations, they nonetheless looked for particular qualities in potential members, and members gained status in the gang for behaving in particular ways. Like young women in Columbus, girls in St. Louis focused on three key features when considering potential members: They had to be trustworthy, committed, and loyal to the gang and be ready and able to "be down" for the gang in whatever that might entail. St. Louis girls, however, seemed more deeply suspicious and skeptical of youths they didn't know well and who were looking to join. Shawanda said one of her concerns about potential members was "can you trust them? You got to get to know them first . . . hang around us a while and see what kind of person they is." Likewise, Yvette was asked about her expectations of youths who wanted to join her gang:

> YVETTE: For real, you can't trust them. We don't really want nobody to be with us for real unless it's somebody that know all of us, like somebody in one of our families . . .
> NV: What if somebody came to you and say I want to join the gang?
> YVETTE: Wanna get friendly? I wouldn't even trust them.

Young women were particularly wary of potential members who wanted to be in the gang just for something to do, those who were capricious, flitting from one group to the next. These youths were seen as problematic because they would not be sufficiently committed to the gang, and thus would be unreliable in one way or another. Pam, for instance, was concerned about young women who got involved in gangs simply because "they want to be known," who would "hang with us and then go back and hang with [another gang]." Moreover, she disapproved of "wannabes":

> PAM: Some of the time, they just want to do something just to be doing it. But you can't do nothing just to be doing it. You do something just to be doing it and they gonna know you doing something just to be doing it, 'cause you ain't gonna be real.
> JM: So how would you distinguish between a wannabe and somebody who is real?
> PAM: Just say if I want to be hard, right? I'm walking around all walking hard, talking hard, you know what I'm saying? But a real hard person ain't got to do all that. I can walk around like a regular person. I ain't got to be all that, letting them know who you are. They already know who you are, what you about, so you ain't got to do all that.

Other young women echoed Pam's concerns. Shiree said, "They'll be talking about it [joining] and then we'll be like, if you want to be down, prove yourself . . . like fight somebody or gank [rob] somebody." Likewise, Latisha explained:

> If you got the heart to do something then you in. If that's what you really want to do. First we got to see if you really, if you just saying that or are you for real or whatever. And we just say if you ain't scared, if you tough, if you a tough person, then it's easy for you to get in. If you down, if you just down for whatever.

Ultimately, as Latisha articulated, being "real" or "down" for the gang meant having a willingness to fight rival gang members and commit other crimes. Neoka observed, "They got to be down, you know what I'm saying. They can't be scared. If you scared then ain't no way you gonna be able to stay in. If somebody do something to one of your homies or something, you got to be down and go back and do whatever." And Tyra concurred, "They got to be down for they set." Specifically describing girls' qualifications for gang membership, Vikkie remarked:

Some girls . . . don't make good [members], you know, 'cause half the time it be these little girls that is cute and stuff like that. They don't want they hair get messed up. If you gonna be in a gang you gotta realize you gonna have to be like a thuggish girls 'cause there ain't no way you gonna be a pretty girl being in a gang. People just gonna be out just to hurt you, scratch on your face or something like that. That's why when I was littler, I used to always be like a tomboy just wear pants and keep my hair tied. I was a tomboy.

However, these weren't hard and fast rules. A number of young women conceded, sometimes to their chagrin, that there were members who did not have the qualities they espoused as important. Yvette said, "Like this one partner, she didn't fight but she was cool. It's just like if you ain't been fighting all your life, you ain't gonna be able to fight." Others expressed more concern, focusing on what they saw as the consequences that could result. Neoka explained: "If I'm getting beat or something and this person I'm with ain't gonna help, then it's something wrong and I don't wanna be with them type of people." Alecia specifically described an incident of this sort:

I got this cousin, she is part of [the gang] too. When we got jumped, she was in 2-1 too, we was at school. She was the only one in 2-1 that did not help us. Everybody else, all the big girls. After we got jumped, all of us went down there and jumped all of the girls and she was the only one that still did not help us. We don't never depend on her.

That Alecia's cousin was viewed as undependable meant she didn't have a high degree of status in the group. In describing those qualities that bring status, young women in St. Louis echoed Columbus girls' discussions of member qualifications with regard to toughness and being down. In addition, they provided comments parallel to those in Columbus about status coming from age and from having been around a long time. But they added a new element, largely absent in Columbus girls' discussions: They also talked about the status that results from success in the drug trade.

The focus on toughness and being down remained a consistent element of girls' discussions. Dionne said that the young woman in her gang who "a lot of people go up to" is "the biggest one, you know, she the toughest and all that stuff. . . . Like bad you know, like rough." Likewise, describing what makes someone a good member of her gang, Vikkie remarked:

What makes them a good member is that you always got to get ahead on yours, don't let nobody diss your set, you know, somebody come over there and be like that, [respond] "Nigger what you saying?" That's what I think. I don't know about anybody else. Can't nobody diss my set in front of me 'cause I'll get 'em in a minute.

Age also came into play. Asked what made her leader influential, Dionne surmised, "First of all, he bein' in longer than them. And he did more than them and I guess, I don't know, he been back and forth to jail and stuff, and they just worship him." Likewise, Latisha said members of her gang look up to "the oldest person of all of us. He around about thirty. We look up to him because he been in it for a long time or whatever." And Brittany said the OGs in her gang got a lot of respect

because they like the older ones, they have been through already what the BGs already been through. They already gone and accomplished what there is, they just OGs. Like they say they want to hit a meal ticket, they just sitting on a high level and the other locs sitting on low levels.

I noted earlier that despite the similarities in criminal versatility between Columbus and St. Louis gangs, gangs in St. Louis appeared to be more deeply immersed in drug sales. This was echoed in their descriptions of status. For instance, Brittany described the girl she looked up to as "a smart gang member. She don't go out fighting and starting stuff. She just chill out and make her money." And Pam said the most influential member of her gang "just don't be tripping. He all about his business." Vashelle, who was one of the only female members in a primarily male gang, described two members of her gang, both now in prison, that everybody looked up to, both because of their success in the drug trade and also because of the flashy lifestyle that resulted:

VASHELLE: They was just like crazy and stuff, you know what I'm saying, had a lot of money, had gals. That's what dudes over there be looking for, got a nice car, money just coming out, and got all gals. They just look for somebody like that. I looked up to them too. . . . I know I look up to them.
RB: Why do you look up to them?
VASHELLE: 'Cause they just ball like that and I'm gonna be up there one day eventually too.
RB: What does ball mean?
VASHELLE: Just have money coming out the butt, you got money to throw away, they got money to burn, put it like that.
RB: That's balling?
VASHELLE: That's balling to me. Two cars that they own, then he got a little house over there on the set where they just straight up boom out of there. They don't even sell dope for real, little BGs out here selling for them and they locked up.

Selling drugs was a routine part of everyday life for a number of gang members in St. Louis, male and female. Like the girls in Columbus, they described their days as spent hanging out in the neighborhood, going to parties, walking around looking for trouble, or dealing with trouble when it came their way. In addition, perhaps because there tended to be more female members in their gangs (see earlier), girls in St. Louis were more likely than girls in Columbus to describe going to the mall, shopping, and going dancing at clubs with other gang members. Illustrating the range of their activities, Shiree explained, "We be going to the show, shopping, we be fighting together, robbing together." Neoka said her gang spent their time "chilling on the block, getting on some highs, everybody be chilling. We don't really trip unless you trip. I mean, we go to the park and play basketball, come back here and sit, just chill all day jawing [talking]. . . . It ain't nothing really that we can say that we did that's really exciting." Sometimes, Neoka explained, they also "went out and robbed people just to get a laugh."

Likewise, asked to describe a typical day, Gwyn surmised that she would:

GWYN: Get something to eat, see who all outside in the neighborhood, then come back in the house, iron my clothes, go outside and go over to everybody house, go to everybody in the 'hood house and see what they gonna do for the day. And then everybody be walking together on the block, and we'll just find something to do.
RB: And that's the whole day?
GWYN: Yeah. And that's every day, all day.

During the school year, she noted, "a lot of us were going to school." She said:

Sometimes if we stayed up at night about 3 [a.m.] . . . we had this little thing at about three, three-thirty, if we up at that time we just stay up for the rest of the night 'cause we have to go to school at six-thirty. Stay up for the rest of the night, from there, go in the house, change clothes, go to school. But if we went in before then, just go in the house about one [a.m.], go to sleep and then the rest of the people that was still outside, they'll come to your house and wake you up for school.

And Shandra described a typical day as follows:

I wake up . . . get dressed, hit the hood, see what they had on the weed, get some weed, sit around and get high, go to one of the homies house and just chill, play dominos, play music and stuff like that. Then more homies would come and that's more weed and drink and that was a typical day for real, we just sat around and just chilled. Wasn't nothing happening. The ones that sold they drugs, they sold they drugs and all that.

Some members dedicated more time to selling drugs; others simply sold when the opportunity arose or when they wanted some cash either to party or to buy something. Comparing her drug sales to those of other members, Shandra continued:

> The times when I sold I only did it for a short while. I only did it to make a little money to do something big. I ain't never really made it a career or nothing like that. But a lot of people, some of them, they sell drugs and they keep on selling, like that's their little hustle, that's what they do.

Like Shandra, Rhonda said she would "just hang out and then we'll walk around the street, do our thing, then I'll make a couple of sales to make some money." Tonya, on the other hand, was more active in drug sales and these were an integral part of daily life. She said she would

> go outside, pretty much stay outside and sell dope. Sell dope all day and then at night, somebody might need a car, and you take [steal] a car and go out driving, chilling, whatever, might get into a fight, come back home, it be like one, two [a.m.], and we still out there in the dark. 'Cause some of the dope fiends come out 24 hours a day. Get high, go in the house and go to sleep, unless you by a dope house and then you go in there and go to sleep.

On the whole, then, drug sales and other criminal endeavors were part of many gang members' activities, but they were not encompassing of their daily lives. Moreover, as I will discuss in Chapter 6, drug sales were not part of the organizational structure of most gangs—that is, members were not selling drugs *for* the gang, but for individual profit. And like in Columbus, much of gang members' time was spent, as Neoka suggested, not doing anything that's "really exciting," but instead hanging out and having fun with one another.

RELATIONSHIPS, PREGNANCY, AND MOTHERHOOD

More so than in Columbus, gang girls in St. Louis talked about girls' relationships with young men and the impact of pregnancy and motherhood on girls' gang involvement. In particular, motherhood appeared a more salient issue in St. Louis because of the greater age span within gangs there. To a limited extent, this was reflected in my sample.[24] As I noted in Chapter 2, gang girls in St. Louis were slightly older on average than gang girls in Columbus. The mean age of gang girls was 14.9 in Columbus and 15.6 in St. Louis. Moreover, while only three Columbus girls (14 percent) were seventeen or older, this was the case for ten of the St. Louis girls (37 percent). This is not to say that only older girls had children, but it was the case that being in gangs that included older members increased the likelihood that young women would have gang friends with children.

In Columbus, I noted that only LaShawna and Keisha reported having a child. Neither of them described living with or actively raising their children. In St. Louis, five young women—Regina, Marie, Latisha, Tyra, and Brenda—were mothers. Brenda was an ex-gang member when she was interviewed, having quit the gang in 1997 several months after her daughter was born. Tyra and Marie were still members, but described curtailing their gang involvement by "not hanging" as much as they had previous to the birth of their children. Regina and Latisha remained active members.

With regard to dating, recall that while ten girls in Columbus (48 percent) described having a boyfriend that was a member of their gang, all of the young women there downplayed the significance of male–female relationships in shaping gang dynamics, and several even spoke of gang rules against dating one another. In contrast, girls in St. Louis were more open about these relationships but were also considerably less likely to describe having a boyfriend who was a member of their gang. While eighteen St. Louis girls (67 percent) had a boyfriend at the time of their interview, only five (19 percent) described that boyfriend as a member of their gang. These included Deborah, Rhonda, Crystal, Cheri, and Mia. Marie had gotten involved in her gang as a result of her relationship with a boyfriend, but they had since broken up. Only Dionne noted that her gang had a rule against members dating one another, the violation of which she again said could result in "chest shots or mouth shots."

Debbie explained that girls in her gang went with boys in the same gang "all the time," but she said they "don't write about it"—that is, don't "tell everybody in the 'hood, you know." Likewise, Yvette said that "a lot of the dudes and girls have kids by each other. . . . Some of them go with each other, live together. One of my partners go with one of the men. She got two sons by him and she got a daughter by another dude from 2-2."[25] In addition, young women mentioned that they sometimes got involved with members of other gangs with which their group was allied. For instance, Alecia said that most girls in her set went with male members of other Crips sets in the area, explaining, "They our peoples too. My friends, they'll try to go with them." Tonya was adamant about the need for monogamy in these relationships:

> If you mess with the dudes in the gang, mess with one dude. If you mess with just one dude, all the rest of them like your brother and that's how it's supposed to be. Look at them like your big brother. When you look at them other ways, like in other ways and you already been with one, if you do have sex with them, then you a wreck.

Tonya's perspective on the need for serial monogamy in male–female relationships, and the stigma attached to perceived sexual promiscuity, parallels findings reported by a number of scholars and has received wide documentation. Moreover, these scholars describe a clear double standard with regard to dating that young women reinforce rather than challenge in their interactions with one another. Anne Campbell explains that girls "not only reject sexual activity outside the context of a steady relationship but even reject friendships with 'loose' girls whose reputations might contaminate them by association."[26] Pam articulated this clearly when she told me, "If [a girl] doing it to everybody in the neighborhood, having sex with them, I don't hang with nobody like that. 'Cause if you hang with somebody like that, you gonna get labeled like she labeled." On the whole, the sexual double standard, enforced by both males and females, tends to disadvantage girls in their relationships with boys, but also interferes with the strength of their own friendship groups by undermining their solidarity with one another. Tonya's and Pam's comments alluded to this, as did young women's discussions of the conflicts that often ensued between girls who found themselves competing for the attention of young men.

Young women acknowledged that male–female relationships were often a source of strife between and among gang members. Most often, they described the source of conflict as two girls fighting over a particular boy, though they also described dating partners having fights that played themselves out in front of the group. Tonya recalled when "this girl named Patricia threatened a girl named Dana 'cause she tried to take her dude." Prior to the fight, "They were best friends." Alecia said members of her gang, the 2-1s, often fought with female members of the 2-2s (with which, recall, 2-1 was afilliated) because young women in both groups competed for the attention of male members of 2-2. She explained: "Them girls from 2-2, the same group, they make the girls in 2-1 jealous and they want to fight the girls in that group. . . . They gonna fight for real for making 2-1 girls jealous." Pam said that a couple of the members of her gang have kids together from when they were involved when they were younger, but she said relations in the gang were better when members didn't date one another. She believed dating one another caused unnecessary problems. For instance, if a guy from the gang dated a girl from the gang but then started bringing a new girl around, that girl would get jumped and beaten up by the girl from the gang. Then once she jumped the girl, the others would jump in and beat her too to support their fellow gang member.

These sorts of fights were not limited to young women in different gangs, but sometimes involved girls in the same set. For example, Yvette said one of the "partners that I be around talk[ed] about my man, like 'I'll take her man.' I had a fight with one of my partners over stuff like that." The situation eventually resolved itself, in part through the intervention of the other young women in the gang: "She said a couple of other things about me but we cool now for real. My other partners be like, 'Y'all don't need to be fighting over nothing like that.' They'll try to break it up."

Although young women were more likely to recall fights between girls over the attention of young men, several also described fights between males and females, resulting, as Tonya explained, when "they get into it with they girlfriends." The following conversation with Alecia is illustrative:

RB: Are there ever any fights between the girls and the dudes?
ALECIA: Yeah, like if they go with them [and] get into an argument with them. They have a lot of fights.

RB: Is there any one particular fight that you can remember between a girl and a dude?

ALECIA: Yeah, a girl Dee-Dee. Ashley was going with Lance, then Dee-Dee, now she go with him. They had a fight because he started trying to talk to Ashley. . . . He still trying to talk to the girl Ashley in Dee-Dee's group. They, so they had a fight because he was trying to talk to his ex.

Although many young women argued that the males in their gang wouldn't be physically aggressive toward the girls in the gang, this position was modified when the male and female in question were romantically involved. Tonya recalled, "I remember one time . . . one of the dude's girlfriends, she had been saying something, he just started whupping her outside the car, beating her all up, pushing on her head." Several girls described having been in physically abusive relationships themselves; it did not appear that boys received any sanctions, informal or otherwise, for physically mistreating their girlfriends.[27]

In addition, some young women in St. Louis indicated that boys were freer to date outside the hood than the girls were, while there was greater control exercised over young women's behavior. Rhonda said one girl in her gang went with someone from another gang and "she got beat up real bad [by] the dudes" for doing so. Asked whether the young men in her gang went with girls from other gangs she contrasted, "If they want to. Can't nobody control them or what they do." Likewise, Brittany said it would be "disrespect" if a girl in her gang went with a boy from another gang, and she would face the wrath of the "dudes and the girls" in her gang. But she said nothing happened to young men who went with girls in other gangs and that the girls had no space to challenge this behavior:

BRITTANY: They can't [say anything] 'cause the guys the ones that got the girls on they feet.

RB: What do you mean?

BRITTANY: They got them to doing [stuff] like selling drugs, they put them in gangs, let they other people take them in. So they [girls] can't really say nothing about it.

Other young women said there weren't explicit rules against dating boys in rival gangs, suggesting instead that the informal rule was simply to keep it quiet and not bring the boy into their territory:

RB: What [happens if a girl goes out with somebody] from a rival gang?

ALECIA: Like a Blood or something? Nothing. As long as they don't come over there, they won't do nothing.

Debbie said the same thing, noting that it was not uncommon for members of her Crips set—male and female—to go with members of rival gangs. Of the boys' involvement with rival girls, Yvette clarified, "I won't say they go with them, they'll have sex with them." Debbie's recommendation for a girl involved with someone from another gang was that the girl "just don't go around" with her boyfriend. She said if a girl from her set brought a rival boy into the 'hood, "They'll beat on the Blood," and the girl will "get a good smack if they come and be like disrespecting the hood." The key to not allowing the relationship to disrupt the member's ongoing relationship with members of her gang was to keep gang business separate from her romantic relationship. Neoka explained: "As long as she don't bring him over there or tell such and such, 'cause once you tell one person, then everybody got to know. Just in case [people think] she might try to tell him something about our, what we trying to do and get set up or something like that."

However, keeping the two parts of their lives separate was easier said than done. Yvette's description of her experiences highlights the various tensions that arise from becoming involved with members of one's own gang, as well as having a boyfriend from a different gang. In her case, tensions that arose from her dating someone outside the gang were exacerbated by the sexual histories she shared with several members of her gang. When asked whether members of her gang got involved with one another, she explained that they did, but in her case, "not no more": "I made the mistake a long time ago. I was like thirteen." She had played around with two different boys in her gang back when she was first beginning to hang around with them. "I had met one of them and then I met another one of them and I went out with him. . . . I didn't know they knew each other though." Yvette said at the time she didn't consider her involvement with either boy a "relationship"; instead, "It was just having fun." However, other members had a long memory, and her past experiences were repeatedly brought up as a means of disrespecting her and challenging her sexual integrity for going with a rival gang member. The following dialogue reveals the difficulties she faced in balancing her gang ties and her ties to her boyfriend.

YVETTE: I go with someone from a different gang. [Members of my gang] got love for me, but some of them be like, they don't like my boyfriend for real. They don't like him, [but] they can't change me. I love my boyfriend. I been with him almost a year now. I feel like sometimes, the dudes, they childish to me or they just old [bring up old experiences]. They don't trip off it cause that was like in '92. If they bring it up, it's like that shit's old. They talk about my boyfriend to me and I love my boyfriend. I know how they is and I know how my man is. But I ain't gonna tell them one way and him one way 'cause that will get somebody killed.

NV: Do they think you are less down because you go out with someone from a rival gang? Do they think you are really with them a hundred percent?

YVETTE: You know what, one of my partners told me like, whatever you do, don't ever put that nigger before us.

NV: Do you agree with that?

YVETTE: I kind of do. I feel like, I trust my man as far as cheating on me. But I know sometimes that he has because he told me. But sometimes I be saying to myself, sometimes he cheat so I'm gonna put my homies before him.

Recently, her boyfriend's conflicts with people around her had become quite serious, potentially lethal, and Yvette found herself in the impossible position of maintaining loyalties both to her "homies" and to her boyfriend. She tried to sustain a "leave me out of it" attitude, but it caused her a great deal of anguish. An incident that occurred the night before her interview is illustrative:

Like my best friend is pregnant by this dude. He is going with one of my partners, the girl, but he is seeing somebody else. But my best friend is pregnant by him now. Him and my boyfriend don't get along for nothing. They just got into it last night. My best friend's boyfriend pulled a gun out on my boyfriend. I'm not gonna let me and her fall out over these niggers because of that incident. But I got to be on my man's side.

What troubled Yvette most was that even though her best friend's boyfriend was not a member of the 2-2s, "Some of them be on his side but they ain't got nothing to do with it." In fact, one of them gave her friend's boyfriend the "strap" that he pulled on Yvette's boyfriend. Tensions escalated as the evening progressed. "My boyfriend last night, he went home and got his gun. All up and down the block they waited on my best friend's boyfriend [to] come through, said he gonna kill him, stuff like that." Although she was distraught over what was happening, Yvette felt helpless to intervene. Any action on her part would be read as disloyalty to someone she cared about. While she said, "They need to let that stuff still for real," it was out of her hands to control. Fortunately, the police showed up and quelled the conflict temporarily, but it was still on Yvette's mind, as she feared it wasn't over.

As these young women's discussions suggest, dating relationships within and outside the gang were complicated and were often the source of a variety of conflicts and tensions. Pregnancy and motherhood added additional layers. As I noted earlier, several more young women in St. Louis gangs described being mothers than in Columbus; moreover, St. Louis girls were more likely to have other gang friends with children. As in Columbus, some girls indicated that becoming a mother provided young women with a route to discontinue or curtail their gang involvement; others suggested that while motherhood could change the nature of girls' gang activities, they often remained actively involved.

Recall that older gang members described changes in their own and their friends' behavior as they aged. These changes included a decline in risk-taking behaviors such as "starting stuff" with rival gang members and a reorientation toward more economic crimes. A number of girls attributed these changes to the impact of having young children. Pam said that "a lot of my friends got kids" and explained that she and her friends were not out confronting people and trying to "stir things up" like they did when they were younger, in part because doing so posed various risks for her partners' children. Nonetheless, Pam noted that while young women with children tended to spend more time at home, when they were out with other gang members, they did the same things as everybody else.

Crystal said that it was common for young women with children to avoid involvement in violence " 'cause she don't want nothing to happen around her baby." Tyra's experiences were illustrative. She still considered herself a member and said when she got pregnant members of her gang "helped me out, buy me baby clothes, gave me money and stuff." However, Tyra "had moved away from there" by the time she had her baby, allowing her to withdraw from the daily activities of her gang. She explained, "I be going over there every once in a while, see how they doing and stuff, but I ain't got time for that no more." Likewise, Tonya suggested that "once a girl get pregnant, she will maybe get out of it . . . not get out of it, but you know, she have to chill, she have to stay inside and all that."

On the other hand, Tonya also suggested that pregnancy could be an asset that gang members used to get away with various crimes: "When she get about six or seven months, when she start really showing a lot, if they showing a lot, if they go car-jacking they'll take them. They'll tell the police they trying to hurry to get to the hospital or so. They'll use them for that." Marie suggested that whether a girl curtailed her gang involvement or stayed active was "up to that female. If she's up to it, then she is." Marie herself "wasn't around them when I got pregnant. I had tried to pull away from it." While some young women like Tyra and Marie decided to pull away, there were also plenty of young women who remained active and even, as Tonya described, "have they babies out and everything. They have they babies outside with them when they selling drugs. There isn't no change, after they have the baby they back to normal." Regina was a case in point. She stayed actively involved during her pregnancy and after the birth of her daughter and even described having fought rival gang members when she was pregnant. Ultimately, young women concurred that it was the girl's decision—she was free to continue her gang activities, as Crystal noted, "if she feel like it," or she could just as readily "tell the people in the gang she a mother now" to curtail her involvement.

CONCLUSION

This chapter and the last have detailed the many differences and similarities in girls' gang experiences in Columbus and St. Louis. While there have been few comparative qualitative studies of gangs across cities, and even fewer on young women's gang involvement,[28] the utility of such an approach is that it provides useful information about those aspects of gang life that are context specific and those that appear to be generalized. My findings, supported as well by other available evidence from the two cities, suggest important differences between Columbus and St. Louis. Most notable among these were variations in gang structures and cultural influences on gangs in the two cities. To begin with, more girls in St. Louis described gangs with a sizeable number of female members, while in Columbus girls were almost always a clear minority in their gangs. As I will detail in Chapter 8, these differences appeared to have a significant impact on girls' relationships with one another and the meanings they attributed to their gang involvement.

Other aspects of gang structure varied as well. Columbus gangs exhibited almost uniformly what Klein and Maxson call a compressed structure—they were small, without subgroupings, and with a comparatively narrow age range. There was more diversity in girls' gang structures in St. Louis; moreover, the predominant type among the girls interviewed there was neotraditional rather than compressed. Most girls described larger gangs, with some age-based subgrouping and a wider age range of active members, including a larger proportion of young adults than described in Columbus. Perhaps because of this wider age range, motherhood was a more salient issue among girls in St. Louis: More gang girls had children whom they were raising, and even when they didn't have kids themselves, they were more likely to have friends with children in the gang.

Finally, many organizational features of gangs in the two cities were quite distinct. Emergent gangs in Columbus but not St. Louis were influenced by Chicago gang style. In St. Louis but less in Columbus, gangs often emerged out of preexisting neighborhood friendship groups. Consequently, such things as leadership, initiations, and rule enforcement were more formalized in Columbus, while their character in St. Louis was of a more informal nature. Despite these seeming indications of organization, gangs in St. Louis were probably better organized and more cohesive than those in Columbus, in part because of the stronger neighborhood character of these groups in the former.

Despite these differences, several common themes emerged across both cities. Among these were features of the gang itself: the adoption of gang colors and signs, participation in versatile patterns of delinquency, and the existence (albeit varied) of territoriality among gangs in both places. Many of girls' discussions of member qualifications and status issues were parallel as well. Gang members preferred youths who were loyal to the group and who were "hard," willing to engage in crimes for the gang and with gang members. Girls in both places lamented that their preferences were not always realities. In addition, they described high-status members in much the same ways—members who were older and had been around for a long time were looked up to, as were members who were particularly daring and confrontational, who had put in a lot of "dirt" for the gang. In St. Louis, success in the drug trade was frequently noted as well.

In addition, although Columbus girls were more reticent to talk about problems that arose out of dating relationships, the same themes emerged in both places and paralleled those documented by a number of scholars. Specifically, they described the operation of a sexual double standard in their gangs in whi:h greater control was exercised over girls' behavior than that of boys' and observed that many of the girls' conflicts with one another resulted from competition for the attention of young men. There was also evidence in both sites of male-on-female violence. These are important themes that will be carried through in my discussions of victimization in Chapter 7 and gender dynamics in Chapter 8. First I turn my attention to delinquency.

6

Gangs, Delinquency, and Violence

M uch gang research in the last decade has been triggered by recognition of the strength of the relationship between gang membership and participation in crime. Several important studies have shown that gang youths account for a disproportionate amount of delinquency, particularly serious and violent acts. For instance, based on data from the Rochester Youth Development Study, Thornberry and Burch report that while gang members were only one-third of the sample, they accounted for 86 percent of all serious delinquent acts reported in the interviews, including 69 percent of all violent crimes and 70 percent of all drug sales.[1] Moreover, studies show that gang membership has a facilitation effect on delinquency—that is, youths' participation in delinquency increases dramatically when they join gangs, and it declines significantly once they leave their gangs.[2]

Research examining young women's involvement in gangs and crime suggests similar, but more complex, patterns. Notably, these studies suggest that young women in gangs have higher rates of delinquency than their nongang peers, both female *and* male. But despite gang girls' greater involvement in delinquency, it is still the case that young men in gangs are more extensively involved in the most serious of gang crimes.[3] In fact, Fagan reports a bimodal distribution for gang girls but not gang boys: Approximately 40 percent of the gang girls in his study were only involved in petty delinquency, while one-third were involved in multiple index offending, compared to 15 percent and 56 percent, respectively, for young men in gangs.[4] Several studies have also documented "the structural exclusion of young women from male delinquent activities" within gangs, as well as young women's decisions to exclude themselves from such behavior.[5]

This attention to the association between gang membership and delinquency has overlooked an equally important relationship: that between gang membership and victimization risk. Although few studies have been attentive to this question,[6] there are reasons to consider it an important one. For instance, there is strong evidence that participation in delinquency increases youths' risk of victimization.[7] Given ample evidence linking youths' participation in gangs with increases in delinquency, as well as research that shows that the primary targets of gang violence are other gang members,[8] it seems self-evident that gang membership likely increases youths' victimization risk. Moreover, evidence of gender inequality within gangs, as well as of young men's greater participation in serious gang crime, suggests that victimization risk within gangs is likely shaped by gender. In this chapter and the next, I examine these issues for young women in gangs in Columbus and St. Louis. Here I will discuss young women's participation in delinquency and gang-related crime. In Chapter 7, I return to issues of victimization risk and exposure to violence, exploring the ways they are structured by gang involvement and shaped by gender.

YOUNG WOMEN, GANG INVOLVEMENT, AND DELINQUENCY

Given what the literature suggests, it is not surprising that the gang girls in Columbus and St. Louis reported greater involvement in delinquency than their nongang counterparts did. Tables 6-1 and 6-2 compare gang members' and nongang girls' responses to questions about their participation in a va-

Table 6-1 Prevalence of Self-Reported Delinquency

	Gang Members (N = 48)	Nongang Members (N = 46)
Minor Delinquency		
Run away	36 (75%)	26 (57%)
Skipped class	45 (94%)	35 (76%)*
Lied about age to get into someplace or to buy something	33 (69%)	13 (28%)*
Loud/rowdy in public	30 (63%)	19 (41%)*
Avoided paying for things	19 (40%)	9 (20%)*
Stole $5 or less	21 (44%)	16 (35%)
Moderate Delinquency		
Drunk in public	28 (59%)	6 (13%)*
Damaged/destroyed property	33 (69%)	10 (22%)*
Stole $5 to $50	22 (46%)	17 (37%)
Used car without permission	30 (63%)	7 (15%)*
Thrown objects at people	39 (81%)	27 (59%)*
Hit someone with the idea of hurting them	36 (75%)	28 (61%)
Serious Delinquency		
Carried hidden weapon	38 (79%)	14 (30%)*
Stole $50 to $100	20 (42%)	8 (17%)*
Stole over $100	17 (35%)	9 (20%)
Stole a motor vehicle	25 (52%)	4 (9%)*
Attacked someone with a weapon or to seriously hurt them	33 (69%)	13 (28%)*
Participated in gang fight	43 (90%)	4 (9%)*
Committed robbery	14 (29%)	4 (9%)*

*$p < .05$.

Table 6-2 Prevalence of Self-Reported Alcohol and Drug Involvement

	Gang Members (N = 48)	Nongang Members (N = 46)
Substance Use		
Drank beer or wine	40 (83%)	23 (50%)*
Drank hard liquor	32 (67%)	14 (30%)*
Smoked marijuana	47 (98%)	24 (52%)*
Used other drugs	7 (15%)	2 (4%)
Drug Sales		
Sold marijuana	28 (58%)	5 (11%)*
Sold crack cocaine	27 (56%)	3 (7%)*
Sold other drugs	11 (23%)	1 (2%)*

*$p < .05$.

riety of delinquent behaviors, classified as minor, moderate, or serious delinquency; substance use; and drug sales. Here young women were asked if they had *ever* engaged in these activities. Minor delinquency includes the following items: running away, skipping class, lying about one's age, being loud or rowdy in public, avoiding paying for things, and stealing five dollars or less. Six items were classified as moderate delinquency: being drunk in public, damaging or destroying property, stealing items valued between five and fifty dollars, using a car without permission, throwing objects like bottles or rocks at people, and hitting someone with the idea of hurting them. Finally, serious delinquency included the following: carrying a hidden weapon, stealing items valued between $50 and $100 and over $100, stealing a car, attacking someone with a weapon or with the intent to seriously injure them, participating in a gang fight, and committing a robbery.[9]

As Table 6-1 shows, gang girls were more likely than were nongang girls to have committed each of the delinquent acts they were asked about, regardless of the seriousness of the offense. In fact, the only acts gang girls were not significantly more likely to have engaged in were to have run away from home, stolen items worth less than $50 or over $100, or to have hit someone with the idea of hurting them.

The most prevalent forms of delinquency among gang girls—activities that two-thirds or more girls reported—included minor offenses such as running away from home, skipping classes, or lying about their age; moderately serious activities such as damaging or destroying property, throwing bottles or rocks at people, and hitting people; more serious forms of delinquency such as carrying a hidden weapon or being involved in a gang fight, as well as drinking alcohol and smoking marijuana. Notably, young women in St. Louis who reported carrying weapons were asked why they did so, and all of them said their primary reason was for protection.[10]

I found few variations in the prevalence rates of delinquency when comparing gang girls from Columbus and St. Louis.[11] The only significant differences were for running away (90 percent of the Columbus girls had done so, compared to 63 percent of the St. Louis girls) and being drunk in public (81 percent versus 41 percent, respectively). On the other hand, while 89 percent of St. Louis girls described having carried a hidden weapon, only 67 percent of Columbus girls had. For all other offenses, reports across the two sites were comparable. For instance, 33 percent of girls in Columbus and 37 percent of girls in St. Louis had stolen over $100; 52 percent of girls in both places had stolen a car; 29 percent of girls in Columbus and 30 percent in St. Louis had committed a robbery.

As with other forms of delinquency, gang members were significantly more likely to report drinking and smoking marijuana, as well as being involved in drug sales. Notably, while all but one gang girl reported smoking marijuana, relatively few reported that they had used other drugs. What Table 6-2 does not show is that a larger percentage of gang girls in Columbus described drinking alcohol (all said they had drank beer or wine, three-fourths hard liquor). In contrast, a sizeable minority of gang girls in St. Louis smoked marijuana but did not consume alcohol: 30 percent didn't drink wine or beer, and 41 percent didn't drink hard liquor. These differences in drinking patterns likely explain the difference between the two sites with regard to girls reporting they had been drunk in public. Around half of the gang girls in Columbus had sold marijuana (52 percent) and crack (48 percent), compared to 63 percent of gang girls in St. Louis for both offenses.

To examine the level of girls' involvement in delinquency, I compared the mean number of different minor, moderate, and serious crimes that young women reported having engaged in from the offenses listed in Table 6-1. This provides a sense of the variety of acts in which young women engaged. In addition, I examined girls' reports of how many times in the last six months they had committed these offenses and sold drugs.[12] These are reported in Table 6-3. Of the six items classified as minor delinquency, on

Table 6-3 Mean Level and Frequency of Participation in Minor, Moderate, and Serious Delinquency

	Gang Members (N = 48)	Nongang Members (N = 46)
Level of Participation		
Minor delinquency	3.83	2.57
Moderate delinquency	3.92	2.07
Serious delinquency	3.88	1.22*
Frequency of Participation (Last Six Months)		
Minor delinquency	75.17	31.84*
Moderate delinquency	30.15	4.28*
Serious delinquency	42.21	2.70*
Drug sales	53.72	4.17*

*$p < .05$.

average gang girls had committed 3.83 of these, compared with 2.57 for nongang girls. Six items were classified as moderate delinquency. On average, gang girls had committed 3.92 of these acts, compared to 2.07 for nongang girls. Likewise with the seven items classified as serious delinquency: Gang girls averaged 3.88 of these acts, compared to 1.22 for nongang girls.

Gang girls committed all of these offenses—minor, moderate, and serious delinquency, as well as drug sales—with greater frequency than nongang girls. These differences were most striking for serious delinquency and drug sales. On average, gang girls had committed 42.21 serious offenses in the last six months (averaging about seven serious crimes per month), compared to only 2.7 for nongang girls (less than one every two months). However, it's important to note that the bulk of gang girls' frequent serious offending was carrying hidden weapons. When this item was removed from the count, gang girls committed an average of 13.78 serious crimes in the last six months—just over two per month.

The comparison of gang and nongang girls' frequency of participation in drug sales shows even more disparate patterns. On average, gang girls sold drugs 53.72 times in the last six months, or about twice a week.[13] In fact, one nongang girl reported selling marijuana every day. If these sales ($n = 180$) were removed from the calculation of nongang girls' mean frequency of participation in drug sales, all nongang girls combined reported selling drugs a *total* of twelve times in the last six months (for a mean of .26). In contrast, gang members participated in drug sales with more frequency than any other type of delinquency. In sum, gang girls were involved in a greater range of delinquent activities, especially serious ones, and engaged in these activities much more often than nongang girls.

I noted earlier that in terms of prevalence rates, there were few differences between gang girls in Columbus and St. Louis. This was also the case when I compared the number of minor, moderate, and serious delinquent acts in which girls had engaged. However, there were striking differences across the two sites with regard to the frequency of their involvement in delinquency and drug sales. Table 6-4 reports these differences. On average, gang girls in Columbus had committed three and a half times more minor delinquency, twice the amount of moderate delinquency, and just over three and a half times more serious delinquency in the six months prior to our interview.[14] In fact, Columbus gang girls committed, on average, approximately twenty-two minor, seven moderate, and twelve serious delinquent acts per month; compared to six, three, and three, respectively, for gang girls in St. Louis. On the other hand, girls in St. Louis were more frequently involved in drug sales. On average, gang girls in St. Louis had sold drugs eleven times per month in the last six months, compared to just over six times for girls in Columbus.[15]

The mean scores in Tables 6-3 and 6-4 do not show another important dimension of gang girls' delinquency—the wide variation in their frequency of offending. As I noted earlier, research on female gang members' delin-

Table 6-4   Mean Level and Frequency of Participation in Minor, Moderate, and Serious Delinquency—Gang Members

	Columbus (N = 21)	St. Louis (N = 27)
Level of Participation		
Minor delinquency	4.19	3.56
Moderate delinquency	4.10	3.78
Serious delinquency	3.76	3.96
Frequency of Participation (Last Six Months)		
Minor delinquency	133.12	35.76*
Moderate delinquency	42.10	20.50*
Serious delinquency	73.71	20.38*
Drug sales	38.14	66.31

*$p < .05$.

quency has found that a portion of girls are quite delinquent, while others remain involved only in sporadic or minor offending. This is clearly the case with the young women I interviewed, as illustrated in Table 6-5. Here I will limit my discussion to serious delinquency and drug sales: Nearly one-fourth of the girls interviewed had committed no serious delinquent acts in the last six months; the same number said they had committed serious delinquency fewer than six times during this period. On the other hand, just over one-fourth of the girls described involvement in serious delinquency on more than a weekly basis—with six girls (13 percent) reporting involvement in these activities as an everyday phenomenon. Likewise with drug sales: Half of the girls interviewed had not sold drugs in the last six months; on the other hand, 27 percent sold drugs more than once a week, including seven girls (17 percent) who sold drugs on a daily basis. Some young women in gangs are quite delinquent, while others seem to temper their routine involvement in criminal offending, particularly offending of a serious nature.

One other notable difference emerged in comparing gang girls in Columbus and St. Louis. As I discussed earlier, research has shown that gang membership has a facilitation effect on youths' involvement in delinquency, par-

Table 6-5   Gang Members' Frequency of Participation in Delinquency

	Minor* (N = 42)	Moderate (N = 47)	Serious (N = 47)	Drug Sales (N = 48)
Frequency in Last Six Months				
None	5 (12%)	5 (11%)	11 (23%)	24 (50%)
Less than once a month	8 (19%)	15 (32%)	11 (23%)	6 (13%)
Once a month to once a week	11 (26%)	15 (32%)	13 (28%)	5 (10%)
More than once a week	18 (43%)	12 (26%)	12 (26%)	13 (27%)

*Some missing cases; rounding error means not all columns add to 100 percent.

ticularly serious offending. That is, the level of their involvement in delinquency increases once they join their gang. This facilitation model suggests that "the norms and group processes of the gang . . . facilitate involvement in delinquency."[16] There are two other arguments posed about the relationship of gangs to youths' delinquency. One is a selection model, which suggests that "gangs recruit or attract individuals who are already involved in delinquency and violence."[17] The second is a mixed model, which suggests that "both selection and facilitation effects are at work"[18] in explaining the relationship of gang involvement and youths' delinquency.

Although my sample is such that I can only speculate about the differences I found, it appears that more of a mixed model fits girls' experiences in Columbus, while a facilitation model fits girls' experiences in St. Louis. Specifically, when I asked girls about their participation in delinquency I also asked about the onset of these behaviors—that is, how old they were the first time they engaged in them. Young women in Columbus were more likely than those in St. Louis to describe having been involved in (mostly minor) offending prior to joining their gangs. For example, of those girls in Columbus who reported having committed the following acts—running away, skipping classes, being loud or rowdy in public, avoiding paying for things, stealing items worth $50 or less, throwing bottles or rocks at people, hitting people, drinking beer or wine, and smoking marijuana—half or more had first engaged in these activities *prior* to joining their gangs. The same was not true for girls in St. Louis. The only delinquent activity that half of the gang girls in St. Louis had engaged in before they joined their gang was throwing bottles or rocks at people.

The most straightforward explanation of these differences may be sampling—that Columbus girls were more likely to be drawn from the detention center or a residential facility—but it likely also results from differences in patterns of territoriality and entrée into gangs in the two cities. As I have noted in previous chapters, St. Louis gangs have a much stronger neighborhood base than Columbus gangs. Young women in St. Louis were much more likely to grow up in a neighborhood with gangs and subsequently join those neighborhood gangs. They also described gang members' hesitancy to let youths who weren't from their neighborhood join their gangs. Girls in Columbus, to a greater extent, joined gangs that their friends were in or that they came into contact with outside of their neighborhood, sometimes even during a period they spent in detention or a residential facility. This suggests that some girls in Columbus were more likely, as a result of their previous involvement in minor delinquency, to come into contact with gangs or gang members and subsequently decide to join.

Nonetheless, for both groups of girls, gang membership clearly had a facilitation effect on their involvement in more serious crimes, which few girls reported committing prior to their gang involvement. For both groups of girls, more serious offending tended not to occur until after they had joined their gangs. For instance, of those girls who reported that they had stolen items over $100, only three girls (two in Columbus and one in St. Louis) had done so prior to joining their gang. Only one young woman (in St. Louis) had committed a robbery before she joined her gang, and only four girls had sold marijuana (one in Columbus, three in St. Louis) or crack (two in each city) before they joined their gangs. Nine girls (three in Columbus, six in St. Louis) had carried a hidden weapon prior to their gang involvement, and nine (two in Columbus, seven in St. Louis) had attacked someone with a weapon or with the intent to seriously injure them.

In sum, gang girls in Columbus and St. Louis were significantly more delinquent that their nongang counterparts, with a majority of gang girls having committed serious acts of delinquency. However, there was, as others have discussed, considerable variation in gang girls' participation in delinquency. A small number of girls were routinely involved in serious delinquency on an ongoing basis, but more engaged in delinquency on an infrequent basis. Next I turn my attention to the context of delinquency in girls' gangs, focusing on young women's accounts of the nature of gang conflict and crime.

THE CONTEXTS OF GANG CRIME

Researchers distinguish between two types of gang crime. First are those offenses committed with a gang-related motive (e.g., crimes based on retaliation; protection of territory; "representing" the gang through colors, graffiti, signs; and so on). The second are gang member crimes—crimes committed by members of a gang but without a specific gang motivation behind the offense.[19] Being in a gang is a precursor for the vast majority of gang-motivated crimes,[20] but other crimes committed by gang members often are facilitated by youths' membership as well. Scholars who discuss the facilitation or enhancement effects of gangs on youths' delinquency emphasize the strength of gang members' associations with peers who are also involved in delinquency, but also gang norms and group processes that encourage youths to engage in these activities.[21] In fact, Klein and Crawford suggest that delinquency is more than just an outcome of gang membership; instead, it serves as a source of group cohesion for its members. That is, participation in delinquent activities (particularly gang-motivated ones) reinforces gang members' conception of themselves as a unified group, banding together against common enemies.[22]

My previous discussions of status hierarchies in Columbus and St. Louis gangs bear this out. Repeatedly, young women described respected members of their gang as those who had "done dirt" for the gang (e.g., committed gang-motivated crimes such as assaulting or confronting rivals), but also respected were those who were particularly criminally sophisticated and made a lot of money from their crimes. In St. Louis especially, success in the drug trade—a gang member but not necessarily gang-motivated crime[23]—

brought members respect and admiration from their peers. Describing a young woman she admired, Brittany surmised, "She's a smart gang member. She don't go out fighting and starting stuff, she just chill out and make her money." Success in criminal endeavors, regardless of their explicit motivation, allowed youths in both cities to build reputations as tough, hard, and not to be messed with. Young women admired these qualities in both males and females, and many aspired to these qualities themselves. I asked Diane about the young women in her gang that had status or influence, and she provided a detailed account:

I think I have a influence in the set because my mind is so much on makin' money. See, I don't care about if you're a Blood or if you're a Crip. I mean, I know I'm a Crip. I'm over any Blood anyways. You respect me. You either bounce or you get bounced. You respect me or you gonna get messed up. That's how I see it. But my mind goes past that. My mind's all about money. Because I love money. . . . And people look up to me because I'm always, I've always got a way. "Oh, I found this lick, we're gonna do this." "This time we'll do this." People look like, Diane, you're only fifteen. Look at all this. I mean my name is in the book of the Crips for doin' so much dirt. So I think, I know people look up to me.

People look up to Janeen just 'cause she's so crazy. People just look up to her 'cause she don't care about nothin'. She don't even care about makin' money. Her, her thing is, "Oh, you're a Slob? You're a Slob? You talkin' to me? You talkin' shit to me?" Pow, pow! And that's it. That's it. She don't care. But this, I'd say females, we don't even talk nothin'. When it comes down to fightin' or whatever, no more of that talk, it completely shuts up. It's all about the fists. It's all about doin' what you gotta do. We all learn that. We learn that from her.

Diane highlighted both of the themes I mentioned earlier—status resulting from physical prowess and a willingness to confront rivals in the name of the gang and from success in money-generating criminal endeavors. While most young women admired and aspired to these qualities, it's also important to note that many girls saw these qualities as existing on a gendered continuum, believing that young men were those most likely to display them in their fullest capacity. This is illustrated most clearly in patterns of gang leadership. As I discussed in Chapters 4 and 5, gangs with established leaders described this leadership as almost exclusively male. In fact, a number of girls stated explicitly that only male gang members could be leaders. The qualities attributed to leaders were the same as those attributed to high-status members—individuals who were hard, able to fight, and willing to "do dirt" for the gang. Leadership emerged in part from having proven oneself on these grounds. Most girls saw males as the group members most likely to carry through these activities at their most extreme.

Distinguishing young women from young men, Tonya exclaimed, "We ain't no supercommando girls!" And Keisha noted, "The guys, they just harder." She explained, "Guys is more rougher. We have our Gs' back, but it ain't gonna be like the guys, they just don't give a fuck, they gonna shoot you in a minute." Vikkie said that males and females

> really all do mostly the same things. But except for the girls don't do no jobs like, well I did, I robbed somebody but it wasn't too much of a robbery. The boys might do a robbery or something, car-jacking, stuff like that. The girls mostly don't. We probably stole a couple cars. We jump people and pump up our set or whatever.

In some cases, these gender differences resulted in girls devaluing the contributions of other girls to the gang. But in other cases their gendered perceptions of status and behavior simply meant that they held girls and boys to different standards. It's also the case, as I will discuss as the chapter unfolds, that some young women valued girls' lesser willingness to use the same lethality of violence in the name of their gang and recognized particular benefits for themselves in being different than the boys.

Girls certainly *could* gain status in the gang by being particularly hard, true to their set, and criminally involved.[24] Diane was a case in point. In fact, by her own account and in comparing her self-reported delinquency with that of other girls, Diane was probably the most widely criminally active young woman. Among other things, she was involved in street-level drug sales on a daily basis and reported having committed around thirty serious assaults and twelve robberies in the last six months (one of which she had just been arrested for when we spoke[25]). But, as I noted earlier, there was tremendous variation in girls' participation in delinquency. Only about one-third of the young women were involved in ongoing serious delinquency and/or drug sales, while the majority (67 percent) were not. In all, sixteen girls (33 percent, including eight in Columbus and eight in St. Louis) were routinely involved in some of these activities.[26] Even among these young women, the nature of their involvement varied. Diane was involved in a range of activities; Chantell described being involved in assaults and robberies regularly, but only sporatic marijuana sales; Stephanie reported assaults as the bulk of her serious crimes; Rhonda and Yvette described frequent assaults and drug sales; LaShawna reported marijuana sales and stealing more than $100; while the rest (ten girls—Keisha, Angie, Jennifer, and Monica in Columbus; Vashelle, Toni, Shawanda, Mia, Tonya, and Debbie in St. Louis) described concentrating their efforts primarily on drug sales and avoiding these other serious kinds of gang crime.[27]

Turning to the context of girls' offending within gangs, there are several key points I want to make. First, with the exception of regular drug-selling, most of the gang delinquency youths were involved in was "happened upon" rather than organized or planned. Sometimes youths went out "looking for trouble" or to "start something," but even then crime routinely was not of a planned variety. Instead, it was something to do, and particular crimes occurred as opportunities presented themselves. At other times, groups of youths came looking to make trouble with these youths and fights or confrontations ensued. Regardless, very little crime was well planned-out ahead of time.

The second important point, as I've alluded to, is that youths' involvement in gang crime is shaped—but not determined—by gender. The kind of activities girls were routinely involved in and the level of their involvement, as well as the kinds of activities they didn't engage in—each of these was influenced by gang members' perceptions of what "femaleness" or "maleness" brought to their interactions and behavior. I will explore each of these points more fully in the context of three facets of gang delinquency: girls' general description of the types of crimes gang members are involved in, conflicts with rival groups, and involvement in the drug trade.

To begin with, I was interested in young women's general perceptions of whether particular types of gang crime were the exclusive purview of males or females. Initially, I did this in a roundabout way by asking girls whether members of their gang engaged in a list of particular crimes. Once they responded, I went back through the list and asked whether female members of the gang engaged in these same crimes. The results are displayed in Table 6-6. There is general uniformity in girls' characterizations of all members' delinquency versus female members' delinquency. In most categories young women were slightly less likely to report female involvement (except for petty theft, where girls were described as more likely[28]), but for the most part young women described girls as participating in the same delinquent endeavors as boys. Despite their recognition and discussion of gender differences in various places throughout the interviews, when specifically asked about gender differences most girls were firm on the point that they were equals—that members of the gang participated in the same activities regardless of gender or any other social category. As Chantell commented, "It's the same set, so why should we do different things?" In some cases, as

Table 6-6 Gang Delinquency (*N* = 42)*

	Committed by Gang Members	Committed by Female Members
Steal things worth less than $50	16 (38%)	22 (52%)
Steal things worth more than $50	31 (74%)	28 (67%)
Joyride in stolen cars	40 (95%)	33 (79%)
Damage or destroy things	31 (74%)	29 (69%)
Intimidate or threaten people	33 (79%)	33 (79%)
Rob people	32 (76%)	27 (64%)
Attack people with the intent to seriously hurt them	26 (62%)	23 (55%)
Sell marijuana	37 (88%)	32 (76%)
Sell other drugs	33 (79%)	29 (69%)

*Six missing cases.

I've said, this was true. In other cases, what Table 6-6 isn't able to capture is variations in the frequency of activities or variations in the behavior of different female members of the same gangs.

Table 6-6 also illustrates the broad range of delinquent activities in which gang members engaged. While I will spend the bulk of this section discussing the crimes we typically think of when we think of gangs—intergang conflict and drug sales—young women in fact described gang members engaging in a wide variety of delinquent activities—some of them gang-motivated, others clearly not. Veronica's description of a typical day with her gang illustrates this well:

> I was leavin' out of here [going AWOL from shelter care] to go over to my cousin's house all the time, and everyday my OG would be over there. And it just seemed like we always had been, it just seemed like every day that I was over there we'd get in a fight with somebody or somethin'. Somebody end up gettin' stabbed or cut or somethin' or some of the boys be out startin' trouble with people. Sit there and robbin' people for no, just to be doin' it, just doin' little stupid stuff. That's, they had jacked the pizza man. They had stolen the car. They took a cab over to my cousin's house and didn't pay for it. Just let somebody else pay for it, I don't know who paid for it. And then, some of the girls, like some of the girls that ain't in but they just hang around us, they stole a car. And one of 'em went to jail for it. It was just bein' stupid. One of them jacked this girl for a dollar. I was like, "Y'all are so stupid."

Veronica's description also illustrates the unplanned, spur of the moment nature of much of gang members' crime. I described in Chapter 4 that many young women in Columbus described their routine involvement in delinquency in these ways. As Erica surmised, "If somebody's bored and they have nothin' to do, then they'll start a fight." St. Louis girls said much the same thing. For instance, Vikkie described a recent robbery in which she was involved. She and her friends were hanging out as a woman walked by, and her friends spontaneously decided to jack the woman. Asked what happened, she explained:

> VIKKIE: I don't really want to say it was fun but it was funny.
> RB: It was funny, why?
> VIKKIE: Because. I didn't want to laugh but the look on her face made me laugh. I didn't want to laugh because I didn't want to do it, but [my friends] were like, come on, come on . . . we gonna do this. I just did it.

These examples describe a variety of crimes than can only loosely be called gang-related, in that they are activities with no clear gang-related motive but come about through youths' associations with their gang friends. Next I turn to probably the most obvious kind of gang-motivated delinquency—conflicts with rival gangs. As I will discuss, confrontations with rivals often come about in the same unplanned, happened-upon ways.

INTERGANG CONFLICTS

Recall from Chapters 4 and 5 that the gang members I interviewed in Columbus included youths in primarily in Folks, Crips, and Bloods sets, while in St. Louis they were primarily Crips and Bloods. In Columbus, Crips and Folks sets are allied with one another, typically referring to each other as "cousins." Both consider Bloods their "enemies." In St. Louis, Crips and Bloods consider themselves enemies, but there are also conflicts between various Crip sets and between various Blood sets. An important element of gang life involves spending time and energy challenging and fighting with rival gangs; it is often at the level of these antagonisms that youths stake out the identity of their gang in opposition to their enemies. I noted earlier that Klein and Crawford suggest it is primarily through conflicts with rival groups that gangs build cohesiveness among themselves: Having common enemies facilitates members' perceptions of themselves as a unified group. Decker and Van Winkle note:

> The bonds between gang members allow them to overcome any initial reluctance about joining the gang, and ultimately enable them to overcome constraints against violence. Thus, the threat of a gang in a geographically proximate neighborhood serves to increase the solidarity of the gang, compels more young men [sic] to join their neighborhood gang, and enables them to engage in acts of violence they might not otherwise have committed.[29]

Opposition to rival gangs is a central theme in the cultural imagery and symbolism that gang youths adopt. Gang members announce and promote their gang identity through the use of a variety of symbols—colors, flags, hand signs, graffiti, tattoos. Often these displays are quite innovative and imaginative.[30] Young women described regularly wearing their gang colors and flags around the neighborhood and also in other public settings. Traci described, "It seems like everything I do be blue. When I get my hair done I get blue stuff in it and everything." And LaShawna explained, "I don't like the color dred [red]; I just wear black all the time." Tamika said:

> Like we'll go to the mall and I'll have on my blue khakis outfit, my blue rag, you know, my pager and everything. And everybody be like, "Dag!" 'Cause my pager is blue. Everybody be like, "Dag!" My shoes is blue. My outfit is blue. They be like, "Dag, dag, she blued out!"

Often confrontations with rivals were a consequence of these displays. Encounters with rival gang members typically occurred either when one group entered the other's territory looking to cause trouble or because youths bumped into each other in the types of places where young people congregate—at school, in shopping centers, or at skating rinks, for instance. Heather explained, "You can just be in the mall and somebody can, you know, just mostly be throwin' up their signs, and you see somebody throwin' up their Blood sign then you'll throw up your Folk sign." Even at the detention center, Lisa said, "Staff can't watch you 24-7. So you know, we be goin' and in the windows you can tell the boys be throwin' up Bloods or whatever, we be throwin' up BK [Blood Killer]." Monica described a similar encounter with a young woman in her school:

> One time I got this girl, oh man, this girl was in the bathroom and I was writin' BK all over the bathroom and she came in the bathroom. She was like, "What you writin' BK for? Are you a Crip or somethin'?" I was like, "Yeah, I'm a Crip. Fuck them Slobs." And she was, she was like, "whatever." Then the next day I saw her comin' into the school sportin' a red rag.

It's telling that the two young women were not involved in a violent altercation at the time, though if the young woman affiliated with Bloods had returned Monica's challenge a fight likely would have ensued. Instead, she chose to avoid a direct confrontation, challenging Monica in a less direct way by wearing her gang colors to school the next day. Many young women said when they encountered rivals, as long as they weren't met with a direct challenge, they were happy to leave it alone. Pam explained:

> We going to the show or skating, to the mall. We be seeing some of our enemies too when we do those things, clubs and stuff, we be seeing a lot of our enemies. [If] they don't say nothing to us, we don't say nothing to them. They say something to us, we say something to them. So that way everybody just go they own little way if they don't want nothing to happen.

Many young women echoed Pam's account. Often gang members didn't perceive themselves to be looking for trouble and tolerated the presence of enemies as long as they weren't directly challenged. One way rival gang members directly challenged the gang was by coming into their hood dressed down or calling out the rival gang's name. Doing so, Crystal explained, was tantamount to "diss[ing] the set." She explained, "If a Blood come on our set and we Crips, as long as they come on our set saying, 'What's up Blood,' they . . . just gonna start a fight. 'Cause they diss us by coming on our set and saying what's up Blood. There ain't nobody no Blood over there." Vashelle concurred:

> They'll just, they walking through the hood, I mean it's just all back luck for them. . . . By them being over in the neighborhood, they just totally disrespecting coming in somebody else hood. Then you wear your colors, you know what I'm saying. . . . A dude come over there [from a rival gang], he know what kind of hood it is to begin with. Any dude that come over there from a gang and know that's a Blood hood, you try to come over there Cripped out [wearing Crip colors, symbolism], you know you gonna eventually have it some way.

These actions—coming into a rival territory to challenge the gang—are what Decker calls mobilizing events.[31] In providing a direct challenge, they are perceived as an external threat, for which members come together and to which they respond. Marie explained, "There's not that many fights unless something really bad [e.g., a mobilizing event] happens." To function as a mobilizing event, however, the challenge typically had to be viewed as deliberate. Neoka explained that members of her gang don't "really do nothing unless [the rival] comes over there looking for some trouble for real. I mean, it ain't nothing like we waiting on somebody to come over there so we can start something. If you don't come over there with no trouble then you leave with no trouble." Shandra told much the same story:

As long as they didn't disrespect nobody they was cool. If we already knew them and we already have static with them, then you know, they probably gonna get killed or something like that. But if they ain't got no problems with us and we ain't got no problems with them and they don't disrespect us or nothing then nothing gonna happen to them. Just tell them, "burn out," leave or something like that.

The following conversation with Erica is also illustrative:

ERICA: Just the other day, we saw a group of Bloods walkin' around. Only reason why we knew, for one, they had a rag on. And for two, they were just all in red in this one group, walkin' around. We just knew it. [Laughs]
JM: So what did you do?
ERICA: We couldn't do anything. We were in a van. I'm sure if we were out in the streets there would have been a fight 'cause we were wearing blue rags and here they are wearing red. And, I could see us walking right on the same street, by the crosswalk. That wouldn't go too well.

Erica and her friends' opportunity for a direct challenge was hindered by their being in a staff van of the residential facility rather than on the streets. Nonetheless, as they drove by they engaged in excited discussions of what would have happened if they had been walking down the street instead of "stuck" in their van. The event functioned to build solidarity without the necessity of a violent encounter.

Not surprisingly, direct challenges were more likely to come in a group context rather than when an individual was alone or outnumbered. Young women insisted that to be a "true" member you should stand up to rivals no matter what the odds against you were. Recall from Chapter 4 that Cathy told me being true meant "[if] you got a whole bunch of people comin' up in your face and if you're by yourself they ask you what you're claimin', you tell 'em. Don't say 'nothing.'" Easy enough to say, but in practice it typically wasn't the case. For instance, Dionne said: "One day I was with my friends, you know, we was in a car and the dude was walking down the street and my friend, he say, 'What's up Blood, where you from?' And old boy looks back but he didn't say nothing, he just kept walkin' so we drove off." Likewise, Erica said when she was alone or with a few other members in a situation where they were likely to be outnumbered, they wouldn't wear their gang flags or otherwise bring attention to their affiliation. Pam described the contexts in which challenges were more or less likely to occur as follows:

> I see [rivals] all the time, every day. Some days they just don't say nothing. Some days there be a lot of them outside and they want to say something. But when it be like about two or three of them or one of them by theyself they won't say nothing for real. It's a lot of them that want to say something at different times. They don't be saying nothing when they by theyself or when they ain't got a lot of people with them. Other than that, they just be saying everything.

In most cases, confrontations with rivals did not result in serious violence. As Nikkie explained, "They'd fight 'em but they wouldn't try to kill 'em because they got on some flu [blue] or they stackin' [throwing hand signs] in they face, but they will fight 'em." Occasionally, however, mobilizing events were more serious—such as when a member of the girls' gang was injured or attacked by rival members. In these cases, the event would lead to an escalation of activities, like calling members together for a meeting to plan a retaliation or riding down on the rivals' hood looking for trouble. Catharsis comes through a violent event such as a shooting or an attack on a rival. Decker concludes that these "violent events typically are short-lived and de-escalate rapidly . . . [but] may be only a respite before the next retaliation."[32]

GENDER AND GANG CONFLICT

Gender differences most clearly emerged in girls' discussions of these serious events. Most serious affronts to the gang were committed by young men. When girls were involved, young women reported that except for in very unusual circumstances male gang members left retaliation against the rival girls to young women in the gang. Tonya described once when members of her gang "had a beef with this girl named Shaunna." Someone spotted the girl up the street, and Tonya explained, "My brother said 'you better go up there yourself and check on this perpetrator' . . . so I had to go buck her." Asked what she meant by buck, she continued:

> Punch her, beat her up. That mean go knock her, hit her in the face, try to knock her out for real. I was scared to death. The girl was bigger than me. At the time I was little, I was really skinny. I just ran up on her, bam! Picked up a bottle and started hitting her in the head with it. We scarred this girl bad.

Her little friends came over there and one girl stabbed my friend. Then they took her knife and they cut her all up and the police came and we ran down an alley.

In addition to young men leaving fights with rival females to the girls in the gang, a number of girls remarked that male gang members were less aggressive in their encounters with rival females than they were with rival males. Lisa told me: "Girls don't face [as] much violence as [guys]. They see a girl, they say, 'We'll just smack her and send her on [her way].' They see a guy—'cause guys are a lot more into it than girls are, I've noticed that—and they like, well, 'We'll shoot him.' "[33] One young woman[34] also said male members of her gang ordinarily left confrontations with rival females to the girls in her gang, explaining that the males "don't wanna go waste their time hittin' on some little girls. They're gonna go get their little cats to go get 'em." However, she also described one attack on a girl that didn't turn out as she'd expected. Characterizing the events leading up to the attack, she explained:

The female was supposingly goin' with one of ours, went back and told a bunch of [rivals] what was goin' on and got the [rivals] to jump my boy. And he ended up in the hospital, OK? They beat him up real bad. He had like fractured skull bones, I mean they beat him up bad. Baseball bats, cut him, everything. He was in the hospital for [about two months].

Members of her gang later saw the girl walking down the street, kidnapped her, and brought her to a house where the gang hung out. Initially, and in keeping with how assaults on rival females typically took place, she said the male gang members turned the girl over to her and her friends. After "a group of us [girls] already done beat her up," much to this young woman's surprise and horror the young men in her gang took over the assault, one of them began ripping the girl's clothes off, and the young men proceeded to gang rape her. She continued:

They really hurt her. I think, she's gonna have, I mean you don't understand. Four guys are makin' her, carryin' her in, I mean I don't wanna be vulgar, but in this, to talk about this you gotta be vulgar, grab her by her hair, stickin' their dick in her mouth, makin' her suck their dick, makin' her, punchin her, boom! "You better suck, try to bite!" I remember she bit one of my boys and she just got beat and he brought her face up again. He was like, "Suck!" Callin' her "little [rival] bitch" and all that stuff. I was like, "Whoa!" I was like, my people do some violence. But she, she was suckin' this dude's dick. The other one put his stuff in her butt. So she's screamin' like "Ah! Ah!" So she's screamin' and so after he, the one got his nut off, the other one spread her legs and started doin' it in the front. And then I was just sittin' there like, "Oh my goodness." I mean, me and a group of us already done beat her up, we already beat her up so she was all beat up plus they were beatin' on her, callin' her names, callin' her [a derogatory name for her gang], fuckin' her every which way. I mean, and then we just drug her out, put her in the trunk and dropped her off [in this park]. I don't know what happened to her. Maybe she died. Maybe, maybe someone came and helped her. I mean, I don't know.

In characterizing the event, this young woman made an important distinction between male gang members' attacks on young men versus the girl in her story: "I mean, we coulda just shot her," she explained. "You know, it coulda been just over. We coulda just taken her life. But they went farther than that." I'll return to this event again in Chapter 7. Although it was a unique attack and brutality of this nature was rare, it nonetheless sheds light on the gendered nature of gang violence. Had it been a young man, members presumably would have "just shot" him.[35] Male-on-female violence, when it did occur, was instead sometimes sexual in nature, differing from both male-on-male and female-on-female violence.

Female-on-female violence within gangs, on the whole, involved fists or weapons such as knives rather than guns. In fact, only one young woman I talked to reported having shot a rival, and only three—Keisha, Diane, and Heather—said they had participated in a drive-by shooting. In St. Louis, girls were asked whether females ever participated in the gang's drive-by shootings, and only seven (25 percent) said they did. Instead, girls said young men were more likely to use guns in their confrontations with rival gang members.[36] Crystal noted, "Girls don't be up there shooting unless they really have to." Likewise, Tonya said, "I ain't never carried no strap [gun] before. I was too nervous. I ain't used no guns." And Regina explained, "I just carry a knife, that's all. I don't carry no gun or something."

Young women in St. Louis were asked specifically about weapons, and 70 percent described carrying knives, sometimes in addition to razors, mace, or other household items that could be used to stab (scissors, forks, screwdrivers). Only seven girls (26 percent) described carrying guns; of these, only four carried guns as their weapon of choice. Vashelle was one of these. She reported that she "just keep[s] a strap on me at all times . . . a little bitty .22." She said, "I done got robbed before by a dope fiend. I mean I had to pull [the gun] out before but I ain't never used it, just to scare people off."

Explaining why girls used fists and knives rather than guns, Pam suggested it was because "we ladies, we not dudes for real." She continued:

We don't got to be rowdy, all we do is fight. A dude, he quick to go get a gun or something, a girl she quick to pull out a knife. Still, [girls] just be wanting to fight one-on-one. Don't no girl want they face hurt all up, bruised up and stuff, so they just fight and whoever beat somebody up, she get mad, can't take it, she gonna stick me or something with a knife and that's how that kick off. She stick me, I'm gonna stick [her] back.

Girls' discussions of young men's greater use of lethal violence were double-edged. On the one hand, some were happy to exclude themselves from such behavior, as it shielded them from the dangers inherent in such events, and in some cases it was behavior they found morally troubling. Veronica, preferring to fight with her fists, commented, "I think it's dumb that they have to use weapons and everything." Often, however, girls didn't choose to exclude themselves so much as the young men in the gang excluded them. Contradicting her earlier comment, Veronica described a drive-by her gang was involved in:

VERONICA: They [male members] went to go do a drive-by on, um, all of them [people they had fought with]. They wouldn't let us [females] go. But, we wanted to go, but they wouldn't let us.

JM: What'd they say?

VERONICA: They was like, "All of y'all stay here in the house just in case some of 'em try to come down here, y'all have to have you all's gats [guns] and stuff ready so if they come down here and try to shoot up the house, y'all be in the house and y'all can call the police and everything and y'all can get away." They'd be the ones to get caught, so.

JM: Why do you think they—

VERONICA: So we won't go to jail if they was to get caught. Or, if one of 'em was to get shot, they wouldn't want it to happen to us.

When young women were excluded from participation, this exclusion was often framed under the guise of protection. For instance, Sonita told me, "If they wanna go do somethin' bad and they think one of the females gonna get hurt they don't let 'em do it with them. . . . Like if they was involved with shooting or whatever, [girls] can't go." LaShawna, who was involved in a lot of gang crime herself (and reported having shot someone), said "We don't want our females to get hurt, you know, and boys is, they just crazy and everything." When I pointed out the contradiction between what she said and her own behavior, she explained:

Yeah, I do a lot of stuff 'cause I'm tough. I likes, I likes messin' with boys. I fight boys. Girls ain't nothing to me, I just knock them out, it's just a thang. That's the way I was raised. Don't let no nigger put hands on you. . . . I got, I got a couple of girls in there that's tough like me so we roll a lot. We roll a lot. But I still have to look out for 'em.

Diane also said girls were typically excluded from drive-bys for their own protection and because they might not be as capable as the young men:

For maybe a drive-by they might wanna have a bunch of dudes. They might not put the females in that. Maybe the females might be weak inside, not strong enough to do something like that, just on the insides. . . . If a female wants to go forward and doin' that, and she wants to risk her whole life for doin' that then she can. But the majority of time, that job is given to a man.

Although some girls didn't mind being excluded from such events, others found their exclusion frustrating because they recognized that it was partly driven by young men's beliefs in girls' lesser competence. Describing encounters with rival male gang members, Chantell commented, "They think that you're more of a punk, or that there's a hole in you . . . that they can go right through you. That you just another punk." And Pam lamented, "Some dudes [in rival gangs], they be tripping with you 'cause they know you from the other side and they be trying to slap you or something." Brandi's comments pertained to her own gang:

JM: Is there anything about the gang you dislike?
BRANDI: Not really. Sometimes I dislike that the boys, sometimes, always gotta take charge and they think sometimes, that the girls don't know how to take charge 'cause we're girls, we're females, and like that.
JM: Can you describe something like that, like what happens?
BRANDI: Like, a guy'll say, like, they're going to have, like a shoot-out. I'll be, the girl'll be like sayin', "Well this is what we'll do." Then the guy will take charge: "Well, you're a girl, you don't know nothin' about that." Then like we'll get really offended and stuff. But he's just playin', he says he's just playin' around or somethin'.
JM: And so do you ever get to take charge, do you fight to—
BRANDI: No, not really. We just let him go ahead. And, 'cause he's been in longer, he knows more about it and he's been through more stuff than we have.

These findings about girls' exclusion from certain gang crimes are similar to those reported in studies with young men in gangs. Just as the girls articulated, young men describe excluding girls from serious crime, both under the guise of protecting them from danger and because they perceive girls as untrustworthy and weak.[37] Perhaps what's most interesting is that these themes about girls being untrustworthy and weak were also mirrored in some girls' accounts of young women in gangs. Many young women, though perhaps frustrated by their own exclusion, on the whole agreed with these statements about girls, and thus supported their exclusion from certain activities.

It's also the case that many young women described excluding themselves from serious criminal involvement, as I've noted, both because it was seen as too risky and because they felt some ambivalence about these aspects of gang life. Angie reported being involved in street-level crack sales and carrying a hidden weapon to protect herself on a daily basis. Of involvement in other gang crime, she explained: "I don't be gettin' involved, no I don't get involved like that. Be out there goin' and just beat up people like that or go stealin', things like that. That's not me. The boys, mostly just the boys do all that, the girls we just sit back and chill, you know." And Dionne said, "I hate bein' around when they havin' shoot-outs and stuff like that. That's what I hate about it. And when they get into it and stuff." Likewise, though Stephanie described committing twenty serious assaults in the last six months, when I asked what things she disliked about the gang, she told me, "Violence, stealing, I don't like a lot of it." Noting the contradiction, I asked why she was involved if she disliked those things and she replied, "'Cause I want to. I don't go rob and steal. I stay at home or I watch out. And I don't get nothing out of robbin' or stealin'." Lisa commented:

> I don't think most the girls would go out there and kill somebody. It just depends on how crazy you are and how much you hate that person. But I don't really think, I don't think they would do it as much as the boys would do. I wouldn't. I wouldn't go out there and kill somebody just 'cause they wearin' that color. I wouldn't do that. I might beat 'em up or get me, I might get beat up. But I would never go out to that certain extent to kill 'em.

GIRLS' INVOLVEMENT IN STREET-LEVEL DRUG SALES

As I discussed earlier, about half of the gang girls in Columbus described having ever sold marijuana (52 percent) and crack (48 percent). Around 63 percent of the girls in St. Louis had sold both of these drugs. In all, fourteen girls were involved in drug sales on at least a weekly basis, including six from Columbus and eight from St. Louis. However, as Table 6-4 showed, girls in St. Louis had a mean frequency of drug sales that was considerably higher than girls in Columbus. I noted in Chapter 5 that gangs in St. Louis appeared to be more deeply involved in drug sales than gangs in Columbus. This was especially apparent when young women talked about status in the gang. Girls in Columbus did not mention success in the drug trade as a key element of members' status ratings, while girls in St. Louis did. Making money through drug sales, and the flashy lifestyle that results, gained St. Louis gang members respect in the eyes of their peers. In fact, five young women in St. Louis (19 percent) sold crack on a daily or near-daily basis, while only one young woman in Columbus did.[38] Given these differences, here I discuss girls' drug-selling in each city separately, beginning with St. Louis.

Young women in St. Louis who described selling drugs routinely emphasized that it was a key element of their gang activities. Tonya said that "mostly dudes was . . . selling guns and jacking cars and stuff like that. But everybody selling drugs." As I described in Chapter 5, older girls emphasized the economic benefits of the gang, especially vis-à-vis drug sales, viewing younger members as more caught up in rivalries and the like. Latisha explained:

> We done what gangs did but we spent all our time on the corner selling drugs, making money. We don't just be standing outside, "What's up Blood" and all

that, throwing up little signs or whatever. Cars come by, they know what we claim or whatever, but we all making our money. We don't be looking for trouble or whatever.

Asked to describe a typical day, she remarked: "From the time I wake up, you know . . . I just dress up in my little colors or whatever then go out, just sit in the front or on the corner or whatever and make my little sales or whatever, sell my drugs or whatever I got to do." In fact, Mia went so far as to say that "the gang don't mean nothing to me, it's the money that means something to me . . . [from] selling drugs." While she said the gang facilitated her ability to sell drugs, she attributed her success to herself, explaining it was "'cause I got the hustle in me." Likewise, in the following conversation, Vashelle described the role of drug sales in her daily life:

RB: Describe for me how you spend a typical day, like for example, how did you spend yesterday?
VASHELLE: Yesterday, went to school, slept all day, went down there and went to work [sold drugs] for an hour, went home, got high, went to sleep, fell asleep for the rest of the day. On any other day, sit on the set [in the neighborhood], get high, go in the house, and go to sleep.
RB: Why do you sleep all day?
VASHELLE: I sit outside selling. When I get high I just be sleepy all the time. But yesterday, I didn't get that much sleep, I sat out on the set all night and then went in the house, went to sleep, came to school the next day, was still tired. I slept in all my classes. . . .
RB: So were you sleepy because you was out selling dope?
VASHELLE: Yeah, sleepy because I just sit out all night, doing nothing, just sitting out.
RB: So how much money did you usually make in a night?
VASHELLE: Like over there in my 'hood, you can make two or three in one night, two or three hundred dollars in one night.

As Vashelle indicated, young women viewed their drug-selling as a viable means of making money. Tonya said members of her gang sold drugs in order to have money to party. She explained, "We . . . have like times when we would all go kicking and stuff and you got to have money for that. So originally, even if you didn't do it in the beginning, you end up selling dope, you see what I mean?" Even so, several young women indicated that their drug-selling was sporadic rather than an everyday phenomenon, indicating some difference between their activities and those of young men. Shandra said: "The times when I sold I only did it for a short while. I only did it to make a little money to do something big. I ain't never really made it a career or nothing like that. But a lot of people, some of them they sell drugs and they keep on selling, like that's their hustle, that's what they do." Likewise, Pam explained:

> The dudes . . . [I] got to say they got the most clout, the most reputation selling drugs. . . . Some girls just sell some drugs and then they'll quit. They just sell it just to get them some money 'cause they need some. Whatever they need they'll make they money and then probably won't sell drugs no more until they need something else. And then they'll go buy them some drugs and sell it and that's it. The dudes, they keep on, keep on, keep on. They like to sell it and stash they money.

Recall from Chapter 5 that Yvette was in a female set affiliated with a local mixed-gender set. A number of the older girls in her gang had children, and she explained that they sold drugs in order to support their kids and also to get the things their families couldn't provide:

> Some of them got like two and three babies and stuff like that. My cousins, they got kids now. Most of my partners, they got families for real. They sell drugs to support they family, pay the bills with it, like that. I mean, I know it ain't right, but you got to survive out here. If you go to school, they ain't paying you. . . . We make $200 or $300 a month, something like that. We don't do higher and bigger things. My momma can't do all this, she got bills and all that. I'm gonna have to make it myself.[39]

Notably, while some young women reported that they often got their supply of drugs from older members of the gang, their drug sales were for individual profit.[40] Vashelle explained:

> Like the dude that I told you we look up to [see Chapter 5], it's like dudes like that [who we get our drugs from]. They come over there, everybody like, one person be like, I need to go recop [get more drugs to sell], somebody will page him, be like so and so, we need this, come meet us on the set on the little back porch. He'll bring it over there. It like he got a suitcase, he'll have it already wrapped up in the plastic and stuff and give it to them and they have to go cut they own stuff down.

However, the choice to sell was the individuals', and they sold to put money in their own pockets. The following conversation with Tyra illustrates this distinction:

> RB: You said before that you sold crack and marijuana. Was the gang involved in selling drugs at all?
> TYRA: Everybody is. Everybody make money for they set.
> RB: Did they make money and bring it back to the gang, or they just made it for themselves?

TYRA: For theyself. When they need something and they don't have no money they have to sell it.

Pam said if members chose not to sell, it wasn't an issue in her gang:

> You don't got to sell drugs if you don't want to. If you want to carry some money, have nice things, and that's what you want to. Or you might go get you a job. It's just all about being real. It ain't about how much money you got, it ain't about what you got, how you got it, or nothing like that. Just how you get yours. You don't have to worry about nobody else but how you get yours.

Despite some of their involvement in drug sales, young women in St. Louis saw their gender as a double-edged sword when it came to selling drugs. On the one hand, to be successful in their drug-selling, they often had to rely on their male peers to ward off potential predators. On the other hand, they felt because they were female they were more likely to be invisible to the police, making their sales less risky. Mia said the young men in her gang assisted in her drug sales: "Like they'll be saying, 'This is my little sister,' make sure don't nobody do nothing to take nothing from me when I'm on the streets." Likewise, Pam explained that it was more difficult for young women to sell drugs on the street because females were viewed as particularly easy targets for drug robberies:

> A dude, they [robbers] ain't too quick to run up on you and rob you, take your stuff. See, you a girl, they be like, "Well she ain't gonna do nothing, she ain't got no clout [reputation], she ain't nothing but a girl. All I got to do is tell her to up it and she gonna give it here." They just can't come up to a dude like that, especially if he know them and he got some clout. They be scared to run up on you if he a dude. By you being a girl, they'll rob you quicker, take everything, your drugs, your money, anything else they want.

Consequently, she said one of the precautions girls would take when dealing drugs would be to "have somebody standing by, one of your boys or something."

On the other hand, several young women commented that being female allowed them to avoid police scrutiny, as the following conversation with Vashelle indicates:

RB: Don't you have to worry about like the police and other gangs and stuff?

VASHELLE: The police, they don't be on the girls for real, females, but if they see a whole crowd of niggers sitting out, they gonna get down on them. But I'm saying if there are niggers out there and I'm with them too they gonna shake me too. If I'm walking up the street by myself they ain't gonna trip off me cause I'm a gal but a crowd of niggers just walking, they gonna get on them. You know how the police is.

RB: How do you avoid getting caught when you're out there selling dope?

VASHELLE: Don't sit out with a crowd. I sit out by myself. That's why I try to go out early in the morning like on the weekends and stuff and I'll be the first one up in the morning getting up early cause that's when the fiends start coming through for real, during the morning time and stuff, I just sit over there until about ten o'clock. That's when everybody start coming out. I be getting up early. Sometimes I won't even go in the house on the weekend. I'll be up all weekend and sleep all day Sunday, get up and go sit outside.

RB: Do you have the dope on you usually?

VASHELLE: No. Like have a car in my garage and I hide the stuff in the car and just sit on the back and when people come I just get up in the car. And the police, as far as me sitting on the back porch, I don't worry about them because they don't mess with me for real. Just because I'm gal. Say if I'm sitting on the corner, then they gonna say something because they don't like that, I mean, they don't let you sit on the corner.

Other young women echoed Vashelle's comments about the police. Latisha noted that if "you be a girl, the police think that if you selling dope or something, a girl, you smoking it, stuff like that and that's not true." In fact, in a recent paper based on interviews with women crack sellers in St. Louis, Bruce Jacobs and I reported similar findings. Many of the women in our study described using similar approaches to selling as Vashelle—not selling on the corner in ways that called attention to themselves and using police officers' beliefs about gender to conceal their activities and avoid being caught.[41]

Most young women in Columbus who talked about girls' involvement in drug sales described it in more circumscribed ways. As I discussed earlier, girls in both cities said gun use and drive-bys were principally the purview of young men. In Columbus, many young women also described drug sales, especially street-level crack-selling, as primarily a male endeavor. The vast majority of young women in Columbus emphasized that girls were typically excluded (or excluded themselves) from crack-dealing or that they needed to rely on male protection to do so successfully. Even young women who sold crack themselves noted that their involvement was unique. In fact, Diane was the only girl in Columbus who didn't note gender differences in drug sales among members of her gang.[42] Cathy said while some of the guys sold, mostly the girls didn't. And Nikkie, who didn't sell herself, said, "It be like three girls that do it. And mostly all the boys do it." Of her drug sales Tamika explained, "I sell bud a little bit. But that ain't really nothin'. I don't sell like crack and all that."

Young women in Columbus gave two accounts for why girls usually didn't sell crack: first, that girls made the decision not to, and second, that it was frowned upon and girls weren't typically permitted to do so. Keisha explained, "You can do it if you want to. If you choose to do it you can. If you choose not to, you don't. Like, I'm the only girl that's in it that is sellin'." Nikkie said girls were more likely to get money from other sources, making drug sales less necessary, "because they moms 'n stuff be givin' 'em stuff. Some of 'em on welfare 'cause they have babies or they got jobs or somethin'." Similarly, Leslie said most girls chose not to because they weren't as caught up in conspicuous consumption as young men were:

> The guys will be, you know, walkin' around with gold around their neck, drivin' a big bad car. And guys are like, "Whew, I want that!" And girls aren't like that. I mean, if I'm gonna get that, I'd rather do it the right way. So, if the police run up at my house they won't take everything 'cause it's related to drugs. . . . I want to be able to, like, "Look I bought this with this money 'cause my check was last week." Instead of all of the sudden you pop up with gold teeth and gold on the fingers, big boomin' system in you car, a [new] car, I mean things like that. I didn't want it like that 'cause then the police can see, well yeah, they're not doin' anything good.

Monica sold crack and other drugs because of her desire for money and material goods. In the following conversation, she discussed her involvement in drug sales, as compared to other young women's in the gang. Monica and I had already talked about a young woman in her gang, Andrea, to whom she refers in this dialogue. Andrea was repeatedly mistreated by the male members of their gang, and Monica was frustrated because she never stood up for herself (more about Andrea in Chapter 7):

JM: Are there very many females sellin' like you?
MONICA: Two. Me and Andrea. She sell because they tell her to.
JM: She doesn't seem like she would be very effective.
MONICA: She gets, she gets her money.
JM: Really?
MONICA: She gets her money. 'Cause she knows if she mess up they money she will get hurt. So she gets the money. Like she supposed to. But um, nobody else wanna do it. They're like, "No, I ain't gonna do it." Like, "I'm scared I'm gonna get caught. I'm scared I'm gonna get caught." If you think about gettin' caught, you're gonna get caught. That's why I don't need to think about it. I wear my big ol' Starter coat out there. I have all my stuff up in my coat, so that won't nobody, so that if, I wouldn't have all of it in my hand or holdin' it, somethin' like that. I keep it undercover where it's supposed to be. And, I mean, they [the other females] don't wanna take the risk. If you want the money bad enough you will take the risk.

Monica was the only young woman in her gang who routinely sold drugs because she wanted to. Andrea was made to sell by the men in the gang, while the other young women chose (and were permitted to choose) not to.

Other young women in Columbus said girls typically weren't permitted to sell drugs or were permitted to only under particular circumstances. Jennifer, a member of an all-female gang, said members of her gang "just [sell] bud. They don't go into the crack and heroine and stuff like that. No. We're not allowed to. If we get caught, with the OG, [with] stuff like that, then we're not allowed to be in the gang no more. Just bud. 'Cause she don't want us strung out on something." And LaShawna told me, "We don't really let the females do that unless they really wanna and they know how to do it and not to get caught and everything." Asked why girls would be less likely to know how, she explained, "Like they don't get taught. 'Cause some females in mine don't know how, don't even know how to make dope or whatever." Erica said when girls in her set sold drugs, they did so in the company of young men:

It's mostly the guys that does all the selling and the, uh, buying. And um, with us, as far as females when it goes to selling, we're always supposed to have a male with us. Always. Or, at least two or three males with us all the time. That way, we can't get robbed or anything. Or if something was to go down, we would always have somebody there with us, instead of by ourselves.

As in St. Louis, Columbus gang members recognized that gender played a factor in young women's success in the drug trade. Even when selling marijuana on the streets, Jennifer said this was a concern for which her members took precautions:

Everybody would think that if some boys were goin' to buy some bud from us, the first one that comes to mind, "I ain't paying her for it, I'm gonna jack her for it." But then they see how many girls, like when we go out we always have like three or four girls with us 'cause, especially with the tiny people. Like I'm one of the tinier people. So I have to have a couple big people with me. And usually, the girls, I mean, we fight dudes. I mean, we fight everything.

Jennifer described what happened once when several young men tried to rob one of the girls in her gang:

One time one of my friends, well one of the members, she got, they tried to jack her out of her car and they didn't see the car behind her full of girls. So. [Laughs] And the girls, they jumped out and they started boxing with 'em. And we left with our stuff. They didn't get none of theirs. We got their money, but they didn't get none of the product.

In sum, girls in both cities recognized that being female posed potential risks to their success in the drug trade. Many young women in Columbus read this as a cue to define crack sales as something to leave to the boys. Ironically, despite the vastly different tone that young women in Columbus and St. Louis took when they described girls' involvement in crack sales, the majority of girls in both places did not sell the drug on a regular basis. Asked about whether they'd sold crack in the last six months, seventeen girls in St. Louis (63 percent) and fourteen girls in Columbus (67 percent) had not. It appears that, in principle, girls in St. Louis saw crack-selling as an avenue more open to them regardless of whether they chose to act on it, while girls in Columbus viewed crack sales as primarily an activity of young men.

CONCLUSION

In this chapter, I have detailed gang girls' involvement in delinquency, focusing particularly on how gender shapes their activities. Not surprisingly, gang girls were significantly more criminally involved than their nongang peers. But there was also a great deal of variation in gang girls' criminal endeavors. Many chose to avoid involvement in serious delinquency, while a sizeable minority were routinely involved in at least some of these activities. In addition, girls' discussions highlighted that with the exception of some income-generating activities, most notably drug sales, most gang members' crime was happened upon rather than well planned-out or organized. Moreover, crime was shaped and facilitated by group processes within girls' gangs, and this was as much the case for young women as has been previously documented for young men.

Nonetheless, young women drew distinct boundaries between young men's crime and young women's crime. In St. Louis and Columbus, girls noted that gun use and drive-by shootings were activities most likely to be engaged in by the males in their gangs, while young women confronted rivals with fists or, less often, knives. In Columbus, girls also felt that crack-selling was an activity mostly left to young men. In addition, except in unusual circumstances, gang confrontations were intragender, with females fighting females and males fighting males.

As I noted in the introduction to this chapter, what this emphasis on gang delinquency often overlooks is that gangs also increase youths' likelihood of victimization and exposure to violence. Given my findings about how gender shapes delinquent involvement among girls in gangs, it also makes sense that gender would shape girls' victimization and exposure to violence. I take up these issues in Chapter 7, and examine the overlapping nature of gangs, offending, and victimization. Here I will further address how gendered structures and ideologies shape girls' participation in gangs, focusing finally in Chapter 8 on young women's perceptions of self and gender within gangs.

Gender and Victimization in Gangs

In Chapter 3, I described the violence that many young women in gangs reported in their home lives. Nearly half of the gang girls I spoke with reported having been abused by adults in their families growing up (twenty-two of forty-eight, or 46 percent), and even more (twenty-seven of forty-eight, or 56 percent) described witnessing adults in their homes hit one another. In fact, fully 69 percent of the gang girls in this study (thirty-three of forty-eight) reported either being abused, witnessing family violence, or both. As I have discussed, my research and that of other scholars have emphasized that young women in gangs have disproportionate histories of childhood victimization prior to joining their gangs. Moreover, there is evidence that girls turn to gangs, in part, because these groups are seen as offering a respite from violence and other problems in the family.[1]

These "blurred boundaries" between young women's involvement in gangs and crime, and their experiences of victimization, are an important insight that feminist scholars have brought to bear in their work on women and crime.[2] However, it's also the case that gang involvement itself opens up young women to additional victimization risk and exposes them to violence, even when they are not the direct victims, that is sometimes haunting and traumatic in its own right. In this chapter, I examine girls' victimization and exposure to violence within gangs, examining both intragang and intergang conflicts. Throughout, I focus in particular on how victimization risk is shaped by gender.

EXPOSURE TO VIOLENCE AND VICTIMIZATION

As I noted in Chapter 6, there is strong evidence that "adolescent involvement in delinquent lifestyles strongly increases the risk of both personal and property victimization."[3] In fact, Lauritsen and her colleagues found that, as a predictor of victimization risk, gender decreases in significance when participation in delinquent lifestyles is controlled for. That is, much of young men's greater victimization risk (with the exception of sexual assault) can be accounted for by their greater involvement in offending behaviors.[4] Given gang members' greater involvement in delinquency, it is thus not surprising that the gang girls I spoke with were more likely both to report having been victimized and to have witnessed violent acts against others than their nongang counterparts.

Table 7-1 Exposure to Violence and Victimization

	Gang Members (*N* = 48)	Nongang Members (*N* = 46)
Exposure to Violence		
Seen attack	41 (85%)	41 (89%)
Seen sexual assault	7 (15%)	5 (11%)
Seen stabbing	27 (56%)	10 (22%)*
Seen guns shot	46 (96%)	31 (67%)*
Seen someone shot	38 (79%)	19 (41%)*
Seen drive-by shooting	29 (60%)	12 (26%)*
Seen someone killed	31 (65%)	12 (26%)*
Victimization		
Attacked	20 (42%)	12 (26%)
Sexually assaulted	25 (52%)	10 (22%)*
Threatened with a weapon	27 (56%)	9 (20%)*
Stabbed	16 (33%)	1 (2%)*
Shot	4 (8%)	1 (2%)

*$p < .05$.

Table 7-1 compares gang members' and nongang girls' exposure to a variety of violent acts and their experiences of victimization. Here young women were asked if they had ever witnessed or been the victim of a number of violent acts. As the table shows, young women in gangs were significantly more likely to report having seen physical violence involving weapons and also were significantly more likely to have been sexually assaulted, threatened with a weapon, and stabbed. In fact, the numbers are alarming. Two-thirds of the young women in gangs had actually witnessed at least one homicide in their lives, and 79 percent had seen someone shot. Over half of the gang girls had been sexually assaulted and threatened with a weapon, and fully one-third of them had been stabbed. There were no significant differences between gang girls in Columbus and St. Louis. However, a larger percentage of girls in St. Louis reported witnessing shootings (89 percent versus 67 percent in Columbus) and killings (74 percent and 52 percent, respectively), and more young women in St. Louis (41 percent versus 24 percent in Columbus) had been stabbed.

Young women in St. Louis (but unfortunately not in Columbus) were also asked how old they were the first time these violent acts occurred. Nearly half (46 percent) of the girls who had seen an attack, guns shot, and someone shot in their presence had witnessed these events for the first time prior to their gang involvement.[5] In addition, 56 percent reported witnessing a drive-by shooting for the first time before they joined their gang. Likewise, over half (54 percent) had been attacked before they became a gang member, and two-thirds had been sexually assaulted before they joined the gang. Other acts of violence were more likely to occur after they joined the gang. Of young women who had witnessed a stabbing, 81 percent reported this happened for the first time after they joined their gang; 84 percent first witnessed a homicide after they joined their gang. In addition, 87 percent were threatened with a weapon after they joined, and 91 percent first were stabbed after they became gang-involved. Most of the violence they reported occurred in their neighborhoods. It is clear that these young women were growing up in volatile environments, as witnessed by the amount of violence they were routinely exposed to as children. Nonetheless, gang involvement itself increased their exposure to violence—specifically to witnessing lethal violence and being victims of weapons threats and knife assaults.

It appears, then, that gang involvement raises the risk of particular sorts of victimization, specifically those kinds of violence that are indicative of girls' gang activities. As I described in Chapter 6, the vast majority of young women described confrontations with rival gang members that involved either fists or knives, but not guns. Thus it is not surprising that only a handful of girls had been shot, while a sizeable minority had been stabbed. In fact, of the four young women who reported having been shot (three in Columbus, one in St. Louis), two of these were accidental shootings that occurred when they were children. All four had been shot by young men. Again, these findings are indicative of the gendered nature of weapons use and also of weapons assaults within gangs.

Before I move on, sexual assault merits comment. In all, twenty-five gang girls had been sexually assaulted (thirteen in Columbus and twelve in St. Louis) a total of thirty-five times. Seven girls had been sexually assaulted multiple times, including two who had been molested by the same family member more than once and five who had been raped on more than one occasion by different people. For instance, Heather had been sexually assaulted by her grandfather, her mother's boyfriend's brother, her uncle, and an acquaintance.

As I described in Chapter 3 and as Heather's example illustrates, most of the sexual victimization young women reported occurred in the context of their families. In all, twenty-three of the thirty-five incidents described (66 percent) were committed by family members or men whom young women were exposed to through their families. Eight of these assaults were committed by immediate family members (e.g., girls' fathers, brothers, and in one case her mother). Eight were committed by extended family (e.g., Heather's grandfather, girls' cousins and uncles), and seven were committed by individuals that young women came into contact with through their families. For instance, Tamika was raped by her stepfather's brother, Vikkie by her mother's boyfriend's friend, Yolanda by her uncle's friend, and Brittany by her aunt's boyfriend.

Of the twelve sexual assaults not involving family, seven young women were raped by acquaintances or friends, including Sonita, who was raped by a member of her gang; three were raped by strangers, and two by boyfriends. As I noted earlier, most girls in St. Louis who were sexually assaulted had been raped or molested before they joined their gangs. While I did not specifically ask this question of girls in Columbus, many of the sexual assaults they described also appeared to have occurred when they were younger, particularly those involving family. On the whole, the gang context did not seem to increase girls' risk of sexual assault in the ways that it increased their risk of other violent crime. Instead, they were at tremendous risk for sexual assault in other arenas of their lives, and perhaps saw the gang as a space of relative shelter from the sexual aggressors around them. However, as I will discuss later, this is not to suggest that sexual assaults within gangs did not occur or that other forms of sexual exploitation were not present—forms that girls were less likely to recognize or classify as sexual assault.

Table 7-2 further explores the relationship of gang members' victimization risk and involvement in delinquency. I ran bivariate correlations between the frequency of victimization and exposure to violence (measured as never, once, a few times, many times) and the frequency of serious offending and crack sales (measured as the number of times young women reported having committed these offenses in the last six months). Here serious offending includes stealing items valued between $50 and $100 and over $100, stealing a car, attacking someone with a weapon or with the intent to seriously injure them, participating in a gang fight, and committing a robbery.[6] As this table shows, frequent involvement in serious delinquency is significantly correlated with a number of types of victimization and exposure to violence, including having been threatened with a weapon and stabbed and having witnessed guns shot, stabbings, shootings, drive-bys, and homicides. Frequent involvement in crack sales is correlated with having been stabbed, seen guns fired, and witnessed drive-by shootings.

Table 7-2 Correlations between Frequency of Victimization, Serious Offending, and Crack Sales among Gang Members

	Frequency of Serious Offending	Frequency of Crack Sales
Frequency of Exposure to Violence		
Seen attack	.181	.170
Seen sexual assault	.281	−.111
Seen stabbing	.523*	.084
Seen guns shot	.333*	.362*
Seen someone shot	.354*	.137
Seen drive-by shooting	.309*	.482*
Seen someone killed	.321*	.235
Frequency of Victimization		
Attacked	−.177	.034
Sexually assaulted	−.204	−.219
Threatened with a weapon	.490*	.100
Stabbed	.445*	.535*
Shot	−.056	−.143

*$p < .05$.

I noted in Chapter 6 that young women who were involved in serious crime tended either to engage in a range of serious offending or to specialize in crack sales. Although I can only report simple bivariate relationships here, my findings suggest that girls' patterns of offending shape their exposure to violence. Those girls involved in serious offending appear more likely to be exposed to a wider variety of violent acts than are girls who limit their routine offending to crack sales. Although young women involved in regular crack sales were clearly involved in street life, they were less likely than girls involved in a range of serious offending to have witnessed stabbings, shootings, and homicides or to have been threatened with a weapon. These findings imply that there needs to be further exploration of the various types of delinquent acts that gang members may be involved in and of the ways that this participation shapes their risk of victimization and exposure to violence.

Much of the violence that gang members engage in is targeted at rival gang members or other individuals involved in street life. Likewise, with the notable exception of sexual assault, the bulk of girls' exposure to violence came from both their gang involvement and from spending time on the streets around their neighborhoods. In fact, 36 percent of the incidents of violence girls said they witnessed were committed by their friends and fellow gang members. An additional 19 percent was committed by acquaintances, 7 percent by relatives, and 6 percent by known rival gang members. Finally, 32 percent of the violent acts girls witnessed were committed either by people they didn't know or by individuals they were unable to identify (e.g., drive-by shootings), though the bulk of these acts occurred around the girls' neighborhoods.

Not surprisingly, when young women described who physically attacked, threatened, or stabbed them, the majority (thirty-eight of the sixty-seven incidents described, or 57 percent) said it was rival gang members or acquaintances they didn't get along with. Nine were assaulted by friends or boyfriends, five by family members.[7] An additional one-fifth of the incidents girls described were committed by people they didn't know, again mostly around the neighborhood. The irony of gang involvement is that although many young women suggest one thing they get out of gang membership is a sense of protection,[8] gang membership itself means exposure to certain kinds of victimization risk and even a willingness to be victimized. In the next sections, I explore this contradiction further, examining in particular the ways that victimization risk appears to be shaped by gender.

GANGS, PROTECTION, AND RISK

Because intergang rivalries and delinquency are important elements of gang activities, some level of victimization risk is an expected part of gang life. As I've discussed in previous chapters, members recognized that they may be the target of rival gang members and were expected to "be down" for their gang at those times, even when it meant being physically hurt. In fact, as I have described, initiation rituals and internal rules within gangs were structured in ways that individuals were expected to submit and be exposed to violence. Young women's descriptions of the qualities they valued in members revealed the extent to which being able to handle violence was deemed an important part of successful gang involvement. Recall that members were expected to be tough, able to fight and to engage in criminal activities, and also to be loyal to the group and willing to put themselves at risk for it. Gang initiations were deemed a measure of these qualities, since they typically involved the individual submitting to a beating at the hands of the gang's members or the commission of a relatively serious crime.

However, despite the violence that was a structured and expected part of gang membership, many young women described their gang involvement as providing a sense of empowerment. Young women in both cities focused on the camaraderie of having a group of friends, as Lisa said, who "got my back," and also on the sense of self that developed from constructing an identity as "hard" or, as Leslie said, as "Miss Bad Butt." Erica explained, "It's like you put that intimidation in somebody. . . . They don't bother you." Neoka concurred, "I know I have somebody behind my back at all times." Perhaps because of some St. Louis girls' greater involvement in the drug trade, they also mentioned the empowerment that came from economic self-sufficiency and independence. Toni said, "[I] can't go home and be like, 'Mama I need these new shoes that's coming out' because they cost like a bill [hundred] forty-nine. I'll get it myself. If I need these shoes I'm gonna sit outside all night and try to make enough money to go out and get the shoes." And Shawanda explained:

> I'm independent. I don't depend on nobody. I mean nobody, my mom, nobody, my man, nobody, nobody give me no money, no nothing. That's one thing about me, I'll go out and hustle before I got to think I got to sit around and wait on some nigger to give me some money. . . . I'm independent, I don't depend on nobody but myself. I make sure I make my own money. Just like I don't see my mama or my daddy at all hardly and I ain't nothing but sixteen. But it's cool.

An important element of the empowerment that gangs provided was that which came from having a group of people that could offer protection, back-up, and retaliation—necessities for success in the drug trade, but also in negotiating the ins and outs of daily life on the streets. As Tonya explained, "Shoot, you ever need to fool with anybody, you can call your homies up and they'll just be there, they won't mess with you or whatever. If you ever get hurt, in any danger, need a ride, they be there to come pick you up." In particular, many young women in both cities articulated a specifically gendered sense of protection that they felt as a result of being a member of a group that was predominantly male. Gangs operate within larger social milieus that are characterized by gender inequality and sexual exploitation. This is clearly evidenced by widespread sexual abuse young women had experienced outside of their gangs. In part, they saw the gang as a refuge from these dangers.

Being in a gang with young men meant at least a semblance of protection from, and retaliation against, predatory men in the social environment. Heather noted, "You feel more secure when, you know, a guy's around protectin' you." She explained that as a gang member, because "you get protected by guys . . . not as many people mess with you." Likewise, Tonya said her older brother, who was in her gang, watched over her and his girlfriend. "Me and my partner Mimi . . . Mimi was my brother's girlfriend and I was my brother's sister so we always had protection over us." Rhonda said that often people didn't mess with her "'cause they know if they try to take advantage of the girls then it gonna be a problem." Brittany said members of her gang "look after me like I'm they little sister." She said, "If somebody disrespect me they'll correct 'em." Being in a gang, Erica said, young men "don't look at you as a doormat so much." Of the young men in her gang, she explained, "They're like protectors over us. When it comes to girls in the set, they're like our protectors."

Other young women concurred, saying that male gang members would retaliate against specific acts of violence against girls in the gang. As I noted in Chapter 6, Pam lamented that "some dudes, they be tripping with you 'cause they know you from the other side and they be trying to slap you or something." When this occurred, she said, "You don't want to say nothing to no dudes 'cause you know you can't beat them or nothing. So you be like, 'Yeah wait 'til my boys come, they gonna get you.'" Likewise, Shandra explained: "The guys in rival gangs, they'll disrespect you to no end. . . . Say like one of the females get into it with the guys that's not from her gang, then the guys from her gang, they gonna jump on that gang for messing with their homegirl." Nikkie had a friend who was raped by a rival gang member, and she said, "It was a Crab [Crip] that raped my girl in Miller Ales, and um, they was ready to kill him." Finally, Keisha explained, "If I got beat up by a guy, all I gotta do is go tell one of the niggers, you know what I'm sayin'? Or one of the guys, they'd take care of it."

Young women also recognized that they brought particular benefits to the young men in the gang. In particular, they felt their presence could shield suspicion from the actions of their gang. Vashelle described this with regard to her drug-selling in Chapter 6. Because the police targeted young men in their crackdowns on drug sales, she felt she could sell with less fear of apprehension than young men. Likewise, Tonya explained:

> Like when we in a car, if a girl and a dude in a car, the police tend not to trip
> off of it. When they look to see if a car been stolen, police just don't trip off of
> it. But if they see three or four niggers in that car, the police stop you auto-

matically, boom. . . . When my brother was gonna be locked up, the police was looking at my cousin Janeeta, she [was in the car with him]. She got a nice little body and face. He let my brother go. . . . He was trying to make on her, you know what I'm saying. Little ways that we got to get them out of stuff sometimes, we can get them out of stuff that dudes couldn't do, you know what I'm saying. So they need us girls, they need us.

The irony is that while young women viewed the gang as offering protection, being a gang member also involved a willingness to open oneself up to the possibility of being victimized. It may be useful to understand this contradiction by thinking about how gang-related violence differs from other forms of victimization in young women's lives. Gang violence, as I have discussed, is governed by rules and expectations. As such it doesn't involve the same kind of vulnerability that being on the streets without a gang might entail in high-crime neighborhoods. Moreover, in principle it provides a contrast to many young women's previous experiences of victimization in their home and family lives, where many found themselves vulnerable and unable to control the actions of the adults who victimized them. Gang violence is structured violence.[9] Youths can't necessarily predict when an encounter with rival gang members will escalate into violence, but they know which situations put them at risk, that there are known methods for response, and that they aren't in it alone. Because of its structured nature, victimization risk within gangs may be perceived as more palatable for many young women. In particular, the gendered nature of the streets and of girls' vulnerability elsewhere may make the empowerment available through gang involvement an appealing alternative to the individualized vulnerability they otherwise face.

Moreover, as I mentioned in Chapter 6, young women could use gender within gangs to shield and control their exposure to gang violence, at least to a certain extent. Because status hierarchies in most of their gangs were male-dominated, young women actually seemed to have greater flexibility in their gang activities than young men did.[10] Young women had fewer expectations placed on them—by both female and male peers—with regard to involvement in criminal activities such as gun use, drug sales, and other serious crimes. As I discussed in Chapter 6, the majority of girls in both cities were not routinely involved in serious crime and drug sales, and few young women used guns. These limitations in their activities, both imposed by young men and by choice, functioned to decrease their exposure to gang-related victimization risk compared to more seriously delinquent gang youths because they were able to avoid activities likely to place them in danger. Erica explained, "Sometimes when they fight, I mean, you don't really expect a girl to be like a guy when it comes to fighting. So that's good for us. We don't have to worry about that."

Recall from Chapter 6 that young men's perceptions of girls as lesser members typically functioned to keep girls from being targets of serious violence at the hands of rival young men, who instead left routine confrontations with rival female members to the girls in their own gang. Young men's main concern was with rival gang males. Shawanda reiterated, "A nigger and another nigger, it ain't gonna be no talk thing, you know what I'm saying, it's just some static [confrontation] or something. But a nigger and a girl, no."

In addition, the girls I interviewed suggested that, in comparison with young men, young women were less likely to resort to serious violence, particularly gun violence, when confronting rivals. Thus, when girls' routine confrontations were more likely to be female-on-female rather than male-on-female, girls' risk of serious victimization was lessened further. As Vashelle explained, "Most girls, they ain't gonna do nothing for real but try to stab you, cut you or something like that. As far as coming by shooting and stuff like a dude would do, no." Getting stabbed, while a serious assault, is much less likely to be lethal than getting shot.

In accepting that young men were more central members of the gang, at least when it came to certain activities, young women could more easily participate in gangs without putting themselves in jeopardy. They could involve themselves more in the routine, everyday activities of the gang, like hanging out, listening to music, and smoking bud. As Tyra explained, "if you wanted to do what the boys did, you did it. But if you didn't, you just sit back and smoke your blunt or something." Of course, some young women didn't choose to "just sit back," and as Table 7-2 indicated, those who chose to be involved in serious delinquency also were more likely to encounter serious gang violence. Young women who made this choice recognized what they were getting themselves into. As Diane noted, "It's dangerous, you know, bein' involved with violence, you're gonna see violence and all that stuff."

The Dangers of Gang Life

Young women were in agreement, despite their discussions of the protections offered by the gang or their attempts to avoid risky behaviors, that being in a gang posed dangers to their well-being. Because of the gendered nature of gang activities, on the whole, girls didn't see themselves as facing the same threats as young men. But they also recognized that being with other gang members increased their chances of being at the wrong place at the wrong time, and some also discussed the gender-specific risks they faced as a result of perceptions of female gang members as weak.

Young women were most concerned about their safety when they were alone or had the potential to be outnumbered. Brittany explained: "You got to always look behind your back. Have to always worry about, 'Hope this dude don't run up on me,' 'Hope this person don't run up on me.' You just in hell, always looking behind your back." In a group context, she felt more secure. "When they sitting in a park, believe me, it's people all around that just got people's backs, they just look out for each other." She said she also tried to avoid violence by staying away from the gang when they were engaged in risky activities. "When they do stuff I scatter, I ain't nowhere around. When they do their little dirt, Brittany is at home."

Other young women also said they tried to avoid danger by keeping out of those activities that could lead to trouble. Keisha said, "I don't do nothin' like, I don't do nothin' to start nothin'." Her best advice on how to avoid danger was "don't let yourself get in a fucked up situation. You know what I'm sayin'? You know where to stop." Likewise, Lisa said, "I don't go into other territories. I be stayin' right there in mine." Yolanda expressed the same sentiment, saying gang involvement wasn't particularly dangerous for her "'cause we don't do nothing, we don't go around fighting over no gang stuff." Notably, she was in an all-female gang that didn't have ongoing rivalries with mixed-gender gangs in St. Louis.

Likewise, Jennifer was a member of the Gangster Girlz in Columbus, and she believed her gang's activities lessened their risks of danger. In her case, this was not because her gang wasn't involved in crime but because she felt they were better organized, more careful, and also didn't let gang rivalries interfere. She explained, "We're not as sloppy as the Bloods and Crips and stuff. . . . Like Bloods, if they do somethin', they're gonna write their name on the wall. That, I mean, what point is that? You're tellin' on yourselves." Her gang didn't adopt colors or symbolism. Consequently, she explained, "If we's walkin' down the street, you couldn't tell we was in a gang. You'd think we were just a group of girls going to the mall or something." In contrast, she said other gangs were "sloppy" and "foolish": "You know how boys are. They just, especially teenage boys. They're all out to get attention, see who could do the most dirt. Who can do the most girls, and stuff like that. That's really what all them are about. That's why they're so sloppy."

Part of young women's concern about violence was of running into rival gang members, but it was also because many of them lived in dangerous neighborhoods where threat was ever-present. Rhonda explained, "I worry about [violence] all the time and it's like, violence is gonna be here until the day everybody kill one another, until God comes down from heaven and takes over." Tyra agreed: "Growing up on the North Side [of St. Louis] . . . everywhere you look, you turn around and somebody is getting killed. I don't care what nobody say, I think the North Side is worse than any side." Erica felt that living in the shelter care facility where she resided in Columbus helped to minimize her risk. On the streets, she said, "You gotta live your life day to day, everyday, watching your back. I think if I was out there I'd be really spooked. I mean, out there. But, since I'm in here, I mean, there are no Bloods that actually live on this campus." Though she AWOL'ed from the campus regularly, she said sometimes it was "scary" because the facility was located in a Bloods neighborhood:

ERICA: I think it would be kind of scary for two girls to be out walking around by themselves out on the streets, especially at night. In a rival gang area by, just them two by themselves. I think it would.

JM: So that usually doesn't happen?

ERICA: Nnhnn. Not supposed to. Now, when we AWOL from here, we have no choice. I mean . . .

JM: Yeah, I was gonna say . . .

ERICA: We have no choice. I mean, there's four of us, or sometimes just two that AWOL. But usually what happens with us, we run and we meet up at [a nearby housing project]. Or we'll have someone come pick us up at the entrance.

JM: And how far away is the [housing project]?

ERICA: It's about, oh, about fifteen minutes from here.

JM: So it's a pretty good walk.

ERICA: Yeah. We have to, we can't go down, we don't go down [the main street exiting campus]. We just walk straight up. But it's, I mean, it's scary sometimes.

JM: Are there any Bloods around here?

ERICA: Uh, yeah. There's some that live on [the main street] actually.

JM: Which is why you don't go down there?

ERICA: Mmhmm.

JM: So what kind of precautions do you take?

ERICA: As far as running from here?

JM: Yeah.

ERICA: When we're out and we know that we're in a rival gang area like [the street exiting campus] we don't wear our flags. We won't wear 'em. Because there're only two of us, and if somethin' were to break out, I'm sure we can't take all of 'em.

JM: Right. You'd be outnumbered.

ERICA: So, we just, we don't wear our flags until we get out with the rest of the set, then we put 'em back on. But, when we leave here we take 'em off.

While part of Erica's concern was about being a young woman alone in a dangerous neighborhood, she also recognized that gangs exacerbated the threat that was already present by making young women known targets when they were with or displaying their affiliation with their gang. Likewise, Brandi explained, "Sometimes you might be walkin' down the street with your flag out of your pocket or somethin' like that. And, they might, they might, like, you might get shot. Or, they might be shootin' another person and shoot you." Tonya concurred, saying she worried about "sitting outside and some Crips come in shooting at you or going down to the corner and they gonna gank [attack] you and shoot at you." Leslie said that even though she tried to avoid danger by not "doin' all that they was doin'," nonetheless she recognized that, being in the gang, "You can get shot when you're sittin' on the porch. I mean, you can get hurt anywhere you are, you can still get hurt. It doesn't matter where you are or what you're doin' you can get hurt." As Crystal said, when "you got one gang member that got a problem with another person, they'll shoot at the whole set or whatever. . . . A whole bunch of them will start shooting at people that got nothing to do with it."

As these descriptions suggest, young women did not fear being the specific target of rival gang members who were shooting. Instead, they recognized the danger of being shot as a result of being in a group context where someone opened fire. As I discussed in Chapter 6, young women believed that gunfire was the purview of male-on-male violence. They ran the risk of stray bullets striking them if a rival gang opened fire. However, on the whole they didn't feel being in the gang was life-threatening in the ways it was for young men, who were more likely to run the risk of being specific targets of a rival gang's hit. The vast majority of gang homicides involved young men, and the young women I talked to were clearly aware of this. In fact, in an analysis of gender and gang homicide in St. Louis, based on police case files, Scott Decker and I found support for their beliefs. Women were just 8 percent of gang homicide victims, versus 17 percent of nongang homicide victims. Moreover, the vast majority of gang homicides involving female victims were shootings in which the woman was not the intended target.[11]

As a consequence, when young women talked about gang homicides and shootings, they talked mostly about the worry and sorrow of having young men they cared about killed in gang violence. Marie noted, "My partner, my best friend, he got shot, was sixteen years old. He was a Blood. He shouldn't have gone out like that." As I mentioned in Chapter 3, Lisa described worrying about her older brother, the leader of her set who was very active in gang crime. She explained, "My brother, when he was little, he was a little geeky little kid that wore glasses. But now he's like, you know, and I don't understand it but uh, I wish he was still a little kid that wore glasses." Three of Tamika's male friends had been killed. She was present when one of her partners was shot at a local mall in Columbus. Members of her Crips gang were hanging with members of a Folks gang when the incident occurred:

We was all kickin' it and everything. And they seen this Blood right, there's a whole bunch of Crips and Folks and we seen about five or six Bloods. And, you know, Chaos [the young man who was killed], Chaos just, we's all playin'. We's like, "Oooh, look at all that little B-town [bloods] right there." And we was walkin' through the mall like, "It's C-town for life, it's C-town." And then the dude looked at Chaos and then Chaos was like, "What, what?" Like that. And he was like, "Yeah, you marked. I got you marked. I got you marked." He's like, "I'm gonna catch you." He's like, "Don't let me catch you slippin'." So then, you know, um, Chaos was goin', OK. Then we was all [at] the pizza shop. Chaos was comin' down the escalators to see us and old dude was comin' up. He was like, and him and his boy was like, "Yeah, that's that punk ass nigger that tried to, tried to gaffle [jump] me." And he shot him. I was like, "Aw, man." And then everybody just started shootin'. I felt, I thought I was gonna die that day. I really did. I was like. . . . Then I was like, oh, man, I just started crying 'cause I ain't know what to do, you know? I'm like, 'cause I ain't think, you know, I tell, I tell my brother and them, I was like, you know, "I ain't think he was gonna come back like that." You know, I thought, you know, no matter what in life, I was like, "I know he's gonna come back, you know, y'all might, Chaos might get jumped or somethin'." I didn't think he was gonna come back like that, though. Shoot him. I'm like, "Dag!"

In addition, Tamika had a friend Tyrell who had only recently been shot, and she described making trips to his grave. She said, "When I heard Tyrell got shot and I knew, and I heard who did it, I ain't gonna lie. I wanted to shoot him so bad. But I ain't have it in my heart." Monica was also friends with Tyrell. She said:

The worse thing about [gang life] is, like, when you get a call sayin', "Well, your boy got hurt." Like that. Because my boy Tyrell got shot a while, well, not even a while back. This is like two or three weeks ago. It hurt me so bad because this is by another Crip. . . . They was beefin' about somethin' that happen between them. So Doughboy shot Tyrell so Tyrell's set went shootin' at Doughboy. I mean, and it was Crip against Crip and that hurt me so bad. I was like, "It ain't even supposed to be like this."

Their friend Tyrell was "shot in the head." Monica commented, "We went to his funeral. He didn't even look like the same person. One side of his head was just all swoll up and he didn't even look like the same person. But that's the worst thing, when you hear about one of your people gettin' hurt." There typically hadn't been fights between Crips sets in Columbus where Monica was a gang member, though there were fights between these groups in St. Louis. I asked her whether this recent incident would likely change the climate, especially since Tyrell's set was retaliating. She said no, because Tyrell's set was "just [after] Doughboy." Further, she explained that "Doughboy's set was mad at him for doin' that. 'Cause they said you don't shoot your own cuz. You handle that. That's family. You handle that. And his set was mad at him so he don't got nowhere to turn."

Vashelle also reported that her cousin had recently been shot, and she described losing another male friend as well. She explained:

[My cousin] just got shot about four weeks [before our interview], paralyzed from the waist down. Doctor told him he wasn't gonna never walk no more. Then my little partner Cain, he got killed on the South Side. . . . Shot him in the head three times. . . . My cousin, he got shot over some gang stuff. My partner Cain got shot over a dice game.

Vashelle said she considered pulling out of gang life "because of all the stuff that's been happening as far as my cousin and all that." In addition, as a result of all she had witnessed, Vashelle said she had become desensitized to violence and was somewhat concerned because she no longer had an emotional reaction to it; if she did react, she recognized her emotions as inappropriate:

VASHELLE: If I see somebody get hurt or something I wouldn't care. I don't know, I got a little messed up attitude I guess because I like seeing people die. I like seeing people suffer too as long as it's not nobody close to me. I love to see somebody get hurt.

RB: Have you seen people get . . .

VASHELLE: Yeah. It excites me, bring joy into my, I don't know what it is, I just got a messed up attitude, I just got a messed up mind too. I need to talk to a counselor for real I think that's what I need. But if something happen to somebody close to my family I'll be ready to straight up hurt somebody but if I see something happen to somebody else, I feel like, so?

RB: Is there a particular incident that you can remember that made you feel like, so?

VASHELLE: Yeah. Cause my little partners be killing people and stuff. It don't bother me. I be like, yeah. I think that's why stuff keep on happening to people in my family I guess. But me, myself, I don't care about nobody but myself, that's how I feel, and my little brothers and sisters. As far as somebody off the street, I could care less about them. One of my homies get killed or something I'll trip off of it, but as far as somebody being from another hood, anybody else getting killed, I'll just look at it like, so?

RB: Is there a particular incident that you can remember somebody getting hurt or somebody suffering and you were there?

VASHELLE: Yeah, we was sitting down on the porch. It was like a little vacant house. Like it's all bushes right here and you can't see for real. As you are coming down the street you just see all bushes. It's like a house pushed all the way to the back. My partner ran up into the house one day and drug the little dude up out of there. A little Crip dude. But I thought it was stupid. But once I seen the little dude get killed it was like funny to me. I didn't care.

RB: How did they kill him?

VASHELLE: Drag him up out of the house and shot him in the head.

RB: Right in front of you?

VASHELLE: Right in front of me.

RB: How did you feel?

VASHELLE: I didn't feel nothing. I didn't care. It made me laugh, that's what I did. I like watching people get hurt. Not people close to me. I be trying to slow down that's all cause something could happen to me.

Vashelle had not engaged in such violence herself. She said, "I ain't never hurt nobody seriously like that. I done beat up somebody bad, you know, jumped on somebody bad, me and a couple of my partners, but as far as straight killing somebody, no." Although she did not describe violence within her family, she said her pathway into the gang, which she joined at age eleven, came from brothers, sisters, uncles, and cousins in gangs and from growing up in a neighborhood with gangs. She said she wasn't close to her mother and didn't know her father, but she was otherwise vague about life in her family. To have developed such a callous attitude about death and suffering, I suspect her vagueness was covering aspects of her early life she chose not to recount to us.

Importantly, not all young women shared Vashelle's attitude. In fact, as I described in Chapter 6, many young women were ambivalent about, and even morally troubled by, the serious violence associated with gang life, even when they were caught up in it themselves. As Vikkie explained, "Being a Blood is hard. Half of the stuff you did want to do and half of the stuff you really didn't want to do and half the stuff you did want to do. But half the stuff I know sometimes I did not want to do . . . because half the stuff I thought was wrong." This ambivalence is likely felt by young women and young men alike; however, my hunch is that young women have greater latitude in acting on their ambivalence by avoiding serious gang violence—but at a cost.

GIRLS' DEVALUATION AND GENDER-SPECIFIC RISK

The previous section has provided a general discussion of the dangers associated with gang life for girls, with an eye toward the ways gender can function as a protective factor for girls. However, as I mentioned earlier, young women also recognized the gender-specific risks they faced in the gang. For instance, because status hierarchies within gangs were male-dominated, young women frequently had to contend with the perception of them as weak. As Chantell described in Chapter 6, rival gang members often "think that you're more of a punk, or that there's a hole in you . . . that they can go right through you. That you just another punk." Dionne concurred: "People from other gangs, the dudes and stuff, they think that we punks 'cause we girls and we can't protect ourselves and stuff like that."

While on the one hand this typically meant that rival males didn't target girls for gang retaliations, there were occasions when young women were targeted specifically because they were seen as weak. Marie explained that sometimes a male would "tak[e] a female just because it's a female. He think she can't do nothing because she's a female." As I discussed in Chapter 6, some young women said it was more dangerous for girls out on the streets, particularly when they were selling drugs, because as Shandra described, "Girls just quicker to get robbed. . . . It's more dangerous for them because the guys tend to think that they are easier targets than another guy." Likewise, Pam explained that rival males will "trip on us before they trip with the dudes because they know they got more ammunition and stuff like that so they don't even trip with them. They just know we gonna fight with our hands and they'll try to pull something on us."

Young women also faced sexual derogation at the hands of rival males. Shiree, a member of an all-female gang, said that while her gang didn't necessarily have rivals, they still faced "being disrespected, getting called whores and bitches and stuff or dykes and you know getting jumped on by the boys . . . getting raped." She said because "the boys off in they own little world, they think girls can't be about it like them." Of the mixed-gender gang also in her neighborhood, she described, "sometimes we do [get along] and sometimes we don't. It all depends on if they start set tripping and disrespecting. Because of our being called N.W.O, they be calling us N.W. Hos. They be, 'Look at them hos.' That's when we get into it."

The difference, when gang violence (or verbal assaults like Shiree described) was male-on-female rather than male-on-male, was that these assaults were likely to be sexual in nature. Recall the young woman's discussion (in Chapter 6) of the gang rape her partners committed in her presence. She was clear that "we coulda just shot her . . . but they went farther than that." In fact, the incident really shook her up, in part because it made her aware of her own vulnerability:

> It scared me. I don't never want anythin' like that to happen to me. And I pray to God that it doesn't. 'Cause God said that whatever you sow you're gonna reap. And like, you know, beatin' a girl up and then sittin' there watchin' somethin' like that happen, well Jesus, that could come back on me. I mean, I felt, I really felt sorry for her even though my boy was in the hospital and was really hurt.

I asked her whether it bothered her to know that her friends could viciously rape a young woman, and though she said it didn't, she was clearly torn between her loyalty to her fellow gang members and her identification with the young woman as another female:

> Did it bother me that it was my friends doin' it to a female? Not really, no. Just because of the fact of what she did. If it was any other female I think it would have bothered me. I think I woulda had to say something. But since it was her and I know the situation. You gotta look at the situation we was in. I was in the wrongs anyways, I had just gotten done beatin' the girl up. Beatin' her bad up. So what am I gonna do? "Oh stop! Oh stop!" That'd be such a hypocrite of me. And they'd be lookin' like, "Stop what? She wasn't tellin' her, the [rivals] to stop when old boy was gettin' beat in his face and he was gettin' slammed and you know when he was doin' all that." So basically I had no place to say nothin'. And how I feel about it is, I feel that it was the most brutal thing I've ever seen in my life and pray to God nothin' ever happens to me like that. And I pray I don't have to witness anything like that [again].

While it is true that this gang rape was an unusual event, this does not take away from the fact that it was a gendered act that took place specifically because, in the eyes of young men, girls are not perceived as equals.

The young men who gang raped this girl were not just enacting vengeance on a rival but on a *female*. Had the victim been an "equal," the attack would have remained a physical one. In fact, young men we interviewed in a related study of male gang members' perceptions of gender told much the same story. Although they typically didn't target female gang members for attack, when they did the attack was often sexual in nature.

A number of young men suggested that because females were perceived as easier targets than males, young women were at risk for being kidnapped and sexually assaulted by rival gang members specifically when they were looking to send a message or retaliate against *male* gang members. Although apparently rare, young men saw these attacks as a particularly effective form of retaliation against rival males because of the emotional turmoil they created. Will explained: "If the boy Crip think that the boy Blood more tougher than the girl, he might go off on the girl just to hurt the other gang member, see what I'm saying. It be the same way if somebody catch your cousin, it's gonna hurt you more than killing you, that's your cousin. You gonna have the same feelings."

Describing such incidents, Lamont said, "Say my homeboys, when we need to, gang members will kidnap women who you associate with to get information or even to send a message. They won't kidnap no male, they'll kidnap a female to send a message, beat her up, rape her, do whatever to send a message." Thomas agreed, "The girls, more stuff can happen to her. Like another gang might try to kidnap a girl or something like that and anything can happen then." Travis described the same scenario:

> If she in a gang and I know her, say I'm in this one gang and I'm on her, I'll probably know her brother and I'll know she in a gang. Like if I can't get to him, and you in a gang, the same gang, I'm gonna get to you first. You more easier to get to, you a female. . . . We just snatch them up real quick 'cause we got more power over them. You can tie them up or something, stab 'em, shoot 'em, whatever you want.

In fact, three young women in the current sample—two nongang girls and one gang member—reported that they had been gang-raped by a group of gang members. In addition, several months after our interviews in St. Louis were complete, there was a brutal gang-related assault on a woman that received quite a bit of local news coverage. The woman was apparently not a gang member but was associated with a local Gangster Disciples gang.[12] A group of gang members pistol-whipped the woman, beat and sodomized her with a broomstick, cut her and poured bleach into the open wounds, and poured boiling water over her head. She suffered second and third degree burns over her face and head. Police said one version of the events they heard was that the woman was tortured because the group was angry that she had done a striptease for another group of men. Notably, four of the eleven members said to be involved in the torture were women.[13]

That young women were involved in the assault is terrible, but not entirely surprising. I described in previous chapters that my work, as well as that of other scholars, documents many gang girls' adherence to a sexual double standard and their repudiation of young women whom they perceive as behaving in sexually inappropriate ways. As I will discuss further later, many of the young women I spoke with held quite negative attitudes about women, and these came to bear in such assaults on other young women. Again, the brutal attack on this woman was an extremely unusual event, but it sheds light on the ways that gang loyalties intersect with beliefs about women to make such atrocities possible.

Gender Dynamics and Victimization Risk within the Gang

Much of the gender-specific violence I've discussed thus far has been tied to intergang rivalries and conflict, and I've noted that all indications are that these assaults, while especially brutal, were relatively rare. Another layer of girls' mistreatment in gangs was more routinized, that is, various forms of abuse they faced at the hands of their own gang peers. As I described in Chapter 6, many girls didn't participate in serious gang crime, not just because they chose to avoid it, but also because they were excluded by young men. Although girls' exclusion from some gang crime was framed as protective (and thus likely reduced their victimization vis-à-vis rival gangs), it also served to perpetuate the devaluation of female members as less significant to the gang—as weak, not as tough, true, or down for the gang as male members. Describing the masculine basis of status hierarchies within her gang, Shawanda surmised, "They dudes, so there ain't none of them girls that they look up to." Likewise, Sheila noted, "The dudes think they run it all."

Within their gangs as well, some young women found the perception of them as weak a frustrating one. Marie said the males in her gang "think that you can't do the same things as a male can. . . . You have to show them that you can." Beliefs that girls were weaker than boys meant that young women had a harder time proving that they were serious in their commitment to the gang. Diane explained: "A female has to show that she's tough. A guy can just, you can just look at him. But a female, she's gotta show. She's gotta go out and do some dirt. She's gotta go whip some girl's ass, shoot somebody, rob somebody, or something. To show that she is tough." In terms of gender-specific victimization risk within the gang, the devaluation of young women meant several things. It could lead to the mistreatment and victimization of girls by members of their own gang, especially when they didn't have specific male protection in the gang (e.g., a brother or boyfriend) or when they weren't able to stand up for themselves to male members.

This was exacerbated by activities that led young women to be viewed as sexually available. The most obvious example was the existence of "sexing-in"—having sexual relations with multiple male members of the gang—as an initiation practice. Other members of the gang, both male and female, viewed young women initiated in this way as promiscuous and sexually available, thus increasing their subsequent mistreatment. In addition, the stigma could extend to female members in general, creating a sexual devaluation with which all girls had to contend.

Connections to influential, high-status males shielded some girls from the more blatant mistreatment that other young women sometimes experienced, as did being someone, like Diane, who had proven herself as a qualified member by male standards. Describing a young woman in her gang with a lot of respect, Alecia said, "She fights dudes, she strong. . . . They say he-man or something, that's what they be calling her."[14] Monica had status and respect in her gang, both because she had proven herself through fights and criminal activities and because her older brothers were members of her set. In the following conversation, she contrasted her own treatment with that of another young woman in the gang, Andrea, whom I mentioned in Chapter 6.

MONICA: I am taken very seriously. Everybody knows what I am capable of and what I will and will not do. And they take me very seriously. I'm not tryin' to sound bad or nothin' but they, they really do. Nobody in my set disrespects me by callin' me a bitch or anything like that. And nobody in my set sit there while I'm around and talk about females like that or nothin' because they know I will get a little attitude with 'em. So I'm taken very seriously because they know what I'm all about.

JM: And do you think it has something to do with your relationship with your brothers?

MONICA: Yeah. I think it has a lot to do because they just be puttin' the other girls off. Like Andrea, man. Oh my God, they dog Andrea so bad. They like, "Bitch, go to the store." She like, "Alright I be right back."

JM: This is a girl in your set?

MONICA: Yes. She will go to the store and go and get them whatever they want and come back with it. If she don't get it right they be like, "Why you do that, bitch." I mean, and one dude even smacked her. And, I mean, and, I don't, I told my brother once. I was like, "Man, it ain't even like that. If you ever see someone tryin' to disrespect me like that or hit me, if you do not hit them or at least say somethin' to them, I will tell my dad. I'll be threatenin' them with my dad all the time. I'll be like, "I'm gonna tell daddy on you all." And they know I will. So my brothers, they kinda watch out for me and it's, I mean, they don't overprotect me but they make sure that if I need them then I got 'em. It's like that.

JM: So, now, like other girls like this girl you said, Andrea, why does she let the guys treat her that way?

MONICA: Because she's stupid. No, seriously, because I don't, I guess she don't know no better. I guess she, I mean, she might be scared to say something. I don't know what that girl's problem is. But I tell her all the time. I'm like, "Andrea, if it was me, they would not do me like that. You need to start standing up for yourself." And she be like, "Alright. Whatever, whatever, whatever." And she don't never do it. I can't make her stand up for herself. And I'm not trying to get in the middle of what's goin' on with them. That's like gettin' in the middle of somebody's family business. You don't do that. So I'm not tryin' to get in the middle of it so I just let her, when I see it I let her know it. I be like, "Andrea, you need to stand up for yourself." She be like whatever and I see it happenin' again. I know that she ain't gonna take my advice so I stop givin' it to her. I just quit.

JM: Yeah. And how many other girls are in the set?

MONICA: About five or six I think. Five or six.

JM: And how are they treated?

MONICA: Andrea is the only one they treat really terrible. The other ones, I mean, they play around with everybody, but I don't know what it is about Andrea. 'Cause they know Andrea ain't gonna say nothin'. I think that's why they do Andrea like they do her. 'Cause they know that girl's not gonna say nothin'.

JM: And the other girls, if they tried that with them would they stand up to them?

MONICA: They never tried it with them, though. I mean, Snoop called Shawna a bitch one time and she went off. She just went off. Didn't nobody call her a bitch from then on. I mean, it's like that. If she wanted to get her respect she stand up and say somethin'. So I just put, I put that on her. They ain't gotta do her like that. But she don't gotta let them do her like that either.

It was both Monica's connection to her brothers and her ability to stand up for herself that allowed her to avoid being mistreated by the men in her gang. Andrea's fear of standing up for herself meant she was viewed as weak, thus her mistreatment was seen as partially deserved because she didn't exhibit the valued traits of toughness and a willingness to fight that would allow her to defend herself. What Monica speaks to, which is important to recognize, is the tremendous variation in girls' experiences within gangs. Some young women are able to carve a niche for themselves that puts them, if not exactly in the same standing as young men, at least on par in terms of their treatment. Other young women, like Andrea, are severely mistreated, and there is a range of experiences in between.

As Monica did, other young women would blame girls for their mistreatment, rather than holding the young men accountable. Sometimes young women's negative characterizations of supposed female traits like having big mouths or being troublemakers were used to justify their mistreatment.[15] Brittany said that "some girls . . . just talk too much and make the dudes just want to hit them in they mouth." Likewise, Keisha explained, "If the female goin' on so much, she gonna have to get her ass beat, she gonna have to suffer the consequence. But it's different for the guys. They know how our mouth is. We keep goin' and goin' and goin' until we push the limit." As I described in Chapter 5, Tonya recalled when "one of the dudes" in her gang assaulted his girlfriend in front of them. "She had been saying something, he just started whupping her outside the car, beating her all up, pushing on her head."

In fact, the handful of young women in the sample who were in all-female gangs said part of the reason they were in all-female rather than mixed-gender gangs was because of the mistreatment some young women experienced at the hands of male gang peers. Jennifer made this point, distinguishing between her female OG and the male leaders of mixed-gender sets:

> They're, it's like when they're in control they know it. So they're gonna take advantage of it. They like tell [girls to do] stupid things. Like, I know, for example, about a part of the Crip gang, the OG got mad at one of the members and um made her have sex with like five different guys, just 'cause he was mad at her about something, somethin' petty. Like with our OG, she's not like that.

Jennifer was not a member of a mixed-gender gang, so clearly her comments are coming from an outsider looking in. However, she did have a number of friends in mixed-gender gangs and members of her gang sometimes associated with these groups, giving her some basis for her interpretation. She commented again later in the interview, "Most of the girls that I've seen in different gangs, they have no respect for themselves. They're, they're too easily taken advantage of because they're with a boys' group."

Sexing-In and the Sexual Mistreatment of Girls in Gangs

The clearest example of some young women's mistreatment within mixed-gender gangs is the acceptance of sexing-in as an initiation practice. None of the young women we interviewed explicitly said they were sexed into their gangs, and only two in St. Louis—Brenda and Yolanda—gave vague descriptions alluding to having been sexed in, in Yolanda's case to a gang she was involved in before she joined N.W.O. As Erica noted, "If they have [been sexed in], they ain't saying nothing."[16] The reason for the silence had to do with the intense denigration that resulted from having been sexed in—something young women who were sexed in weren't fully aware of until it was too late. Tonya explained:

> Girls either get beat in or sexed in. When you a girl, you don't get no respect when you get sexed in, you don't get no respect. Only way you sell dope is you cop money and cop it yourself 'cause they don't give you no dope. *They tell you big lies, they tell you all kinds of stuff,* you don't get no respect [my emphasis].

In contrast, she said, "If you get beat in, you be like, 'Oh that's my nigger, that's my homey,' you be all proud. . . . If you do have sex with them, then you a wreck."

Getting sexed into the gang placed young women in a position that increased their risk of ongoing mistreatment at the hands of their gang peers. This included extensive verbal abuse and sometimes ongoing sexual abuse as well. Young women described girls who were sexed in as "nasty" and "hos" in Columbus, "wrecks" and "hood rats" in St. Louis. Asked to define what she meant by wreck, Shawanda explained, "They don't care about they body. They just let everybody get something off of them." Shandra said once a young woman was sexed into the gang, "After that they might want to have sex with you again. And if you tell them no or something like that then you might get put out of the gang or get taken out of the 'hood or whatever like that." Likewise, according to Keisha, "If you get sexed in, you have no respect. That means you have to go ho'in' for 'em; when they say you give 'em the pussy, you gotta give it to 'em. If you don't, you gonna get your ass beat." One young woman in her set was sexed in and Keisha observed that the girl "just do everything they tell her to do, like a dummy." Nikkie reported that two girls who were sexed into her set eventually quit hanging around with the gang because they were harassed so much:

> Everybody told 'em too. They was like, "Why y'all get done it in?" They used to just say "stop askin' us about that." So they just stopped hanging out with us. . . . They know that they was gettin' looked at as hos. We just look at 'em. Sometimes we tell 'em too, we be like, "Ooh y'all look, y'all some little hos," or, "Why y'all do that?" They be like, "So." They be like, "That's our business." And when we say that to them and they ain't never come around no more.

In fact, Veronica said the young men in her set purposely tricked girls into believing they were being sexed into the gang and targeted girls they didn't like:

> If some girls wanted to get in, if they don't like the girl they have sex with 'em. They run trains on 'em or either have the girl suck their thang. And then they used to, the girls used to think they was in. So then the girls used to just come try to hang around us and all this little bull, just 'cause, 'cause they thinkin' they in.

Our continuing dialogue on the topic is illustrative of the derision these girls faced, not just by male members but also by female members like Veronica:

VERONICA: You can't get sexed in. . . . They're playin' with girls' heads. And then, once they leave them girls, them girls be gettin' mad.
JM: So, basically, it's just a game to just let the girls think they can be let in?
VERONICA: Mmhmm. Yep. Can't get sexed in. I don't know why they, ooh, that's nasty, why would you even wanna do, oooh, that's nasty. [Laughs] That's nasty.

JM: So, has that happened in your set? Where they've tricked a girl into thinking that she's—

VERONICA: Mmhmm. Yep. They used to do it all the time. All the time. I used to think it was funny. If girls wanna be dumb and fall for it, let 'em. They used to just think they was in. Used to always just, just, try to come hang around us.

JM: And then what would happen?

VERONICA: I mean when all the, once all the boys done, you know, rammed up in 'em, when they through with 'em, they just find them with another girl and them girls be gettin' mad. 'Cause, if, if a girl thinkin' they get sexed in, they gotta do whatever, whatever the boys tell 'em to do when they want 'em to do it, right then and there, in front of whoever. And I think that's just sick. That's nasty, that's dumb.

Although Veronica was extremely judgmental of young women who were sexually abused by male gang members, she said the young men's sexual behavior didn't matter to her, "as long as they hardcore." Likewise, Keisha blamed the young woman who was sexed into her gang for the ongoing exploitation she faced, rather than the young men: "She brought that on herself, by bein' . . . sexed in." Young women who were sexed into the gang were viewed as weak, sexually promiscuous, degraded and not "true" members. They were subject to revictimization and mistreatment and were viewed as deserving of abuse by other members, both male and female.

Part of the reason girls were disrespected for being sexed in was because they were perceived to have chosen what Heather described as "the easy way in." Tamika explained, "That don't make you no woman . . . to let four or five niggers run train on you just to get put into the gang. To me, it makes you a woman if you gonna be bold enough to let someone hit you in your head or in your chest six times." Likewise, Diane said that girls chose to be sexed in "because they're weak. 'Cause they're too, they're too weak to take a beat down." As Chantell elaborated, this could pose a real physical threat to other girls in the gang:

> [Being sexed in]'s just showin' how good you can fuck. But if its just us, we have to have each other's back. You don't know how good she can fight, because you never seen her fight, you've just seen how good she can fuck. . . . Like, just say there was three girls that had sex in, and there was one girl that fought in. And if we went to the mall, we seen all these Slobs, and they came to us. We don't know, and I'm just by myself, I don't know how good they could fight. They prob'ly can't fight and I get beat down, because of them.

On the other hand, Tamika described a girl who was sexed in, stigmatized as a result, but successfully fought to rebuild her reputation:

> Some people at first, they called her "little ho" and all that. But then, now she startin' to get bold. . . . They be like, "Ooh, look at the little ho. She fucked me

and my boy." She be like, "Man forget y'all. Man, what? What?" She be ready to squat [fight] with 'em. I be like, "Ah, look at her!" . . . At first we looked at her like, "Ooh man, she a ho man." But now we look at her like she just our kickin' it partner. You know, however she got in that's her business.

However, this typically was not the case. Moreover, the fact that there was such an option as sexing-in served to keep all girls disempowered on some level because they were always faced with the question of how they got in and of whether they were "true" members. The practice challenged the integrity of all girls in mixed-gender gangs. As Denise, a nongang girl who affiliated with an all-male gang, told me: "I mean they tell you that [they weren't sexed in], but you don't know how they *really* got in." Monica said she faced this question often when she encountered young people who were not in gangs:

MONICA: The problem that I faced, everybody was like, "Well you probably got sexed in. You probably got sexed in." . . . And I was like, "No, I really didn't."
JM: And who would say that?
MONICA: Girls at school. Like, "Oh, you a ho. How'd you get put in?" I was like, "None of your business." They was like, "You probably got sexed in." I was like, "No I really didn't." Like that.

Likewise, Yvette explained, "I mean like some people, like the police right, they think that you a girl, you in a gang, the niggers taking advantage of you, they think they fuck you any time they want to, they treat you like sluts. It's not like that. The police, they don't know what the fuck they talking about."

However it wasn't just outsiders who were affected. The practice of sexing-in contributed to a milieu in which young women's sexuality was seen as exploitable. The following conversation with Vikkie is illustrative:

VIKKIE: Like some gangs if they see a girl in there they want to mess with them and make them into a rat or whatever. . . .
RB: What do you mean by [make] them into a rat?
VIKKIE: Like, you know . . . by being in a gang and you mess with all them little boys, you practically trying to talk to all them boys and you gonna sleep with all of them. That's making you a rat from the set, from the hood.
RB: What are some of the problems girls face by being in the gang?
VIKKIE: Harassment, rape.
RB: By who?
VIKKIE: You can be harassed by your own members. . . . [But] I don't worry about my people raping me. I worry about other gang-bangers trying to do something.

Young women who were privy to male gang members' conversations reported that male members routinely disrespected the girls in their gang by disparaging them sexually, though they typically did so outside of the girls' presence. For instance, despite Monica's comment that "nobody in my set sit there while I'm around and talk about females like that or nothin' because they know I will get a little attitude with 'em," later in the interview she conceded that it did occur.

> I mean the guys, they have their little comments about 'em. Because I hear more because my brothers are all up there with the guys and everything and I hear more just sittin' around, just listenin'. And they'll have their little jokes about, "Well, ha I had her," and then and everybody else will jump in and say, "Well I had her too." And then they'll laugh about it.

Likewise, Sonita said that males in her gang had "little man talk, and then the females find out about it and get mad." Yvette found herself being disparaged by young men after she had been involved with more than one from the same gang. She said, "That taught me not to mess with them no more." In fact, Sonita learned firsthand how little respect young men in the gang had for young women when she was raped by one of the boys in her gang. No one in the gang stood up for her, and there were no repercussions for his behavior, despite the gang's rules about not hurting members of the group. As a result of the incident she had severed her ties from her gang when we spoke. Like Monica, Leslie had firsthand knowledge of how young men talked about girls in their gang when they weren't around. Her boyfriend was a member of the same gang, and being around him allowed her to directly observe young men's behavior. She was highly critical of male gang members' disrespect of young women. At one point in the interview, she made the comment that "the girls are mainly used for sex," and I asked her to elaborate:

LESLIE: The talk I was hearin', 'cause they would talk about, like, 'cause whenever I was with the males I would be, my boyfriend would be right there. I was never around the males by myself. So, and they didn't refer to me like they referred to them [other girls] because I, 'cause I had a boyfriend that was in there. They referred to the girls that didn't. They talked, "Yeah, I'm gonna get her," and all this. "Yeah, uh huh, we need to take her out," and all this 'n stuff. And, I thought that was very disrespectful. . . . I mean, 'cause, they, gangs, I mean, our leader had respect for us. But, the guys that were in the gang didn't have respect for us.
JM: And did the other girls know it? Or, were they only disrespectful when they weren't around?
LESLIE: They were disrespectful mainly when they weren't around. Sometimes they would call 'em bitches 'n stuff. But, they would just shrug

it off like, ah, he's just playin'. But, I was never talked to like that. But, I mean, if I was, see, I don't like, that's why I don't like the B-word. I don't, I mean, if I don't call you one, I, you don't call me one. And, they, they, they are, were very disrespectful. Very disrespectful to women.

JM: So, like, the girls, well, 'cause you had a boyfriend. The other ones, did they see themselves as primarily, as only there to give sex to the guys?

LESLIE: They thought they were, like, one of the, one of the niggers. That's what they said. They was one of the guys. They should act like a guy and all this. So, guys were doin' it to everybody so they would do it to everybody. So, they actually didn't see what was goin' on. They were walkin' like they had blindfolds on. And, bein' where I was, I could see everything that was goin' on. So, that's, I was, nnhnn.

JM: So, you kinda had the inside—

LESLIE: Right.

JM: Because of your boyfriend.

LESLIE: If I didn't have him, I'da been just like one of them.

JM: And, now, were you friends with the other girls?

LESLIE: Oh, I was friends. I would tell 'em, I'd be like, "Y'all are stupid. Y'all just need to find one and just be with that one instead of doin' it to every, anything and everybody." And they would, "Oh, girl, they just jokin' around. We just be doin' it on," they call it "the low-key" so don't nobody know about it. But, when they say "low-key" or whatever, when they're actually the girls aren't around and the guys are sittin' there talkin'. They're not low-key no more 'cause the guys are braggin', "Well yeah, she did this to me," and all this. I mean, it's just stupid.

JM: So, the girls thought that the guys were being quiet but they really weren't.

LESLIE: Right. They was really tellin' everybody and anything about what they did. And, even if they wanted to they added a couple little pieces that didn't happen.

JM: And, then, how would the guys be when the girls were around?

LESLIE: "Oh, hey baby, how ya doin'?" And, just real, real respectful when they were around. But, very disrespectful when they weren't. So, they were bein', like, very two-faced. . . . [The girls] thought that they were being like the guys, or 'they respect me as a guy.' . . . And that really wasn't what happened.

CONCLUSION

In this chapter, I have shown that gender plays a complicated role in shaping young women's risk of victimization within gangs. Among the young women in my sample, being in a gang increased young women's risk of some forms of serious violence, like being threatened with a weapon or stabbed, and also exposed them to such brutalities as witnessing and losing loved ones to homicide. On the other hand, a number of gang girls had been sexually assaulted prior to their gang involvement. Being in a gang did not seem to increase their risk of sexual assault, and young women actually felt more protected from such violence because of their gangs. Nonetheless, other forms of sexual abuse and exploitation were present within many gangs.

Gender dynamics in mixed-gender gangs are complex and thus have multiple and contradictory effects on young women's risk of victimization. Participation in the delinquent lifestyles associated with gangs clearly places young women at risk for victimization. Many of the acts of violence that young women described would not have occurred had they not been in gangs. It seems, however, that these young women in gangs had traded unknown risks for known ones—that victimization at the hands of friends, or at least under predictable conditions, was an alternative preferable to the potential of individual vulnerability. Moreover, the gang offered both a semblance of protection from others on the streets, especially men, and a means of retaliating when victimization occurred.

On one hand, young women could call upon gender as a means of avoiding exposure to activities they found risky, threatening, or morally troubling. Doing so meant they were somewhat insulated from the risk of assault at the hands of rival gang members. However, this insulation was double-edged, as it fit with perceptions of female gang members, and of women in general, as weak. Consequently, this contributed to more routinized victimization at the hands of the male members of their gang. Moreover, sexual exploitation in the form of sexing-in exacerbated definitions of young women as sexually available, contributing to the likelihood of repeat victimization unless young women could stand up for themselves and fight to gain other members' respect.

The gender inequalities that govern gang life shape young women's interactions with one another and also come with particular costs and benefits—among them the structuring of victimization risk. In the final chapter, I explore why young women participate in gangs despite these decidedly negative elements of gang life. I attempt to make sense of the contradictory nature of gang life for young women—particularly their support for gender inequalities within gangs even as they endeavor to define themselves as "equals."

8

Gender Strategies in Youth Gangs

In Chapter 7 I suggested that gender could serve as both a protective factor and a risk factor for gang girls with regard to victimization. Here I further explore the meanings of gender for young women within gangs. I began this book by suggesting that our attempts to understand young women's place in gangs have been hindered by the tendency to focus either on girls' victimization or on their agency rather than, as David Curry has suggested, to recognize these as dialectical processes.[1] Research that emphasizes gender differences and conceptualizes girls' participation in gangs and delinquency primarily as gendered resistance doesn't sufficiently account for variations in young women's experiences, including within-gender differences and overlaps between the experiences of young women and young men. Moreover, these accounts don't sufficiently deal with some young women's support of and participation in the mistreatment of other females. On the other hand, work that suggests that gang involvement and other delinquency are illustrative of "liberation" fail to account for the continuing significance of male domination on the streets, as well as in other arenas of women's lives.[2]

To explore these issues further, in this chapter I focus more attention on the contradictory gender dynamics that operate within street gangs. My conversations with gang girls shed light on these dynamics: On the one hand was a predominant "myth system" of gender equality; on the other hand, a distinct gender hierarchy within gangs, which young women themselves often upheld. My goal here is to explore how and why these contradictions operate. Specifically, how is it that young women participate in a group that they themselves perceive as justly hierarchical by gender, and yet describe it as one in which young women and young men are equals?

GENDER EQUALITY AS A NORMATIVE FEATURE OF GANGS

As I described in Chapters 4 and 5, the vast majority (88 percent) of young women in this study were in groups that they characterized as mixed-gender. Only three girls were in all-female gangs, while three in St. Louis were in an all-female Crips set that was affiliated with a mixed-gender set in the same neighborhood. Young women in mixed-gender gangs, as well as the girls in the affiliated group, articulated a strong belief that males and females were equals in their gangs with regard to their activities as well as their treatment by other members. Girls were insistent that their groups were a space of gender equality and were quite resistant to my questions about gender inequality, emphasizing instead that everyone in the gang was "all the same." Sonita explained, "They give every last one of us respect the way they give the males." This was a prevailing discourse throughout the interviews, even as the same young women described activities to the contrary.

For instance, Monica answered a series of questions with the same response. When I asked if there were differences in the activities of males and females, she said, "They basically do the same thing." I asked about member qualifications and she responded, "It's basically the same for both sexes." And of the benefits of gang membership, "It's basically the same for both of 'em." However, recall from Chapter 7 that Monica in fact did make distinctions between the treatment of various girls in the gang and was also aware of how the men in her gang talked about the young women in her gang outside of their presence. I'll return to Monica's resolution of these contradictions later in the chapter; my point now is to highlight her desire to see the gang as a space of gender equality.

Chantell actually became frustrated with my line of questioning and repeatedly cut me off or "talked back," as I described in Chapter 2, in response:

JM: You said before that the gang was about half girls and half guys? Can you tell me more about that? Like you said you don't think there are any differences in terms of what—
Chantell: There isn't!
JM: OK, can you tell me more—
Chantell: Like what? There isn't, there isn't like, there's nothing—boy, girl, white, black, Mexican, Chinese.
JM: Everyone does the same thing.
Chantell: Yeah.

Likewise, Yvette explained, "The boys, the girls are no different for real, we all the same," and Debbie noted, "It's all the same." Regina also said that the boys and girls are "the same," and there was "nothing" that stood out in her mind that differentiated between what young men did and what young women did. Marie said, "I get treated the same way," and Dionne noted, "The girls do everything they do. Like the girls carry weapons like they do. They sell drugs and stuff like they do. Like my friend Kiki [would] tell you, there ain't nothin' that they can do that she can't do. There ain't nothin' they can do that she can't do." Erica even made specific reference to the women's movement in response to a question I asked about whether young women in gangs are perceived differently than males: "I mean, a lot of people I know look up to it. They call it the women's rights civil group or somethin' like that they call it. It's funny. . . . They say that 'it's about time you got some women involved around here!' [Laughs] It's funny, they say that though."

For girls in mixed-gender gangs, the fact that the group was integrated, rather than segregated by gender (or exclusively male), was seen as evidence of this equality. As Chantell noted, "It's the same set, so why should we do different things?" Shawanda said, "If she consider herself as a gang member, then she gonna be treated like a gang member," and she concluded, "You can't really judge it on the boys or the girls, it ain't based on that." Likewise, Latisha explained: "We just like dudes to them. We just like dudes, they treat us like that 'cause we act so much like dudes they can't do nothing. They respect us as females though, but we just so much like dudes that they just don't trip off of it."

As Latisha's comment implies, part of girls' discussions of their equality within the gang was not so much by suggesting that all women should be treated equally, but by differentiating themselves from young women who were not in gangs.[3] Brandi explained that girls in gangs are different from other girls because they "act more, more like guys. Not like guys, guys, guys, but act different from most girls." Veronica concurred:

A lot of girls get scared. Don't wanna break their nails and stuff like that. So, ain't no need for them to try to be in no gang. And the ones that's in it, most of the girls that's in act like boys. That's why they in, 'cause they like to fight and stuff. They know how to fight and they use guns and stuff.

Shawanda said the girls in her gang "had a one-track mind, and they mind was basically they started being thugs." Returning to Latisha's discussion, she continued: "I was the girl who done everything the dudes done. I wasn't scared of nothing. I was just like, I was just like a dude in a girl's body or whatever." Explaining what made *gang* girls unique, she said, "There wasn't that many girls that had heart like we did . . . [that] ain't scared."

In sum, young women described themselves as equals within their gangs, particularly by describing themselves as different from young women who were not in gangs and constructing an identity as "one of the guys." As I will discuss in the next section, gang girls differentiated themselves from girls who were not in gangs on a number of fronts, mostly by drawing on negative characterizations of other young women, as well as through their resistance to the narrow confines of "appropriate" femininity. Consequently, some young women felt that girls' equality within the gang was earned or justified because they were not like other girls, who they saw as less deserving of this treatment.

However, often their descriptions of other young women applied not only to girls who were not in gangs but also to other gang members. In doing so, their discussions reveal their support of the gangs' gender hierarchies, even as they describe their own status as one of an "equal." Moreover, young women often provided contradictory discussions within the course of their conversations. For instance, while Vashelle insisted that "gals gonna do whatever dudes do over there," only a few minutes later in the same conversation she just as vehemently declared, "Ain't no girl over there doing it like the dudes." In fact, despite young women's insistence that males and females were "the same" and girls were treated with equal respect, without exception young women provided evidence to the contrary. In previous chapters, I have documented a distinct gender hierarchy within mixed-gender gangs that includes male leadership, a double standard with regard to sexual activity, the sexual exploitation of some young women, and most girls' exclusion from serious gang crime—specifically those acts that build status and "rep" within the group. The goal of this chapter is to make sense of these contradictions.

CONTRADICTORY ATTITUDES ABOUT WOMEN

Researchers have suggested that young women's gang involvement provides a means of resisting limitations placed on them by narrow social definitions of femininity, which girls recognize as limiting their options in an environment in which these options are already quite restricted. Campbell, for instance, argues that "gang girls see themselves as different from their peers. Their association with the gang is a public proclamation of their rejection of the lifestyle which the community expects from them."[4] In fact, a number of young women in the current study talked about social pressures to be more like "girls," as well as their resistance to these pressures. Alecia said that people "think girls should be doing something better than being in a gang." And Vashelle explained, "Some people just don't think it's ladylike, you know what I'm saying. I'm ladylike, I like being ladylike most of the time. I know people are down on gals as far as being in the gang." Yvette said, "I used to wear a lot of blue, baggy pants. . . . I used to be dressed like that for real. But it ain't cute to me no more. My mother and sister did not like having me in boys' clothes. They be saying it crazy."

Trina said, "They call me a tomboy 'cause we go play basketball, we play football in the backyard. We do most everything." She explained:

They [gang members] just treated me like a little boy. . . . I got to do what dudes usually do. I got to be like dudes. 'Cause my mama used to try everything. My mama used to tell me like that type of stuff. I ain't like to wear earrings and stuff and she say, "Girl, you ain't no boy! Girls got to wear earrings." I say, "I want to be a tomboy."

Trina was only twelve, and she looked her age. The physicality of tomboyness—for instance dressing "like a boy"—was not adopted by all young women, and tended to be embraced more by younger than older girls. Later in the interview, Trina described a similar incident, this time involving a stranger, in which she also felt and resisted social pressure to be more "ladylike."

Monday I was at a park and a woman come over and sit down watching us play. . . . She called me over there. I'm like, what you calling me for? I ignored her and then she called again. I kept on ignoring her and then she came over there to us. I'm like, oh no. She talking about, are you in a gang? I was like, no. Then she said, "You look like you kind of little to be in a gang." Because me and Terrell had said something when I was looking at her strange. I was like, "What? You better go." She said "You a young lady, how you claim [a gang], you should be at home playing with a little doll." I started cussing, I was cussing up a storm. I was like, "Man what you coming at me with that stuff for?" 'Cause my mama do that. She'll come up to me, "You need to be playing with some dolls."

In describing themselves as "one of the guys," young women highlighted what they perceived to be the importance of being tough and physically aggressive and of not being preoccupied with "feminine" concerns. As Veronica noted earlier, girls who "get scared" or "don't wanna break their nails and stuff like that" don't belong in gangs. This was one of several predominant themes young women raised to differentiate themselves from other girls. Tonya complained about girls who "don't fight, ones that think they too cute to fight, ones that be scared to sell drugs, just scared. . . . You can't be scared and be a gang member." Likewise, describing girls who don't belong in gangs, Vikkie noted:

These little girls that is cute and stuff like that, they don't want they hair getting messed up, if you gonna be in a gang you gotta realize you gonna have to be a thuggish girl 'cause there ain't no way you gonna be a pretty girl being in a gang. People just gonna be out to hurt you, scratch on your face or something like that. That's why when I was littler I used to always be like a tomboy, just wear pants and keep my hair tied. I was a tomboy.

In fact, a number of young women described that "cute" girls often looked down on young women in gangs. The following conversation with Rhonda is illustrative:

RHONDA: I wouldn't hang out with popular girls, too popular, think they too cute, I don't hang out with those types of girls.
RB: Why wouldn't you hang out with them?
RHONDA: 'Cause they think they too much. They ugly for real. They might think they good but on the inside they ugly.

Recall from Chapter 7 that Monica described being harassed by nongang girls in her school, who assumed because she was in a gang she was sexually promiscuous. Sheila described these girls as "snakes": "They talk about you and they laugh in your face." Likewise, Shawanda described these girls as "all prissy, two-faced." Shiree said she didn't like such girls' "attitude": "They stuck up, they think they all that." And Brandi told me, "I don't get along with girls that much." When I asked her why, she explained, "I mean some of the girls, just because I'm in a gang, they think, 'Oh well I don't like her.'" Dionne said there were girls who "be talkin' behind my back. . . . They be like, 'She think she bad, she think she hard, she, you know all that.'"

Brittany surmised that this was "because most females don't feel that they should have to be in a gang. Most females, like around my little neighborhood anyway, they like school and they like working." Recall from Chapter 3 that Brittany described turning to the gang, in part because she "didn't have no friends" at school and the other girls teased and made fun of her. Other scholars have discussed these kinds of hierarchies among adolescent girls.[5] It is likely that some of young women's distaste for other girls had to do with their perception that they were looked down upon and judged by these girls; with their gang friends, they could turn this around and look down on other girls for not having the qualities that *they* value.[6]

In fact, some young women emphasized in their interviews that they preferred the company of young men. Brandi, as I noted, said, "I don't get along with girls that much." She commented, "I don't have that many girlfriends. . . . I hang out with guys, I always, I've been raised with guys and stuff. I've hung out with guys basically all my life." Likewise, Veronica said, "I never really hang out around a whole bunch of girls, I just mostly hang out with a whole bunch of guys." Vashelle explained, "I don't hang out with girls. . . . They start too much stuff, they get into too much stuff. They fight over stupid stuff for real." And Marie noted, "I don't hang around girls." Leslie, though critical of young men's mistreatment of girls in gangs (see Chapter 7) was equally, if not more, critical of young women:

> I don't like girls 'cause, I mean, I'm the type of person that I'll talk, I like guys, I mean, I like to be around guys 'cause you can tell a guy, I mean, you can tell a guy some stuff and then you can tell a girl somethin' and next week anybody and everything know it. And with a guy, it's more than likely they're gonna be, I mean, either they forget about it or somethin'. But they don't tell it. Then a girl's mouth is movin' fifty miles an hour, they're just "aaah," tellin' everything. And they're always in the middle of something. They wanna argue, fight, all the time. That's all they wanna do. And talk about each other behind their back. And, that's why I don't like girls. Girls get too much stuff started. They always in somethin'. I mean, I have a couple of girls as friends. But, that's only, I have two. And I don't trust them that well because girls are just. Their mouth. If, I don't think, if God didn't make girls with mouths they would be just fine and dandy. They wouldn't be as much problems as they are and if their mouth was just zipped up and shut they wouldn't have as much problems as they have.

Leslie's comments refer not just to girls who aren't in gangs, but to girls in general—including other young women in gangs. One complaint about girls, as Leslie suggested, was "their mouths." Describing a young woman she didn't like, Trina noted, "She talk too much, she'll go tell another set what we be doing and what we be saying." She concluded, "I don't like girls that talk too much, they starting stuff all the time." And Latisha said she didn't like "girls who got a lot of mouth." Vikkie said she tried to limit the girls who were allowed to join her set because of this problem: "I told them I didn't want too many females in here 'cause I know half of them females on my block and they was snakes, and some of them snitches. And I don't trust snitches and I don't trust snakes." Asked why there weren't more girls in her gang, Shawanda explained: "'Cause girls and girls don't get along that well. They be different. It's the same with dudes, but dudes, I think they be more cooler, because girls talk too much. I know I do. I always got to tell if somebody say something, you know what I'm saying? Dudes ain't like that. It's all on them, you know?" Likewise, Tyra noted that she didn't really hang around with girls "because they start stuff," and Yvette commented, "You can't trust 'em." Even Shiree, who was in an all-female gang, said her gang remained small "because we don't get along with females."

Part of young women's distrust of other girls had to do with their competition with one another over the attention of young men, which many young women found frustrating and tiresome.[7] Yolanda described these as "silly girl fights." Asked what she meant, she explained, "He say–she say stuff, or over ɔoyfriends, stupid stuff." Brittany noted, "Girls, they all crazy. They'll just run up on you, knock on your door and pull you out of your own house, just silly. . . . Girls are lowly." Recall Vashelle's comment that girls "fight over stupid stuff." Asked to elaborate, she explained, "I mean the gals over there banging over a dude. You all over here banging over him but he probably ain't even existed for you right now. They [fight] over a dude, stupid stuff and dudes. My partner, the gal who I used to hang with, she used to be cool, she got stabbed in the head over a dude." Alecia described, "Like we will go to a party and then the girls, you know how the girls look at you all like she jealous or something. They be like, 'Here are some 2-1s [Alecia's gang], we got to help fight her,' and then all of them jump her."

As Campbell has aptly noted, young women's competition with each other tends to undermine the strength of female–female relationships within gangs.[8] In particular, as I detailed in Chapter 7, young women were very judgmental of girls who were seen as sexually promiscuous, and they held especially harsh attitudes about young women who had been sexed into gangs. Keisha commented again, "There's really no hope for them. . . . I mean it's just trifling, that's just downgrading yourself." In addition, their problems with one another, and negative attitudes about girls in general, undermined their claims and desire for "equality" within their gangs because these attitudes also led them to express the belief that young men were often "better" members, as well as the idea that gangs were masculine enterprises.

This notion that gangs are—or should be—masculine enterprises was vividly reflected when I talked to girls in mixed-gender gangs about their perceptions of all-female gangs. Veronica recalled one all-female gang, which she called "stupid," and said the boys referred to it as "pussy-infected." She noted, "They try to have their own little girl group goin' on. [Laughs] It was silly." The following conversation with LaShawna was also illustrative:

JM: Do you know of any gangs in Columbus that are all females?
LASHAWNA: Aw, no! No.
JM: Why do you think that's the case?
LASHAWNA: I don't know, I guess they need somebody to protect 'em or something. But I don't know, I ain't never seen it.
JM: You haven't heard of any?
LASHAWNA: No.
JM: OK. What do you think the reaction would be if there were?
LASHAWNA: I'd probably *laugh* or something. 'Cause I ain't never seen it.
JM: OK. And why would you laugh?
LASHAWNA: 'Cause! What they gonna do? They can't do nothin' about it. Nothin' about nothin'! They probably could be, though, they probably could be hard or whatever. But they wouldn't have no props. They wouldn't get no props.
JM: What do you mean by props?
LASHAWNA: Like you know, "Yeah, I heard they be doin' all this stuff man." You just get your props, you know, like, "Yeah, they bad." "You gotta watch out for them," or somethin' like that. Naw, it's not like that.
JM: So they wouldn't get any kind of respect?
LASHAWNA: Naw.

There was a moment where LaShawna was torn, admitting that an all-female gang could be "hard," but her general reaction, like Veronica's, was to laugh. Importantly, part of the reason that both found the notion of an all-female gang "silly," to use Veronica's term, was because they believed that without males, the group would not be respected. Moreover, their comments reflect the belief that young women need young men in gangs in order to maintain the credibility and respect necessary to negotiate their activities and place on the streets. In fact, it is because of reactions like these that I resist calling girls' groups "female gangs." While other scholars insist upon the use of this term,[9] the vast majority of girls in my study did not see themselves as being in "female gangs"; moreover, they were resistant to such a classification because of what they saw as its negative implications.

As I discussed in Chapter 7, LaShawna's comment about girls needing "somebody to protect 'em" was a theme in many interviews. Despite their desire to see the gang as a space of gender equality, most young women still felt that girls needed protection and that young men were the best providers of this. Several girls' comments, in fact, were quite exaggerated, as when Lisa suggested that "fifty girls [would] have to get on five guys" in order to win a fight. Erica noted, "When you think of a girl, you think of her bein' all small and fragile." She argued that young men were integral to the gang because "they're stronger. Just imagine what if one of us got wounded. They would have to carry us. We couldn't carry ourselves! [Laughs]" Her comments are perhaps most ironic, as she was a very large, strong girl, nicknamed, as I noted in Chapter 3, "Iron Mike." No doubt, she was probably stronger than a number of young men in her set. As much as these girls' comments reveal negative beliefs about young women's capabilities, they are also a reflection of the recognition that gangs are primarily male-dominated, masculine groups. Tonya explained that if the gang were all girls, "If some other dudes from another territory come and try to take over our set, they could easily take us." The irony is that if Jennifer's description of her all-female gang, the Gangster Girlz, is any indication, all-female groups are capable of being very "hardcore," able to take care of themselves and fend off potential predators and be involved in serious economic crime.[10]

While these themes predominated girls' discussions, it is important to note that some young women—though surprisingly few—discussed their relationships with other girls in their gangs as a significant source of support and friendship in their lives. This was especially the case for girls in all-female gangs and gangs with a sizeable number of female members. Girls in minority-female gangs were the least likely to describe the importance of other gang girls in their lives. In addition, such descriptions were more common in St. Louis than in Columbus, most likely a reflection of the greater proportion of girls in their gangs there (see Chapter 5). Recall from Chapter 3 that gang girls in St. Louis were also more likely to describe the strong influence of *female* relatives—sisters, aunts, cousins—on their decisions to join. Perhaps it is because of these female familial ties, as well, that girls there were more likely to articulate the value they placed on their relationships with other young women in their gangs.

Shiree, a member of an all-female gang, noted that the most important expectations she had of a member of her gang were not that they be tough or down for the gang; rather, it was their "friendship" and trustworthiness that she valued. She explained, "You can't trust nobody" outside the gang. Likewise, describing the importance of the other young women in her set, Yvette said, "Almost everybody that I know for real, I know from the same clique, in the same gang. It's just part of life for me. . . . They my only partners for real, you know what I'm saying. I got friends, but they the only ones that I trust." Recall that Yvette was a member of a female gang that affiliated with a neighborhood mixed-gender gang. Pam's gang was mixed-gender, but half the members were female. She surmised, "Most of the girls for real is family and friends. We went to school together, grew up together, so it was already a group before it was a gang." She said her friendships—having people trust her to share their secrets—were the most valuable benefits she gained from being in the gang.

MAKING SENSE OF GENDER CONTRADICTIONS

Perhaps part of the reason more young women didn't express this sentiment about the importance of their female peers, while many were quite critical of other young women, was a result of the structures of their gangs. The gender composition of the gang—specifically the number and percentage of female and male members—appears to impact young women's attitudes and experiences. In an important article on how organizational structure shapes gender dynamics, Rosabeth Moss Kanter suggests that the *"relative* numbers of socially and culturally different people in a group are . . . critical in shaping interactional dynamics."[11] In fact, there is preliminary evidence that the gender composition of gangs results in different patterns of delinquency: In a recent study of gang youth in fourteen cites, it was found that youths in mixed-gender gangs that were predominantly male had higher rates of delinquency than youths in gender-balanced groups, as well as youths in all-female and all-male gangs. Notably, this pattern held for both gang boys *and* gang girls.[12] Thus it should not be surprising that gender composition might affect girls' attitudes as well.

As I described in Chapters 4 and 5, the majority of girls in mixed-gender gangs were in gangs that were predominantly male. In all, thirty-one of the forty-two girls in mixed-gender gangs (74 percent) described their gangs as having more males than females; about one-third were in gangs in which females were only one-fifth or fewer of the members. Kanter's work provides some insight into the effects of these gendered patterns. She distinguishes between skewed groups, in which "there is a large preponderance of one type over another"[13] (such as gangs with one-fifth or fewer girls), and tilted or balanced groups, in which women have a larger and sizeable representation in the group. In skewed groups, women are "token" members, and Kanter found that women tokens were subject to three perceptual phenomena: "visibility (tokens capture a disproportionate awareness share), polarization (differences between tokens and dominants are exaggerated), and assimilation (tokens' attributes are distorted to fit preexisting generalizations about their social type)."[14]

Ironically, while her discussion of these perceptual phemonema differed from my findings, her description of women's responses to being tokens are quite similar to girls' accounts. Rather than standing out as different from their male peers, as Kanter found women in the workplace experienced, girls who were tokens in primarily male gangs tended to adopt "honorary male" status—as Latisha suggested, "a girl in a dude's body." In fact, the young men we spoke to in the study mentioned in Chapter 7 said much the same thing. This difference is likely attributable to differences with regard to qualifications for entrée. For instance, in the workplace, women's male coworkers have little or no choice in the hiring of women, while young men in gangs can control whether and which young women they allow to join.

Nonetheless, as I noted, Kanter's findings with regard to women's responses to being tokens parallel gang girls' descriptions. About one-third of the girls in this study were in gangs that could be classified as skewed; the others were in tilted or balanced groups. Kanter suggests that when groups "begin to move toward less extreme distributions . . . dominants are just a majority and tokens a minority. Minority members are potentially allies, can form coalitions, and can affect the culture of the group."[15] However, when women are tokens, they typically adopt two responses: overachieving according to the "masculine" standards of the group and attempting to become "socially invisible"—to "minimize their sexual attributes so as to blend unnoticably into the predominant male culture."[16]

This helps explain why girls who were tokens in predominantly male gangs (for instance, Veronica, Brandi, and Vashelle) spoke about girls in the most negative ways, while girls in groups with a more balanced gender ratio or girls in female gangs (e.g., Pam, whose gang was half female; Yvette; and Shiree) were more likely to talk about the strength of their friendships with other girls. Kanter suggests:

> In both macroscopic and microscopic analysis, sex and gender components are sometimes confounded by situational and structural effects. . . . Conclusions about "women's behavior" or "male attitudes" drawn from such situations may sometimes confuse the effect of situation with the effect of sex roles; indeed such variables as position in opportunity and power structures account for a large number of phenomena related to . . . behavior that have been labeled "sex differences."[17]

In fact, Kanter suggests that women in token positions are subject to loyalty tests and "expected to demonstrate loyalty to the dominant group":

> For token women, the price of being "one of the boys" is a willingness to turn occasionally against "the girls." There are two ways by which tokens can demonstrate loyalty and qualify for closer relationships with dominants. First, they can let slide or even participate in statements prejudicial to other members of their category. They can allow themselves to be viewed as exceptions to the general rule that others of their category have a variety of undesirable or unsuitable characteristics. . . . Tokens can also demonstrate loyalty by allowing themselves and their category to provide a source of humor for the group. Laughing with others . . . is a sign of a common definition of the situation; to allow oneself or one's kind to be the object of such laughter signals a further willingness to accept others' culture on their terms.[18]

Let me return now to Monica's discussion in Chapter 7 with regard to male gang members' mistreatment and sexual disrespect of girls in her gang. Recall she told me repeatedly that "it's basically the same for both sexes." However, she admitted that "the guys, they have their little comments about 'em [girls in the gang]." When I asked how she felt about being a young woman and hearing how they talked about females, she described a process in which she learned to silence herself and eventually shift the responsibility to the girls involved:

> At first, when I first ever started listening to them talk, it made me mad and I would jump in and say my little piece. And my brother would look at me like, "Are you going to sit here and join the conversation or just butt in when you get mad?" So I just learned to just sit back and just keep mine to myself.

Monica revealed her struggle between challenging male sexism, which risked alienating her from the group, and accepting it, which risked self-alienation. She continued:

> I mean, it's like, I be hearin' guys talk about girls so much. I haven't heard no guys talk about me or nothin' like that. I know, I mean, there will be guys that will talk about me but I've never heard it myself. Because I hang around guys most the time. And they'll sit back and they'll be like, "Yeah, she's a ho. I know all about her." And they'll sit back and discuss it with me like, "Yeah, she did all of this for me and she did this and this and this and then I told her to get up and go home." I mean, stuff like that. So, I be like, "Oh, you did, for real?" And I just learned to say, "Mmhmm. Alright. Mmhmm. Yeah. Whatever." I mean, and just listen.

In order to participate "equally" in the gang, she silenced herself and accepted members' disrespect of young women. Ultimately, she did so by placing most of the responsibility for disrespect in the hands of individual girls: "I mean, I've heard about two or three other girls and I couldn't even do it. Nnhnn. It ain't even me." Recall also her description of Andrea, the girl in her gang who was often abused and mistreated by male members: "I put that on her. They ain't gotta do her like that, but she don't gotta let them do her like that either." Blaming the victims of male gang members' mistreatment allowed her to explain why girls were mistreated in a way that did not challenge her belief in her own importance to the group, where she said she was "taken very seriously." Nonetheless, Monica said her exposure to these conversations left her skeptical of other young men:

> I mean, I can tell how a guy's gonna be on the first time I meet him. I can tell how he's gonna be. Like, oh, I met a guy like you before. The guy's like, "No you didn't. You ain't met nobody like me." And come to find out he's just exactly like the person I met before. I mean, it's like that because you learn how guys will do and, oh my God, most of the guys use the same lines all the time. And I be like, "Oh, I heard that one before." I be like, "Come with a new one," somethin' like that and, um, I mean, it just make you look at 'em like, I know I can't trust him. I know I can't trust him or him. And then when you finally do find somebody that you can trust you know that you be able to trust 'em. Like that.

The young woman who witnessed her fellow members brutally gang rape a rival gang girl provided a similar discussion of her struggle to reconcile herself to their behavior:

> I was talkin' to my boy. . . . He was one of the ones who did it. I was talkin' to him like, "Did you get off on that?" He's like, "I got off on that fact because my boy is on a life line." I was like, "OK, I can understand what you're saying. You know, our boy's in the hospital 'cause of her. OK, I can understand what you're saying." But I was lookin' like, "Wow." That's, that's I mean, I've seen people get shot. I've seen people get stabbed, cut, anything. But that is the most brutal thing I've ever seen. That's like something worse than O. J. Simpson could have done to Nicole Simpson. I mean, that's something really brutal I seen.

As I described in Chapter 7, she felt that she would be a "hypocrite," having beaten up the girl, to challenge the young men's behavior. And she knew that the young men would challenge her loyalty to the group—and to her friend in the hospital—if she disapproved. To reconcile the situation, she emphasized that the event was unique, justified by the girl's prior actions, and even tried to convince herself that her friends who participated were not sexually aroused during the assault. Nonetheless, it's clear that the incident continued to haunt her.

To maintain a sense that they were valued members of their gangs, young women had to be able to explain why girls were mistreated, and to do so in a way that didn't challenge their central belief in their own significance and importance to the group. To rectify discrepancies between the norm of gender equality and features of gender *in*equality within their gangs, young women drew on two types of frames, as the young woman who witnessed her friends gang rape the girl illustrated. First, they individualized acts they recognized as involving the mistreatment of females, describing them as unique or exceptional cases. When this was not possible—for instance, when the mistreatment was recurring or routine—they sought ways to hold young women accountable for their mistreatment.

The former of these—individualizing mistreatment—was how Sonita made sense of having been raped by a member of her gang. She described the event as atypical and aberrant, not representative of the overall value system of the gang or its members. Sonita resisted talking about gender differences in her interview, insisting that young women received the same respect in her gang as young men. However, she had previously explained to me that she was raped by one of the young men and had quit spending time with the gang after the OG didn't punish him. In the following dialogue, I reminded her of the sexual assault as a means of eliciting a discussion about gender inequality:

> JM: Do girls face any particular kinds of dangers?
> SONITA: Gettin' shot at, that's about it. Goin' to jail.

JM: What about like what happened to you? Is that, remember on Monday you told me about when one of the gang members raped you?

SONITA: Mm hmm.

JM: Is that something that's a—

SONITA: That only happened once, to me, and I was the only female it ever happened to, so.

JM: So it wasn't something that was a danger for girls usually?

SONITA: [Shakes head]

JM: It was just like an isolated incident?

SONITA: Yep.

As I noted in Chapter 7, it does not appear to be the case that gang membership increased girls' risk of sexual assault; most of the rapes young women described occurred outside the context of the gang. However, the OG's failure to punish the young man indicated something about Sonita's value to the group. In addition, as I described in Chapter 7 some young women were clearly sexually victimized in gangs in other ways. However, as with the young woman who took solace in her belief that her companions only once took part in a brutal gang rape and didn't enjoy it sexually, Sonita did not believe her own sexual assault reflected on male gang members' attitudes and treatment toward young women in the gang.

As I noted earlier, the second means by which young women made sense of girls' mistreatment was to justify particular acts as deserved because of the behaviors of the young women in question. Sometimes this was because of a specific act, such as when the young woman was gang raped in retaliation for setting up a rival gang boy. More often, young women's negative characterizations of female "traits" came into play. Girls were perceived to have brought about what happened to them because they were "big mouths," troublemakers, weak, or—as I discussed in Chapter 7—"hos" or "wrecks." In adopting these justifications, which singled out and blamed the victims of mistreatment, young women were adopting methods that are part of larger cultural traditions in the United States. In this sense, there is nothing particularly unusual about the cultural frames young women drew upon. Routinely, women continue to be held responsible for their victimization in both popular discourses about violence against women and legal response; this is particularly the case with sexual abuse.[19] Thus it should come as no surprise that young women in gangs culled from these same cultural traditions when they described and evaluated the exploitation of young women around them.

"BARGAINING" WITH PATRIARCHY

To understand the contradictions between girls' assertions of equality and their descriptions of and participation in gender inequality within their gangs, it is also necessary to examine the gang within its larger social contexts. Specifically, this requires an exploration of the benefits young women get out of both their gang affiliation *and* gang members' mistreatment of young women, given the milieu in which gangs operate. In a seminal article, Kandiyoti coined the concept of "bargaining with patriarchy"—women's strategies of action as they arise within particular sets of gendered constraints. She notes that "different forms of patriarchy present women with distinct 'rules of the game' and call for different strategies to maximize security and optimize life options with varying potential for active or passive resistance in the face of oppression."[20] Gangs are not uniquely "sexist" groups, and they do not stand alone in their patterns of gender inequality. Instead, they are shaped by the larger social worlds that they inhabit. Situating girls' experiences in gangs within the broader contexts of their lives helps make sense of their experiences in gangs.

In the best of circumstances, adolescence is a time fraught with contradictory gender expectations and meanings. Relationships with peers increase in significance, and this is magnified, especially for girls, with increased self-consciousness and sensitivity to others' perceptions of them.[21] In addition, this time is characterized by a "shift from the relatively asexual gender system of childhood to the overtly sexualized gender systems of adolescence and adulthood."[22] Young women find themselves in a contradictory position. Increasingly, they receive status from their peers via their association with and attractiveness to males, but they are denigrated for their sexual activity and threatened with derogatory sexual labels.[23]

These adolescent contexts are further complicated by circumstances associated with racial and class inequalities for young women living in inner-city neighborhoods. There is, as I noted in Chapter 1, extensive evidence that gender inequality is a salient feature of the urban street scene. Moreover, recent evidence suggests that structural factors such as unemployment and unbalanced gender ratios in inner-city communities increase cultural support for the victimization of women.[24] Particularly with the influx of crack cocaine into urban settings, the exploitation and degradation of at least some women have been intensified, including in public spaces.[25] This environment—where the victimization and exploitation of women are both widespread and highly visible—is one in which gang girls must negotiate.

These contexts are further entangled with young women's personal histories. As I discussed in earlier chapters, more than half of the gang girls in the study described having been sexually abused or assaulted, 46 percent reported beir.g abused by family members, and 56 percent witnessed physical abuse among adults in their families. Moreover, while over half of the girls described regular drug use in their homes, ten girls (21 percent) specifically talked about what they experienced as the devastation resulting from their mother's crack or heroin addiction.[26] Given the intense degradation of many drug-using women on the streets, these particular young women likely dealt with the trauma of having knowledge of or even witnessing such events. Moreover, as Chapter 7 revealed, these young women had witnessed a tremendous amount of interpersonal violence in their neighborhoods.

For all of these reasons, it is apparent that the world around gang girls is not a particularly safe place, physically or psychically. While the specific nature of gender relations in gangs (with the exception of autonomous female gangs) may be distinctive, the overarching gender hierarchy in girls' gangs is quite similar to most other social settings these young women see and experience. In fact, to the extent that there is normative space within these groups for "gender equality," however narrowly defined, participation in gangs may actually provide young women with a means of empowerment and self-definition not available in other contexts. Recognizing this helps to explain girls' acceptance of, and even participation in, structured inequalities. Here I return to two sets of gender beliefs notable in girls' discussions, which I have discussed in previous chapters. These are the acceptance of a sexual double standard and the idea that young women are "weaker" than young men. I return to these to detail how such beliefs can operate simultaneously with a belief in equality as well as to explore what benefits and costs young women appear to get out of the "bargain."

The Sexual Double Standard and "Sexing-In"

As I discussed in Chapter 7, the practice of "sexing" girls into gangs is one that challenges the integrity of all girls in mixed-gender gangs. As Denise, a nongang girl who affiliated with an all-male gang, told me: "I mean they tell you that [they weren't sexed in], but you don't know how they *really* got in." Because of this, gang girls' vilification of girls who were sexed in was necessary to distance themselves from the practice and to maintain an identity as a "true" member—as someone who had not been sexed into the gang. The more vocally girls spoke of these *other* girls as "hos" and "wrecks," the more successful they were, or hoped to be, in creating a rigid dichotomy between themselves and girls who were sexed in.

In addition, there were also practical considerations in young women's disdain for girls who were sexed in. As I described in previous chapters, being in a gang comes with the expectation that you will encounter rival gang members and that these encounters pose a potential threat to your physical safety. As Erica noted, "When you join [the gang], you might as well expect that there's gonna be fights." The typical route for joining involved some form of physical confrontation, whether it was being "jumped in" by members, taking "blows" to the head and chest, fighting a rival gang member, or committing a risky crime. As I discussed in Chapter 7, part of the reason girls were disrespected for being sexed in was because they had chosen "the easy way in," and this could pose a real physical threat to other girls in gangs. Recall that Chantell expressed concern about what would happen if she were out with girls from the gang who were sexed in and they were confronted by rival gang members. In her estimation, she risked being outnumbered and injured because she couldn't count on the other girls to back her up. Because they were sexed into the gang, she was unsure of their fighting skills, which raised concern for her own safety.

Given the dangers involved, why didn't gang girls challenge the practice? Ironically, denigrating girls who were sexed in or exploited, rather than holding the young men accountable, was the key to maintaining the tenuous but vital belief that the male gang members viewed them as equals. Creating this dichotomy allowed girls to conclude that the boys in their gang treated and discussed *other* young women in sexually derogatory ways—young women who deserved it because they were "nasty." On the other hand, they could believe that the boys considered them, as Leslie put it, "one of the niggas," or one of the guys. It was a difficult balance to maintain, as my conversation above with Monica suggests. Challenging the practice, or the general tendency of some young men to mistreat other girls or talk about them in sexually derogatory ways, risked being ostracized from the group. The young woman who witnessed her friends gang rape another girl made these risks apparent in her conversation. It also meant having to confront rather than deny or justify the fact that girls were not "equals" in the eyes of their male gang peers. Given the importance of their gangs in many young women's lives, it appears the only viable options were to either find a way to come to terms with these activities or give up the group. For the time being at least, most of the young women I talked to had chosen the former.

Males Are Harder, Females Are Softer

The second gender belief to which young women most routinely subscribed—that male members tend to be "harder" than females—is more difficult to make sense of with regard to its incongruity with the notion of gender equality in the gang. However, its benefits for young women are much more apparent. While girls' sexual denigration of females is aimed at *other* girls, with only a few exceptions their beliefs that female members aren't as tough as males are aimed at themselves as well, as Tonya's exclamation, "We ain't no supercommando girls!" makes clear (my emphasis). Despite the incompatibility of this belief with their assertion of equality, it nonetheless provided a number of advantages for gang girls. It meant accepting protection and retaliation on their behalf from male members of their gangs in recognizably dangerous environments, it furnished a justification for avoiding or limiting participation in those aspects of gang involvement that were dangerous or morally troubling, and finally, it allowed young women to view the gang as less central to their long-term life plans and instead define their gang involvement as a primarily adolescent commitment.

As I noted earlier, gangs operate within larger social milieus that are characterized by gender inequality and sexual exploitation. Being in a gang with young men meant at least the semblance of protection from and retaliation against other young men in the social environment. I explored this benefit in detail in Chapter 7, noting girls' discussions of this as an important feature of their gangs. Moreover, young men's protection was particularly useful when girls were engaged in crime. Recall from Chapters 6 and 7 that a number of young women suggested that females were viewed as particularly easy targets on the streets, especially when they were selling drugs. Young men could aid in their success in these endeavors by making sure they had backup and weren't messed with. Young women recognized that males had greater resources at their disposal to commit a variety of crimes— what Hagan and McCarthy call criminal capital.[27] As Tonya explained, "They can get us strapped [armed] quicker, they can get dope quicker. So girls need dudes in the gang."

More than just providing young women with the semblance of protection, girls' perceptions that males were more central to the gang allowed them to limit the level of their criminal involvement. This is a theme I explored in detail in Chapter 6. In particular, young women's acceptance of the notion that participation in the most serious forms of crime (e.g., shootings, armed robberies) was primarily a male endeavor provided them with a means of avoiding participation in those aspects of gang life they found risky, threatening, or troubling in some way. Obviously, as I described in Chapter 6, there were young women involved in serious gang crime. However, they were the exception rather than the rule. Most girls tended to avoid involvement in serious crime, at least on a regular basis. While partly this was because young men excluded them, it was also the case that many young women made their own decision to exclude themselves because they felt ambivalent about this aspect of gang life.

Finally, the acceptance of the gang as male-dominated, even while claiming equality, provided young women with an additional benefit: They were able to define their gang commitment as more transitory than that of young men. Let me return to Diane's description of how her gang handled the commission of serious crimes:

For maybe a drive-by, they might wanna have a bunch of dudes. They might not put females in that. Maybe the females might be weak inside, not strong enough to do something like that, just on the insides. . . . If a female wants to go forward and doin' that, and *she wants to risk her whole life for doin' that*, then she can. But the majority of the time, that job is given to a man [my emphasis].

Diane was not simply alluding to the notion that males were harder than females, though it was clearly part of what she said. In addition, her inference was that young women were able to avoid committing serious crime more than young men because a girl shouldn't have to "risk her whole life" for the gang. In defining young men as more central members of their gangs, young women were able to view their time in the gang as an adolescent undertaking, rather than a way of life.

As I described in Chapters 4 and 5, motherhood was often an event that allowed young women to move away from their gangs.[28] In addition, the girls I interviewed nearly all said they expected to leave their gangs when they reached adulthood, and most had career aspirations, ranging from wanting to be hairdressers or nurses to probation officers or lawyers. There is evidence that these kinds of career aspirations are more common for young women in gangs than they are for young men, who have a more difficult time leaving their gangs and criminal ties behind.[29] As I noted in Chapter 1, research also indicates that young women tend to get into gangs at younger ages and exit earlier than young men do. Perhaps part of the way they are able to do so is by defining their gangs as part of their adolescent life, rather than as an ongoing commitment. It may also be that some young women become disillusioned with their gangs over time, as Leslie and Sonita both described, because of their experiences of gender inequality within the group.

Gang girls struck a situationally specific "patriarchal bargain" within their gangs, which allowed them to draw many of the social benefits of gang affiliation while avoiding or negotiating which of the gang's riskier sides they would take part in. There were, of course, costs associated with the bargain. As I noted with regard to the practice of "sexing-in," its sheer existence meant that all gang girls contended with others' perceptions of them as sexually available or promiscuous. This served to keep girls disempowered because they always faced the question of how they got in and whether they were "true" members. In fact, several scholars have noted the long-term stigma some women face even in adulthood as a result of their adolescent gang involvement, because of perceptions of their supposedly "spoiled" sexuality.[30] Moreover, allowing that males were "harder" than females perpetuated the devaluation of female members as less significant to the gang—not as tough, true, or "down" for the gang as the young men were. As I discussed in Chapter 7, the assumption that girls were weaker meant they had to fight harder to prove how tough they were, and it also placed them at greater risk of being mistreated by male gang members when they were viewed, as Chantell lamented, as "just another punk." Perhaps the most significant cost of the bargain, however, was the way in which it perpetuated girls' negative perceptions of other young women, alienating girls from one another.

A number of recent studies have examined women's gender strategies in a variety of settings, explicating why and how women often participate in the maintenance of gender oppression, instead of or in addition to resisting it.[31] This is a useful avenue of inquiry for understanding aspects of young women's gang involvement as well. Young women in gangs live in social worlds where gender oppression is both fierce and highly visible. Many have been victimized themselves or know other women in their lives who have been. Although the gang reproduces some of these same structures of gender inequality, it also provides normative space for equality, which the young women I spoke to clearly valued.

Although understandable, it is unfortunate that the notion of equality that many young women adopted was not one that encouraged solidarity with other young women, but instead was a version suggesting that females with the "right stuff" could be accepted as "one of the guys." This meant being willing to denigrate or accept the denigration and mistreatment of other girls, making gang girls' equality contingent on being different than other young women—namely, those who were weak, easily exploitable, or sexually "promiscuous". Many young women's means of resisting gender oppression within gangs tended to be an individualized response based on constructing gendered gang identities as separate from and "better than" those of the girls and women around them in their social environments. It meant internalizing and accepting masculine constructs of gang values.

Even as they defined themselves as equals, young women revealed the myriad ways in which they continued to face forms of disempowerment in relation to young men in gangs. However, it is important also to recognize the benefits they gained. On the whole, gender inequality within gangs did not appear to be substantially different than it was in other areas of these young women's lives, but gang membership *did* provide them with a sense of empowerment and the semblance of protection from others on the streets. The fact that most of the sexual assaults they experienced occurred prior to or outside of the context of their gangs is evidence of this. Moreover, girls' marginalization relative to males in their gangs allowed them to view their involvement as comparatively transitory. These young women lived in social worlds in which women were devalued; their means of resisting their own devaluation was not to challenge the premise of this treatment, but instead to define themselves as outside of its boundaries, while simultaneously drawing what advantages they could from the gender hierarchies within their gangs. Ultimately, as with any "patriarchal bargain," young women's participation in and support of oppressive gender structures, while understandable, ultimately helped to maintain their inequality.

CONCLUSION

In this chapter, I have attempted to make feminist sense of young women's contradictory attitudes about gender equality and women. Much to my initial chagrin, I did not encounter many of the gang girls that other scholars have described—girls who expressed the importance of "sisterhood" or close familial-like bonds with other young women in their gangs. Instead, young women drew on many of the same cultural frames found in the larger society with regard to negative characterizations of women, including, most notably, victim-blaming attitudes toward young women's mistreatment.

However, I believe their discussions make sense when placed in the context of the primarily male-dominated structures of their gangs, as well as the larger contexts of young women's lives. Recognizing the devaluation of women around them, young women appreciated the normative space of "equality" available in gangs, even when it was not always a reality. Identifying with dominant beliefs about women while rejecting such images for themselves allowed many young women to construct themselves as "one of the guys." Being one of the guys, as Kanter notes, sometimes meant doing so at the expense of "the girls." However, young women's gender strategies allowed them to draw particular advantages from their gangs that were less available in other social spaces.

9

Conclusion

In Chapter 1, I suggested that our studies of girls in gangs and women's involvement in crime would be strengthened by several insights found in the feminist literature outside of criminology. First is recognition of the limitations of either a "gender differences" or a "gender similarities" approach for understanding women's lives. The former tends to essentialize differences between women and men, fails to account for similarities in their experiences, and also overlooks important differences *between* women—including, but not limited to, differences resulting from race, class, and age. On the other hand, the "gender similarities" approach often results in a failure to be attentive to the importance of gender, which, despite my call for caution in overemphasized gender differences, continues to play a primary role in creating the opportunities and constraints that frame young women's daily lives.

Old paradigms continue to resurface within our scholarship, albeit in new ways. For instance, the "hapless" victim characteristic of early writings on girls in gangs and women who offend has been replaced by a "resisting" one. Here women's criminal offending and girls' participation in gangs are characterized as response or resistance to victimization. And this is no doubt part of what's going on. Nonetheless, it's only part. The overemphasis on women's gendered victimization—and with it, the accentuation of gender differences—continues to permeate much of the feminist literature on women and crime, to the exclusion of other important issues. Instead, I have argued that we need to grapple with women's harmful actions toward others in ways that go beyond defining these acts simply as resistance or response to gendered victimization. This does not mean being *in*attentive to the importance of gender or victimization, but it does mean taking into account broader motives and rewards for involvement in crime—including those shared with men. While it's true that we're either female or male—and in our culture, that means a lot—it's also true that we're all human. And thus we have to expect overlap in the experiences and considerations that shape our activities.

Casting women's involvement in crime in the ways I propose may seem a dangerous proposition to many, and perhaps it is so. We live in a time in which individual responsibility dominates the rhetoric on crime and justice, and feminism is experiencing a backlash—particularly, as I described in Chapter 1, in accounts of women's offending. Thus the threat that our work be misused is ever-present. Nonetheless, if our goal truly is to understand women's lives, then we must take the full range of their experiences into account. Not doing so limits our ability to gain a complex understanding of the richness of women's lives and actions—both good and bad—and it leaves our work easily discountable for those who wish to do so. Moreover, I emphasize the importance of resisting easy "gender differences" approaches at a time when this alarm is clearly in need of sounding. Evolutionary and biological approaches have begun to regain popularity in the field, and this is even the case among some feminist criminologists.[1] To me, the tendency toward reductionism in these approaches poses a much greater threat than does opening up our understanding of women's crime, even as it means grappling with what it means to hold women accountable for their harmful actions toward others. I remain convinced that we can do so in ways that remain stalwartly feminist.[2]

Throughout my discussion of girls in gangs, I have attempted to keep each of these insights at the forefront, while remaining keenly focused on the impact of gender on gang girls' lives. Perhaps most important in facilitating this approach has been my stress on the insights to be gleaned from a comparative perspective. I built a number of comparative strategies into both data collection and analysis. Most obvious are the comparisons of gang and nongang girls—the focus of Chapter 3—and of Columbus and St. Louis, the focus of Chapters 4 and 5. In addition, by drawing on the literature on young men's involvement in street gangs, as well as on girls' insights about the significance of gender in gangs, I have worked to provide comparative insights about girls' and boys' experiences within youth gangs. Finally, I have emphasized differences *among* girls in gangs, most notably by highlighting levels of criminal involvement, commitment to their gangs, attitudes about girls, and differences I suggest emerge from the gender compositions of girls' gangs. Taking this approach has allowed me to be attentive to the complexities of gang life, the importance of a variety of contexts, and the similarities in gang life across gender. Nonetheless, I believe my approach has remained thoroughly feminist—remaining attentive to gender, but drawing my conclusions based on insights emerging from empirical discoveries, all the while remaining open to the possibility that there may be situations in which *gang* contexts are more relevant than or interact with *gender* in explaining girls' experiences, motives, and activities.

In Chapter 3, I detailed young women's accounts of getting into gangs, focusing on three important dimensions: neighborhood and friendship networks, problems within the family, and the influence of gang-involved family members. Not only did these factors distinguish gang girls from nongang girls living in similar communities, but they also emerged in gang girls' own descriptions of the processes by which they chose to join gangs. There were overlaps in girls' accounts of getting into gangs with what we know of young men's gang involvement, particularly with regard to the importance of neighborhood and peer networks. In some of their discussions, "Erica could easily be Eric,"[3] or Veronica, Ronald.

However, there were also important differences, most notably many young women's troubled family lives and experiences of abuse. No doubt, many young men also experience family problems and abuse, but as Moore's work makes clear, this appears to be a stronger tipping point in drawing girls into gangs.[4] Moreover, there were differences across young women's accounts: Some focused on the influence of significant family members, others did not; some recounted sexual abuse within the family, others did not; still others emphasized the overwhelming impact of having drug-addicted mothers and the feelings of abandonment that resulted. I tried to tell their stories in ways that captured the overlapping nature of their experiences, but also took seriously their differences.

Chapters 4 and 5 focused on the nature of gangs in Columbus and St. Louis, with an eye toward the similarities and differences emerging across community contexts. Young women in the two cities gave similar accounts of many aspects of gang life, for instance, status hierarchies, dating relationships, and the impact of motherhood on young women's gang involvement. However, Columbus gangs appeared to be more strongly influenced by cultural diffusion from Chicago gangs, resulting in a greater emphasis on organizational elements of the gang such as leadership, initiations, and meetings. In contrast, because of the preexisting strength of neighborhood boundaries in St. Louis, gang territoriality and membership requirements there appeared to be more clearly delineated and tied to youths' neighborhood identities. And while my study methodology and sampling limit my ability to make conclusive statements about the differences across these two sites, the work of other scholars in Columbus and St. Louis gives credence to my findings.[5]

Columbus and St. Louis, however, are both specific types of gang cities. Future comparative work could yield even greater insights—particularly about the impact of race and ethnicity, community contexts in cities outside of the Midwest, and how different types of gangs and gang cities shape young women's experiences. Columbus and St. Louis are both relatively new gang cities, with relatively new gangs. Comparative studies including more traditional gang cities, with long histories of gangs and gangs with long histories, can provide important additional insights. Moreover, while gangs in Columbus and especially St. Louis are predominantly African American, as were the young women I spoke with, there is evidence that the nature and structure of young women's gangs are influenced by ethnicity—an issue I was unable to fully explore. For instance, some research suggests that autonomous female gangs appear more common among African Americans, while Latina and Chicana gang members are more likely to describe their groups as auxiliary female gangs.[6] The vast majority of girls in my study were in neither of these types of groups.

In Chapter 6, I turned my attention to young women's participation in delinquency. Here I highlighted gang girls' greater likelihood than their non-gang counterparts to be involved in a variety of delinquent activities as well as the variations among young women in gangs. As I described, only about one-third of the girls in my study were involved in ongoing serious delinquency or drug sales, while the majority were not. Moreover, young women discussed the ways that gender shaped or differentiated young women's gang crime from young men's. They highlighted that gun use was primarily the purview of young men, while knives and fists were the purview of young women. Many young women expressed moral ambivalence about the gun use and homicides associated with gangs and also described being excluded from such behavior by young men. Drug-selling, especially crack sales, was also seen as primarily a male endeavor, though young women in St. Louis were less likely to express this opinion than were young women in Columbus.

Nonetheless, important similarities across gender emerged in Chapter 6, buttressed by girls' discussions of status issues and gang rivalries. Most notably, although their confrontations with rival gang members tended to manifest themselves in different ways—in their most extreme forms, girls rarely use guns or participate in drive-by shootings—girls' confrontations, like those of boys, were motivated by gang processes. This provides important information that challenges the tendency, documented in Chapter 1, to describe girls' use of violence in gangs as resulting from protective or defensive responses to gendered vulnerability. Instead, girls described participating in attacks based on retaliation, protection of gang territory, and "being down" for their gangs and gang friends. Even when describing crimes less in keeping with recognized gang motives, girls' accounts highlighted the importance of peer contexts in facilitating their delinquency. Despite the gendered nature of girls' crime, their participation was often a function of gang processes.

In keeping with my position here, elsewhere I have made the argument that differences in males' and females' patterns of offending do not always result from differences in their motivation to commit crime.[7] Again, to talk about situational motives is not the same as talking about larger etiological questions; instead, I am referring to the foreground of offending.[8] Girls' descriptions of their reasons for involvement in crime, and the circumstances in which it occurred, were very much in keeping with what we know about crime among male gang members. The striking gender differences girls described with regard to the types and levels of their criminal involvement did not appear to result from differences in the reasons they committed gang crime. Rather, they were in part a reflection of the practical choices girls made, as well as male gang members' exclusion of girls, in the context of gangs that were gender-stratified and male-dominated.

With an eye toward the impact of these features of gangs, Chapter 7 focused on victimization risk, particularly the ways in which gang involvement structures this risk for girls. Gang girls were more likely than their nongang peers both to have been victimized and to have witnessed serious violence. Part of this exposure appeared related to gang involvement, while other violence, most notably sexual assault, did not. On the whole, young women recognized that being in a gang meant exposure to victimization risk; nonetheless, many girls emphasized the protection they received within their gangs. Some young women limited their involvement in risky behaviors, which also decreased their likelihood of being victimized or witnessing serious violence, particularly at the hands of rival gang members or others on the street. Because they were less likely to be involved in gun violence, young women did not report the fear of being killed; rather, they feared losing their male loved ones. Combined, my findings in Chapters 6 and 7 suggest that while protection from gendered vulnerability clearly *was* a feature of girls' gang involvement, this does not preclude their participation in gangs and gang crime for a range of other reasons.

On the other hand, young women's lesser involvement in serious gang crime also increased the likelihood that they would be mistreated by their own gang peers when they were seen as unlikely to stand up for themselves. For instance, I documented the existence of sexual mistreatment within gangs, most notably in the form of sexual initiations. Although only two young women in the sample alluded to having been sexed in, many knew young women who had gone through such an initiation, and they noted that it typically led to the girl's subsequent mistreatment by gang members. Moreover, the existence of the practice created problems and stigma with which all gang girls had to contend. In addition, young women's lesser participation in serious gang crime strengthened perceptions of them as less capable, less "true" members. This contributed to more routinized mistreatment at the hands of male gang members. Ultimately, it appears that these young women chose to trade unknown risks for known ones. The gang offered protection from and retaliation against others on the streets in exchange for the acceptance of violence under more or less predictable conditions.

Finally, in Chapter 8 I attempted to make feminist sense of young women's contradictory attitudes about gender equality and women. Much to my initial chagrin, I did not encounter many young women who expressed the importance of "sisterhood" or the importance of bonds with other young women in their gangs, as a number of other scholars have suggested. Instead, young women drew on many of the same cultural frames found in the larger society with regard to negative characterizations of women. However, I believe their discussions make sense when placed in the context of the primarily male-dominated structures of their gangs, as well as the larger contexts of young women's lives. Recognizing the devaluation of women around them, young women appreciated the normative space of "equality" available in gangs, even when it was not always a reality. Identifying with dominant beliefs about women but rejecting such images for themselves allowed many young women to construct themselves as "one of the guys." Being one of the guys, as Kanter notes, sometimes meant doing so at the expense of "the girls." Nonetheless, young women's gender strategies—what Kandiyoti aptly terms "patriarchal bargains"—allowed them to draw particular advantages from their gangs that were less available in other social spaces.

In this book, I most often have placed young women's gang involvement within the context of crime and criminology, specifically within the broader criminologica l literature on youth gangs. I stand by having done so, as I believe I've situated girls' gangs within the space that the young women I spoke to placed them. In addition, this approach has allowed me to make important contributions about both overlaps and differences in girls' and boys' experiences within gangs. While I have highlighted the broader contexts of their lives, particularly in Chapter 3, I believe nonetheless that there's more to be done in this regard. I have worked to reveal the humanity of the young women who took part in this study and have taken particular effort to situate them in a more complex way within their gangs. However, with my approach inevitably came sacrifices, most notably, a limited ability to describe these young women's histories and lives beyond "life in the gang." Future work should further broaden our understanding of the life contexts of girls in gangs. My hope is that the insights provided here, and those drawn from feminist scholarship in other disciplines, will help frame the parameters of future research—bridging the gender similarities/differences divide and documenting girls' victimization, resistance, *and* agency in ways that capture their full humanity.

Gang-Involved Study Participants (*N* = 48)

Name*	City	Race	Age (Years)	Joined at Age (Years)	Affiliation†
Traci	Columbus	African American	12	12	Crips
Nikki	Columbus	African American	13	12	Bloods
Brandi	Columbus	African American	13	13	Folks
Lisa	Columbus	White	13	13	Folks
Chantell	Columbus	African American	14	12	Crips
Keisha	Columbus	African American	14	13	Folks
Sonita	Columbus	African American	14	13	Folks
Stephanie	Columbus	African American	14	14	Folks
Angie	Columbus	African American	15	11	Crips
Diane	Columbus	White	15	11	Crips
Veronica	Columbus	African American	15	11	Folks
Heather	Columbus	White	15	12	Folks
Tamika	Columbus	African American	15	15	Crips
Monica	Columbus	African American	16	13	Crips
Cathy	Columbus	White	16	14	Bloods
Leslie	Columbus	Biracial	16	14	Folks
Jennifer	Columbus	White	16	15	Gangster Girlz
Kim	Columbus	African American	16	15	Folks
LaShawna	Columbus	African American	17	12	Folks
Erica	Columbus	African American	17	15	Folks
Michelle	Columbus	African American	17	16	Folks
Trina	St. Louis	African American	12	11	Bloods
Regina	St. Louis	African American	13	11	Crips
Crystal	St. Louis	African American	13	12	Crips (all-girls set)
Tyra	St. Louis	African American	14	10	Crips
Vashelle	St. Louis	African American	14	11	Bloods
Neoka	St. Louis	African American	14	12	Crips
Alecia	St. Louis	African American	14	12	Crips (all-girls set)
Vikkie	St. Louis	African American	14	13	Bloods
Yolanda	St. Louis	African American	14	13	N.W.O.
Shandra	St. Louis	African American	15	12	Crips
Rhonda	St. Louis	Multiracial	15	13	Unavailable
Brittany	St. Louis	African American	15	14	Bloods
Toni	St. Louis	African American	15	15	Bloods
Shawanda	St. Louis	African American	16	12	Crips
Latisha	St. Louis	African American	16	12	Bloods
Marie	St. Louis	Multiracial	16	13	Gangster Disciples

Name*	City	Race	Age (Years)	Joined at Age (Years)	Affiliation†
Dionne	St. Louis	African American	16	14	Bloods
Cheri	St. Louis	Multiracial	17	11	Crips
Gwyn	St. Louis	African American	17	13	Crips
Sheila	St. Louis	African American	17	13	Crips
Tonya	St. Louis	African American	17	13	Crips
Yvette	St. Louis	African American	17	13	Crips (all-girls set)
Mia	St. Louis	African American	17	14	Crips
Brenda	St. Louis	African American	17	15	N.W.O.
Pam	St. Louis	African American	18	13	Crips
Shiree	St. Louis	African American	18	18	The Outlaws
Debbie	St. Louis	African American	20	10	Crips

*Pseudonyms.

†Specific gang names have been excluded or, in the case of all-female gangs, changed.

NOTES

Chapter 1

1. Short and Strodtbeck, *Group Process and Gang Delinquency*, p. 242. Notably, this quotation in Short and Strodtbeck's book was based on the observations of an African American female graduate student who was a research assistant on the project.
2. This passage was taken from a story on female gang involvement by ABC news correspondent Karen Burnes, which ran on *World News Tonight* in February 1990.
3. For a thorough discussion of the problems of victimization, agency, and volition in relation to female offenders, see Maher, *Sexed Work*.
4. Daly and Chesney-Lind, "Feminism and Criminology." See also Kruttschnitt, "Contributions of Quantitative Methods to the Study of Gender and Crime, or Bootstrapping Our Way into the Theoretical Thicket."
5. Spergel and Curry, "The National Youth Gang Survey," p. 359; also see Curry et al., "Estimating the National Scope of Gang Crime from Law Enforcement Data"; Klein, *The American Street Gang*; and Maxson et al., "Street Gang Migration in the United States." Gang proliferation is only part of the answer to the question of why the academic study of gangs has been reborn. Bursik and Grasmick point out that "criminology has been characterized by ongoing paradigm shifts concerning the role of group dynamics in the etiology of crime" (p. 113). Renewed interest in gangs is thus partly a result of a shift away from individual-level theories of crime and delinquency, which dominated criminological research during the 1970s and early 1980s. See Bursik and Grasmick, *Neighborhoods and Crime*; Bookin and Horowitz, "The End of the Youth Gang." In addition, funding priorities—namely, the widespread availability of federal funds for cities with gang problems—may have contributed to the reclassification of youth crime problems into "gang" problems in some communities. See, for example, Zatz, "Chicano Youth Gangs and Crime."
6. Klein, *The American Street Gang*.
7. Brotherton, "'Smartness,' 'Toughness' and 'Autonomy'"; Campbell, "Female Participation in Gangs"; Curry, "Selected Statistics on Female Gang Involvement"; Fagan, "The Social Organization of Drug Use and Drug Dealing among Urban Gangs"; Joe and Chesney-Lind, "'Just Every Mother's Angel'"; Klein and Maxson, "Gang Structures, Crime Patterns, and Police Responses"; Sullivan, "Getting Paid."
8. For instance, in their "Gang Crime and Law Enforcement Recordkeeping," Curry et al. found that some law enforcement policies officially exclude female gang members from their counts. Controlling for data from these cities, they still found that females were only 5.7 percent of gang members known to law enforcement agencies. Part of law enforcement's underestimation of girls' gang involvement

is likely attributable to male gang members' greater likelihood of being involved in serious gang crimes, as well as law enforcement's greater attention to older offenders. See Curry, "Proliferation of Gangs in the U.S."

9. For instance, based on a stratified sample of youths in high-risk, high-crime neighborhoods, Bjerregaard and Smith actually found that a slightly larger percentage of females (22 percent) than males (18 percent) claimed gang membership when self-definition was used as a measure. See their "Gender Differences in Gang Participation, Delinquency, and Substance Use." Notably, while this was the case in the early waves of their study, examination of later waves showed that young women quickly dropped out of gangs, suggesting that much of girls' gang involvement takes place in early adolescence and desists shortly thereafter.

   Based on a sample of eighth graders in eleven cities, Esbensen and Deschenes report that the prevalence rate for gang membership was 14 percent for males and 8 percent for females. See their "A Multi-Site Examination of Gang Membership" Other recent studies have examined the gender ratio among gang members; these inquiries estimate that young women approximate between 20 and 46 percent of gang members. See Esbensen and Huizinga, "Gangs, Drugs and Delinquency in a Survey of Urban Youth"; Winfree et al., "The Definition and Measurement of 'Gang Status.'" Esbensen and Winfree suggest that both methodological differences and differences in the age of youth included in gang studies explain varying estimates of girls' gang involvement. See their "Race and Gender Differences between Gang and Non-Gang Youth" for a discussion.

10. See Klein, *Street Gangs and Street Workers*; Moore, *Going Down to the Barrio*. Moreover, Moore's work, as well as Fishman's—both historical analyses of gangs in earlier decades—reveal that girls' roles in these groups were broader than the literature from those periods suggest. See Fishman, "The Vice Queens." See also Brown, "Black Female Gangs in Philadelphia."

11. Battin et al., "The Contribution of Gang Membership to Delinquency beyond Delinquent Friends"; Esbensen et al., "Gang and Non-Gang Youth"; Esbensen and Huizinga, "Gangs, Drugs, and Delinquency in a Survey of Urban Youth"; Esbensen and Winfree, "Race and Gender Differences between Gang and Non-Gang Youth"; Fagan, "Social Processes of Delinquency and Drug Use among Urban Gangs"; Huff, "Comparing the Criminal Behavior of Youth Gangs and At-Risk Youths"; Thornberry and Burch, "Gang Members and Delinquent Behavior"; Thornberry et al., "The Role of Juvenile Gangs in Facilitating Delinquent Behavior."

12. Bjerregaard and Smith, "Gender Differences in Gang Participation, Delinquency, and Substance Use"; Esbensen and Winfree, "Race and Gender Differences between Gang and Non-Gang Youth"; Fagan, "Social Processes of Delinquency and Drug Use among Urban Gangs"; Thornberry et al., "The Role of Juvenile Gangs in Facilitating Delinquent Behavior"

13. For example, see Cloward and Ohlin, *Delinquency and Opportunity*; Cohen, *Delinquent Boys*; Klein, *Street Gangs and Street Workers*; Moore, *Homeboys*; Short and Strodbeck, *Group Process and Gang Delinquency*; Thrasher, *The Gang*. This emphasis on male gang members has continued in some contemporary research as well. For recent examples, see Hagedorn, *People and Folks*; Jankowski, *Islands in the Streets*; Padilla, *The Gang as an American Enterprise*; Vigil, *Barrio Gangs*.

14. For feminist critiques of criminology's treatment of women, see Campbell, *Girl Delinquents*; Klein, "The Etiology of Female Crime"; Leonard, *Women, Crime and*

Society; Smart, *Women, Crime and Criminology*. For critiques of gender bias in early gang research, see Campbell, *The Girls in the Gang*, "Female Participation in Gangs," and "On the Invisibility of the Female Delinquent Peer Group"; Chesney-Lind and Shelden, *Girls, Delinquency and Juvenile Justice*; Fishman, "The Vice Queens"; Taylor, *Girls, Gangs, Women and Drugs*.

For vivid illustrations of the mischaracterization of women offenders throughout criminology's history, see Cowie et al., *Delinquency in Girls*; Konopka, *The Adolescent Girl in Conflict*; Lombroso and Ferrero, *The Female Offender*; Pollock, *The Criminality of Women*; Thomas, *The Unadjusted Girl*.

15. For overviews of feminist contributions to criminology, see Daly, "From Gender Ratios to Gendered Lives"; Daly and Chesney-Lind, "Feminism and Criminology"; Daly and Maher, "Crossroads and Intersections"; Kruttschnitt, "Contributions of Quantitative Methods to the Study of Gender and Crime, or Bootstrapping Our Way into the Theoretical Thicket"; Simpson, "Feminist Theory, Crime and Justice."

16. See Adler, *Sisters in Crime*; Simon, *Women and Crime*.

17. Daly and Chesney-Lind, "Feminism and Criminology," p. 514.

18. See, for instance, Bjerregaard and Smith, "Gender Differences in Gang Participation, Delinquency, and Substance Use"; Esbensen and Deschenes, "A Multi-Site Examination of Gang Membership."

19. Kruttschnitt, "Contributions of Quantitative Methods to the Study of Gender and Crime, or Bootstrapping Our Way into the Theoretical Thicket," p. 141. See also Smith and Paternoster, "The Gender Gap in Theories of Deviance."

20. See Pearson, *When She Was Bad*.

21. See Simpson, "Feminist Theory, Crime and Justice," pp. 610–611; Steffensmeier and Steffensmeier, "Trends in Female Delinquency."

22. For a discussion, see Chesney-Lind, *The Female Offender*; Chesney-Lind et al., "Girls, Delinquency, and Gang Membership."

23. Sampson and Wilson, "Toward a Theory of Race, Crime and Urban Inequality"; Wilson, *When Work Disappears*. With regard to gangs specifically, see Hagedorn, *People and Folks* and "Gangs, Neighborhoods and Public Policy"; Jackson, "Crime, Youth Gangs and Urban Transition"; Klein, *The American Street Gang*; Moore, "Gangs and the Underclass"; Moore and Vigil, "Barrios in Transition"; Padilla, *The Gang as an American Enterprise*; Short, "New Wine in Old Bottles?"; Sullivan, "Getting Paid"; Zevitz and Takata, "Metropolitan Gang Influence and the Emergence of Group Delinquency in a Regional Community."

24. See Baumer et al., "The Influence of Crack Cocaine on Robbery, Burglary, and Homicide Rates."

25. For instance, in *Casualties of Community Disorder*, Baskin and Sommers examined arrest data for violent crime in New York City from 1980 to 1994 and noted that women's "arrests for robbery and aggravated assault increased 77.5 percent and 56 percent, respectively" during this period (p. 19). Moreover, they suggest that women's proportion of violent increased during this period as well—while women were 6.4 percent of robbery arrestees and 13.1 percent of assault arrestees during the period between 1980 and 1984, they were 8.9 percent and 15.1 percent, respectively, during the period between 1990 and 1994.

While they do document increases in women's proportions of these two types of violence, these changes are arguably slight and are not indicative of a wide movement of women into serious violent crime. Moreover, they make less of their data on women's arrests for homicide, which are clearly less likely to be influenced by police decision making. In fact, their data show that women's participation in homicides declined during the study period, both in terms of actual numbers (468 female arrestees from 1980 to 1984 versus 347 from 1990 to 1994) and as a proportion of arrestees (7.7 percent in the earlier period versus 5.2 percent in the later period) (p. 20).

26. Baskin et al., "The Political Economy of Violent Female Street Crime," p. 413.
27. Baskin et al., "The Political Economy of Violent Female Street Crime," pp. 415 and 417, respectively.
28. Bourgois, *In Search of Respect*, p. 213.
29. Taylor, *Girls, Gangs, Women and Drugs*, pp. 8, 10, and 23, respectively.
30. Federal Bureau of Investigation, *Crime in the United States, 1995*.
31. Daly and Chesney-Lind, "Feminism and Criminology," p. 515.
32. See note 25 for a description of one such example.
33. Hill and Crawford, "Women, Race and Crime"; Maher, *Sexed Work*; Simpson, "Caste, Class and Violent Crime"; Simpson and Elis, "Doing Gender."
34. Campbell, "Female Participation in Gangs"; Fishman, "The Vice Queens"; Joe and Chesney-Lind, "'Just Every Mother's Angel'"; Lauderback et al., "'Sisters Are Doin' It for Themselves.'" A number of studies of young men's gang involvement highlight these issues as well. See Hagedorn, *People and Folks*; Padilla, *The Gang as an American Enterprise*; Vigil, *Barrio Gangs*.
35. Maher, *Sexed Work*, p. 18.
36. See Anderson, *Streetwise*; Oliver, *The Violent Social World of Black Men*; Miller, "Up It Up"; Steffensmeier, "Organizational Properties and Sex-Segregation in the Underworld"; Steffensmeier and Terry, "Institutional Sexism in the Underworld."
    With regard to gender inequalities in gangs, see Campbell, *The Girls in the Gang* and "Female Participation in Gangs"; Moore and Hagedorn, "What Happens to Girls in the Gang?"; Portillos, *Doing Gender in Chicano/a Gangs*; Portillos et al., "Machismo and Chicano/a Gangs"; Swart, "Female Gang Delinquency." For further discussion, see Chapters 7 and 8.
37. Wilson, *When Work Disappears*.
38. See Inciardi et al., *Women and Crack Cocaine*; Maher, *Sexed Work*; Maher and Curtis, "Women on the Edge of Crime"; Maher and Daly, "Women in the Street-Level Drug Economy"; Miller, "Gender and Power on the Streets"; Ratner, *Crack Pipe as Pimp*.
39. See Jacobs and Miller, "Crack Dealing, Gender, and Arrest Avoidance"; Miller, "Up It Up."
40. See Hagan et al., "The Class Structure of Gender and Delinquency"; Hagan et al., "Class in the Household"; Heimer and De Coster, "The Gendering of Violent Delinquency."
41. See Daly, "From Gender Ratios to Gendered Lives."
42. West and Fenstermaker, "Doing Difference," p. 21; see also West and Zimmerman, "Doing Gender."
43. West and Zimmerman, "Doing Gender," p. 147.
44. Simpson and Elis, "Doing Gender," p. 50. See also Messerschmidt, *Masculinities and Crime*; Newburn and Stanko, *Just Boys Doing Business?*
45. See Simpson, "Feminist Theory, Crime and Justice"; Simpson, "Caste, Class and Violent Crime"; Simpson and Elis, "Doing Gender."
46. Braithwaite and Daly, ""Masculinities, Violence and Communitarian Control," p. 190.

47. Daly, "Women's Pathways to Felony Court," p. 14.
48. Arnold, "Processes of Victimization and Criminalization of Black Women"; Campbell, *The Girls in the Gang*; Chesney-Lind and Rodriguez, "Women under Lock and Key"; Daly, "Women's Pathways to Felony Court"; Gilfus, "From Victims to Survivors to Offenders"; Richie, *Compelled to Crime*. With regard to gangs, see Joe and Chesney-Lind, " 'Just Every Mother's Angel' "; Moore, *Going Down to the Barrio*.
49. Chesney-Lind, *The Female Offender*.
50. Maher, *Sexed Work*, p. 95.
51. Maher, *Sexed Work*, pp. 95–96.
52. Campbell, *Men, Women and Aggression*, p. 131–132.
53. Campbell, *Men, Women and Aggression*, p. 133.
54. Joe and Chesney-Lind, " 'Just Every Mother's Angel,' " pp. 424–425, 428.
55. In their "The Gendering of Violent Delinquency," Heimer and De Coster provide what to me is the most compelling way out of this conundrum. Their theory and the evidence they present keep gender at the forefront, but in ways that can account for differences among girls *and* similarities between boys and girls, as well as cross-gender differences. Unlike traditional "generalizability" approaches, they highlight and empirically test how various theoretical constructs may apply differently across gender, but at the same time, they recognize and can account for situations in which gender is not the most salient factor shaping offending.
56. Maher, *Sexed Work*, p. 63.
57. See Heimer and De Coster, "The Gendering of Violent Delinquency"; Miller, "Up It Up"; Simpson, "Caste, Class and Violent Crime"; Simpson and Elis, "Doing Gender." In fact, there is evidence of this in a number of studies of girls' gang activities. See Brown, "Black Female Gangs in Philadephia"; Fishman, "The Vice Queens"; Giordano, "Girls, Guys and Gangs"; Quicker, *Homegirls*. I will discuss these themes in greater detail in Chapters 4–6.
58. Simpson and Elis, "Doing Gender," p. 51.
59. Simpson and Elis, "Doing Gender," p. 71.
60. In fact, the need to pay attention to intersections such as race, class, and gender is something that feminist criminologists have been discussing for some time. For instance, see Daly, "Women's Pathways to Felony Court" and "From Gender Ratios to Gendered Lives"; Daly and Maher, "Crossroads and Intersections"; Maher, *Sexed Work*; Rafter and Heidensohn, *International Feminist Perspectives in Criminology*; Schwartz and Milovanovic, *Race, Gender, and Class in Criminology*.
61. Simpson, "Feminist Theory, Crime and Justice," p. 618. See also Hill and Crawford, "Women, Race and Crime"; Simpson, "Caste, Class and Violent Crime."
62. Sampson and Wilson provide an important argument about the ways that the structural underpinnings of racial and economic inequalities shape cultural adaptations. Arguably, their findings apply to women as well as men in these communities. See their "Toward a Theory of Race, Crime and Urban Inequality." See also Baskin et al., "The Political Economy of Violent Female Street Crime"; Baskin and Sommers, *Casualties of Community Disorder*; Miller, "Up It Up"; Sommers and Baskin, "The Situational Context of Violent Female Offending." In fact, urban African American women's disproportionate involvement in serious violent crime is evidence of the significant link between underclass conditions and crime. For instance, Hill and Crawford report that structural indicators appear to be most significant in predicting the criminal involvement of African American

women, while social-psychological indicators are more predictive for white women. See their "Women, Race and Crime." For additional evidence regarding race, gender, and crime, see Ageton, "The Dynamics of Female Delinquency, 1976–1980"; Laub and McDermott, "An Analysis of Serious Crime by Young Black Women"; Mann, "Sister against Sister."

63. Thorne, *Gender Play*, p. 29.

64. Thorne, personal correspondence, September 17, 1998.

65. See Short, "The Level of Explanation Problem Revisited—The American Society of Criminology 1997 Presidential Address."

66. See Battin et. al., "The Contribution of Gang Membership to Delinquency beyond Delinquent Friends"; Klein and Crawford, "Groups, Gangs and Cohesiveness"; Short and Strodtbeck, *Group Process and Gang Delinquency.*

67. See Fausto-Sterling, *Myths of Gender*; Thorne, *Gender Play.*

68. As I described in note 55, perhaps the best illustration of what I am arguing for is Heimer and De Coster's "The Gendering of Violent Delinquency." Their analysis of young women's and young men's participation in violence accounts for between-gender differences and similarities and within-gender differences, while maintaining gender as a central category of analysis.

69. See Campbell, "Female Participation in Gangs" and *The Girls in the Gang*, for a discussion of these early studies.

70. Brotherton, " 'Smartness,' 'Toughness' and 'Autonomy' "; Campbell, *The Girls in the Gang*, "Girls' Talk," and "Self Definition by Rejection"; Giordano, "Girls, Guys and Gangs"; Harris, *Cholas*; Joe and Chesney-Lind, " 'Just Every Mother's Angel' "; Lauderback et al., " 'Sisters Are Doin' It for Themselves' "; Moore and Hagedorn, "What Happens to Girls in the Gang?"; Nurge, "Female Gangs and Cliques in Boston"; Portillos, *Doing Gender in Chicano/a Gangs*; Portillos et al., "Machismo and Chicano/a Gangs"; Quicker, *Homegirls*; Swart, "Female Gang Delinquency."

In fact, a critical dimension of feminist research involves recognizing and validating women's understandings of their experiences. See Collins, *Black Feminist Thought*; Harding, *Feminism and Methodology*; hooks, *Talking Back*; Lather, *Getting Smart*; Smith, "Women's Perspective as Radical Critique of Sociology."

71. Campbell, "Female Participation in Gangs," p. 173.

72. Curry, "Female Gang Involvement."

73. See, for instance, Fleisher, *Dead End Kids*; Taylor, *Girls, Gangs, Women and Drugs*, for examples at opposite poles of the continuum.

74. But see Campbell, "Self Definition by Rejection."

75. Fleisher, *Dead End Kids.*

76. Moore, *Going Down to the Barrio*, p. 52. See also Miller and Brunson, "Gender Dynamics in Youth Gangs."

77. See Miller, "Gender and Victimization Risk among Young Women in Gangs." This will be explored further in Chapter 7.

78. See Moore, *Going Down to the Barrio*; Moore and Hagedorn, "What Happens to Girls in the Gang?" In fact, recent attention to gangs is partly the result of (and contributes to) increased punitiveness toward juveniles, particularly youths of color. See Krisberg et al., "The Watershed of Juvenile Justice Reform," for a discussion of changes in the treatment of juveniles; Tonry, *Malign Neglect*, for a discussion of the impact of race. Klein, "Attempting Gang Control by Suppression"; Klein and Maxson, "Street Gang Violence"; and Molina, "California's Anti-Gang Street Terrorism Enforcement and Prevention Act," detail the punitive orientation driving much contemporary gang policy.

79. Taylor, *Girls, Gangs, Women and Drugs*, p. 23.
80. Lauderback et al., " 'Sisters Are Doin' It for Themselves,' " p. 57.
81. Lauderback et al., " 'Sisters Are Doin' It for Themselves,' " p. 62.
82. Lauderback et al., " 'Sisters Are Doin' It for Themselves,' " p. 68.
83. See Curry, "Selected Statistics on Female Gang Involvement"; Nurge, "Female Gangs and Cliques in Boston." Walter Miller was the first to suggest this tripartite classification of young women in gangs (e.g., autonomous, mixed-gender, "auxiliary"; see his *Violence by Youth Gangs and Youth Groups as a Crime Problem in Major American Cities*). While I use it myself, I should note that a number of scholars, including Nurge, are critical of this typology, arguing that it misses some of the complexity of gang formations for girls. In addition, while young women's gangs are routinely classified according to their gender composition, young men's gangs are defined more broadly—in terms of their activities, structures, and criminal endeavors. See Hagedorn and Devitt, "Fighting Female."

   There is also some evidence that the nature and structure of young women's gangs are influenced by ethnicity. For instance, autonomous female gangs appear to be more common among African Americans, while Latina and Chicana gang members are more likely to describe their groups as auxiliary female gangs. See Brotherton, " 'Smartness,' 'Toughness' and 'Autonomy' "; Joe and Chesney-Lind, " 'Just Every Mother's Angel' "; Joe-Laidler and Hunt, "Violence and Social Organization in Female Gangs"; Lauderback et al., " 'Sisters Are Doin' It for Themselves' "; Harris, *Cholas*; Moore, *Going Down to the Barrio*; Moore and Hagedorn, "What Happens to Girls in the Gang?"; Quicker, *Homegirls*.
84. See Campbell, *The Girls in the Gang* and "On the Invisibility of the Female Delinquent Peer Group"; Joe and Chesney-Lind, " 'Just Every Mother's Angel.' "
85. Campbell, "Self Definition by Rejection," pp. 463–464.
86. Campbell, *The Girls in the Gang* and "Female Participation in Gangs."
87. Bourgois and Dunlap, "Exorcising Sex-for-Crack"; Goldstein et al., "From Bag Brides to Skeezers"; Inciardi et al., *Women and Crack Cocaine*; Miller, "Gender and Power on the Streets"; Ratner, *Crack Pipe as Pimp*.
88. But see Allen, "Rendering Them Harmless"; Daly, "Women's Pathways to Felony Court."
89. Kelly, "Unspeakable Acts," p. 13.
90. Kelly, "Unspeakable Acts," p. 13.
91. Handler, "In the Fraternal Sisterhood," p. 236.
92. Feminist sociologists have theorized about this aspect of gender oppression in a wide variety of contexts. For examples, see Ebaugh, "Patriarchal Bargains and Latent Avenues of Social Mobility"; Hey, *The Company She Keeps*; Kandiyoti, "Bargaining with Patriarchy"; Kibria, "Power, Patriarchy and Gender Conflict in the Vietnamese Immigrant Community."
93. Simpson, "Caste, Class and Violent Crime," p. 118.
94. I use the term "at risk" in part because it is a familiar one used widely by other researchers and practitioners, but also because I believe it connotes concern for understanding the detrimental social conditions that affect young women's lives. However, the term has been critiqued by others, who suggest that "the at risk label . . . [has a] tendency to shift attention away from the social conditions that place adolescents at risk and locate the risk within the adolescents themselves." See Taylor et al., *Between Voice and Silence*, p. 21.
95. See Klein, *The American Street Gang*, for a discussion of the unique features of southern California and gangs.

96. Southern California has been a particularly popular setting for studies of girls in gangs. See Bowker et al., "Female Participation in Delinquent Gang Activities"; Bowker and Klein, "The Etiology of Female Juvenile Delinquency and Gang Membership"; Harris, *Cholas*; Moore, *Going Down to the Barrio*; Quicker, *Homegirls*. Likewise, Campbell's *Girls in the Gang* was based in New York, another traditional gang city.
97. For exceptions, see Brown, "Black Female Gangs in Philadelphia"; Fishman, "The Vice Queens"; and, more recently, Brotherton, " 'Smartness,' 'Toughness' and 'Autonomy' "; Lauderback et al., " 'Sisters Are Doin' It for Themselves' "; Taylor, *Girls, Gangs, Women and Drugs*. Joe and Chesney-Lind provide one of the few examinations of girls in Asian and Pacific Islander gangs. See their " 'Just Every Mother's Angel.' "
98. Decker and Van Winkle note that gangs have waxed and waned in St. Louis throughout the century, though the recent reemergence of gangs there is new. See their *Life in the Gang*.
99. See Moore and Hagedorn, "What Happens to Girls in the Gang?" See also note 9.

Chapter 2

1. See Hagedorn, *People and Folks*; Spergel and Curry, "The National Youth Gang Survey."
2. See Hagedorn, *People and Folks*; Huff, "Youth Gangs and Public Policy;" Klein, *The American Street Gang*, Chapter 4.
3. Hagedorn, *People and Folks* and "Gangs, Neighborhoods and Public Policy"; Moore, "Gangs and the Underclass"; Moore and Vigil, "Barrios in Transition"; Padilla, *The Gang as an American Enterprise*; Short, "New Wine in Old Bottles?"; Sullivan, *"Getting Paid"*; Zevitz and Takata, "Metropolitan Gang Influence and the Emergence of Group Delinquency in a Regional Community."
4. Wilson, *The Truly Disadvantaged* and *When Work Disappears*. However, some research suggests that the "underclass" explanation may be better suited to describe the experiences of inner-city African Americans than Latinos. See Moore and Pinterhughes, *In the Barrios*.
5. Hagedorn, *People and Folks* and "Homeboys, Dope Fiends, Legits and New Jacks"; Klein, *The American Street Gang*; Moore, "Gangs and the Underclass" and *Going Down to the Barrio*.
6. Jackson, "Crime, Youth Gangs and Urban Transition," p. 379.
7. See Klein, *The American Street Gang*. Socioeconomic factors do remain important, however, even in smaller cities and suburbs. For instance, Johnstone's research on suburban gangs shows a high correlation between the number of poverty-level families in a suburban community and the amount of gang activity there. See his "Youth Gangs and Black Suburbs."
8. See Decker and Van Winkle, *Life in the Gang*, pp. 85–89; Klein, *The American Street Gang*, pp. 205–212; Klein et al., "Introduction to Section II." In fact, there is evidence that the American gang culture has spread, through music videos, movies, and books, to European gang youth. In October 1998 I participated in a Eurogang Conference in Schmitten, Germany, attended by a number of scholars from around the United States and Europe. Gang-involved youths there have adopted

American gang names (e.g., Crips and Bloods), as well as the symbolism, colors, and graffiti of gangs here.

9. Klein et al., "Introduction to Section II," p. 110.
10. Spergel and Curry, "The National Youth Gang Survey," p. 398.
11. Klein and Crawford, "Groups, Gangs and Cohesiveness." See also Klein,"Attempting Gang Control by Suppression"; Short and Strodbeck, *Group Process and Gang Delinquency*. It is notable that some individuals who work with adolescents recognize that the adoption of gang style by nongang youths is widespread and poses problems for the identification of gang members. See Bursik and Grasmick, *Neighborhoods and Crime*, p. 116; Miller, "Struggles over the Symbolic."
12. See Maxson et al., "Street Gang Migration in the United States."
13. Rusk, *Cities without Suburbs*, p. 47.
14. Rusk, *Cities without Suburbs*, p. 47.
15. Rusk is referring here to cities with a central city population that is greater than 100,000. Other midwestern cities with zero elasticity include Chicago, Cincinnati, Cleveland, Detroit, Minneapolis, Pittsburgh, and St. Paul. Other cities in the Midwest characterized as having high or hyper elasticity are Indianapolis, Kansas City (Kansas), Kansas City (Missouri), Madison, and Wichita.
16. In 1876, St. Louis voters approved a legal separation of the city of St. Louis from its county, principally for economic and tax reasons—namely, they did not want to be encumbered by infrastructural improvements in the more rural regions of the county. See Phares and Louishomme, "St. Louis."
17. Neither St. Louis nor Columbus have much racial diversity beyond African Americans and whites. In each, the largest additional group is Asian Americans, who are 2.4 percent of the Columbus population and .9 percent of the St. Louis population. Hispanics and American Indians are less than 1 percent of the population in both cities.
18. Rusk, *Cities without Suburbs*, p. 21. In fact, from 1980 to 1990, Franklin County was the only one of Ohio's eight largest counties to experience significant growth. See Columbus Metropolitan Human Services Commission, *State of Human Services Report—1995*.
19. Rusk, *Cities without Suburbs*, p. 17.
20. Decker and Van Winkle, *Life in the Gang*, p. 32.
21. Decker and Van Winkle, *Life in the Gang*, p. 32.
22. Rusk, *Cities without Suburbs*, p. 30.
23. Decker and Van Winkle, *Life in the Gang*, p. 33.
24. Rusk, *Cities without Suburbs*, pp. 39–42.
25. Columbus Metropolitan Human Services Commission, *State of Human Services Report—1995*, pp. 9–10.
26. Rusk, *Cities without Suburbs*, p. 36.
27. In addition, while median household income has increased in Franklin County for both whites and African Americans, the income gap between the two groups has grown since 1979. See Columbus Metropolitan Human Services Commission, *State of Human Services Report—1990*, pp. 12–13, 17.
28. For continuity's sake, I use the singular "I" in this section. While I conducted all of the interviews in Columbus, in St. Louis I benefited from the help of two research assistants who conducted most of the interviews there.
29. In Columbus, young women were referred primarily from one of two agencies: the Franklin County juvenile detention center and a privately run shelter care

facility. The shelter care program provides emergency housing for young women placed there by Franklin County Children's Services for unruly behavior or abuse and neglect, with referrals from both the juvenile court and parents. While it is designed to provide temporary placement, many of the young women I spoke to had been in the facility for several months or more. While the facility does provide care for dependency-only cases, only one young woman in my sample fell exclusively into this category. Because she lived in a neighborhood with gang activity, she still fit the criteria for my sample. In addition, three respondents in Columbus were interviewed at a school for youths labeled as severe behavioral problems, housed within the same facility as the shelter care program. Three more respondents came from a private agency that provides individual and family services to at-risk youths; a young woman whom I interviewed at the school referred one additional respondent.

St. Louis respondents were much more likely to come from agency referrals within the community, rather than residential facilities. Just under one-third of the young women were interviewed at the detention center, in addition to five girls referred by their probation officers. Another third of the St. Louis sample came from three local community agencies, including one street outreach program that targeted primarily high-risk youths such as gang members. The remainder of young women interviewed in St. Louis came from a local public high school designated to serve youths suspended or expelled from other settings.

In Columbus, I contacted numerous additional agency personnel in an effort to draw the sample from a larger population base, but most efforts remained unsuccessful despite repeated attempts and promises of assistance. None of the agencies I contacted openly denied me permission to interview young women; they simply didn't follow up and quit returning my phone calls. Fortunately, I was more successful in St. Louis in gaining the cooperation of personnel from a number of community agencies and was able to rely much less on girls who were locked up or in residential care. This is no doubt a result of the long-standing working relationships that faculty in my department at the University of Missouri–St. Louis have with agencies across the city. In Columbus, I was quite concerned about the limited sources of respondents in the sample. Some investigation suggests that there is less cause for concern than I originally believed.

First, I was particularly worried that the majority of gang members came from the juvenile detention center, versus only one-fourth of the nongang girls. I did not want a sample that characterized gang members as more seriously delinquent than nongang youths by virtue of their greater numbers in detention. However, a snapshot view of the detention center taken in June 1995 for the Ohio Department of Youth Services indicates that the detention center does not engage in careful risk assessment to screen for serious offenders, and instead is routinely used to house nonserious offenders prior to their adjudication. The report revealed that 33 percent of youths locked in the facility were on motions or probation violations, and nearly half of these had been placed on probation for unruly or misdemeanor offenses in the first place. See Sanniti, "Snapshot View of Detention." Moreover, while only six nongang girls were interviewed at the detention center, survey interviews showed that eighteen of them had been arrested in the last year, as compared to eighteen of the gang members.

My second concern was with the comparability of the shelter care facility and detention center, particularly as they compared with community agencies that did not refer girls for the project. I have reason to believe that there is a great deal of overlap between the young women I interviewed at these settings, as well as with girls at other agencies. All of the agencies serve populations of girls deemed "at risk." While my interviews at the shelter care facility and detention center were dispersed over large periods of time, I nonetheless encountered girls at one setting that I had interviewed at the other. In addition, a number of the young women I interviewed reported overlaps with the agencies from which I was unable to gain cooperation. For instance, several girls were on probation, and a few had spent time at a shelter for teen runaways. This evidence tempers many of my initial concerns, although it's still the case that my selective sample makes generalizability problematic.

30. In Columbus, two young women described themselves as former gang members—one who quit after a friend was shot, the other after she became pregnant. In addition, one girl still considered herself a member, but quit hanging out with the gang after she was raped by one of its members. In St. Louis, nine girls described themselves as former members, including five who had quit a year or more before taking part in the study. One additional girl was still a member, but hadn't hung out with her gang since she had a baby. In some cases, these girls consistently slipped into the present tense when talking about their gangs and may have said they were former members to avoid incriminating themselves.

31. In all, 86 percent (eighteen of twenty-one) of the gang members in Columbus had been arrested; 59 percent (sixteen of twenty-seven) of the gang members in St. Louis had been arrested. In both cities, the majority of these arrests were for nonviolent offenses, although arrests for violent crimes were only 22 percent of the arrests reported by gang members in Columbus, while they were 45 percent of the arrests in St. Louis. Seventeen gang members in Columbus (81 percent) had been in the detention center, compared to thirteen (48 percent) of the gang members in St. Louis.

    Among nongang girls, 64 percent (sixteen of twenty-five) of the girls in Columbus had been arrested; and 38 percent (eight of twenty-one) of the nongang girls in St. Louis had been arrested. Twelve (48 percent) of the nongang girls in Columbus had been in the detention center, versus seven (33 percent) of the nongang girls in St. Louis. In Columbus, 33 percent of nongang girls' arrests were for violent offenses, as were 50 percent of nongang girls' arrests in St. Louis. Part of the reason for these differences among girls across the two cities likely results from Columbus girls' greater likelihood of being arrested for status offenses such as running away and truancy. In all, 25 percent of gang girls' arrests in Columbus were for status offenses, versus only 8 percent for gang girls in St. Louis. Similarly, none of the nongang girls in St. Louis described having been arrested for a status offense, while 25 percent of the nongang girls' arrests in Columbus were for status offenses.

32. Approximately a quarter of the way through the survey, after a series of questions about their family, school, activities, and friends, young women were asked, first, whether they consider their group of friends to be a gang and, second, whether they consider themselves to be gang members. I chose to identify gang members through self-nomination for a combination of reasons. First, I didn't want to limit my sample to girls who had been officially labeled as gang members. Research on gangs that relies on law enforcement data may oversample those gang members most seriously involved in crime and experienced with

formal intervention. In addition, although using agency referrals has generally proven successful in accessing gang members, this still poses the potential problem of targeting only officially labeled youth. Although my sample came from agencies working with youths, I did not specifically target agencies working with gang members, nor did I simply attempt to generate a pool of girls known to be gang members. The comparative research design meant that I asked agency personnel to refer me both to girls they believed were gang-involved and girls living in neighborhoods where they might have contact with gangs; consequently, some of the gang members in the sample were not recognized as such by agency staff.

A second reason for using self-nomination has to do with the context of my study—namely, my focus on two emergent gang cities. Gangs are widely recognized by scholars as relatively transitory groups with fluid and changing memberships (see Klein, *The American Street Gang*). Given the changing nature of gangs as they em rge and diversify in new cities, I felt that self-nomination would provide the be it means of applying a limited definitional criteria in order to capture what may be a varied phenomenon. See Horowitz, "Sociological Perspectives on Gangs," for a discussion of the benefits of limited definitional criteria; for evidence of gang emergence and diversification, see Curry and Spergel, "Gang Involvement and Delinquency among Hispanic and African American Adolescent Males"; Klein and Maxson, "Gang Structures, Crime Patterns, and Police Responses"; Spergel and Curry, "The National Youth Gang Survey."

A number of scholars now use self-definition as a measure of gang membership, either alone or in conjunction with more restrictive guidelines. Some researchers suggest that only youths who are members of groups involved in illegal activities should be classified as gang members (this is regardless of the individual youths' delinquency or lack thereof). For example, see Esbensen et al., "Gang and Non-Gang Youth"; Esbensen and Huizinga, "Gangs, Drugs, and Delinquency in a Survey of Urban Youth." Additional criteria sometimes used include that the youth be able to provide a gang name and report more than six members. For example, see Bjerregaard and Smith, "Gender Differences in Gang Participation, Delinquency, and Substance Use"; Thornberry et al., "The Role of Juvenile Gangs in Facilitating Delinquent Behavior."

Research suggests that using restrictive measures does not change substantive conclusions concerning gang members' behaviors when comparing self-defined gang members to those members who meet more restrictive definitions. In fact, Winfree et al. found that the "self-reported definition of gang membership proved to be a better predictor of gang-related crime than the more restrictive definition," which they speculate may be a result of fringe or wannabe members' efforts to "demonstrate their gang membership." See Winfree et al., "The Definition and Measurement of 'Gang Status,'" pp. 34–35.

Additional evidence of the robustness of self-definition as a measure of gang membership comes from those studies that have found large and stable differences between self-identified gang members and nongang youths (including nongang serious offenders) in their rates of involvement in delinquency, and specifically serious crime. In addition to studies previously listed in this note, also see Fagan, "Social Processes of Delinquency and Drug Use among Urban Gangs."

33. In Columbus, three nongang but gang-affiliated girls completed in-depth interviews as well. One was affiliated with an all-male gang; one hung out primar-

ily with members of one gang, but had friends in other gangs; the third hung out exclusively with gang members—including her brother and boyfriend—but from different gangs.

34. Because the project was partially supported by funds from the National Institute of Justice, respondents' confidentiality was protected by federal law. In addition, we maintained the anonymity of respondents by not eliciting or recording their names, except as needed to schedule follow-up interviews. Completed interviews were kept in a locked file box or file cabinet. Respondents were told not to make statements about intentions to harm others in the future, as I may be required to report such statements to the authorities. No such incidents occurred.

Parental consent is routinely required when interviewing individuals under the age of eighteen. This poses a danger for gang youths, as the act of seeking parental consent risks informing parents of their child's gang membership. Previous research has documented gang youths' reluctance to reveal their gang membership to their parents and their success at concealing it (see Decker and Van Winkle, *Life in the Gang*). To deal with this dilemma, I sought and was granted a waiver of parental consent by the Institutional Review Boards at the University of Southern California and the University of Missouri–St. Louis. In each site, this waiver was contingent on the appointment of a youth advocate to serve as a surrogate guardian for respondents. The advocates were each chosen based on their experience working with at-risk youths. Potential respondents were given the advocate's name and phone number and were provided with the opportunity to contact her prior to making a decision to participate (although in neither city did this occur).

Because parental consent was waived, great diligence was required to assess youths' voluntary participation and informed consent. Girls under age twelve were excluded from the study, and particular care was taken with girls under age fourteen to assess their competence to provide informed consent. At the Detention Center in St. Louis, we were required to obtain passive parental consent. We mailed letters to parents asking permission for their child to participate in a study of "youth violence" and they were provided a seven-day window to contact us to refuse permission.

Another concern regarding confidentiality was the risk of soliciting reports of ongoing child abuse. It is critical to assess exposure to violence as a risk factor for gang membership, particularly for females. Neither Ohio nor Missouri law requires mandatory reporting of abuse for researchers; however, I chose to make decisions concerning the reporting of abuse on a case-by-case basis. Fortunately, because the girls in the sample came from agency referrals, some intervention had previously taken place, making these decisions unnecessary for me.

There was, however, one particularly troubling case in St. Louis. One of the young women interviewed at the detention center reported that a young man in her neighborhood repeatedly threatened and sexually assaulted her when he saw her on the streets. My research assistant and I had numerous conversations about how to proceed with our colleague David Curry, who serves on the Institutional Review Board at UM–St. Louis. For personal reasons, the young woman was not willing to file a report about the incidents, so we ultimately chose simply to provide her with information about local agencies that provide assistance to sexual assault and abuse victims. However, we remained troubled about our inability to do more to protect her.

35. Young women were initially approached about the project by agency staff, who briefly described the study and asked if they might be willing to speak to me. Once we were face-to-face, I read the description, which provided general information about the study goals, the confidentiality agreement, payment for participating, and methods for getting in touch with me. Potential respondents were told that they did not have to participate, could refuse to answer any question, and could terminate the interview at any time. In addition to the small monetary incentive, it is likely that a number of girls participated simply for something to do—particularly those girls housed in facilities.

36. The survey I used was a variation of several instruments currently being used in a number of cities. These include the Gang Membership Resistance Survey (in San Diego and Long Beach), the Rochester Youth Development Study, and the Denver Youth Survey. It asks detailed questions about such things as family structure, relationships and problems; educational attainment and work status of adults in the family; commitment to school and school performance; community activities and involvement; peer relationships and peer delinquency; individual delinquent involvement and arrests; exposure to violence and abuse; sexual experience; self-esteem; and measures of perceived blocked opportunities related to class, race, and gender. In developing an instrument that adopts many of the questions and scales currently in use in other research, I benefited from the previous examination of issues of validity and reliability concerning the interview questions. However, my use of these instruments is not *survey* research, given the purposive sampling and comparatively small number of cases in my project.

37. Four gang members were not reinterviewed, and one additional girl (Angie) became uncomfortable talking about her gang during the course of the in-depth interview; we talked about her discomfort and decided to terminate the interview. Of the four who were not reinterviewed, only one refused the second interview. One was released from the detention center before the second interview could be scheduled. Two were lost after circumstances required me to terminate my interviews at the residential facility in Columbus because of a problem that arose there with one of the girls.

    Each girl's in-depth interview was assigned the same numeric code as her survey interview; this provided multiple sources of data for each respondent. Combining qualitative interviewing with the survey provided complementary information about young women in gangs. In tandem, the surveys and in-depth interviews provided a wealth of information about the personal, familial, social, and community contexts in which girls' gang involvement occurs.

    An additional strength of the combined methodology was that the survey interviews provided a means for me to triangulate my findings from the in-depth interviews. The use of multiple sources of data allows for more systematic and rigorous analyses and increased confidence in the validity and reliability of research findings. See Marshall and Rossman, *Designing Qualitative Research*. For this project, additional collaborative evidence came in the form of conversations with agency personnel, as well as comparisons across interviews. For instance, although I did not disclose information about interviews with agency staff, they frequently revealed information about the girls that I interviewed. In addition, I was sometimes able to compare interviews and conversations with girls who were either in the same gang, or in gangs that associated with one another, to check for consistencies in what they told me.

I only came across two obvious discrepancies. The first was from a young woman I interviewed in Columbus at the shelter care facility. During the survey interview she told me she was affiliated with a Bloods set, though several other gang members there told me she was a Folk, and I saw for myself that the girls she hung out with were Folks and Crips. She appeared very committed to her gang, and I believe she attempted to mislead me to protect herself and her gang. Unfortunately, we were unable to complete the in-depth interview (see earlier), at which time I planned to discuss the discrepancy. The second incident involved a gang member who referred me to a friend of hers, who she claimed was a member of her set. The friend ended up being affiliated with the set, but not a member. In this case, I believe the motivation was monetary, as—in an attempt at snowball sampling—I had agreed to pay girls ten dollars for referring me to their gang-involved friends.

38. See Elkind and Bowen, "Imaginary Audience Behavior in Children and Adolescents"; Pesce and Harding, "Imaginary Audience Behavior and Its Relationship to Operational Thought and Social Experience"; Simmons et al., "Disturbance in the Self-Image at Adolescence."

39. See Simmons et al., "Disturbance in the Self-Image at Adolescence"; Taylor et al., *Between Voice and Silence.*

40. Singer and Singer, *Psychological Development in Children.*

41. Pseudonyms are used throughout to disguise the identity of young women. In addition to supplying names for the young women, I also changed the names of individuals they talked about and of their set names and any streets to which they made reference. I quote from young women extensively throughout the book and present their discussions verbatim. However, I sometimes remove repetition of words or phrases when doing so does not change the content of what is said but helps to make their discussions more understandable. When words might be unfamiliar to the reader, I indicate in parentheses my sense of what the words mean as girls use them.

   Let me also comment on my own use of words. Quantitative researchers are sometimes skeptical of such seemingly loose language as "many" or "a number of"—terms that are frequently used in qualitative writing. I use the words "most" or "the majority" to indicate more than half, "the vast majority" to indicate approximately three-quarters or more. I typically use "many" to indicate a sizeable minority (over one-third), while "a number" is roughly one-fourth or more. I use "several" or "a few" to highlight themes mentioned by a small number of girls, but more than two.

42. See Charmaz, "Between Positivism and Postmodernism"; DeVault, "Ethnicity and Expertise"; Fine and Sandstrom, *Knowing Children*; Riessman, *Narrative Analysis*; Taylor et al., *Between Voice and Silence.*

43. Taylor et al., *Between Voice and Silence*, p. 36.

44. See Charmaz, "Between Positivism and Postmodernism," p. 54; see also Adler and Adler, *Membership Roles in Field Research*; Glassner and Loughlin, *Drugs in Adolescent Worlds*; Harding, *Feminism and Methodology*; Spradley, *The Ethnographic Interview*; Strauss, *Qualitative Analysis for Social Scientists.* For a critical discussion of this approach, see Miller and Glassner, "The 'Inside' and the 'Outside.'"

45. For a discussion, see Dunlap et al., "Studying Crack Users and Their Criminal Careers"; Lofland and Lofland, *Analyzing Social Settings*; Miller, "Researching Violence against Street Prostitutes."

46. For a discussion of this technique, see Spradley, *The Ethnographic Interview.*

47. Blumer, *Symbolic Interactionism*, p. 22. See also Glassner and Loughlin, *Drugs in Adolescent Worlds*, p. 36.

48. Most of the girls I interviewed assumed that I was in my early twenties. In fact, at the school where I interviewed in Columbus, I was once stopped by a staff member and asked for my hall pass because she assumed I was one of the students.

49. Brunson, "Pumping Up the Set."

50. Currie and MacLean, "Measuring Violence against Women," p. 178. These authors suggest that when women internalize ideologies that blame women for their victimization, they may be particularly uncomfortable sharing their experiences with other women, whom they believe will judge them.

51. Previous research I conducted concerning violence against street prostitutes provides some support for this interpretation. When I interviewed women engaged in prostitution, I *was* in my early twenties. I found that women in my age range— particularly the African American women I spoke with—were often more uncomfortable discussing their experiences with me than were older women, who could more easily view me as nonthreatening, and consequently could respond to me as a naïve young woman whom they were educating. See Miller, "Researching Violence against Street Prostitutes." In the current project, our perceived age similarity, probably coupled with gender, had another effect. While Rod was asked by several respondents for assurance that he wasn't a police officer (or in one case, a member of the secret service), no young women ever appeared to be suspicious of me on these grounds.

52. Taylor et al., *Between Voice and Silence*, p. 36.

53. Collins, *Black Feminist Thought*.

54. Richardson, *Writing Strategies*, p. 23. See also Mishler, *Research Interviewing*; Riessman, *Narrative Analysis*.

55. Schmitt, "Cornerville as Obdurate Reality," p. 126.

56. Agar, "Ethnography in the Streets and in the Joint."

57. Klein, *Street Gangs and Street Workers*, p. 85.

58. The most obvious example was many young women's insistence on the presence of gender equality within their gangs, even though they provided evidence to the contrary. See Chapter 8 for a discussion.

59. See Miller and Glassner, "The 'Inside' and the 'Outside.'"

Chapter 3

1. See Decker and Van Winkle, *Life in the Gang*, Chapter 3.

2. There was slight variation across site. While 78 percent of the St. Louis girls (twenty-one of twenty-seven) described joining their gangs by age thirteen, only 57 percent of the Columbus girls (twelve of twenty-one) did so.

3. Rhonda, Marie, and Stephanie were the only young women I spoke with who described their boyfriends as also being partially responsible for facilitated their gang involvement. Given their small number, I did not provide a separate dimension for this factor in the diagram.

4. See Chapter 6 for a detailed discussion of how I classified girls as serious delinquents and of gang girls' participation in delinquency in general.

5. See Cloward and Ohlin, *Delinquency and Opportunity*; Cohen, *Delinquent Boys*;

Hagedorn, *People and Folks*; Jackson, "Crime, Youth Gangs and Urban Transition"; Klein, *The American Street Gang*; Moore, *Homeboys* and *Going Down to the Barrio*; Thrasher, *The Gang*; Vigil, *Barrio Gangs*.

6. See Campbell, *The Girls in the Gang* and "Female Participation in Gangs"; Fishman, "The Vice Queens"; Joe and Chesney-Lind, " 'Just Every Mother's Angel' "; Quicker, *Homegirls*; Taylor, *Girls, Gangs, Women and Drugs*. Although not about young women in gangs, Baskin and Sommers also provide a useful account of how neighborhood and peer contexts facilitate women's involvement in violent crime. See their "Females' Initiation into Violent Street Crime."

7. Joe and Chesney-Lind, " 'Just Every Mother's Angel,' " p. 411.

8. This information was collected by asking young women to provide the names of two intersecting streets very near to where they live, and then gathering data on neighborhood characteristics based on measures from the 1990 census. In Columbus, I relied on census tract data; in St. Louis, I used data aggregated at the neighborhood level (see Community Development Agency, *Neighborhood Demographic Profiles*). Tracking this information based on street addresses would have provided a more precise means of measuring neighborhood characteristics, but I chose not to take this approach in order to more fully ensure respondents' confidentiality. In addition, my use of 1990 data does not provide as up-to-date a picture as would more recent data. For instance, there is evidence that the city of St. Louis has experienced further decline in the last decade, including continuing population loss and population shifts (see Bray and Rosenfeld, "The Impact of Neighborhood Disadvantage and Racial Composition on Youth Homicide"). Moreover, the vast majority of girls I spoke with described quite a bit of residential instability, which a measure from one moment in time does not capture. Nonetheless, these measures remain a useful proxy for understanding generally the character of the neighborhoods in which gang girls resided.

9. Six girls in St. Louis described neighborhoods that the 1990 data indicate were less than 20 percent African American; however, evidence of population shifts in south St. Louis in recent years indicates that a number of these neighborhoods now have a larger African American population. See Bray and Rosenfeld, "The Impact of Neighborhood Disadvantage and Racial Composition on Youth Homicide."

10. See Bursik and Grasmick, *Neighborhoods and Crime*; Wilson, *The Truly Disadvantaged*.

11. Significance levels are based on chi-square tests. It's important to note here that while I use statistics to make comparisons throughout the book, my sample is purposive in nature and thus violates key assumptions regarding random or representative sampling. While technically statistical methods are inappropriate for my sample, I use these methods not in an attempt to generalize to a larger population, but to highlight the strength of the patterns I uncovered.

12. Quicker, *Homegirls*, p. 80. See also Joe and Chesney-Lind, " 'Just Every Mother's Angel.' "

13. See Decker, "Collective and Normative Features of Gang Violence"; Joe and Chesney-Lind, " 'Just Every Mother's Angel' "; Lauderback et al., " 'Sisters Are Doin' It for Themselves.' "

14. Jennifer was the only member of an all-female gang that I was able to interview in Columbus. She described the OG, who was in her mid-twenties and had started the gang several years before Jennifer joined, as very careful about whom she al-

lowed to join. This was not in keeping with the overall pattern in Columbus, where gangs tended to be fluid and loosely defined groups (see Chapter 4).

15. In their study of St. Louis gangs, Scott Decker and Barrik Van Winkle describe in similar ways the strength of neighborhood ties in the city, which they suggest have been quite longstanding—existing long before the recent reemergence of gangs there. See their *Life in the Gang*.

16. See Bjerregaard and Smith, "Gender Differences in Gang Participation, Delinquency, and Substance Abuse"; Bowker and Klein, "The Etiology of Female Juvenile Delinquency and Gang Membership"; Campbell, "On the Invisibility of the Female Delinquent Peer Group" and "Female Participation in Gangs"; Giordano, "Girls, Guys and Gangs"; Morash, "Gangs, Groups and Delinquency" and "Gender, Peer Group Experiences, and Seriousness of Delinquency."

17. See Canter, "Family Correlates of Male and Female Delinquency"; Cernkovich and Giordano, "Family Relationships and Delinquency"; Hagan et al., "The Class Structure of Gender and Delinquency"; Hagan et al., "Class in the Household"; Joe and Chesney-Lind, " 'Just Every Mother's Angel' "; Moore, *Going Down to the Barrio*; Singer and Levine, "Power-Control Theory, Gender, and Delinquency"; Smith and Paternoster, "The Gender Gap in Theories of Deviance."

18. Joan Moore documented myriad factors within families that contribute to the likelihood of gang involvement for young women. These include the following: childhood abuse and neglect, wife abuse, having alcohol or drug addicts in the family, witnessing the arrest of family members, having a family member who is chronically ill, and experiencing a death in the family during childhood. Her conclusion, based on comparisons of male and female gang members, is that young women in particular are likely to come from families that are troubled. See Moore, *Going Down to the Barrio*. Mark Fleisher's ethnographic study of gangs in Kansas City, Missouri, documents intergenerational patterns of abuse and neglect, based on his observations of the interactions of gang members, their young children, and their parents. See Fleisher, *Dead End Kids*.

Joe and Chesney-Lind observed that the young women they spoke with sometimes had parents who worked long hours or parents who were unemployed or underemployed—circumstances that they suggest affected girls' supervision and the quality of their family relationships. See their " 'Just Every Mother's Angel.' " Esbensen and Deschenes, in a multisite study of risk factors for delinquency and gang behavior, found that lack of parental supervision was associated with gang membership for male and female gang members but that maternal attachment was more predictive of gang membership for males than females. See Esbensen and Deschenes, "A Multi-Site Examination of Gang Membership."

Bjerregaard and Smith found that neither parental supervision nor parental attachment was significantly correlated with gang membership for girls. However, it may be that these factors, particularly parental attachment, are not accurate measures of family problems. For instance, a number of young women in my study described feeling close to adults in their family despite abuse and mistreatment. Perhaps the most profound example was Sonita, who spent much of her childhood in various foster homes because of her mother's drug addiction and time in jail. Moreover, Sonita spent over a year on the streets as a runaway, which is when she joined her gang, and had been sexually assaulted by both her father and brother. When asked questions about her family, however, Sonita described her relationship with her mother as a close and trusting one and her family as one that had "a great deal" of fun together. This contradiction may partly be accounted for by the fact that she and her mother were in counseling together at the time that we spoke; nonetheless, it raises serious concerns about the extent to which attitudinal measures can adequately capture family dynamics.

19. These are included in my measure of abuse in Table 3-3 when a family member committed the assault, but not when it was someone else the girl was exposed to through her family.

20. Huff, "Gangs in the United States"; but see Decker and Van Winkle, *Life in the Gang*.

21. Perhaps this is why Esbensen and Deschenes found that although male and female gang members reported similar levels of commitment to negative peers, this was a stronger explanatory factor for gang involvement for females than males. See Esbensen and Deschenes, "A Multi-Site Examination of Gang Membership." There is some evidence that young women are more likely than young men to join gangs in a search for emotional attachments. For example, Chesney-Lind and Paramore ranked male and female gang members' perceptions of why youths join gangs, and girls' number one response was "family problems—to fit in and feel wanted and loved." In comparison, this response did not rank in the top five reasons young men listed. These included: (1) show off—to be cool and popular, (2) to have protection and back up, (3) to act bad, (4) to gain respect/think tough, and (5) peer pressure and influence. Nonetheless, the rest of female gang members' reasons paralleled young mens and included: (2) show off—be cool and popular, (3) to have protection and back up, (4) to act bad, and (5) to gain respect/think tough. It is important to keep in mind that these responses were not based on asking gang members to articulate *their* reasons for joining but to offer their perceptions of why "kids" join gangs. See Chesney-Lind and Paramore, "Gender and Gang Membership."

22. There is a growing body of literature that supports the link between childhood maltreatment and youths' subsequent involvement in delinquency. See Smith and Thornberry, "The Relationship between Childhood Maltreatment and Adolescent Involvement in Delinquency"; Widom, "Child Abuse, Neglect, and Violent Criminal Behavior."

23. See Bourgois and Dunlap, "Exorcising Sex-for-Crack"; Maher, *Sexed Work*.

24. Other research offers support for the relationship between girls' gang involvement and that of their family members. Moore's study of Chicano/a gang members in Los Angeles suggests that female gang members are often likely to have joined gangs because of a relative's association. In their interviews with gang members, Joe and Chesney-Lind report that 90 percent of the girls (twelve of thirteen) and 80 percent of the boys (twenty-eight of thirty-five) reported having a family member who was in a gang; usually this was a sibling. Although Lauderback and his colleagues argue that this pattern does not hold for African American females, whom they suggest are more likely to organize and join gangs independently, my research suggests that gang-involved family members are important contributors to African American girls' gang involvement. See Moore, *Going Down to the Barrio*; Joe and Chesney-Lind, " 'Just Every Mother's Angel' "; Lauderback et al., " 'Sisters Are Doin' It for Themselves.' "

Geoffrey Hunt made an important observation about gangs and "family" during my presentation of a paper based on this study at the 1998 meetings of the American Sociological Association. While scholars typically talk about the gang as a "surrogate" family for young people, in fact there are many cases in which both "real" and "fictive" kin are members of girls' gangs. Thus, when young women speak of the familial nature of their gang relationships, they sometimes are literally speaking about their blood relatives.

25. See Collins, *Black Feminist Thought*; Hill, *The Strength of Black Families*; Scott and Black, "Deep Structures of African American Family Life"; Stack, *All Our Kin*.

26. Fortunately, when Dionne was interviewed for this project she was no longer living in her mother and uncle's home. She was living with her father, whom she described as "always giving her attention," and was in counseling to cope with what had happened to her.

27. Moore, *Going Down to the Barrio*. See note 18 for more details.

28. Hagan and McCarthy, *Mean Streets*, p. 81. See also Short, "The Level of Explanation Problem Revisited."

Chapter 4

1. Diane was initiated into a Crips set. Some of the symbolism involved in her initiation merits note. It is widely known, thanks in part to the 1988 film *Colors*, that Crips typically adopt the color blue and Bloods the color red. Some additional symbols are less familiar. In Columbus, Crips and Folks (whose color is black) both adopt a six-point star as one of their symbols. The number six thus has symbolic meaning, and Diane's sixty-second beating is illustrative. Bloods adopt a five-point star; thus a timed beating for a Blood initiate would involve the number five. As I will describe, other initiations involve being punched five (for Bloods) or six (for Crips and Folks) times. In addition, Crips and Folks wear indicators of their gang affiliation—hats, flags, pushed-up pants legs, earrings—on or toward the right, while Bloods wear theirs to the left. Thus Diane knelt on her right knee during her initiation and had her flag placed on her right shoulder. Flags, also called rags or scarves, are appropriately colored bandanas that members wear, typically tied to a belt loop, to indicate their gang affiliation. The blessing, Diane explained, "means they say a prayer over you. You gotta repeat the prayer."

2. As I will describe, all of the girls in Columbus described taking part in some sort of initiation. This was not the case in St. Louis, where only 63 percent of girls said there was an initiation when they joined. More on these site differences will be discussed in Chapter 5.

3. See Horowitz, "Sociological Perspectives on Gangs."

4. Klein, *Street Gangs and Street Workers*, p. 13.

5. James Short, personal communication, quoted in Klein, *The American Street Gang*, p. 26. See also Jensen, "An Interview with James F. Short, Jr." Another critique of the use of crime as a defining feature is that it can be tautological when a potential *outcome* of gangs (crime) is part of the definition (see Short, "New Wine in Old Bottles?"; Bursik and Grasmick, *Neighborhoods and Crime*, Chapter 5). However, defining gangs as groups that are involved in crime does not preclude the examination of variations in criminal involvement, including the types, extent, or seriousness of illegal activities. Instead, as I noted, it simply highlights that crime is a focal point of the group, one that brings status and recognition (see also Decker, "Collective and Normative Features of Gang Violence"). Nonethe-

less, it remains important to recognize that gangs are not simply criminal groups—that they have functions and meanings in youths' lives that go beyond providing opportunities to commit crime. Indeed, as I will highlight, gang members sometimes resist perceptions of their groups as mere criminal enterprises.

6. Given this, what's perhaps most striking is in fact how little variation I uncovered, across gangs and even across the two sites. Relying on self-definition also allowed me to take Horowitz's ("Sociological Perspectives on Gangs") criticisms of gang definitions to heart. She has been the strongest advocate of the need to keep definitional criteria unrestricted in order to keep debate open and to capture gang variations.

7. When asked, all of the girls in Columbus (100 percent) and twenty-six of the girls in St. Louis (96 percent) provided evidence that their gangs were involved in criminal activities. This is not surprising. A number of studies that define gangs based on self-nomination without specifying crime as a defining feature nonetheless have found serious criminal involvement as a factor that distinguishes gangs from other groups of youths. See Fagan, "Social Processes of Delinquency and Drug Use among Urban Gangs"; Thornberry et al., "The Role of Juvenile Gangs in Facilitating Delinquent Behavior"; Winfree et al., "The Definition and Measurement of 'Gang Status.'"

8. Twelve of the young women I spoke with (57 percent) were Folks, six (29 percent) were Crips, and two (10 percent) were Bloods. These are the groups most common in Columbus, according to law enforcement. Bloods, in fact, are a much stronger presence than my interviews reflect. I can't account for why these particular young women didn't turn up in my sample with more regularity, since all of the young women I interviewed—Bloods, Crips, and Folks alike—described Bloods gangs as mixed-gender.

Folks gangs have an interesting story, and they appear to be a curious offshoot of Chicago's Gangster Disciples. Chicago's many gangs align themselves under one of two "nations"—the People and the Folks. Gangster Disciples gangs fall under the Folks umbrella, but do not explicitly adopt the gang name "Folks." For some reason, gang proliferation into a number of midwestern cities, among them Columbus and Cleveland, has resulted in the emergence of gangs who identify themselves as Folks and trace their lineage at least loosely to Chicago. As I will discuss in greater detail, diffusion of gang culture has resulted in the filtering down of Chicago gang lore into Columbus gangs, but much of it is sketchy if not inaccurate. For discussions of Chicago gang nations, see Gang Prevention Incorporated, *The Street Gang Identification Manual*; Perkins, *Explosion of Chicago's Black Street Gangs*.

With regard to autonomous female gangs such as the Gangster Girlz, most of the young women I interviewed were not familiar with the existence of these groups, and, if they were familiar, typically denigrated them (more on this in Chapter 7). I also spoke with several officers from the Columbus Police Department's gang unit about their knowledge of autonomous female gangs. They had information on five small all-female gangs in Columbus, including the Gangster Girlz, all of which they described as relatively harmless. According to the officers, the major problems these groups got into were jumping and fighting other girls in and around schools and at bus stops, along with some minor theft and drug sales. This was in keeping with the officers' general picture of female gang involvement: On the whole, they viewed serious gang problems as primarily a male phenomenon even though they recognized that most gangs in Columbus had female members or affiliates.

Jennifer painted a more sophisticated portrait of her gang, and I found her depiction a convincing one. Unfortunately, despite a great deal of effort on my part, I was unable to interview any other young women from her gang or from other all-female gangs in Columbus. Jennifer had been referred to me by her best friend Rachel, who hung out with gang members, including those from Jennifer's and LaShawna's gangs, but was not a gang member herself (see Chapter 3). Jennifer's OG didn't know she had spoken with me, and Jennifer felt strongly that she wouldn't have approved. Consequently, she was leery of approaching other members to participate, and my chain referral ended there.

9. Huff, "Youth Gangs and Public Policy." See also Mayhood, "Blood Spills over Hand Signs" and Mayhood and LaLonde, "A Show of Colors."

10. LaLonde, "Police Trying to Contain Gang Problem"; Mayhood, "Officials Organize to Combat Gangs." These figures are from 1995, and are up from the 1992 results of the Maxson-Klein gang migration survey, at which time police in Columbus reported an estimated ten to twenty-five gangs with over two hundred members. See Maxson et al., "Street Gang Migration in the United States."

11. It is important to note that gangs have fluid, changing boundaries with regard to membership and affiliation and that I base my size estimates on those provided by young women at one point in their gangs' histories. For an excellent illustration of these membership issues, see Fleisher, *Dead End Kids.*

One young woman I interviewed in Columbus did not provide information on her gang's structure, composition, or organization. Another provided this information, but was uncomfortable answering questions about her gang's criminal endeavors. Consequently, there will often be one missing case in the information I provide about Columbus.

12. An oversight in the Columbus portion of the research, which was rectified in St. Louis, was that I didn't gather specific data in the survey about the racial composition of girls' gangs. Instead, I glean this information primarily from our conversations during the in-depth interviews. Consequently, I cannot provide precise data on the topic. Police estimates in Columbus characterize gangs as 90 percent African American, 8 percent Latino, and 2 percent white (Maxson et al., "Street Gang Migration in the United States"). Other reports and my research suggest that a number of gangs in Columbus are racially mixed groups, although with a majority of African American members. See Mayhood and LaLonde, "A Show of Colors."

13. In his 1975 report, *Violence by Youth Gangs and Youth Groups as a Crime Problem in Major American Cities,* Walter Miller classified female gang involvement into three types: (1) auxiliary groups associated with male gangs, (2) mixed-gender gangs with male and female members, and (3) independent or autonomous female gangs. However, most research on young women's gang involvement either has not specified the gendered structure of their gangs, has focused on female gangs as auxiliary groups, or, less often, has looked at autonomous female gangs. Consequently, relatively little is known about mixed-gender gangs. This may be related to ethnicity—for instance, most studies of female auxiliary gangs have been based on research with Latinas or Chicanas, while my study is one of the few on primarily African American gangs.

In addition, there is some debate about whether scholars should classify female gang involvement with regard to its gendered structures. For instance, in their "Fighting Female," Hagedorn and Devitt argue that this focus is a carry-over of the male bias that has plagued gang research since its inception. Male gangs have been classified broadly, in terms of their behaviors and activities, while female gangs have been defined narrowly, only in relation to male gangs. While I believe the point is well taken, I would take it in a different direction and argue that we need to be more attentive to the gendered nature of gang involvement for both females *and* males, rather than purposively ignoring gendered gang structures when studying females.

14. In all, six girls (30 percent) were in gangs in which one-fifth or fewer of the members were female, eight (40 percent) were in sets with one-fourth to one-third of the membership female, two described gangs where girls were around 45 percent of the members, two were in gangs with equal numbers of males and females, and one described her gang as two-thirds female and one-third male. The Gangster Girlz had twenty-three members, all of whom were in their late teens, except for the OG, who was in her early twenties.

15. Only Diane alluded to gender differentiation within her gang. She explained, "We're all together, but in a way we're split just because, 'cause we're ladies and they're the males. We're Lady Crips and they're the Crips." Interestingly, Diane was a member of what I would characterize as one of the more organized gangs in Columbus, with a comparatively long history in the city (seven or eight years at that point) and more sophisticated involvement in economic crimes than many other groups I learned about. Diane said her OG was originally from Los Angeles, where he had been a member of a Crips gang. It could be that he brought a particular notion of what the gender organization of his set should be, based on the organization of his gang in LA.

16. For various configurations of these definitional criteria, see Bjerregaard and Smith, "Gender Differences in Gang Participation, Delinquency, and Substance Use"; Esbensen et al., "Gang and Non-Gang Youth"; Esbensen and Huizinga, "Gangs, Drugs, and Delinquency in a Survey of Urban Youth"; Klein, *The American Street Gang*; Thornberry et al., "The Role of Juvenile Gangs in Facilitating Delinquent Behavior"; Winfree et al., "The Definition and Measurement of 'Gang Status.'" See note 32, Chapter 2, for a further discussion.

17. Angie's pronoun usage is notable in this passage—the gang is "we" and "us" when she speaks of its size and popular status, but "them" when she describes violence. Part of this is gender-based—as I'll discuss in further detail, young women appear to be better able than young men to distance themselves from the antisocial aspects of gang involvement. I think her distancing was also partly attributable to some apprehension about being interviewed, particularly at the detention center. Angie was the only young woman in the sample who asked that we terminate the in-depth interview partway through.

Two other young women resisted the characterization of their gangs as *only* criminally involved. Leslie lamented that people "just concentrate on the bad stuff that [gangs] are doin'. 'Cause as soon as they hear about a gang doin' somethin' bad, they're, whew, on it . . . [while] it's very rare that you hear about a gang doin' somethin' good." Likewise, Tamika described a gang shooting she had witnessed, then to correct the impression she created, she remarked:

[People] just stereotype gang members to be hardcore and to always be shootin' at somebody. They don't stereotype people that could be a gang member but still they could go to school and get straight As. That's stereotyping because I know, I know a few gangbangers who go to school, get straight As, hit the books, but still when they on the street, you know, they take good care of theirs. But they, they takin' care of theirs in school and they takin' care of theirs on the street and I don't think that's right to stereotype people.

18. *Throwing it up* refers to throwing hand signs that signify the gang. *Stacking* is a more elaborate form of throwing signs that entails throwing your gang up and rival gangs down through a sequence of gestures.

19. These Columbus gangs are characteristic of what Maxson and Klein, in "Investigating Gang Structures," refer to as compressed gangs, which are small, with a narrow age range, and which may or may not be territorial. I will say more on these structural issues in Chapter 5. Notably, the Gangster Girlz were one of two gangs described as nonterritorial; Angie's was the other. Had we completed the entire in-depth interview, it may have come out that her gang claimed a territory, as it is clear from her other descriptions that the gang was neighborhood-based (see Chapter 3).

20. "Slob" is a derogatory term for Bloods, used by Crips and Folks members. Bloods call Crips "crabs" and Folks "forks" to disrespect them. An additional form of disrespect is to either refuse to use the letter B if you're a Crip and C if you're a Blood, or if you write the letter, to put an X through it. Occasionally during the survey interviews, girls would request that I cross out their rival gangs' letters when I recorded their responses.

21. Huff, "Youth Gangs and Public Policy." Hagedorn reports similar findings for Milwaukee, as do Decker and Van Winkle for St. Louis. See Hagedorn, *People and Folks*; Decker and Van Winkle, *Life in the Gang*. See also Laskey, "Gang Migration."

22. My question was based on information LaShawna had provided during the survey portion of the interview.

23. *Lits* and *knowledge* refer to stories about the gang, hand signs, symbolism, and the like. *Queen* is a rank or designation assigned to gang members, to be discussed further later in the chapter.

24. This question refers to the set that Lisa's brother was in prior to his decision to start his own set after they moved to a new neighborhood.

25. See Knox and Fuller, "The Gangster Disciples"; Spergel, "Community Action Research as a Political Process."

26. Knox and Fuller, "The Gangster Disciples"; Tyson, "Journey of Chicago's Ultimate Street Tough" and "True Colors."

27. In fact, Columbus youths' adherence to gang lore is not unique; Hoover is something of a mythical hero among Chicago gang youths as well, who are no more likely to have contact with him. See Tyson, "Journey of Chicago's Ultimate Street Tough." Nonetheless, it is notable that gang members in Columbus call themselves "Folks" rather than "Gangster Disciples," an indication that their ties to these Chicago gangs are perhaps more ephemeral than they are led to believe by those members who claim to have direct ties to Chicago gangs.

28. Hagedorn, *People and Folks*, p. 78.

29. In Columbus gang vernacular, *false flagging* refers to an individual saying they are a gang member when they are not. This is not the same as *claiming*, or affiliating, with a set, which is an acceptable practice. The difference is that false flaggers assert membership status (which youths who are claiming or affiliating do

not) without having gone through an initiation. Young women told me that youths who are caught false flagging are typically beaten up.

30. Recall in Diane's case that she got down on her right knee, while Veronica got down on her left knee. Both are in gangs whose symbolism favors the right side, and in fact, both of their gestures, though opposite, can be interpreted as supporting this symbolism. For Diane, being prostrate on her right knee was a means of favoring the right side; for Veronica, being down on her left knee was the equivalent of throwing down her rivals' symbolism.

31. In most cases, being sexed in required sexual intercourse with multiple male gang members—it could be five for Bloods, six for Crips or Folks; it could be all of the male members, or those male members who were present at the time of the initiation. It was only in cases like Trish's—the girlfriends of the OG—that girls described a sexed-in initiate only engaging in intercourse with one member. More on sexual initiations in Chapters 7 and 8.

32. As I will discuss later in the chapter, various gangs had their own sets of rankings and the titles that went along with them. Trish's rank as a queen was not equivalent to LaShawna's queen ranking; their gangs simply adopted the same term. In fact, Diane also had a designation of queen in her gang's ranking system.

33. See Decker and Van Winkle, *Life in the Gang*; Klein, *Street Gangs and Street Workers* and *The American Street Gang*.

34. Leslie called the leader of her set Governor, as the title OG was reserved for the "leader of all sets" in Chicago.

35. Young women who described adult OGs were Angie, Cathy, Diane, Erica, Jennifer, Keisha, Kim, Leslie, Michelle, Monica, and Sonita. Of the girls with OGs under twenty-one, only Veronica had an OG who was twenty. Brandi, Chantell, Heather, LaShawna, Lisa, Nikki, Stephanie, Tamika, and Traci were in gangs with an OG nineteen or younger.

36. I was never offered evidence that something like this actually happened, that is, that an OG ordered a young woman to kill someone. In fact, given young women's discussions of their participation in gang violence (see Chapter 6), it is doubtful. Instead, it seems to be part of the mythology of gang rules and violence. See Decker and Van Winkle, *Life in the Gang*; Decker, "Collective and Normative Features of Gang Violence"; Klein, *The American Street Gang*.

37. The Gangster Girlz did not have ranks like those described by girls in mixed-gender gangs. The OG had founded the gang; otherwise, all of the members engaged in the same activities, often directed by the OG.

38. See LaLonde, "Police Trying to Contain Gang Problem"; Mayhood and LaLonde, "A Show of Colors." In fact, this may be changing. During the course of my interviews, the general impression of gangs conveyed to me by gang officers with the Columbus Police Department was that Columbus gangs were not as visibly active on the streets as gangs in many other cities, and were more easily approached and confronted by police than gang members in "tougher" cities. One detective told me that Columbus gang members "talk the talk, but can't walk the walk," concluding that "a lot of these kids don't have the heart to be gangsters." However, in the spring of 1996 as my research was wrapping up, this same detective expressed concern that there had been a recent increase in serious gang crime—at the time he was working three gang homicides in as many weeks. He was cautious about attributing this to a change in gang behavior, how-

ever, as he pointed out that the department previously had not made a serious effort to investigate whether homicides involving young people were gang related.

39. This phrase is borrowed from Decker and Van Winkle's monograph of the same name.
40. See Klein, *The American Street Gang* and *Street Gangs and Street Workers*; see also Hagedorn, *People and Folks*, p. 94; Jensen, "An Interview with James F. Short, Jr."
41. See Jacobs, *Dealing Crack*. However, as Decker points out, how individuals talk about drugs does not necessarily correspond to their behavior. See his "Legitimating Drug Use."
42. Decker and Van Winkle, *Life in the Gang*, p. 100.
43. This included Angie, Keisha, Kim, LaShawna, Leslie, Lisa, Stephanie, Tamika, Traci, and Veronica.
44. See Campbell, *The Girls in the Gang*; Horowitz, *Honor and the American Dream*; Moore, *Going Down to the Barrio*.
45. See Fleisher, *Dead End Kids*, for a discussion of the frequency of miscarriages in gangs.
46. In fact, in the survey portion of the interview, young women were asked a series of questions about things they valued in life. Asked how important being a mother was to them, twelve (57 percent) of the gang girls in Columbus said "not important at all," compared to only three (12 percent) of the nongang girls. Eighteen of the nongang girls (72 percent) said motherhood was very or pretty important to them, compared to only eight (38 percent) of the gang members.
47. In their chapter "Breaking the Bonds of Membership," Decker and Lauritsen discuss some of the myths surrounding exiting the gang: Once a member, always a member; in order to get out you have to shoot your mother. In reality, they found members could leave their gangs with relative ease. Likewise, a number of young women in both Columbus and St. Louis said they or young women they knew left their gangs when they became pregnant, and none reported any repercussions from having done so.
48. A number of gang girls in Columbus used the term *cousin* to denote the affiliation of members of their gangs.
49. Campbell, *The Girls in the Gang*.

Chapter 5

1. Maxson et al., "Street Gang Migration in the United States."
2. Decker and Van Winkle, *Life in the Gang*, p. 85.
3. Huff, "Denial, Overreaction, and Misidentification"; Zatz, "Chicano Youth Gangs and Crime."
4. This information comes from their response to a survey conducted by the National Youth Gang Center. According to David Curry, who provided me with the information, a notation in the file indicates that the officer queried provided this "official" statement, but noted that as recently as that very afternoon he had talked with Columbus gang members. Curry, personal correspondence, August 13, 1998.
5. The 1992 data come from Maxson et al., "Street Gang Migration in the United States." My information on 1998 comes from Curry, personal correspondence.

As I noted in Chapter 1, this underestimation of female gang involvement is typical of law enforcement. In fact, in their "Gang Crime and Law Enforcement Recordkeeping," Curry and his colleagues found that some law enforcement agencies have policies that officially exclude female gang members from their counts. Even controlling for data from these cities, they still found that females were only 5.7 percent of gang members known to law enforcement agencies. Part of this underestimation is likely attributable to male gang members' greater likelihood of being involved in serious gang crimes. This is an issue I will discuss in greater detail in Chapter 6.

6. As I detailed in Chapter 2, the representativeness of my sample is unknown, both because young women were drawn from agencies rather than the community at large and because the parameters of the total population of female gang members in each city has not been ascertained. Thus, my conclusions about the differences in the two sites can only be speculative in nature. However, one benefit of having chosen Columbus and St. Louis as my study sites is that other gang research has been done in both cities. Because many of my findings parallel existing research, I have greater confidence in having uncovered real differences between gangs in the two cities, rather than differences that are artifacts of sampling.

7. Traditional gangs are found in cities with longer histories of gangs: they have a history spanning twenty years or more, more than one hundred members, a wide age range (twenty to thirty years), subgroupings, and are territorial with versatile crime patterns. Neotraditional gangs also are characterized by subgrouping, territoriality, and versatile crime patterns, but they are somewhat smaller (fifty to one hundred members) and have a narrower age range and a shorter duration. Compressed and collective gangs do not have subgroups, may or may not be territorial, and have versatile crime patterns. While compressed gangs are small (under fifty members) with a narrow age range (typically under ten years) and short duration, collective gangs are larger (fifty or more members), have a wider age range (typically greater than ten years), and their duration can be somewhat longer. Finally, specialty gangs, which I found in neither city, specialize in particular types of crimes (such as drug distribution) and are less social in nature; they typically do not have subgroups, are quite territorial, and are small, with a narrow age range and short duration. See Klein and Maxson, "Gang Structures, Crime Patterns, and Police Responses" and Maxson and Klein, "Investigating Gang Structures."

8. Maxson and Klein, "Investigating Gang Structures," p. 34.

9. The issue of gang size is the only area in which my findings diverge substantially from Decker and Van Winkle's study of St. Louis gangs. Based on research conducted in the early 1990s, they report an average gang size of around two hundred members. I have talked with Scott Decker at length about these issues (Decker, personal correspondence), and we concluded that there are several possible explanations for these differences. First, we may have sampled youths from different gangs. While this may be the case, it probably doesn't account for the vast divergence in size we found. Recall that in 1998, police estimates were of seventy-five gangs, with around thirteen hundred active members–an average size of around seventeen (male) members. Decker notes that since the time of his study, there is evidence that gang participation has declined in St. Louis, and a number of gangs have splintered. In addition, some differences likely result from

how young people define the boundaries of their gangs. Providing information on their individual set or subgroup (which many of my respondents did) results in smaller numbers than when members give estimates based on the size of the larger group that shares the same name.

10. See Hagedorn, "Homeboys, Dope Fiends, Legits and New Jacks" and *People and Folks*; Klein, *The American Street Gang*; Moore, *Going Down to the Barrio*.
11. See also Decker and Van Winkle, *Life in the Gang*.
12. It's likely, in addition, that the decline in gang involvement in St. Louis over the last several years (see note 9) has contributed to gang members' shifting behaviors.
13. Decker and Van Winkle, *Life in the Gang*.
14. Maxson and Klein, "Investigating Gang Structures," p. 39.
15. Maxson and Klein, "Investigating Gang Structures," p. 40.
16. Recall that while most girls provided smaller numbers, they typically were referring to the size of their age-based clique.
17. In their report on gang structures in 201 cities, Klein and Maxson report that approximately one-third of the sites surveyed described having one gang type, one-third had two gang types, and approximately one-sixth had three gang types. There were not patterns with regard to the combination of structures that co-occurred in any given city. Neither St. Louis or Columbus were part of their sample. See their "Gang Structures, Crime Patterns, and Police Responses."
18. Decker et al., "A Tale of Two Cities," p. 423.
19. See also Decker and Van Winkle, *Life in the Gang*.
20. Decker and Van Winkle report that young women were unlikely to do more than property crimes for their initiations. And while male gang members described the sexual initiation of some female members, the young women they spoke to disputed these claims. However, for young men as well they found some flexibility in the form initiations took. They report that 90 percent of the gang members they spoke with described going through initiations, most of which consisted of being beaten in. However, several said their initiations involved going on a "mission" (committing a crime), several were tattooed, and, when there were relatives involved, a number reported that no initiation was required. See their *Life in the Gang*.

    These more lenient attitudes toward gang initiations in St. Louis were also reflected in the lesser concern girls there expressed about false flaggers—youths who claim gang membership without having been formally initiated. In fact, while this phrase was commonly used among the girls I spoke with in Columbus, St. Louis gang members did not use it or any other phrase to single out youths who falsely claim gang membership. Membership flowed from being in and of the gang's neighborhood: Youths from the neighborhood who hung out with the gang were viewed as part of the gang to a greater extent than in Columbus. However, St. Louis girls did talk about *perpetrators*, a semiparallel to Columbus' false flaggers. This term was used to refer to kids who moved back and forth across gang affiliations and kids who claimed to have committed serious crimes but had not.
21. Marie explained that she was blessed in because she was only thirteen at the time. Older members were required to be beaten in.
22. This information is missing for Toni and Cheri, who did not participate in the in-depth interview.

23. For a detailed look at this kind of diffuse gang leadership, see Fleisher, *Dead End Kids*. See also Decker and Van Winkle, *Life in the Gang*; Klein, *Street Gangs and Street Workers* and *The American Street Gang*.
24. This was also reflected in the survey findings about the importance of being a mother. Whereas the majority of gang girls in Columbus said being a mother was not important at all, only 19 percent of the gang girls in St. Louis said so. In contrast, ten St. Louis gang members (37 percent) said being a mother was very important. This included four of the five young women who were mothers when interviewed. In fact, a larger percentage of nongang girls in St. Louis (38 percent) said motherhood was not important at all, while only two said it was very important. See note 46, Chapter 4, for details on Columbus girls' responses.
25. In his *Dead End Kids*, Fleisher provides an in-depth look at gang girls' relationships with gang boys, including how these relationships ebb and flow over time. He also discusses how pregnancy and parenthood affect gang youths' relationships with one another and others in their gang.
26. See Campbell, "Self Definition by Rejection," p. 452. Also see her *The Girls in the Gang* and "Female Participation in Gangs"; Fishman, "The Vice Queens"; Horowitz, *Honor and the American Dream*; Moore, *Going Down to the Barrio*. In my project, this issue emerges with particular clarity in young women's discussions of girls who have been sexed into their gangs. I will discuss this in greater detail in Chapter 7.
27. Fleisher also documents young men's routine use of physical violence against girls in the gang and its lack of sanction. See his *Dead End Kids*; see also Campbell, *The Girls in the Gang*.
28. For exceptions to this general pattern, see Curry, "Selected Statistics on Female Gang Involvement"; Decker et al., "A Tale of Two Cities"; Jankowski, *Islands in the Streets*; Moore and Hagedorn, "What Happens to Girls in the Gang?"

Chapter 6

1. Thornberry and Burch, "Gang Members and Delinquent Behavior." See also Esbensen and Huizinga, "Gangs, Drugs, and Delinquency in a Survey of Urban Youth"; Esbensen et al., "Gang and Non-Gang Youth"; Fagan, "The Social Organization of Drug Use and Drug Dealing among Urban Gangs" and "Social Processes of Delinquency and Drug Use among Urban Gangs"; Huff, "Comparing the Criminal Behavior of Youth Gangs and At-Risk Youths"; Thornberry, "Membership in Youth Gangs and Involvement in Serious and Violent Offending"; Thornberry et al., "The Role of Juvenile Gangs in Facilitating Delinquent Behavior."
2. See Huff, "Comparing the Criminal Behavior of Youth Gangs and At-Risk Youths"; Thornberry et al., "The Role of Juvenile Gangs in Facilitating Delinquent Behavior." However, there is evidence that youths' participation in drug sales often continues after their gang involvement, even as they report declines in other delinquent behaviors. For an overview, see Thornberry, "Membership in Youth Gangs and Involvement in Serious and Violent Offending."

Notably, Battin and her colleagues found that, controlling for the influence of delinquent peers and prior delinquency, gang membership itself contributes to delinquency among gang members. Thus there is something unique about being in a gang that increases the likelihood that youths will be involved in crime. See Battin et al., "The Contribution of Gang Membership to Delinquency beyond Delinquent Friends."

3. Perhaps the best illustration of this comes from the St. Louis Homicide Project. Data from that project show that between 1990 and 1995, there were 207 gang-related homicides in the city. Of these, only *one* involved a female perpetrator— a nongang woman defending her children from local gang members. See Miller and Decker, "Women and Gang Homicide."

For overviews of young women's participation in gang crime as compared to young men's, see Bjerregaard and Smith, "Gender Differences in Gang Participation, Delinquency, and Substance Use"; Esbensen and Winfree, "Race and Gender Differences between Gang and Non-Gang Youth"; Fagan, "Social Processes of Delinquency and Drug Use among Urban Gangs."

4. Fagan, "Social Processes of Delinquency and Drug Use among Urban Gangs."

5. Bowker et al., "Female Participation in Delinquent Gang Activities," p. 516; see also Miller, "Gender and Victimization Risk among Young Women in Gangs" and "One of the Boyz?"; Miller and Brunson, "Gender Dynamics in Youth Gangs."

6. For exceptions, see Huff, "The Criminal Behavior of Gang Members and Non-gang At-Risk Youths"; Miller, "Gender and Victimization Risk among Young Women in Gangs"; Miller and Brunson, "Gender Dynamics in Youth Gangs"; Savitz et al., "Delinquency and Gang Membership as Related to Victimization."

7. Lauritsen et al., "The Link between Offending and Victimization Among Adolescents."

8. See Block and Block, "Street Gang Crime in Chicago"; Decker, "Collective and Normative Features of Gang Violence"; Klein and Maxson, "Street Gang Violence"; Sanders, *Drive-Bys and Gang Bangs.*

9. I categorized offenses as minor, moderate, or serious following the classifications used by Bjerregaard and Smith in "Gender Differences in Gang Participation, Delinquency, and Substance Use." They did not include carrying a hidden weapon, which I classified as serious delinquency.

Running away is always a tricky behavior to classify as "delinquent." In many cases, youths run away from home to escape from abusive or troubled home lives (see Chapter 3), and their attempts to leave are then criminalized. Running away also exposes youths to greater risks and to delinquent peer networks that tend to exacerbate their problems. For a discussion of this problem as it relates to girls, see Chesney-Lind, *The Female Offender.* For the problems of street youths more generally, see Hagan and McCarthy, *Mean Streets.*

10. Unfortunately, young women in Columbus were not asked this question. While all of the young women in St. Louis noted "protection" as their primary reason, seven young women listed a variety of secondary reasons as well: Four noted they also did so to get back at someone, two said it made them feel important, two said they held weapons for others, two did so to scare someone, and three said they carried because their friends did.

11. Although I combined youths across the two cities for this table, it is noteworthy that there were marked differences in self-reported delinquency among nongang girls across sites, with young women in St. Louis reporting less involvement in delinquency than young women in Columbus. This is most likely the case because more youths in Columbus were interviewed in detention and residential

facilities (see Chapter 2, note 29). Although nongang girls in Columbus were more delinquent than their St. Louis counterparts, comparisons of gang and nongang girls in Columbus nonetheless revealed significant differences in their participation in delinquency, particularly in the moderate and serious categories.

12. I do not present a mean score for drug sales because girls were asked whether they had sold marijuana, crack, or the category "other drugs." Because of this last category, presenting a mean score does not indicate how many types of drugs girls had sold.

13. In fact, seven gang girls described selling drugs every day. Each day was counted as an incident of drug sales, rather than each sale, making the mean frequency reported an underestimation of the actual number of times they sold drugs.

14. My initial concern was that these differences in the frequency of offending in the last six months resulted from the fact that more girls in St. Louis described themselves as ex-gang members (see note 30, Chapter 2). However, when I compared the mean frequencies of offending for St. Louis girls who described themselves as current versus ex-gang members, there were not significant differences. In fact, girls who defined themselves as ex-members reported committing an average of 20.88 serious delinquent acts in the last six months, compared to 15.70 for current gang members.

   Another explanation may be sampling. Recall that the Columbus sample was more likely to be drawn from youths in the detention center and a residential facility. On the one hand, this could account for some of the differences in youths' reporting—girls drawn from these places probably have participated in more delinquency to have ended up there. On the other hand, it seems contradictory that girls who are locked up or in a residential facility would have the opportunity to commit more crime. It is important to restate several points I made in earlier chapters for these numbers make more sense. First, the detention center in Columbus does not engage in careful risk assessment and routinely houses youths for short periods of time while they are awaiting their court date. Second, youths in the shelter care facility described frequently going AWOL, spending days or weeks on the streets before returning. I witnessed this myself during the time I was interviewing there. Girls who I had just interviewed took off, and others I had scheduled to interview had to be postponed until girls returned. Thus in neither case were girls in Columbus confined in ways that would considerably hinder their ongoing activities on the streets.

15. While I did not uncover differences in the frequency of other offending when I compared girls in St. Louis who said they were current versus ex-gang members, there were significant differences with regard to frequency of drug sales. On average, current St. Louis gang members had sold drugs 95.24 times in the last six months (approximately sixteen times a month), compared to 11.67 (twice a month) for ex-gang members there. These findings contradict what other research has shown about ex-gang members' patterns of offending. Recall from note 2 in this chapter that other studies—using far superior sampling—suggest that, with the exception of drug sales, youths' involvement in delinquency drops off once they quit their gang association.

16. Thornberry, "Membership in Youth Gangs and Involvement in Serious and Violent Offending," p. 160.

17. Thornberry, "Membership in Youth Gangs and Involvement in Serious and Violent Offending," p. 159.

18. Thornberry, "Membership in Youth Gangs and Involvement in Serious and Violent Offending," p. 160.
19. See Maxson and Klein, "Street Gang Violence."
20. Exceptions to this would include youths who hang with a gang but don't or haven't yet joined, or possibly nongang individuals protecting themselves from gang members.
21. Battin et al., "The Contribution of Gang Membership to Delinquency beyond Delinquent Friends"; Short and Strodtbeck, *Group Process and Gang Delinquency*; Thornberry et al., "The Role of Juvenile Gangs in Facilitating Delinquent Behavior."
22. Klein and Crawford, "Groups, Gangs and Cohesiveness." In fact, they argue that the primary sources of gangs' cohesiveness are external to the group—members' sense of their group as a unified whole is strengthened by negative attention, be it from law enforcement, rival gangs, or other community disapproval.
23. Gang members in both cities described their involvement in drug sales for individual profit, and did not routinely share their earnings with the gang.
24. These findings are also borne out in a recent study of male gang members' perceptions of gender that I completed with Rod Brunson, one of the research assistants on this project (see Miller and Brunson, "Gender Dynamics in Youth Gangs"). We found that on the whole, young men perceived gangs as primarily a "male thing," that girls either had no role in or had limitations in what they could offer. One respondent noted, "It's a male thing. We just strictly about, we want tough dudes in our stuff for real." On the other hand, some young men did leave space in their own rankings of status for young women they saw as sort of 'honorary males': Girls who behaved like young men and were perceived as able to hold their own. Describing one such girl in his gang, one respondent noted, "She not a regular girl, she like a boy for real. She act like a boy and work around the boys. Other girls, I don't think they should be in no gang, they soft for real." It's important to recognize that while gender shapes youths' gang involvement, it does not *determine* their involvement. Informal rules and expectations about gendered behavior can be bent to accommodate particular individuals. See West and Zimmerman, "Doing Gender," p. 139.
25. This was a very profitable commercial robbery, which she proudly told me (and I recalled) had gotten local media coverage at the time.
26. I made this determination by examining individual girls' descriptions of the frequency of their involvement in serious delinquency (those offenses listed in Table 6-1 excluding carrying a hidden weapon) and drug sales in the last six months. I characterize young women as "routinely" involved when they describe any or all of the following: attacking someone with a weapon or with the intent to seriously injure them at least twice a month, committing robberies at least twice a month, stealing more than $100 once a week, selling marijuana at least once a week, selling crack at least once a week, and/or selling other drugs at least once a week. These were actually pretty easy designations to make—young women tended either to report few incidents in the last six months or a large number of them. While gang fights were not included, only Diane and LaShawna reported involvement in these on a regular basis (about twenty times each in the last six months). Only three girls reported stealing a car once a month or more, and none did so more than once a week.

27. The number of girls here who report drug sales on a weekly basis (fourteen) differs from Table 6-5 because I include one girl who reported selling on average once a week, while the last category in Table 6-5 was more than once a week. The number of girls here who report involvement in serious delinquency is lower than in Table 6-5 because it does not include girls whose frequency of serious offending was more than once a week because they carried hidden weapons.

28. What's interesting here is that "female members" are reported to have committed more petty theft than "members." What this is indicative of, I would suggest, is the extent to which girls' concept of their gang is a masculine one. I'll discuss this issue in greater detail in Chapter 8.

29. Decker and Van Winkle, *Life in the Gang*, p. 22.

30. See Miller, "Struggles over the Symbolic." In this study of probation officers' interventions on gang style, I was repeatedly amazed at the imaginative ways that gang members symbolized their gangs, adapting mainstream artifacts and reappropriating their meanings. For instance, one officer who had members of a Crip gang on his caseload was frustrated that members routinely ate at Burger King. Afterwards, they held on to the wrapping and cups because they interpreted the initials—B. K.—to mean Blood Killers. Whereas he could violate a youth for wearing gang colors or symbols on their bodies, he was hard-pressed to attempt to revoke a kid's probation for eating at Burger King.

31. Decker, "Collective and Normative Features of Gang Violence."

32. Decker, "Collective and Normative Features of Gang Violence," p. 262.

33. This is also in keeping with our findings on male gang members' perspectives on gender within gangs. Because young men see the gang as primarily a masculine endeavor, they don't take most girls' involvement as seriously and are less likely to view a challenge from a rival female as a "mobilizing event." Consequently, they also reported few attacks on rival females—except when they did so to send a message or challenge *male* members of the rival gang. See Miller and Brunson, "Gender Dynamics in Youth Gangs."

34. Because the excerpt that follows provides details of a serious crime (perhaps even a homicide), and because demographic information about respondents is available, I have chosen to conceal both the pseudonym and gang affiliation of the young woman who told me the story.

35. I use the phrase "just shot" to illustrate this young woman's take on the event. She described it as "the most brutal thing I've ever seen in my life." I've debated this interpretation of the event with (mostly male) colleagues who suggest that such an interpretation minimizes the seriousness of lethal violence. I suppose it's a debatable question—which is worse, to be shot and killed or brutally gang raped and left for dead. But for this young woman, the answer was clear.

36. In fact, the young men we interviewed in St. Louis appeared much better versed in the language of guns. Asked how the gang provides protection, most young women and young men noted a primary means was through the provision of guns. However, all but one girl in the study said "guns," while many of the young men we interviewed described particular types of guns: 9mms, AK-47s, Mac 11s, Tech 9s, 44 mags, rifles, gauges. See Miller and Brunson, "Gender Dynamics in Youth Gangs."

37. See Bowker et al., "Female Participation in Delinquent Gang Activities"; Miller and Brunson, "Gender Dynamics in Youth Gangs."

38. Three St. Louis girls described selling crack every day, one sold about five times a week, and one sold about four times a week. Only one girl in Columbus sold crack every day, and none sold four or more times a week.
39. For a similar description of a female gang selling drugs to support their families, see Lauderback et al., "Sisters Are Doin' It for Themselves." Their study, however, involved a gang that was into "higher and bigger things" than what Yvette reports.
40. See also Decker and Van Winkle, *Life in the Gang.* About one-third of their sample of St. Louis gang members said their suppliers were gang leaders. Nonetheless, members sold for individual profit. Most research emphasizes that gang members, rather than gangs, are involved in drug sales (see Klein, 1995, for an overview). However, several studies based in Chicago, an atypical gang city because of its high level of organization, describe structured gang-based drug enterprises, in some cases where street-level sellers are paid a wage for their work. See Padilla, *The Gang as an American Enterprise*; Venkatesh and Levitt, "The Political Economy of an American Street Gang."
41. Jacobs and Miller, "Crack Dealing, Gender, and Arrest Avoidance."
42. Recall, however, that she did say that drive-bys were mostly committed by young men.

Chapter 7

1. See Campbell, *The Girls in the Gang*; Joe and Chesney-Lind, " 'Just Every Mother's Angel' "; Lauderback et al., "Sisters Are Doin' It for Themselves"; Moore, *Going Down to the Barrio.*
2. Arnold, "Processes of Victimization and Criminalization of Black Women"; Daly, "Women's Pathways to Felony Court"; Gilfus, "From Victims to Survivors to Offenders."
3. Lauritsen et al., "The Link between Offending and Victimization among Adolescents," p. 265.
4. Lauritsen et al., "The Link between Offending and Victimization among Adolescents."
5. Percentages here are based on the subsample of girls who responded affirmatively about witnessing violence or being victimized, rather than the total sample.
6. Unfortunately, the section of the questionnaire concerning victimization and exposure to violence was not as refined as the section on delinquency, making these comparisons speculative at best. While the measures of frequency of delinquency are for the past six months, no time specification was provided for the victimization/exposure to violence section. Moreover, the measure of frequency (never, once, a few times, many times) is more imprecise than that used for delinquency. Nonetheless, because so few scholars have explored these issues I believe the findings are important and merit further research.
7. Four girls described being attacked or threatened by a friend, three girls were attacked by a family member, two were stabbed by their brothers, and five young women reported being threatened with a weapon by a boyfriend or ex-boyfriend. Combined, these were about twenty percent of the violent attacks against gang girls.

8. See also Decker, "Collective and Normative Features of Gang Violence"; Joe and Chesney-Lind, " 'Just Every Mother's Angel' "; Lauderback et al., " 'Sisters Are Doin' It for Themselves.' "
9. See Decker, "Collective and Normative Features of Gang Violence." He discusses the cyclical and predictable nature of gang conflicts.
10. The extent of young men's flexibility with regard to expectations of their behavior, and the ways that these are shaped by notions of masculinity, are important questions that I can't address in this study. However, our interviews with young men in St. Louis do indicate that young men also believe girls are better able to avoid the most dangerous gang crime (in part because young men exclude them). See Miller and Brunson, "Gender Dynamics in Youth Gangs." Young women's discussions clearly suggest that they believe gender constructions within gangs make dangerous activities more imperative for young men than themselves. However, we need more research on issues of masculinities within gangs from young men's points of view.
11. See Miller and Decker, "Women and Gang Homicide." Again, these findings are also in keeping with our interviews with young men in gangs. Many of them did recognize their gang involvement as life-threatening and knew that there were rival gang members after them individually. Dwayne explained: "If the enemy over there, unless you got a crowd over here and a crowd over here with girls and us, they'll shoot at us first. They'll just ride through and see the girls there, probably keep on rolling, but if they see one of the dudes, they'll shoot." Moreover, young men felt trapped in gang life because their enemies would always remember them, even after they quit their gang involvement. Will explained: "Once you a member, you stuck being a gang member and you got these enemies knowing that you a gang member. I mean you a gang member forever to them." See Miller and Brunson, "Gender Dynamics in Youth Gangs." See also note 3, Chapter 6.
12. Although our study with young men was exploratory in nature, we did find evidence that young women who hang out with gangs but are not members may be at the greatest risk of sexual abuse and exploitation at the hands of male gang members. This is an important question that deserves additional attention. See Miller and Brunson, "Gender Dynamics in Youth Gangs."
13. Bryan, "Woman Is Beaten, Tortured by Gang Members, Police Say."
14. Young men we interviewed also differentiated between most girls and those few young women they deemed worthy of a sort of "honorary male" status. See note 24, Chapter 6.
15. See Fleisher, Dead End Kids, for a similar discussion of male-on-female violence within gangs.
16. Individuals who work with young women in gangs also report that it is difficult to get young women to disclose sexual abuse of this nature. Linda Schmidt, a youth worker in Cleveland, Ohio, describes one case in which she worked with a young woman for nearly a year before the girl finally told her she had been sexed into her gang. As I'll describe, the stigma associated with being sexed in likely keeps young women feeling shameful and silent.

For example, Yolanda did not outright describe having been sexed in, but her comments were readily interpretable as such, given what she and other youths said about the practice of sexing girls in and its consequences (see Chapter 5). Because our study was based on one-time interviews, it is understandable that girls were reticent about disclosing their involvement in a practice that involved ongoing abuse and degradation. Lisa Maher reports similar findings in her study of women in the drug economy, which she was better able to overcome because of the ongoing nature of her field research. Women she spoke with initially denied or downplayed their participation in sex-for-drug exchanges, but over time were more willing to disclose their involvement in these widely denigrated practices (see Maher, *Sexed Work*).

Chapter 8

1. Curry, "Female Gang Involvement."
2. It should go without saying that while my focus is on gender inequality and male domination on the streets and within gangs, I am in no way suggesting that gangs or the urban street world are unique in this regard. As I noted in Chapter 1, gender inequality is embedded within the fabric of American society and orders all of our "social life and social institutions in fundamental ways" (Daly and Chesney-Lind, "Feminism and Criminology," p. 504).
3. See also Campbell, "Self Definition by Rejection."
4. Campbell, "Self Definition by Rejection," pp. 463–464; see also Curry, "Female Gang Involvement"; Harris, *Cholas*.
5. See Brown, *Raising Their Voices*; Hey, *The Company She Keeps*.
6. Brown provides a similar analysis, based on her study of a group of middle-class girls' constructions of themselves in opposition to the "popular" group at school. See her *Raising Their Voices*.
7. See also Campbell, *The Girls in the Gang*, "Girls' Talk," "Female Participation in Gangs"; Joe-Laidler and Hunt, "Violence and Social Organization in Female Gangs."
8. Campbell, "Self Definition by Rejection."
9. See Hagedorn and Devitt, "Fighting Female."
10. Further evidence of this comes from Lauderback et al., " 'Sisters Are Doin' It for Themselves," which I discussed in Chapter 1.
11. Kanter, "Some Effects of Proportion on Group Life," p. 965. Thanks to an anonymous reviewer at *Gender & Society* for bringing the relevance of this article to my attention.
12. See Lynskey et al., "The Impact of Gender Composition on Gang Member Attitudes and Behavior."
13. Kanter, "Some Effects of Proportion on Group Life," p. 966.
14. Kanter, "Some Effects of Proportion on Group Life," p. 965.
15. Kanter, "Some Effects of Proportion on Group Life," p. 966.
16. Kanter, "Some Effects of Proportion on Group Life," p. 974.
17. Kanter, "Some Effects of Proportion on Group Life," p. 967.
18. Kanter, "Some Effects of Proportion on Group Life," p. 979.
19. See Estrich, *Real Rape*; Hatty, "Violence against Prostitute Women"; Schur, *Labeling Women Deviant*; Schwartz and DeKeseredy, *Sexual Assault on the College Campus*.
20. Kandiyoti, "Bargaining with Patriarchy," p. 274.
21. Pesce and Harding, "Imaginary Audience Behavior and Its Relationship to Operational Thought and Social Experience."

22. Thorne, *Gender Play*, p. 135.
23. Eder, *School Talk*; Lees, *Sugar and Spice*.
24. Anderson, *Streetwise*; Rainwater, *Behind Ghetto Walls*; Wilson, *When Work Disappears*.
25. Bourgois and Dunlap, "Exorcising Sex-for-Crack"; Maher, *Sexed Work*.
26. In her *Sexed Work*, Maher provides a detailed critique of the "addiction" model in theorizing women's drug use. However, in keeping with young women's descriptions, I use the term here.
27. Hagan and McCarthy, *Mean Streets*.
28. Although having children may expedite young women's leaving their gangs, doing so does not necessarily increase their chances for successful lives. Partly this is because stable marriages and jobs are less available in the current socioeconomic climate in urban communities throughout the United States. Communities where many gangs are located have dwindling numbers of males in the marriage pool; moreover, skyrocketing rates of incarceration, as well as lethal violence among young people, have greatly contributed to this shortage (see Moore and Hagedorn, "What Happens to Girls in the Gang?"; Wilson, *When Work Disappears*). Considering the high unemployment rates in most gang neighborhoods, many young men have few conventional opportunities and are likely to continue their gang and criminal involvement into adulthood (see Hagedorn, "Homeboys, Dope Fiends, Legits and New Jacks"; Klein, *The American Street Gang*). The bleak futures that await men in their communities often makes marriage no longer a desirable component of gang-involved women's lives. Moreover, attacks on many social programs have negatively affected women's lives subsequent to gang membership. Moore and Hagedorn ("What Happens to Girls in the Gang?") observe:

> Ironically, the most important influence on gang women's future may be the dismantling of the nation's welfare system in the 1990s. This system has supported women and children who want to stay out of the drug marketing system and in addition has provided a significant amount of cash to their communities. Its disappearance will deepen poverty and make the fate of gang women even more problematic.

29. Hagedorn and Devitt, "Female Gang Members."
30. See Hagedorn and Devitt, "Female Gang Members"; Moore and Hagedorn, "What Happens to Girls in the Gang?"; Moore, *Going Down to the Barrio*.
31. See Handler, "In the Fraternal Sisterhood"; Kandiyoti, "Bargaining with Patriarchy"; Kibria, "Power, Patriarchy, and Gender Conflict in the Vietnamese Immigrant Community"; Sanday, *Fraternity Gang Rape*.

Chapter 9

1. See, for example Campbell et al., "Female-Female Criminal Assault."
2. For a critique of biological and evolutionary approaches, see Fausto-Sterling, *Myths of Gender*. As noted in Chapter 1, Heimer and De Coster's "The Gendering of Violent Delinquency" is an illustration of the type of feminist criminology I am calling for. See also Daly, "Women's Pathways to Felony Court," for a discussion of these issues.
3. Thanks to an early anonymous reviewer for this quote, which creatively makes the point about the importance of gender similarities.

4. Moore, *Going Down to the Barrio.*
5. See especially the work of Huff in Columbus and Decker and Van Winkle in St. Louis.
6. See Brotherton, "'Smartness,' 'Toughness' and 'Autonomy'"; Harris, *Cholas*; Joe and Chesney-Lind, "'Just Every Mother's Angel'"; Joe-Laidler and Hunt, "Violence and Social Organization in Female Gangs"; Lauderback et al., "'Sisters Are Doin' It for Themselves'"; Moore, *Going Down to the Barrio*; Moore and Hagedorn, "What Happens to Girls in the Gang?"; Quicker, *Homegirls*; Taylor, *Girls, Gangs, Women and Drugs.*
7. See Jacobs and Miller, "Crack Dealing, Gender, and Arrest Avoidance"; Miller, "Up It Up."
8. See Hagan and McCarthy, *Means Streets*; Short, "The Level of Explanation Problem Revisited—The American Society of Criminology 1997 Presidential Address."

Adler, Freda. 1975. *Sisters in Crime: The Rise of the New Female Criminal.* New York: McGraw Hill.

Adler, Patricia A., and Peter Adler. 1987. *Membership Roles in Field Research.* Newbury Park, CA: Sage Publications.

Agar, Michael H. 1977. "Ethnography in the Streets and in the Joint: A Comparison." In *Street Ethnography: Selected Studies of Crime and Drug Use in Natural Settings,* edited by Robert S. Weppner. Beverly Hills, CA: Sage Publications, pp. 143–156.

Ageton, Suzanne S. 1983. "The Dynamics of Female Delinquency, 1976–1980." *Criminology* 21:555–584.

Allen, Hilary. 1987. "Rendering Them Harmless: The Professional Portrayal of Women Charged with Serious Violent Crimes." In *Gender, Crime and Justice,* edited by Pat Carlen and A. Worrall. Philadelphia: Open University Press, pp. 81–94.

Anderson, Elijah. 1990. *Streetwise: Race, Class, and Change in an Urban Community.* Chicago: University of Chicago Press.

Arnold, Regina. 1990. "Processes of Victimization and Criminalization of Black Women." *Social Justice* 17:153–166.

Baskin, Deborah R., and Ira B. Sommers. 1993. "Females' Initiation into Violent Street Crime." *Justice Quarterly* 10:559–581.

———. 1997. *Casualties of Community Disorder: Women's Careers in Violent Crime.* New York: Westview Press.

Baskin, Deborah R., Ira B. Sommers, and Jeffrey Fagan. 1993. "The Political Economy of Violent Female Street Crime." *Fordham Urban Law Journal* 20:401–417.

Battin, Sara R., Karl G. Hill, Robert D. Abbott, Richard F. Catalano, and J. David Hawkins. 1998. "The Contribution of Gang Membership to Delinquency beyond Delinquent Friends." *Criminology* 36:93–115.

Baumer, Eric, Janet L. Lauritsen, Richard Rosenfeld, and Richard Wright. 1998. "The Influence of Crack Cocaine on Robbery, Burglary, and Homicide Rates: A Cross-City, Longitudinal Analysis." *Journal of Research in Crime and Delinquency* 35:316–340.

Bjerregaard, Beth, and Carolyn Smith. 1993. "Gender Differences in Gang Participation, Delinquency, and Substance Use." *Journal of Quantitative Criminology* 4:329–355.

Block, Carolyn Rebecca, and Richard Block. 1993. "Street Gang Crime in Chicago." *Research in Brief.* Washington, DC: National Institute of Justice.

Blumer, Herbert. 1969. *Symbolic Interactionism: Perspective and Method.* Berkeley: University of California Press.

Bookin, Hedy, and Ruth Horowitz. 1983. "The End of the Youth Gang: Fad or Fact?" *Criminology* 21:585–602.

Bourgois, Philippe. 1995. *In Search of Respect: Selling Crack in El Barrio.* Cambridge, England: Cambridge University Press.

Bourgois, Philippe, and Eloise Dunlap. 1993. "Exorcising Sex-for-Crack: An Ethno-graphic Perspective from Harlem." In *Crack Pipe as Pimp: An Ethnographic Inves-tigation of Sex-for-Crack Exchanges,* edited by Mitchell S. Ratner. New York: Lex-ington Books, pp. 97–132.

Bowker, Lee H., and Malcolm W. Klein. 1983. "The Etiology of Female Juvenile Delin-quency and Gang Membership: A Test of Psychological and Social Structural Ex-planations." *Adolescence* 18:739–751.

Bowker, Lee H., Helen Shimota Gross, and Malcolm W. Klein. 1980. "Female Par-ticipation in Delinquent Gang Activities." *Adolescence* 15:509–519.

Braithwaite, John, and Kathleen Daly. 1994. "Masculinities, Violence and Commu-nitarian Control." In *Just Boys Doing Business?,* edited by Tim Newburn and Eliz-abeth A. Stanko. New York: Routledge, pp. 189–213.

Bray, Timothy M., and Richard Rosenfeld. 1997. "The Impact of Neighborhood Dis-advantage and Racial Composition on Youth Homicide: Race, Place and Risk Re-visited." Paper presented at the Annual Meeting of the American Society of Crim-inology, San Diego.

Brotherton, David C. 1996. "'Smartness,' 'Toughness' and 'Autonomy': Drug Use in the Context of Gang Female Delinquency." *Journal of Drug Issues* 26:261–277.

Brown, Lyn Mikel. 1998. *Raising Their Voices: The Politics of Girls' Anger.* Cambridge, MA: Harvard University Press.

Brown, Waln K. 1978. "Black Female Gangs in Philadelphia." *International Journal of Offender Therapy and Comparative Criminology* 21:221–228.

Brunson, Rod K. 1997. "Pumping Up the Set: Comparing Male and Female Percep-tions of Female Gang Involvement." Paper presented at the Annual Meeting of the American Society of Criminology, San Diego.

Bryan, Bill. 1998. "Woman Is Beaten, Tortured by Gang Members, Police Say." *St. Louis Post-Dispatch,* March 26, p. 1B.

Bursik, Robert J. Jr., and Harold G. Grasmick. 1993. *Neighborhoods and Crime: The Di-mensions of Effective Community Control.* New York: Lexington Books.

Campbell, Anne. 1981. *Girl Delinquents.* New York: St. Martin's Press.

———. 1984. *The Girls in the Gang.* New York: Basil Blackwell.

———. 1984. "Girls' Talk: The Social Representation of Aggression by Female Gang Members." *Criminal Justice and Behavior* 11:139–156.

———. 1987. "Self Definition by Rejection: The Case of Gang Girls." *Social Problems* 34:451–466.

———. 1990. "Female Participation in Gangs." In *Gangs in America,* edited by C. Ronald Huff. Newbury Park, CA: Sage Publications, pp. 163–182.

———. 1990. "On the Invisibility of the Female Delinquent Peer Group." *Women & Criminal Justice* 2:41–62.

———. 1993. *Men, Women and Aggression.* New York: Basic Books.

Campbell, Anne, Steven Muncer, and Daniel Bibel. 1998. "Female-Female Criminal Assault: An Evolutionary Perspective." *Journal of Research in Crime and Delinquency* 35:413–428.

Canter, Rachelle J. 1982. "Family Correlates of Male and Female Delinquency." *Crim-inology* 20:149–167.

Cernkovich, S. A., and Giordano, Peggy C. 1987. "Family Relationships and Delin-quency." *Criminology* 25:295–319.

Charmaz, Kathy. 1995. "Between Positivism and Postmodernism: Implications for Methods." *Studies in Symbolic Interaction* 17:43–72.

Chesney-Lind, Meda. 1993. "Girls, Gangs and Violence: Anatomy of a Backlash." *Humanity & Society* 17:321–344.

———. 1997. *The Female Offender: Girls, Women, and Crime.* Thousand Oaks, CA: Sage Publications.

Chesney-Lind, Meda, and Vickie V. Paramore. 1997. "Gender and Gang Membership: Exploring Youthful Motivations to Join Gangs." Paper presented at the Annual Meeting of the American Society of Criminology, San Diego.

Chesney-Lind, Meda, and Noelie Rodriguez. 1983. "Women under Lock and Key: A View from the Inside." *The Prison Journal* 63:47–65.

Chesney-Lind, Meda, and Randall G. Shelden. 1992. *Girls, Delinquency and Juvenile Justice.* Pacific Grove, CA: Brooks/Cole Publishing Company.

Chesney-Lind, Meda, Randall G. Shelden, and Karen A. Joe. 1996. "Girls, Delinquency, and Gang Membership." In *Gangs in America, 2nd ed.,* edited by C. Ronald Huff. Thousand Oaks, CA: Sage Publications, pp. 185–204.

Cloward, Richard, and Lloyd Ohlin. 1960. *Delinquency and Opportunity.* Glencoe, IL: Free Press.

Cohen, Albert. 1955. *Delinquent Boys.* Glencoe, IL: Free Press.

Collins, Patricia Hill. 1990. *Black Feminist Thought: Knowledge, Consciousness, and the Politics of Empowerment.* Boston: Unwin Hyman.

Columbus Metropolitan Human Services Commission. 1995. *State of Human Services Report—1995.* Columbus, OH: Columbus Metropolitan Human Services Commission.

Community Development Agency. 1993. *Neighborhood Demographic Profiles: 1990.* St. Louis, MO: City of St. Louis.

Connell, R. W. 1987. *Gender and Power.* Stanford, CA: Stanford University Press.

Cowie, John, Valerie Cowie, and Eliot Slater. 1968. *Delinquency in Girls.* London: Heinemann.

Currie, Dawn H., and Brian D. MacLean. 1997. "Measuring Violence against Women: The Interview as a Gendered Social Encounter." In *Researching Sexual Violence against Women: Methodological and Personal Perspectives,* edited by Martin D. Schwartz. Thousand Oaks, CA: Sage Publications, pp. 157–178.

Curry, G. David. 1997. "Selected Statistics on Female Gang Involvement." Paper presented at the Fifth Joint National Conference on Gangs, Schools, and Communities, Orlando, FL.

———. 1998. "Female Gang Involvement." *Journal of Research in Crime and Delinquency* 35:100–118.

———. 1998. "Proliferation of Gangs in the U.S." Paper presented at the Eurogang Workshop, Schmitten, Germany.

Curry, G. David, Richard A. Ball, and Scott H. Decker. 1996. "Estimating the National Scope of Gang Crime from Law Enforcement Data." *Research in Brief.* Washington, DC: National Institute of Justice.

Curry, G. David, Richard A. Ball, and Robert J. Fox. 1994. "Gang Crime and Law Enforcement Recordkeeping." *Research in Brief.* Washington, DC: National Institute of Justice.

Curry, G. David, and Irving A. Spergel. 1992. "Gang Involvement and Delinquency among Hispanic and African American Adolescent Males." *Journal of Research on Crime and Delinquency* 29:273–291.

Daly, Kathleen. 1992. "Women's Pathways to Felony Court: Feminist Theories of Lawbreaking and Problems of Representation." *Review of Law and Women's Studies* 2:11–52.

———. 1998. "From Gender Ratios to Gendered Lives: Women and Gender in Crime and Criminological Theory." In *The Handbook of Crime and Justice*, edited by Michael Tonry. Oxford: Oxford University Press, pp. 85–110.

Daly, Kathleen, and Meda Chesney-Lind. 1988. "Feminism and Criminology." *Justice Quarterly* 5:497–538.

Daly, Kathleen, and Lisa Maher. 1998. "Crossroads and Intersections: Building from Feminist Critique." In *Criminology at the Crossroads: Feminist Readings in Crime and Justice*, edited by Kathleen Daly and Lisa Maher. Oxford: Oxford University Press, pp. 1–17.

Decker, Scott H. 1996. "Collective and Normative Features of Gang Violence." *Justice Quarterly* 13(2):243–264.

———. 1998. "Legitimating Drug Use: A Note on the Impact of Gang Membership and Drug Sales on the Use of Illicit Drugs." Unpublished manuscript.

Decker, Scott H., and Janet L. Lauritsen. 1996. "Breaking the Bonds of Membership: Leaving the Gang." In *Gangs in America*, 2nd ed., edited by C. Ronald Huff. Thousand Oaks, CA: Sage Publications, pp. 103–122.

Decker, Scott H., and Barrik Van Winkle. 1996. *Life in the Gang*. Cambridge, England: Cambridge University Press.

Decker, Scott H., Tim Bynum, and Deborah Weisel. 1998. "A Tale of Two Cities: Gangs as Organized Crime Groups." *Justice Quarterly* 15:395–425.

DeVault, Marjorie L. 1995. "Ethnicity and Expertise: Racial-Ethnic Knowledge in Sociological Research." *Gender & Society* 9:612–631.

Dunlap, Eloise, B. Johnson, H. Sanibria, E. Holliday, V. Lipsey, M. Barnett, W. Hopkins, I. Sobel, D. Randolph, and Ko-Lin Chin. 1990. "Studying Crack Users and Their Criminal Careers." *Contemporary Drug Problems* Winter:455–473.

Duster, Troy. 1987. "Crime, Youth Unemployment, and the Black Urban Underclass." *Crime and Delinquency* 33:300–316.

Ebaugh, Helen Rose. 1993. "Patriarchal Bargains and Latent Avenues of Social Mobility: Nuns in the Roman Catholic Church." *Gender & Society* 7:400–414.

Eder, Donna. 1995. *School Talk: Gender and Adolescent Culture*. New Brunswick, NJ: Rutgers University Press.

Elkind, David, and Robert Bowen. 1979. "Imaginary Audience Behavior in Children and Adolescents." *Developmental Psychology* 15:38–44.

Esbensen, Finn-Aage, and Elizabeth Piper Deschenes. 1998. "A Multi-Site Examination of Gang Membership: Does Gender Matter?" *Criminology* 36:799–828.

Esbensen, Finn-Aage, and David Huizinga. 1993. "Gangs, Drugs, and Delinquency in a Survey of Urban Youth." *Criminology* 31:565–589.

Esbensen, Finn-Aage, and L. Thomas Winfree. 1998. "Race and Gender Differences between Gang and Non-Gang Youth: Results from a Multi-Site Survey." *Justice Quarterly* 15:505–525.

Esbensen, Finn-Aage, David Huizinga, and Anne W. Weiher. 1993. "Gang and Non-Gang Youth: Differences in Explanatory Factors." *Journal of Contemporary Criminal Justice* 9:94–116.

Estrich, Susan. 1987. *Real Rape*. Cambridge, MA: Harvard University Press.

Fagan, Jeffrey. 1989. "The Social Organization of Drug Use and Drug Dealing among Urban Gangs." *Criminology* 27:633–667.

———. 1990. "Social Processes of Delinquency and Drug Use among Urban Gangs." In *Gangs in America*, edited by C. Ronald Huff. Newbury Park, CA: Sage Publications, pp. 183–219.

Fausto-Sterling, Anne. 1985. *Myths of Gender: Biological Theories about Women and Men.* New York: Basic Books.

Federal Bureau of Investigation. 1996. *Crime in the United States, 1995.* Washington DC: U.S. Government Printing Office.

Fine, Gary Alan, and Kent L. Sandstrom. 1988. *Knowing Children: Participant Observation with Minors.* Newbury Park, CA: Sage Publications.

Fishman, Laura T. 1995. "The Vice Queens: An Ethnographic Study of Black Female Gang Behavior." In *The Modern Gang Reader,* edited by Malcolm W. Klein, Cheryl L. Maxson, and Jody Miller. Los Angeles: Roxbury Publishing Company, pp. 83–92.

Fleisher, Mark S. 1998. *Dead End Kids: Gang Girls and the Boys They Know.* Madison: Wisconsin University Press.

Gang Prevention Incorporated. 1994. *The Street Gang Identification Manual.* Chicago Gang Prevention Incorporated.

Gilfus, Mary E. 1992. "From Victims to Survivors to Offenders: Women's Routes of Entry and Immersion in to Street Crime." *Women and Criminal Justice* 4:63–89.

Giordano, Peggy C. 1978. "Girls, Guys and Gangs: The Changing Social Context of Female Delinquency." *Journal of Criminal Law and Criminology* 69:126–132.

Glassner, Barry, and Julia Loughlin. 1987. *Drugs in Adolescent Worlds: Burnouts to Straights.* New York: St. Martin's Press.

Goldstein, Paul J., L. J. Ouellet, and M. Fendrich. 1992. "From Bag Brides to Skeezers: A Historical Perspective on Sex-for-Drug Behavior." *Journal of Psychoactive Drugs* 24:349–361.

Hagan, John, and Bill McCarthy. 1997. *Mean Streets: Youth Crime and Homelessness.* Cambridge, England: Cambridge University Press.

Hagan, John, A. R. Gillis, and John Simpson. 1985. "The Class Structure of Gender and Delinquency: Toward a Power-Control Theory of Common Delinquent Behavior." *American Journal of Sociology* 90:1151–1178.

Hagan, John, John Simpson, and A. R. Gillis. 1987. "Class in the Household: A Power-Control Theory of Gender and Delinquency." *American Journal of Sociology* 92:788–816.

Hagedorn, John M. 1988. *People and Folks: Gangs, Crime and the Underclass in a Rustbelt City.* Chicago: Lake View Press.

———. 1991. "Gangs, Neighborhoods and Public Policy." *Social Problems* 38:529–542.

———. 1994. "Homeboys, Dope Fiends, Legits and New Jacks." *Criminology* 32:197–219.

———. 1998. *People and Folks: Gangs, Crime and the Underclass in a Rustbelt City,* 2nd ed. Chicago: Lakeview Press.

Hagedorn, John M., and Mary L. Devitt. 1998. "Female Gang Members: A Life Course Perspective." Paper presented at the Annual Meeting of the American Sociological Association, San Francisco.

———. 1999. "Fighting Female: The Social Construction of Female Gangs." *Female Gangs in America: Essays on Girls, Gangs and Gender,* edited by Meda Chesney-Lind and John Hagedorn. Chicago: Lakeview Press, pp. 256–276.

Handler, Lisa. 1995. "In the Fraternal Sisterhood: Sororities as Gender Strategy." *Gender & Society* 9:236–255.

Harding, Sandra, ed. 1987. *Feminism and Methodology.* Bloomington: Indiana University Press.

Harris, Mary G. 1988. *Cholas: Latino Girls and Gangs.* New York: AMS.

Hatty, Suzanne. 1989. "Violence against Prostitute Women: Social and Legal Dilemmas." *Australian Journal of Social Issues* 24:235–248.

Heimer, Karen, and Stacy De Coster. 1999. "The Gendering of Violent Delinquency." *Criminology* 37:277–317.

Hey, Valerie. 1997. *The Company She Keeps: An Ethnography of Girls' Friendship.* Philadelphia: Open University Press.

Hill, Gary D., and Elizabeth M. Crawford. 1990. "Women, Race and Crime." *Criminology* 28:601–623.

Hill, Robert B. 1972. *The Strength of Black Families.* New York: Emerson Hall Publishers.

hooks, bell. 1989. *Talking Back: Thinking Feminist, Thinking Black.* Boston: South End Press.

Horowitz, Ruth. 1983. *Honor and the American Dream: Culture and Identity in a Chicano Community.* New Brunswick, NJ: Rutgers University Press.

———. 1990. "Sociological Perspectives on Gangs: Conflicting Definitions and Concepts" In *Gangs in America*, edited by C. Ronald Huff. Newbury Park, CA: Sage Publications, pp. 37–54.

Huff, C. Ronald. 1989. "Youth Gangs and Public Policy." *Crime and Delinquency* 35:524–537.

———. 1990. "Denial, Overreaction, and Misidentification: A Postscript on Public Policy." In *Gangs in America*, edited by C. Ronald Huff. Newbury Park, CA: Sage Publications, pp. 310–317.

———. 1993. "Gangs in the United States." In *The Gang Intervention Handbook*, edited by Arnold P. Goldstein and C. Ronald Huff. Champaign, IL: Research Press, pp. 3–20.

———. 1996. "The Criminal Behavior of Gang Members and Nongang At-Risk Youths." In *Gangs in America*, 2nd ed. edited by C. Ronald Huff. Thousand Oaks, CA: Sage Publications, pp. 75–102.

———. 1998. "Comparing the Criminal Behavior of Youth Gangs and At-Risk Youths." *Research in Brief.* Washington, DC: National Institute of Justice.

Inciardi, James A. D. Lockwood, and A. E. Pottieger. 1993. *Women and Crack Cocaine.* New York: Macmillan.

Jackson, Pamela Irving. 1991. "Crime, Youth Gangs and Urban Transition: The Social Dislocations of Postindustrial Economic Development." *Justice Quarterly* 8:379–396.

Jacobs, Bruce A. 1999. *Dealing Crack: The Social World of Streetcorner Selling..* Boston: Northeastern University Press.

Jacobs, Bruce A., and Jody Miller. 1998. "Crack Dealing, Gender, and Arrest Avoidance." *Social Problems* 45:550–569.

Jankowski, Martin Sanchez. 1991. *Islands in the Streets: Gangs and American Urban Society.* Berkeley: University of California Press.

Jensen, Eric L. 1995. "An Interview with James F. Short, Jr." *Journal of Gang Research* 2:61–68.

Joe, Karen A., and Meda Chesney-Lind. 1995. " 'Just Every Mother's Angel': An Analysis of Gender and Ethnic Variations in Youth Gang Membership." *Gender & Society* 9:408–430.

Joe-Laidler, Karen A., and Geoffrey Hunt. 1997. "Violence and Social Organization in Female Gangs." *Social Justice* 24:148–169.

Johnstone, John W. C. 1981. "Youth Gangs and Black Suburbs." *Pacific Sociological Review* 24:355–375.

Kandiyoti, Deniz. 1988. "Bargaining with Patriarchy." *Gender & Society* 2:274–290.

Kanter, Rosabeth Moss. 1977. "Some Effects of Proportion in Group Life: Skewed Sex Ratios and Responses to Token Women." *American Journal of Sociology* 82:965–990.

Kelly, Liz. 1991. "Unspeakable Acts." *Trouble and Strife* 21:13–20.

Kibria, Nazli. 1990. "Power, Patriarchy, and Gender Conflict in the Vietnamese Immigrant Community." *Gender & Society* 4:9–24.

Klein, Dorie. 1973. "The Etiology of Female Crime: A Review of the Literature." *Issues in Criminology* 8:3–30.

Klein, Malcolm W. 1971. *Street Gangs and Street Workers.* Englewood Cliffs, NJ: Prentice-Hall.

———. 1993. "Attempting Gang Control by Suppression: The Misuse of Deterrence Principles." In *Studies on Crime and Crime Prevention.* Stockholm, Sweden: Scandinavian University Press, pp. 88–111.

———. 1995. *The American Street Gang: Its Nature, Prevalence and Control.* New York: Oxford University Press.

Klein, Malcolm W., and Lois Y. Crawford. 1967. "Groups, Gangs and Cohesiveness." *Journal of Research in Crime and Delinquency* 4:63–75.

Klein, Malcolm W., and Cheryl L. Maxson. 1989. "Street Gang Violence." In *Violent Crime, Violent Criminals,* edited by Neil Weiner and Marvin Wolfgang. Newbury Park, CA: Sage Publications, pp. 198–231.

———. 1996. "Gang Structures, Crime Patterns, and Police Responses." Final Report to the National Institute of Justice.

Klein, Malcolm W., Cheryl L. Maxson, and Jody Miller. 1995. "Introduction to Section II." In *The Modern Gang Reader,* edited by Malcolm Klein, Cheryl L. Maxson, and Jody Miller. Los Angeles: Roxbury Publishing Company, pp. 109–111.

Knox, George W., and Leslie L. Fuller. 1995. "The Gangster Disciples." *Journal of Gang Research* 3:58–76.

Konopka, Gisela. 1966. *The Adolescent Girl in Conflict.* Englewood Cliffs, NJ: Prentice-Hall.

Krisberg, Barry, Ira M. Schwartz, Paul Litsky, and James Austin. 1986. "The Watershed of Juvenile Justice Reform." *Crime and Delinquency* 32:5–38.

Kruttschnitt, Candace. 1996. "Contributions of Quantitative Methods to the Study of Gender and Crime, or Bootstrapping Our Way into the Theoretical Thicket." *Journal of Quantitative Criminology* 12:135–161.

LaLonde, Brent. 1995. "Police Trying to Contain Gang Problem." *The Columbus Dispatch,* September 3, p. 2A.

Laskey, John A. 1996. "Gang Migration: The Familial Gang Transplant Phenomenon." *Journal of Gang Research* 3:1–15.

Lather, Patti. 1991. *Getting Smart: Feminist Research and Pedagogy with/in the Postmodern.* New York: Routledge.

Laub, John H., and M. Joan McDermott. 1985. "An Analysis of Serious Crime by Young Black Women." *Criminology* 23:81–98.

Lauderback, David, Joy Hansen, and Dan Waldorf. 1992. " 'Sisters Are Doin' It for Themselves': A Black Female Gang in San Francisco." *The Gang Journal* 1:57–70.

Lauritsen, Janet L., Robert J. Sampson, and John H. Laub. 1991. "The Link between Offending and Victimization among Adolescents." *Criminology* 29:265–292.

Lees, Sue. 1993. *Sugar and Spice: Sexuality and Adolescent Girls.* New York: Penguin Books.

Leonard, Eileen B. 1982. *Women, Crime and Society: A Critique of Criminological Theory.* New York: Longman.

Lofland, John, and Lyn H. Lofland. 1984. *Analyzing Social Settings: A Guide to Qualitative Observation and Analysis.* Belmont, CA: Wadsworth.

Lombroso, Cesare, and William Ferrero. 1867. *The Female Offender.* New York: Appleton Press.

Long, J. Scott. 1983. *Confirmatory Factor Analysis.* Newbury Park, CA: Sage Publications.

Lynskey, Dana, Finn Esbensen, and Jody Miller. 1999. "The Impact of Gender Composition on Gang Member Attitudes and Behavior." Unpublished manuscript.

Maher, Lisa. 1997. *Sexed Work: Gender, Race and Resistance in a Brooklyn Drug Market.* Oxford: Clarendon Press.

Maher, Lisa, and Richard Curtis. 1992. "Women on the Edge of Crime: Crack Cocaine and the Changing Contexts of Street-Level Sex Work in New York City." *Crime, Law and Social Change* 18:221–258.

Maher, Lisa, and Kathleen Daly. 1996. "Women in the Street-Level Drug Economy: Continuity or Change?" *Criminology* 34:465–492.

Mann, Coramae Richey. 1993. "Sister against Sister: Female Intrasexual Homicide." In *Female Criminality: The State of the Art,* edited by C. C. Culliver. New York: Garland Publishing, pp. 195–223.

Marshall, Catherine, and Gretchen B. Rossman. 1989. *Designing Qualitative Research.* Newbury Park, CA: Sage Publications.

Maxson, Cheryl L., and Malcolm W. Klein. 1990. "Street Gang Violence: Twice as Great, or Half as Great?" In *Gangs in America,* edited by C. Ronald Huff. Newbury Park, CA: Sage Publications, pp. 71–100.

———. 1995. "Investigating Gang Structures." *Journal of Gang Research* 3:33–40.

Maxson, Cheryl L., Kristi Woods, and Malcolm W. Klein. 1995. "Street Gang Migration in the United States." Final Report to the National Institute of Justice.

Mayhood, Kevin. 1995. "Blood Spills Over Hand Signs." *The Columbus Dispatch,* September 4, p. 2A.

———. 1995. "Officials Organize to Combat Gangs." *The Columbus Dispatch,* September 15, p. 3B.

Mayhood, Kevin, and Brent LaLonde. 1995. "A Show of Colors: A Local Look." *The Columbus Dispatch,* September 3, pp. 1–2A.

Messerschmidt, James W. 1993. *Masculinities and Crime.* Lanham, MD: Rowman & Littlefield.

Miller, Jody. 1995. "Gender and Power on the Streets: Street Prostitution in the Era of Crack Cocaine." *Journal of Contemporary Ethnography* 23:427–452.

———. 1995. "Struggles over the Symbolic: Gang Style and the Meanings of Social Control." In Jeff Ferrell and Clinton Sanders, eds. *Toward a Cultural Criminology.* Boston: Northeastern University Press, pp. 213–234.

———. 1997. "Researching Violence against Street Prostitutes: Issues of Epistemology, Methodology and Ethics." In *Researching Sexual Violence against Women: Methodological and Personal Perspectives,* edited by Martin D. Schwartz. Thousand Oaks, CA: Sage Publications, pp. 144–156.

———. 1998. "Gender and Victimization Risk among Young Women in Gangs." *Journal of Research in Crime and Delinquency* 35:429–453.

———. 1998. "One of the Boyz? Girls' Gender Strategies in Youth Gangs." Paper presented at the Annual Meeting of the American Sociological Association, San Francisco.

———. 1998. "Up It Up: Gender and the Accomplishment of Street Robbery." *Criminology* 36:37–66.

Miller, Jody and Rod K. Brunson. 2000. "Gender Dynamics in Youth Gangs: A Comparison of Male and Female Accounts." *Justice Quarterly* 17: .

Miller, Jody, and Scott Decker. 1999. "Women and Gang Homicide." Unpublished manuscript.

Miller, Jody, and Barry Glassner. 1997. "The 'Inside' and the 'Outside': Finding Realities in Interviews." In David Silverman, ed. *Qualitative Research*. London: Sage Publications, pp. 99–112.

Miller, Walter. 1975. *Violence by Youth Gangs and Youth Groups as a Crime Problem in Major American Cities*. Washington, DC: Government Printing Office.

Mishler, Elliot G. 1986. *Research Interviewing: Context and Narrative*. Cambridge, MA: Harvard University Press.

Molina, Alexander A. 1993. "California's Anti-Gang Street Terrorism Enforcement and Prevention Act: One Step Forward, Two Steps Back?" *Southwestern University Law Review* 22:457–481.

Moore, Joan. 1978. *Homeboys: Gangs, Drugs, and Prison in the Barrios of Los Angeles*. Philadelphia: Temple University Press.

———. 1988. "Gangs and the Underclass: A Comparative Perspective." In *People and Folks: Gangs, Crime and the Underclass in a Rustbelt City*, by John M. Hagedorn. Chicago: Lake View Press, pp. 3–17.

———. 1991. *Going Down to the Barrio: Homeboys and Homegirls in Change*. Philadelphia: Temple University Press.

Moore, Joan, and John Hagedorn. 1996. "What Happens to Girls in the Gang?" In *Gangs in America*, 2nd ed., edited by C. Ronald Huff. Thousand Oaks, CA: Sage Publications, pp. 205–218.

Moore, Joan, and Raquel Pinterhughes. 1993. *In the Barrios: Latinos and the Underclass Debate*. New York: Russell Sage Foundation.

Moore, Joan, and James Diego Vigil. 1993. "Barrios in Transition." In *In the Barrios: Latinos and the Underclass Debate*, edited by Joan Moore and Raquel Pinterhughes. New York: Russell Sage Foundation, pp. 27–50.

Morash, Merry. 1983. "Gangs, Groups and Delinquency." *British Journal of Criminology* 23:309–331.

———. 1986. "Gender, Peer Group Experiences, and Seriousness of Delinquency." *Journal of Research in Crime and Delinquency* 23:43–67.

Newburn, Tim, and Elizabeth Stanko, eds. 1994. *Just Boys Doing Business?* New York: Routledge.

Nurge, Dana. 1998. "Female Gangs and Cliques in Boston: What's the Difference?" Paper presented at the Annual Meeting of the American Society of Criminology, Washington, DC.

Oliver, William. 1994. *The Violent Social World of Black Men*. New York: Lexington Books.

Padilla, Felix M. 1992. *The Gang as an American Enterprise*. New Brunswick, NJ: Rutgers University Press.

Pearson, Patricia. 1997. *When She Was Bad: Violent Women and the Myth of Innocence*. New York: Viking.

Perkins, Useni Eugene. 1987. *Explosion of Chicago's Black Street Gangs: 1900 to Present.* Chicago: Third World Press.

Pesce, Rosario C., and Carol Gibb Harding. 1986. "Imaginary Audience Behavior and Its Relationship to Operational Thought and Social Experience." *Journal of Early Adolescence* 6:83–94.

Phares, Donald, and Claude A. Louishomme. 1996. "St. Louis: A Politically Fragmented Area." In *Regional Politics: America in a Post-City Age,* edited by H. V. Savitch and Ronald K. Vogel. Thousand Oaks, CA: Sage Publications, pp. 72–93.

Pollock, Otto. 1950. *The Criminality of Women.* Philadelphia: University of Pennsylvania Press.

Portillos, Edwardo. 1996. *Doing Gender in Chicano/a Gangs: Machismo, Masculinities, and Femininities.* Unpublished master's thesis, Arizona State University.

Portillos, Edwardo, Nancy Jurik, and Marjorie Zatz. 1996. "Machismo and Chicano/a Gangs: Symbolic Resistance or Oppression?" *Free Inquiry in Creative Sociology* 24:175–184.

Quicker, John C. 1983. *Homegirls: Characterizing Chicana Gangs.* San Pedro, CA: International University Press.

Rafter, Nicole Hahn, and Frances Heidensohn, eds. 1995. *International Feminist Perspectives in Criminology: Engendering a Discipline.* Philadelphia: Open University Press.

Rainwater, Lee. 1990. *Behind Ghetto Walls.* Chicago: Aldine de Gruyter.

Ratner, Mitchell S, ed. 1993. *Crack Pipe as Pimp: An Ethnographic Investigation of Sex-for-Crack Exchanges.* New York: Lexington Books.

Richardson, Laurel. 1990. *Writing Strategies: Reaching Diverse Audiences.* Newbury Park, CA: Sage Publications.

Richie, Beth E. 1996. *Compelled to Crime: The Gender Entrapment of Battered Black Women.* New York: Routledge.

Riessman, Catherine Kohler. 1993. *Narrative Analysis.* Newbury Park, CA: Sage Publications.

Rosemont Center Annual Report. 1995. Columbus, Ohio.

Rusk, David. 1995. *Cities without Suburbs,* 2nd ed. Washington, DC: Woodrow Wilson Center Press.

Sampson, Robert J., and William Julius Wilson. 1995. "Toward a Theory of Race, Crime and Urban Inequality." In *Crime and Inequality,* edited by John Hagan and Ruth D. Peterson. Stanford, CA: Stanford University Press, pp. 37–54.

Sanday, Peggy Reeves. 1990. *Fraternity Gang Rape: Sex, Brotherhood, and Privilege on Campus.* New York: New York University Press.

Sanders, William. 1993. *Drive-Bys and Gang Bangs: Gangs and Grounded Culture.* Chicago: Aldine de Gruyter.

Sanniti, Carl V. 1995. "Snapshot View of Detention, Franklin County Detention Utilization, June 12, 1995." Columbus: Ohio Department of Youth Services.

Savitz, Leonard, Lawrence Rosen, and Michael Lalli. 1980. "Delinquency and Gang Membership as Related to Victimization." *Victimology: An International Journal* 5:152–160.

Schmitt, Raymond L. 1993. "Cornerville as Obdurate Reality: Retooling the Research Act through Postmodernism." *Studies in Symbolic Interaction* 15:121–145.

Schur, Edwin. 1984. *Labeling Women Deviant.* New York: Random House.

Schwartz, Martin D., and Walter S. DeKeseredy. 1997. *Sexual Assault on the College Campus: The Role of Male Peer Support.* Thousand Oaks, CA: Sage Publications.

Schwartz, Martin D., and Dragan Milovanovic. 1996. *Race, Gender, and Class in Criminology: The Intersection.* New York: Garland Publishing.

Scott, Joseph W., and Albert Black. 1989. "Deep Structures of African American Family Life: Female and Male Kin Networks." *Western Journal of Black Studies* 13:17–24.

Short, James F. 1990. "New Wine in Old Bottles? Change and Continuity in American Gangs." In *Gangs in America*, edited by C. Ronald Huff. Newbury Park, CA: Sage Publications, pp. 223–239.

———. 1998. "The Level of Explanation Problem Revisited—The American Society of Criminology 1997 Presidential Address." *Criminology* 36:3–36.

Short, James F., and Fred L. Strodtbeck. 1965. *Group Process and Gang Delinquency.* Chicago: University of Chicago Press.

Simmons, Roberta G., Florence Rosenberg, and Morris Rosenberg. 1973. "Disturbance in the Self-Image at Adolescence." *American Sociological Review* 38:553–568.

Simon, Rita James. 1975. *Women and Crime.* Lexington, MA: Lexington Books.

Simpson, Sally. 1989. "Feminist Theory, Crime and Justice." *Criminology.* 27:605–631.

———. 1991. "Caste, Class and Violent Crime: Explaining Differences in Female Offending." *Criminology* 29:115–135.

Simpson, Sally, and Lori Elis. 1995. "Doing Gender: Sorting out the Caste and Crime Conundrum." *Criminology* 33:47–81.

Singer, Robert D., and Anne Singer. 1969. *Psychological Development in Children.* Philadelphia: W. B. Saunders Company.

Singer, Simon I., and Murray Levine. 1988. "Power-Control Theory, Gender, and Delinquency: A Partial Replication with Additional Evidence on the Effects of Peers." *Criminology* 26:627–647.

Smart, Carol. 1976. *Women, Crime and Criminology: A Feminist Critique.* London: Routledge & Kegan Paul.

Smith, Carolyn, and Terence P. Thornberry. 1995. "The Relationship between Childhood Maltreatment and Adolescent Involvement in Delinquency." *Criminology* 33:451–479.

Smith, Dorothy E. 1987. "Women's Perspective as Radical Critique of Sociology." In *Feminism and Methodology*, edited by Sandra Harding. Bloomington: Indiana University Press, pp. 84–96.

Smith, Douglas A., and Raymond Paternoster. 1987. "The Gender Gap in Theories of Deviance: Issues and Evidence." *Journal of Research in Crime and Delinquency* 24:140–172.

Sommers, Ira, and Deborah R. Baskin. 1993. "The Situational Context of Violent Female Offending." *Journal of Research in Crime and Delinquency* 30:136–162.

Spelman, Elizabeth V. 1988. *Inessential Woman: Problems of Exclusion in Feminist Thought.* Boston: Beacon Press.

Spergel, Irving A. 1972. "Community Action Research as a Political Process." In *Community Organization: Studies in Constraint*, edited by Irving A. Spergel. Beverly Hills, CA: Sage Publications, pp. 231–262.

Spergel, Irving A., and G. David Curry. 1993. "The National Youth Gang Survey: A Research and Developmental Process." In *The Gang Intervention Handbook*, edited by Arnold P. Goldstein and C. Ronald Huff. Champaign, IL: Research Press, pp. 359–400.

Spradley, James. 1979. *The Ethnographic Interview.* New York: Holt.

Stack, Carol. 1974. *All Our Kin: Strategies for Survival in a Black Community.* New York: Harper & Row.

Steffensmeier, Darrell J. 1983. "Organizational Properties and Sex-Segregation in the Underworld: Building a Sociological Theory of Sex Differences in Crime." *Social Forces* 61:1010–1032.

Steffensmeier, Darrell J., and Renee Hoffman Steffensmeier. 1980. "Trends in Female Delinquency: An Examination of Arrest, Juvenile Court, Self Report and Field Data." *Criminology* 18:62–85.

Steffensmeier, Darrell J., and Robert Terry. 1986. "Institutional Sexism in the Underworld: A View from the Inside." *Sociological Inquiry* 56:304–323.

Strauss, Anselm L. 1987. *Qualitative Analysis for Social Scientists.* Cambridge, England: Cambridge University Press.

Sullivan, Mercer L. 1989. *"Getting Paid": Youth Crime and Work in the Inner City.* Ithaca, NY: Cornell University Press.

Swart, William J. 1991. "Female Gang Delinquency: A Search for 'Acceptably Deviant Behavior.'" *Mid-American Review of Sociology* 15:43–52.

Taylor, Carl. 1993. *Girls, Gangs, Women and Drugs.* East Lansing: Michigan State University Press.

Taylor, Jill McLean, Carol Gilligan, and Amy M. Sullivan. 1995. *Between Voice and Silence: Women and Girls, Race and Relationship.* Cambridge, MA: Harvard University Press.

Thomas, W. I. 1967. *The Unadjusted Girl.* New York: Harper & Row.

Thornberry, Terence P. 1997. "Membership in Youth Gangs and Involvement in Serious and Violent Offending." In *Serious and Violent Juvenile Offenders: Risk Factors and Successful Interventions,* edited by Rolf Loeber and David P. Farrington. Thousand Oaks, CA: Sage Publications, pp. 147–166.

Thornberry, Terence P., and James H. Burch II. 1997. "Gang Members and Delinquent Behavior." *Juvenile Justice Bulletin.* Washington, DC: Office of Juvenile Justice and Delinquency Prevention.

Thornberry, Terence P., Marvin D. Krohn, Alan J. Lizotte, and Deborah Chard-Wierschem. 1993. "The Role of Juvenile Gangs in Facilitating Delinquent Behavior." *Journal of Research in Crime and Delinquency* 30:75–85.

Thorne, Barrie. 1993. *Gender Play: Girls and Boys in School.* New Brunswick, NJ: Rutgers University Press.

Thrasher, Frederick M. 1927. *The Gang.* Chicago: University of Chicago Press.

Tonry, Michael. 1995. *Malign Neglect: Race, Crime and Punishment in America.* New York: Oxford University Press.

Tyson, Ann Scott. 1996. "Journey of Chicago's Ultimate Street Tough." *The Christian Science Monitor,* December 31 (http://www.csmonitor.com).

———. 1996. "True Colors: Trial of Chicago's 'Disciples.'" *The Christian Science Monitor,* February 27 (http://www.csmonitor.com).

Venkatesh, Sudhir Alladi, and Steven D. Levitt. 1998. "The Political Economy of an American Street Gang." Unpublished manuscript.

Vigil, James Diego. 1988. *Barrio Gangs: Street Life and Identity in Southern California.* Austin: University of Texas Press.

West, Candace, and Sarah Fenstermaker. 1995. "Doing Difference." *Gender & Society* 9:8–37.

West, Candace, and Don H. Zimmerman. 1987. "Doing Gender." *Gender & Society* 1:125–151.

Widom, Cathy Spatz. 1989. "Child Abuse, Neglect, and Violent Criminal Behavior." *Criminology* 27:251–271.

Wilson, Nanci Koser. 1993. "Stealing and Dealing: The Drug War and Gendered Criminal Opportunity." In *Female Criminality: The State of the Art*, edited by C. C. Culliver. New York: Garland Publishing, pp. 169–194.

Wilson, William Julius. 1987. *The Truly Disadvantaged: The Inner City, the Underclass, and Public Policy*. Chicago: University of Chicago Press.

———. 1996. *When Work Disappears: The World of the New Urban Poor*. New York: Alfred A. Knopf.

Winfree, L. Thomas Jr., Kathy Fuller, Teresa Vigil, and G. Larry Mays. 1992. "The Definition and Measurement of 'Gang Status': Policy Implications for Juvenile Justice." *Juvenile and Family Court Journal* 43:29–37.

Zatz, Marjorie S. 1987. "Chicano Youth Gangs and Crime: The Creation of a Moral Panic." *Contemporary Crises* 11:129–158.

Zevitz, Richard G. and Susan R. Takata. 1992. "Metropolitan Gang Influence and the Emergence of Group Delinquency in a Regional Community." *Journal of Criminal Justice* 20:93–106.

INDEX

Adler, Freda, 4, 209
Agar, Michael, 33
Arrest, 24, 33, 51, 83, 112
Attitudes about gender, gang girls, 111,
    131–132, 157, 159, 165, 180–186,
    191, 196
Autonomous female gangs. *See* Gender
    composition of gangs
AWOL, from residential facility, 24, 26,
    70, 134, 160, 161

Banging in Little Rock, 58
"Bargains with patriarchy." *See*
    "Patriarchal bargains"
Baskin, Deborah R., 5
Battin, Sara, R., et.al., 208
Bjerregaard, Beth, 208
"Blurred boundaries" of victimization
    and offending, 8, 71, 151
Bloods, 55, 60, 65, 70, 72, 74, 75, 77, 96,
    99, 101, 103, 104, 117, 118, 131,
    135, 136, 138, 143, 160, 162, 165,
    167
Bourgois, Philippe, 5, 7
Braithwaite, John, 8
Brunson, Rod K., 31, 32
Burch, James H., II, 123, 208
Bursik, Robert J., Jr., 207

Campbell, Anne, 9, 11, 13, 90, 181, 184
Chesney-Lind, Meda, 1, 8, 9, 39
Chicago, Illinois
    as origin of Folk Nation/gang, 72, 74
    Gangster Disciples, 73, 100, 101, 104,
        167
    Larry "King" Hoover, 73
    model, 101, 104, 107, 109, 121, 201
Colors, 103
Columbus, Ohio
    gang drug sales, 84–85, 89, 147–150
    gang initiations, 64, 69, 70, 74, 76, 77,
        79, 86–88, 91, 97
    gang size, 91, 94
    racial composition, 16, 20, 91, 93

socioeconomic context, 16, 21–22, 53
socioeconomic indicators, 19–20
See also Racial segregation
Comparison between Columbus and
    St. Louis
    cultural diffusion. *See* Cultural
        diffusion, in Columbus; Cultural
        diffusion, in St. Louis
    delinquency among gang members,
        100, 124–128
    drug trade. *See* Drug trade, differ-
        ences between Columbus and St.
        Louis
    gang characteristics. *See* Gang
        characteristics, differences be-
        tween Columbus and St. Louis
    gang initiations, 102, 104–105
    gang involvement among family
        members, 35, 51–53
    gang leadership, 106–107
    gender composition of gangs, 93–94
    socioeconomic context, 16–22, 96
Conflicts with rival gangs, 135–138
    and gender, 138–143
    "mobilizing events," 137–138
    See also Delinquency, gang-related;
        Victimization, and conflicts with
        rival gangs
Crack markets, 6, 7
Crack sales. *See* Drug trade
Crime, gang-related, 2, 8, 59, 62, 65, 83,
    85, 91, 97, 123–125, 130, 132, 133,
    181, 195, 202
Crawford, Elizabeth, 19
Crawford, Lois, 211
Crips, 43, 47, 50, 51, 54, 59, 60, 65, 68,
    69, 74, 75, 77, 90, 95, 98, 101, 102,
    103, 104, 115, 117, 131, 135, 157,
    160, 161, 162, 163, 164, 167, 171,
    178
Cultural diffusion of gangs, 18, 69–72
    from Chicago, 101, 104, 107, 109, 121,
        201
    from Los Angeles, 16, 68, 69

Lethal violence in gangs, 83, 138–139,
140–142
and gender, 83
Liberation hypothesis, 1, 4, 10, 12, 13,
178
Locked up. *See* Arrest

MacLean, Brian D., 32
Maher, Lisa, 7, 8
Maxson, Cheryl L., 19, 92, 94, 100
McCarthy, Bill, 63, 195
Meetings. *See* Gang activities
Member qualifications. *See* Gang
characteristics
Menace II Society, 71
Migration. *See* Gang migration
Miller, Walter, 210
Mixed gender gangs. *See* Gender
composition of gangs
Moore, Joan, 12, 62–63
Motherhood, 10, 32, 87–91, 114–120, 121
Motives for joining gangs, 41–45, 49–51,
151

Neighborhood characteristics, of
sample, 36–37, 38–45, 129
Neighborhood peer networks, 35, 37,
42, 43, 45, 200
and exposure to violence, 36
and victimization risk, 123
Nongang girls, reasons for not joining,
57–62
Nurge, Dana, 13
NWO (No Way Out), 99, 101, 104, 105,
166, 171

OG (Original Gangster), 44, 48, 60, 66,
69, 70, 72, 73, 80, 81, 82, 84, 85,
101, 103, 106, 107, 108, 112, 134,
149, 171, 190, 191

Panther, 72
Paramore, Vickie V., 235
"Patriarchal bargains," 192, 196, 203
Potrero Hill Posse (PHP), 13, 14
Pregnancy, 87–91, 114–120
Prevalence, female gang involvement,
13
Proliferation. *See* Gangs, proliferation
Protective functions of gangs. *See*
Gangs, protective functions of
"Putting in work," 82, 83

Quicker, John C., 213

Racial segregation, 20
Ranking systems. *See* Gang characteristics
Research methodology
in-depth interviews, 17, 23, 25, 26, 29,
35, 36
protections of confidentiality, 27,
29–30
rapport-building, 29, 31
sample characteristics, 23–24
sampling, 23–28
self-nomination approach, 24–25, 65
social distances, 29–32
survey interviews, 23, 25, 26, 29, 36
"talking back," 30, 179
Residential instability, 43, 44
Resistance to oppression. *See* "Resistance to victimization"
"Resistance to victimization," 8, 9, 10,
13, 14, 15, 197, 199
Richardson, Laurel, 33
Risk factors for gang involvement,
35–48, 51–53, 121, 129
See also Family; Neighborhood peer
networks
Rules. *See* Gang characteristics
Rule enforcement
"chest shots," 108–109, 193
"mouth shots," 108–109, 193
"violations," 108–109
Rusk, David, 19

Sampson, Robert J., 209
Schmidt, Linda, 241
Short, James F., 11, 65
"Sexing in," 50, 79, 104, 168, 171–174,
184, 193–194, 196, 203
Sexual abuse, 9, 36, 46, 48–49, 56, 63,
152, 153, 154, 155, 157, 172, 173,
177, 191, 192, 197, 201, 203
gang rape, 139–140
rape, 153, 157, 166–167, 175, 194
sexual exploitation, 11–12, 14, 79, 80
within families. *See* Family, sexual
abuse within
See also "Sexing in"; Dating relationships, and sexual exploitation
Sexual assault. *See* Sexual abuse
Sexual double standard, 117–118, 181,
193
Sexual exploitation. *See* Sexual abuse
"Sisterhood," 13, 14, 32, 203
"Slobs," 60, 61, 68, 81, 85, 86, 131, 136,
173
Social injury hypothesis, 12–13